ORIGINAL NARRATIVES
OF EARLY AMERICAN HISTORY

REPRODUCED UNDER THE AUSPICES OF THE
AMERICAN HISTORICAL ASSOCIATION

GENERAL EDITOR, J. FRANKLIN JAMESON, PH.D., LL.D., LITT.D.
DIRECTOR OF THE DEPARTMENT OF HISTORICAL RESEARCH IN THE
CARNEGIE INSTITUTION OF WASHINGTON

NARRATIVES OF EARLY VIRGINIA
BRADFORD'S HISTORY OF PLYMOUTH PLANTATION
WINTHROP'S JOURNAL "HISTORY OF NEW ENGLAND"
    (2 vols.)
NARRATIVES OF EARLY CAROLINA
NARRATIVES OF EARLY MARYLAND
NARRATIVES OF EARLY PENNSYLVANIA, WEST NEW JERSEY,
    AND DELAWARE
NARRATIVES OF NEW NETHERLAND
EARLY ENGLISH AND FRENCH VOYAGES
VOYAGES OF SAMUEL DE CHAMPLAIN
SPANISH EXPLORERS IN THE SOUTHERN UNITED STATES
SPANISH EXPLORATION IN THE SOUTHWEST
NARRATIVES OF THE INSURRECTIONS
NARRATIVES OF THE INDIAN WARS
JOHNSON'S WONDER-WORKING PROVIDENCE
THE JOURNAL OF JASPAR DANCKAERTS
NARRATIVES OF THE NORTHWEST
NARRATIVES OF THE WITCHCRAFT CASES
THE NORTHMEN, COLUMBUS, AND CABOT

ORIGINAL NARRATIVES
OF EARLY AMERICAN HISTORY

EARLY ENGLISH
AND FRENCH VOYAGES

CHIEFLY FROM HAKLUYT

1534—1608

EDITED BY

HENRY S. BURRAGE, D.D.

OF THE MAINE HISTORICAL SOCIETY

New York
BARNES & NOBLE, INC.

COPYRIGHT, 1906
BY CHARLES SCRIBNER'S SONS
COPYRIGHT RENEWED BY BARNES & NOBLE, INC., 1934

All rights reserved

REPRINTED, 1959

PRINTED IN THE UNITED STATES OF AMERICA

NOTE

IN the texts printed in this volume, the modern practice in the use of *u* and *v* and of *i* and *j* respectively has been substituted for the practice of Hakluyt and the other original writers; also, *and* has been printed instead of the sign &. In other respects, the spelling of the originals has been followed.

Special acknowledgments and thanks are due to the Gorges Society for permission to use their text of Rosier's *Relation* of Waymouth's voyage of 1605, and that of the *Relation* of the Popham Colony of 1607-1608. Some typographical errors in the first-named of these have, by permission of Mr. George Parker Winship, been corrected from the text printed in his *Sailors' Narratives of New England Voyages*, published by Messrs. Houghton, Mifflin and Company (Boston, 1906), direct collation with the original having been, at the time of printing, possible to only a small extent.

J. F. J.

CONTENTS

ORIGINAL NARRATIVES OF EARLY ENGLISH AND FRENCH VOYAGES

Edited by Henry S. Burrage, D.D.

	PAGE
Introduction	xvii
The First Relation of Jaques Carthier of S. Malo	1
Introduction	2
Cartier's Approach to Newfoundland	4
His Description of the East Coast	6
The Strait of Belle Isle and the South Coast of Labrador	7
The West Coast of Newfoundland	8
Cartier crosses the Gulf of St. Lawrence	13
From Prince Edward Island he passes north along the New Brunswick and Canadian Coast	17
Gives an Account of the Natives	19
Erects a Cross near the Mouth of the St. Lawrence	24
Explores the Coast of Anticosti	26
Examines further the South Coast of Labrador	27
Returns to France through the Strait of Belle Isle	29
A Shorte and Briefe Narration (Cartier's Second Voyage)	33
Introduction	35
Cartier again reaches Newfoundland	38
Re-enters the Gulf of St. Lawrence	38
Explores the Shores of the Gulf on the North and West	39
Discovers the St. Lawrence River	41
Explores it as far as the Site of Quebec	43
Holds Intercourse with the Natives	46
Ascends the River in Boats to Hochelaga	54
Description of the Town	59
Cartier's Reception by the Indians There	61
Falls in the River prevent his farther Advance	63
Returns to his Vessels; goes into Winter Quarters	64
Faith, Manners, and Customs of the People	66
Description of the Country	69
Cartier loses Twenty-five of his Men by Scurvy	72

CONTENTS

	PAGE
Experiences with the Indians	77
Captures the Chief Donnacona and Some of his Subjects	81
Promises to return the Captives in the next Year	82
Descends the River and sails for France	84
Specimens of the Language of the Indians on the St. Lawrence	86

THE THIRD VOYAGE OF DISCOVERY MADE BY CAPTAINE JAQUES
CARTIER 89
    INTRODUCTION 91
    Cartier returns to the St. Lawrence 93
    Announces the Death of the Captive Indian Chief . . . 96
    The Fertility and Products of the Country 97
    Further Exploration along the River 99
    The Indians Conspire against the French 101
    The Narration abruptly Closes 102

THE VOYAGE OF M. HORE 103
    INTRODUCTION 105
    The Expedition sails from Gravesend 106
    M. Dawbeny's Report to M. Richard Hakluyt . . . 107
    Famine; Seizure of a French Vessel; the Return . . . 108
    Henry VIII. afterward recompenses the Frenchmen . . . 110

THE VOYAGE MADE BY M. JOHN HAWKINS, ESQUIRE . . . 111
    INTRODUCTION 113
    Hawkins sails to the African Coast; secures a Cargo of Slaves . 114
    Sells these Slaves in the West Indies; reaches the West End of Cuba 114
    Passes along the Northern Part of Cuba 115
    Crosses to the Eastern Coast of Florida 117
    Visits the French Huguenot Colony on the St. John River . 119
    Hardships of the French Colonists 122
    The Colonists relieved by Hawkins 124
    Products of the Country 125
    Some of the Animals found There 127
    Hawkins sails homeward by the way of the Newfoundland Fishing
        Grounds 131

THE THIRD TROUBLESOME VOYAGE MADE WITH THE JESUS OF LUBEC 133
    INTRODUCTION 135
    Hawkins again sails for the African Coast 137
    With a Cargo of Slaves he crosses to the West Indies and the Spanish
        Main 139
    Is driven to the Eastern Coast of Mexico 140
    Engages the Spanish Fleet in the Harbor of San Juan de Ulua . 143
    Escapes; returns past Florida to Spain and England . . . 145

THE WORLD ENCOMPASSED BY SIR FRANCIS DRAKE (CALIFORNIA) . 149

CONTENTS

	PAGE
INTRODUCTION	151
On the California Coast	154
Anchors "in a convenient and fit Harbor"	155
The People of the Country	158
Their Manner of Life	161
Their *Hióh* or King	164
Drake's Reception	166
Character of the People	170
A Monument erected as a Token of English Possession	171

REPORT OF THE VOYAGE OF SIR HUMFREY GILBERT KNIGHT, BY MASTER EDWARD HAIES . . . 175

INTRODUCTION	177
The Claim of England to the American Coast	179
Encouragement for English Exploration and Colonization	180
Sir Humphrey Gilbert's First Endeavor	185
His Second Expedition	186
Orders given to the Fleet Captains	189
Gilbert plans to approach by way of Newfoundland	190
Sails from England	192
Arrives in St. John Harbor	196
Takes Possession of the Country	198
Description of Newfoundland and its Products	200
Gilbert proceeds Southward for further Exploration	207
Loss of the *Delight* at Cape Breton	210
Gilbert decides to return to England	214
His Vessel founders; Gilbert is Drowned	219
Character of Gilbert	221

THE FIRST VOYAGE MADE TO THE COASTS OF AMERICA, BY CAPTAIN ARTHUR BARLOWE . . . 223

INTRODUCTION	225
The Expedition arrives in Pamlico Sound	228
The Natives of the Country	230
Their Manners and Customs	231
Their Towns and Neighbors	237
Roanoke Island	240
The Return to England	240

ACCOUNT OF THE PARTICULARITIES OF THE IMPLOYMENTS OF THE ENGLISHMEN LEFT IN VIRGINIA, BY MASTER RALPH LANE . 243

INTRODUCTION	245
Extent of Exploration by the Colonists	247
Pearls and other Commodities for Traffic	249
Conspiracy of the Indians against the English	252

CONTENTS

	PAGE
Inquiry for Minerals	254
A Better Harbor Desired	257
Growing Hostility of the Indians	259
Pemisapan's Conspiracy	262
Pemisapan and his Followers Slain	267
Drake's Fleet arrives and takes the Colonists back to England	268

THE THIRD VOYAGE TO VIRGINIA 273

   INTRODUCTION 275

   Ralegh sends Relief to the Colony, but as the Colonists had returned to England the Relief Ship sails Homeward 276

   Grenville, not finding the Colonists, leaves Fifteen Men with Provisions and returns to England 277

THE FOURTH VOYAGE MADE TO VIRGINIA IN THE YERE 1587, BY GOVERNOR JOHN WHITE 279

   INTRODUCTION 281

   The Expedition proceeds westward by way of the West Indies . 282

   Reaches Roanoke Island; fails to find Grenville's Men . . 287

   Inquiries among the Indians 289

   Friendly Indians attacked under Misapprehension . . . 292

   Governor White constrained to return for Supplies . . . 294

   The Homeward Voyage 295

   Names of all the Men, Women, and Children left at Roanoke Island 298

THE FIFTH VOYAGE OF M. JOHN WHITE 301

   INTRODUCTION 303

   White's Letter to Hakluyt 305

   Sails by way of the Canaries and West Indies 307

   Various Experiences in the West Indies 308

   On the American Coast 313

   Captain Spicer and Six Others drowned at Hatorask . . . 315

   Governor White finds None of the Colonists left at Roanoke Island in 1587 317

   Sails for the West Indies for Supplies, but is driven by a Storm toward the Azores 320

   Reaches the Azores; proceeds to England 321

BRIEFE AND TRUE RELATION OF THE DISCOVERIE OF THE NORTH PART OF VIRGINIA, BY JOHN BRERETON 325

   INTRODUCTION 327

   Gosnold reaches the Coast in Lat. 43°; sails Southward . . 330

   Passing Cape Cod and Martha's Vineyard he lands at Cuttyhunk 331

   In Buzzard's Bay 335

   Trades with the Indians 336

   Loads his Vessel with Sassafras, etc., and sails Homeward . . 339

CONTENTS

	PAGE
A VOYAGE SET OUT FROM THE CITIE OF BRISTOLL, BY MARTIN PRING	341
INTRODUCTION	343
Pring's Landfall on the Maine Coast	345
Sailing south he enters Plymouth Harbor	346
Experiences with the Indians; their Appearance and Boats	347
Products of the Country	349
Loads One of his Vessels with Sassafras	350
Returns to England	351
A TRUE RELATION OF THE VOYAGE OF CAPTAINE GEORGE WAYMOUTH, BY JAMES ROSIER	353
INTRODUCTION	355
Rosier's Preface	357
Waymouth sails from Ratcliffe on the Thames	359
Sights Sankaty Head, Nantucket	361
At Monhegan, driven thither by Contrary Winds	362
Anchors in St. George's Harbor	364
Fishes and Fruits	365
Visited by Indians	367
Waymouth discovers a Great River	369
Traffics with the Indians	370
Description of their Women and Children	373
Waymouth visits the Indians	376
Captures Five Indians in St. George's Harbor	378
Ascends the River in his Vessel	379
Attractiveness and Characteristics of the River	381
Sets up a Cross where the River "trended westward"	386
Reluctantly leaves the River	387
Returns to St. George's Harbor	389
Sails homeward with his Indian Captives	390
Concerning the Products of the Country	393
A RELATION OF A VOYAGE TO SAGADAHOC	395
INTRODUCTION	397
The Popham Colonists sail for the Maine Coast by way of the Azores	399
Land is sighted on the Coast of Nova Scotia	401
The *Mary and John* at Cape Sable	404
The Camden Mountains are Sighted	405
The *Mary and John* anchors in St. George's Harbor; also the *Gift*	406
Chaplain Seymour delivers a Sermon	407
The Vessels sail for the Kennebec; the *Gift* enters the River	408
The *Mary and John* passes to the westward of Seguin, and enters the River Three Days Later	409
The Patent is read and Laws are Promulgated	411
The Colonists explore the Coast to the Westward	412

	PAGE
Pemaquid Indians visit the Colonists	413
Gilbert and Others explore the Coast to the Eastward; also the Sagadahoc River	413
The Relation abruptly Ends	415
Continuation from Strachey; conflict with Sabenoa	416
The Completion of Fort St. George	418
Its Abandonment	419

ORIGINAL NARRATIVES OF EARLY
ENGLISH AND FRENCH VOYAGES

INTRODUCTION

INTRODUCTION

WITH three exceptions, all the voyages recorded in this volume were made by English navigators. These three exceptions — the narratives of Cartier's voyages — were of so much importance in western discovery, however, that they are very properly included here, and for the same reason, doubtless, that they were included by Hakluyt, three hundred years ago, in his *Principall Navigations, Voiages and Discoveries of the English Nation*. Indeed for most of the material contained in this volume we are indebted to Hakluyt's monumental work. This sense of indebtedness, strong even among English-speaking people in Hakluyt's lifetime, was never stronger than in these days when the student of history in his investigations rightly insists on going back to the sources.

Hakluyt was really one of the great men of England in the sixteenth century. He saw, and he saw clearly, that western discovery afforded to his nation a great opportunity for extending English dominion and power. The quality of Hakluyt's mind peculiarly fitted him for a work that made him the repository of large information with reference to various parts of the new world. Born in 1552 or 1553, he was educated at Westminster School and Christ Church College, Oxford, which he entered in 1570, and where he took his B.A. degree February 19, 1574, and his M.A. degree June 27, 1577. Even while a Queen's scholar at Westminster, "that fruitful nurserie," as he tells us, when one day visiting his cousin, Mr. Richard

Hakluyt, "a Gentleman of the Middle Temple," he found upon his table "certeine bookes of Cosmographie with a universal Mappe." These awakened his curiosity and stimulated his desire to know more concerning them. In meeting this desire his cousin cited the passage in the one hundred and seventh Psalm concerning those who go down into the sea in ships. "The words of the Prophet," says Hakluyt, "together with my cousin's discourse (things of high and rare delight to my young nature), tooke so deepe an impression that I constantly resolved, if ever I were preferred to the University, where better time and more convenient place might be ministered for these studies, I would by God's assistance prosecute that knowledge and kinde of literature, doores whereof (after a sort) were so happily opened before me." [1]

That resolution Hakluyt kept, and how well he kept it is indicated by the fact that at length he was made university lecturer on cosmography. In the dedication of his *Divers Voyages*, etc., his earliest printed work for the furtherance of English maritime exploration, Hakluyt, in a dedication of the work to Sir Philip Sidney, says: "In my public lectures I was the first that produced and showed both the olde imperfectly composed and the new lately reformed mappes, globes and spheares." In other words, Hakluyt was a forerunner in such instruction, and we have in this statement a glimpse of the strong workings of his mind in the endeavor to widen his own horizon and to widen the horizon of his countrymen by directing the attention to lands beyond the seas, available for English exploration and colonization. Nothing was more evident than that Spain, because of her western discoveries and possessions, had greatly increased her wealth and influence. But the rights of England to the American continent Hakluyt believed ante-dated those of Spain by reason of the discoveries of Cabot. England, however, had been remiss in making good

[1] Preface to *The Principall Navigations*, etc., published in 1589.

INTRODUCTION

her claim. It is true that there had been voyages like those of Hawkins and Drake; but Hakluyt had in mind something entirely aside from slave-stealing and selling and the plundering of Spanish ships and Spanish settlements. He saw the gain that would come to England by seizing on the American coast the vast territory between the Spanish settlements at the South and the French settlements at the North; and accordingly he sought, in all possible ways, to impress his views upon the minds of influential men in all parts of the kingdom. It was in support of these views that he published in 1582 his first small book, *Divers Voyages touching the Discoverie of America*.

Hakluyt early took clerical orders. Soon after he left Oxford, while he was occupied chiefly with geographical lecturing, the attention of Walsingham, Elizabeth's astute Secretary of State, was directed to the young cosmographer, and a letter of Walsingham to Hakluyt, dated March 11, 1582/3, commended his geographical studies and thanked him for the service he had rendered in his efforts "for the discovery of the Western partes yet unknowen."

In 1584, Hakluyt wrote his *Discourse of Western Planting*, which he designated "A Particular discourse concerning the great necessitie and manifold comodyties that are like to growe to this Realme of Englande by the Westerne discoveries lately attempted."[1] This masterly *Discourse* was written at the request of Sir Walter Ralegh, and inasmuch as a manuscript

[1] At least four manuscript copies of the *Discourse* were made by Hakluyt. It was never printed by him. Indeed no copy was known to have been preserved until the sale of Lord Valentia's library, near the middle of the last century, when one was bought by Mr. Henry Stevens, who later sold it to Sir Henry Phillipps. When President Woods of Bowdoin College was in England, in 1867, in search of materials relating to the early history of Maine, an application to Mr. Phillipps for any such material in his possession revealed the existence of Hakluyt's *Discourse*, and Dr. Woods secured a copy of the manuscript, which he brought to this country. The *Discourse* was published by the Maine Historical Society in 1877, as Volume II. of its *Documentary History of Maine*.

copy of it was presented to the Queen by Hakluyt in the early autumn of 1584, it has been thought that it was designed to secure Elizabeth's support of an enterprise which Ralegh purposed to set on foot under his patent of March 25, 1584. Hakluyt's breadth of view, his great knowledge of what had already been done, and his profound conviction with reference to the favorable opportunity which western planting still afforded to his countrymen, are conspicuous upon every page of this learned *Discourse*.

Already, in 1583, Hakluyt had enlarged his opportunity for prosecuting his favorite studies by accepting an appointment as chaplain to Sir Edward Stafford, English ambassador to France. Accompanying Sir Edward to Paris, Hakluyt remained five years at the French capital, continuing his inquiries with reference to the new world. In 1586, he published in the French language an account of the voyages of Laudonnière and others, which he translated and published in English in 1587, under the title, *Foure Voyages unto Florida*. In the same year he brought out an edition of Peter Martyr's *De Novo Orbe*. This also he translated into English and published under the title, *The Historie of the West Indies*.

As the ripened fruit of the labors of nearly twenty years, Hakluyt, on his return to England, published in 1589 his great work, *The Principall Navigations, Voiages and Discoveries of the English nation, made by Sea or over Land, to the most remote and farthest distant Quarters of the earth at any time within the compasse of these 1500 yeeres*.[1] An enlarged edition in three volumes was published in 1598, 1599, and 1600. Hakluyt had taken pains not only to keep himself informed with reference to the work of navigators and explorers, but to have narrations of their voyages made and to secure copies of such narrations. Because of his wide acquaintance in influential

[1] In Volume II. of the next edition the title-page read "1600 yeres."

circles, his opportunities in this endeavor were great, and he improved them to the utmost extent.

Hakluyt was made a prebendary of Bristol in 1586, rector of Wetheringset in Suffolk in 1590; in 1602 he was made a prebendary, in 1603 archdeacon, of Westminster. He died at Eaton, in Herefordshire, November 23, 1616, and was buried in Westminster Abbey, November 26, 1616. His unpublished papers came into the possession of Samuel Purchas, who used them in the preparation of his well-known *Pilgrimes*.

Hakluyt's *Principall Navigations*, in an edition embracing all the contents of both the edition of 1589 and that of 1598–1600, was reprinted in London in 1809. A part, edited by Edmund Goldsmid, was published in Edinburgh in 1889 and 1890, entitled *The Voyages of the English Nation to America before the Year* 1600. The whole work, after the edition of 1598–1600, in sixteen volumes "with notes, indices and numerous additions," edited by Edmund Goldsmid, was republished at the same time. Messrs. James MacLehose and Sons of Glasgow, the Hakluyt Society of London, and The Macmillan Company of New York and London, have united in the publication (1903–1905) of a very handsome edition of the whole work in twelve volumes with many interesting illustrations.

My grateful acknowledgments are due to Messrs. Dodd, Mead and Company, New York, for an early opportunity of examining the sheets of Mr. Baxter's scholarly work, "A Memoir of Jacques Cartier." In this examination much valuable help was received for the preparation of notes identifying the places visited by Cartier in his three voyages of discovery. For the use of books I am indebted to the State Library in Augusta, the library of Bowdoin College, the library of Colby College, and especially to the library of the Maine Historical Society; and I would not fail to mention the latter's librarian, Mr. H. W. Bryant. The superintendent of the United States

Coast and Geodetic Survey, Mr. O. H. Tittmann, has rendered me prompt and efficient service in the identification of places in the West Indies visited by the early voyagers; and a like acknowledgment is made to Rear-Admiral Albert S. Barker, U.S.N. (retired).

HENRY S. BURRAGE.

THE FIRST RELATION OF JAQUES CARTHIER OF S. MALO, 1534

INTRODUCTION

JACQUES CARTIER was a native of St. Malo, the principal port of Brittany. On fishing voyages in his earlier years he became interested in western discovery, and in 1533, in a letter addressed to Philippe de Chabot, Sieur de Brion, High Admiral of France, he proposed a voyage to the American coast, continuing the discoveries commenced by Verrazano in 1524. Through him the interest of the king was enlisted in the enterprise; and with two vessels, of sixty tons each, Cartier sailed from the port of St. Malo, April 20, 1534. A report of this voyage, written either by Cartier himself or by one of his companions, was preserved in an Italian translation by Ramusio, in the third volume of his *Navigationi*, folio 435 *et seqq.* (Venice, 1556). An English translation by Jean Florio was printed in London in 1580. The French edition published by Raphael du Petit Val appeared in 1598, *Discours du Voyage fait par le Capitaine Jaques Cartier* (Rouen, 1598; reprinted in various editions of Lescarbot, and also at Quebec in 1843 and at Paris in 1840 and in 1865). Hakluyt's account of the voyage appeared first in his edition of 1600. A relation of Cartier's first voyage in manuscript was discovered in the Bibliothèque Nationale in Paris in 1867, and was published the same year. Messrs. Dodd, Mead and Company (New York, 1906) have published *A Memoir of Jacques Cartier* by Hon. James P. Baxter, Litt.D., in which, besides the memoir and a bibliography, will be found a facsimile of this manuscript with annotations — a very valuable work.

H. S. B.

THE FIRST RELATION OF JAQUES CARTHIER OF S. MALO, 1534

The first relation of Jaques Carthier of S. Malo, of the new land called New France, newly discovered in the yere of our Lord 1534.

How M. Jaques Carthier departed from the Port of S. Malo, with two ships, and came to Newfoundland, and how he entred into the Port of Buona Vista.

AFTER that Sir Charles of Mouy knight lord of Meylleraye, and Viceadmirall of France had caused the Captaines, Masters, and Mariners of the shippes to be sworne to behave themselves truely and faithfully in the service of the most Christian King of France,[1] under the charge of the sayd Carthier, upon the twentieth day of Aprill 1534, we departed from the Port of S. Malo with two ships of threescore tun apiece burden, and 61 well appointed men in each one: and with such prosperous weather we sailed onwards, that upon the tenth day of May we came to Newfoundland, where we entred into the Cape of Buona Vista,[2] which is in latitude 48 degrees and a halfe, and in longitude .[3] But because of the great store of the ice that was alongst the sayd land, we were constrayned to enter into an haven called S. Katherins[4] haven, distant from the other Port about five leagues toward Southsoutheast: there did we stay tenne days looking for faire weather; and in the meanwhile we mended and dressed our boats.

[1] Francis I.
[2] A point of land on the eastern shore of Newfoundland between Bonavista Bay and Trinity Bay. It was the point at which the early voyagers aimed in coming to the coast, and from which they took their departure. By some it has been regarded as the *prima vista* of Cabot, while others have found in it the landfall of Cortereal in 1501.
[3] Blank in the original.
[4] Catalina at present.

How we came to the Island of Birds, and of the great quantity of birds that there be.

Upon the 21 of May the winde being in the West, we hoised saile, and sailed toward North[1] and by East from the cape of Buona Vista until we came to the Island of Birds,[2] which was environed about with a banke of ice, but broken and crackt: notwithstanding the sayd banke, our two boats went thither to take in some birds, whereof there is such plenty, that unlesse a man did see them, he would thinke it an incredible thing: for albeit the Island (which containeth about a league in circuit) be so full of them, that they seeme to have been brought thither, and sowed for the nonce, yet are there an hundred folde as many hovering about it as within; some of the which are as big as jayes, blacke and white, with beaks like unto crowes: they lie alwayes upon the sea; they cannot flie very high, because their wings are so little, and no bigger then halfe ones hand, yet they do flie as swiftly as any birds of the aire levell to the water; they are also exceeding fat; we named them Aporath.[3] In lesse then halfe an houre we filled two boats full of them, as if they had bene with stones: so that besides them which we did eat fresh, every ship did powder and salt five or sixe barrels full of them.

Of two sorts of birds, the one called Godetz, the other Margaulx; and how we came to Carpunt.

Besides these, there is another kinde of birds which hover in the aire, and over the sea, lesser than the others; and these doe all gather themselves together in the Island, and put themselves under the wings of other birds that are greater: these

---

[1] Evidently Cartier had no knowledge of a southern entrance to the Gulf of St. Lawrence.
[2] Funk Island.
[3] Perhaps the great auk, then common in that region.

we named Godetz.[1] There are also of another sort, but bigger, and white, which bite even as dogs: those we named Margaulx.[2] And albeit the sayd Island be 14 leagues from the maine land, notwithstanding beares come swimming thither to eat of the sayd birds: and our men found one there as great as any cow,[3] and as white as any swan, who in their presence leapt into the sea; and upon Whitsunmunday (following our voyage toward the land) we met her by the way, swimming toward land as swiftly as we could saile. So soone as we saw her, we pursued her with our boats, and by maine strength tooke her, whose flesh was as good to be eaten as the flesh of a calf of two yeres olde. The Wednesday following, being the 27 of the moneth, we came to the entrance of the bay of the Castles;[4] but because the weather was ill, and the great store of ice we found, we were constrained to enter into an harborow about the sayd entrance called Carpunt,[5] where, because we would not come out of it, we stayed til the ninth of June, what time we departed, hoping with the helpe of God to saile further then the said Carpunt, which is latitude 51 degrees.

The description of Newfoundland, from Cape Razo to Cape Degrad.

The land from Cape Razo[6] to Cape Degrad,[7] which is the point of the entrance of the bay that trendeth from head to head toward Northnortheast, and Southsouthwest, All this part of land is parted into Islands one so nere the other, that there are but small rivers betweene them; thorow the which you may passe with little boats, and therefore there are certaine good harborows, among which are those of Carpunt and Degrad. In one of these Islands that is the highest of them all, being the top of it you may plainly see the two low Islands that are nere to Cape Razo, from whence to the port of Carpunt

[1] Murres, or razorbills. [2] Gannets. [3] *Ursus maritimus.*
[4] Strait of Belle Isle. [5] Quirpon.
[6] Cape Rouge in the French manuscript, and so called at the present time.
[7] Northern extremity of Quirpon.

they count it five and twenty leagues; and there are two entrances thereat, one on the East, the other on the South side of the Island. But you must take heed of the side and point of the East, because that every where there is nothing els but shelves, and the water is very shallow: you must go about the Island toward the West the length of halfe a cable or thereabout, and then to goe toward the South to the sayd Carpunt. Also you are to take heed of three shelves that are in the chanell under the water: and toward the Island on the East side in the chanell, the water is of three or four fadome deepe, and cleere ground. The other trendeth toward Eastnortheast, and on the West you may go on shore.

Of the Island which is now called S. Katherins Island.

Going from the point Degrad, and entring into the sayd bay toward the West and by North: there is some doubt of two Islands that are on the right side, one of the which is distant from the sayd point three leagues, and the other seven, either more or lesse then the first, being a low and plaine land, and it seemeth to be part of the maine land. I named it Saint Katherines Island;[1] in which, toward the Northeast there is very dry soile; but about a quarter of a league from it, very ill ground, so that you must go a little about. The sayd Island and the Port of Castles[2] trend toward North northeast, and South southwest, and they are about 15. leagues asunder. From the said port of Castles to the port of Gutte,[3] which is in the northerne part of the said Bay, that trendeth toward East northeast, and West southwest, there are 12. leagues and an halfe: and about two leagues from the port of Balances,[4] that is to say, the third part athwart the saide Bay the depth being sounded it is about 38. fadomes: and from the said port of Balances to the white Sands[5] toward West southwest there

---

[1] Identified by some as the island now known as Belle Isle and by others as Schooner Island.
[2] Chateau Bay.
[3] Greenish Harbor.
[4] Baie Royal.
[5] Present name.

is 15. leagues, but you must take heed of a shelfe that lyeth about 3. leagues outward from the said white Sands on the Southwest side above water like a boat.

Of the place called Blanc Sablon, or the white Sand: of the Iland of Brest, and of the Iland of Birds, of the sorts and quantitie of birds that there are found: and of the Port called the Islettes.

White Sand is a Road in the which there is no place guarded from the South, nor southeast. But toward South southwest from the saide road there are two Ilands, one of the which is called Brest Iland,[1] and the other the Iland of Birds, in which there is great store of Godetz, and crowes with red beakes and red feete: they make their nestes in holes under the ground even as Conies. A point of land being passed about a league from white Sand, there is a Port and passage found called the Islettes,[2] a better place then white Sand: and there is great fishing. From the said Port of the Islettes unto another called Brest, the circuit is about ten leagues. This Port is in latitude 51. degrees and 55. minutes, and in longitude .[3] From the Islettes to that place there are many other Ilands: and the saide Port of Brest is also amongst those Ilands. Moreover the Ilands do compasse more then 3. leagues from the said Brest, being low, and over them are the other lands above mentioned seene.

How we with our ships entred into the Port of Brest, and sayling onward toward the West we passed amidst the Islettes, which were so many in number, that it was not possible to tell them: and how we named them the Islettes.

Upon the 10. of June wee with our ships entred into the Port of Brest, to furnish our selves with water and wood, and to

---
[1] Named from a well-known port in Brittany; now called Old Fort.
[2] Bradore Bay.   [3] Blank in original.

make us ready to passe the said Bay. Upon S. Barnabas day Service being heard, we with our boats went beyond the said Port toward the west, to see what harboroughes were there: wee passed through the midst of the Islettes, which were so many in number that it was not possible they might be tolde, for they continued about 10. leagues beyond the said Port. We to rest our selves stayed in one of them a night, and there we found great store of ducke egges, and other birds that there do make their nests, we named them all The Islettes.

Of the Port called S. Antonies Port, S. Servans Port, James Cartiers Port: of the river called S. James: of the customes and apparell of the inhabitants in the Iland of White Sand.

The next day we passed the said Ilands, and beyond them all we found a good haven, which we named S. Antonies Haven,[1] and one or two leagues beyond wee found a little river towarde the southwest coast, that is betweene two other Ilands, and is a good harborough. There we set up a Crosse, and named it S. Servans Port:[2] and on the Southwest side of the said Port and river, about one league there is a small Iland as round as an Oven, environed about with many other litle Ilands that give notice to the said Ports. Further about two leagues there is another greater river, in which we tooke good store of salmon, that we named S. James his River. Being in the said river, we saw a ship of Rochel that the night before had passed the Port of Brest, where they thought to have gone a fishing: but the Mariners knew not where they were. We with our boats approched neere unto it, and did direct it to another Port one league more toward the West than the said river of S. James, which I take to be one of the best in all the world, and therefore wee named it James Carthiers Sound.[3] If the soile

[1] Rocky Bay.
[2] Probably Shecatica Bay, which from some points of view has the appearance of a large river.
[3] Cumberland Bay.

were as good as the harboroughes are, it were a great commoditie: but it is not to be called The new Land, but rather stones and wilde cragges, and a place fit for wilde beastes, for in all the North Iland I did not see a Cart-load of good earth: yet went I on shoare in many places, and in the Iland of White Sand, there is nothing else but mosse and small thornes scattered here and there, withered and dry. To be short, I beleeve that this was the land that God allotted to Caine. There are men of an indifferent good stature and bignesse, but wilde and unruly: they weare their haire tied on the top like a wreath of hay, and put a wooden pinne within it, or any other such thing instead of a naile, and with them they binde certaine birdes feathers. They are clothed with beastes skinnes as well the men as women, but that the women go somewhat straiter and closer in their garments than the men do, with their wastes girded; they paint themselves with certaine Roan colours: their boates are made of the barke of birch trees, with the which they fish and take great store of Seales, and as farre as we could understand since our comming thither, that is not their habitation, but they come from the maine land out of hotter countreys, to catch the saide Seales and other necessaries for their living.

Of certaine Capes, that is to say, The double Cape, The pointed Cape, Cape Royal, and The Cape of Milke: of the mountaines of Granges: of the Ilands of Dove houses: and of the great fishing of Cods.

Upon the 13. of that moneth we came to our ships againe with our boats on purpose to saile forwards because the weather was faire, and upon Sunday we caused Service to be saide: then on munday being the 15. of the moneth we departed from Brest, and sailed toward the South to take a view of the lands that there wee had seene, that seemed unto us to bee two Ilands: but when we were amidst the Bay, we knew it to be firme land, where was a great double Cape one above the other, and therefore wee named it The double Cape.[1] In the entrance of the Bay wee sounded, and found it to be an hundred fadome round about us. From Brest to The double Cape there is about 20. leagues, and about five or sixe leagues beyond we sounded againe and found 40 fadome water. The said land lieth Northeast and Southwest. The next day being the 16 of the moneth we sailed along the said coast toward the Southwest, and by South about 35 leagues from the double Cape, where we found very steepe and wilde hilles, among the which were seene certaine smal cabbans, which we in the countrey call Granges, and therefore we named them The hilles of the Granges.[2] The other lands and mountaines are all craggie, cleft and cut, and betwixt them and the Sea, there are other Ilands, but low. The day before through the darke mists and fogges of the weather, we could not have sight of any land, but in the evening we spied an entrance into the land, by a river among the said Hilles of Granges, and a Cape lying toward the Southwest about 3 leagues from us. The said Cape is on the top of it blunt-pointed, and also toward the Sea it endeth in a point, wherefore wee named it The pointed Cape,[3] on the North side of which there is a plaine Iland. And because we would have notice of the said entrance, to see if there were any good havens, we strooke saile for that night. The next day being the 17 of the moneth we had stormie weather from Northeast, wherefore we tooke our way toward the Southwest untill thursday morning, and we went about 37 leagues, till wee came athwart a Bay full of round Ilands like dove houses, and therefore wee named them The dove houses.[4] And from the Bay of S. Julian, from the which to a Cape that lieth South and by West, which wee called Cape Roial,[5] there are 7. leagues, and toward the West southwest side of the saide Cape, there is another that beneath is all craggie, and above round.

[1] High lands beyond Point Rich. Cartier was now passing down the north-western shore of Newfoundland.
[2] Range of mountains on the western coast of Newfoundland.
[3] Cow Head.
[4] Bay of Islands, south of Bonne Bay.
[5] Bluff Head.

On the North side of which about halfe a league there lieth a low Iland: that Cape we named The Cape of milke.[1] Betweene these two Capes there are certaine low Ilands, above which there are also certaine others that shew that there be some rivers. About two leagues from Cape royall wee sounded and found 20 fadome water, and there is the greatest fishing of Cods that possible may be: for staying for our company, in lesse then an houre we tooke above an hundreth of them.

Of certaine Ilands that lie betweene Cape Royall, and The Cape of Milke.

The next day being the 18 of the moneth, the winde with such rage turned against us, that we were constrained to go backe towards Cape Royal, thinking there to finde some harborough, and with our boates went to discover betweene the Cape Royal, and the Cape of Milke, and found that above the low Ilands there is a great and very deepe gulfe, within which are certaine Ilands. The said gulfe on the Southside is shut up. The foresaid low grounds are on one of the sides of the entrance, and Cape Royal is on the other. The saide low grounds doe stretch themselves more then halfe a league within the Sea. It is a plaine countrey, but an ill soile: and in the middest of the entrance thereof, there is an Iland. The saide gulfe in latitude is fourtie eight degrees and an halfe, and in longitude [2] That night we found no harborough, and therefore wee launched out into the Sea, leaving the Cape toward the West.

Of the Iland called S. John.

From the said day untill the 24 of the moneth being S. Johns day we had both stormie weather and winde against us, with such darknesse and mistes, that untill S. Johns day, we

---

[1] Cape St. George.   [2] Blank in original.

could have no sight of any land, and then we had sight of a Cape of land, that from Cape Royal lieth Southwest about 35 leagues, but that day was so foggie and mistie, that we could not come neere land, and because it was S. Johns day, we named it Cape S. John.[1]

Of certaine Ilands called the Ilands of Margaulx, and of the kinds of beastes and birds that there are found. Of the Iland of Brion, and Cape Dolphin.

The next day being the 25. of the moneth, the weather was also stormie, darke, and windy, but yet we sailed a part of the day toward West North west, and in the evening wee put our selves athwart untill the second quarter; when as we departed, then did we by our compasse know that we were Northwest and by West about seven leagues and an halfe from the Cape of S. John, and as wee were about to hoise saile, the winde turned into the Northwest, wherefore we went Southeast, about 15. leagues, and came to three Ilands, two of which are as steepe and upright as any wall, so that it was not possible to climbe them: and betweene them there is a little rocke. These Ilands were as full of birds, as any field or medow is of grasse, which there do make their nestes: and in the greatest of them, there was a great and infinite number of those that wee call Margaulx, that are white, and bigger then any geese, which were severed in one part. In the other were onely Godetz, but toward the shoare there were of those Godetz, and great Apponatz, like to those of that Iland that we above have mentioned: we went downe to the lowest part of the least Iland, where we killed above a thousand of those Godetz, and Apponatz. We put into our boates so many of them as we pleased, for in lesse then one houre we might have filled thirtie such boats of them: we named them The Ilands of Margaulx.[2] About five leagues from the said Ilands on the West, there is another Iland that is about two leagues in length, and so much in breadth: there did we stay all night to take in water and wood. That Iland

[1] Cape Anguille.   [2] Still known as the Bird Rocks.

is environed round about with sand, and hath a very good road about it three or foure fadome deepe. Those Ilands have the best soile that ever we saw, for that one of their fields is more worth then all the New land. We found it all full of goodly trees, medowes, fields full of wild corne and peason bloomed, as thicke, as ranke, and as faire as any can be seene in Britaine,[1] so that they seemed to have bene plowed and sowed. There was also a great store of gooseberies, strawberies, damaske roses, parseley, with other very sweete and pleasant hearbes. About the said Iland are very great beastes as great as oxen,[2] which have two great teeth in their mouths like unto Elephants teeth, and live also in the Sea. We saw one of them sleeping upon the banke of the water: wee thinking to take it, went to it with our boates, but so soone as he heard us, he cast himselfe into the Sea. We also saw beares and wolves: we named it Brions Iland.[3] About it toward Southeast, and Northwest, there are great lakes. As farre as I could gather and comprehend, I thinke that there be some passage betweene New found land, and Brions land.[4] If so it were, it would be a great shortening, aswel of the time as of the way, if any perfection could be found in it. About foure leagues from that Iland toward West-Southwest is the firme land, which seemeth to be as an Iland compassed about with litle Ilands of sands. There is a goodly Cape which we named Cape Dolphin,[5] for there is the beginning of good grounds. On the 27. of June we compassed the said lands about that lie West Southwest: and a farre off they seeme to be little hilles of sand, for they are but low landes: wee could neither goe to them, nor land on them, because the winde was against us. That day we went 15. leagues.

[1] Brittany.
[2] Walrus, sometimes called morse or seahorse.
[3] Now known as Byron Island. The name was given by Cartier in honor of his patron, Philippe de Chabot, Sieur de Brion.
[4] The French manuscript has here "land of the Bretons." A passage between Newfoundland and the island of Cape Breton was with Cartier only a matter of conjecture.
[5] North Point.

Of the Iland called Alezai, and of the cape of S. Peter.

The next day we went along the said land about 10. leagues, till we came to a Cape of redde land, that is all craggie, within the which there is a bracke looking toward the North. It is a very low countrey. There is also betweene the Sea and a certaine poole, a plaine field: and from that Cape of land and the poole unto another Cape, there are about 14 leagues. The land is fashioned as it were halfe a circle, all compassed about with sand like a ditch, over which as farre as ones eye can stretch, there is nothing but marrish grounds and standing pooles. And before you come to the first Cape very neere the maine land there are two little Ilands. About five leagues from the second Cape toward the Southwest, there is another Iland very high and pointed, which we named Alezai.[1] The first Cape we named S. Peters Cape,[2] because upon that day we came thither.

Of the Cape called Cape Orleans: of the River of Boates: of Wilde mens Cape: and of the qualitie and temperature of the countrey.

From Brions Iland to this place there is good anckorage of sand, and having sounded toward Southwest even to the shoare about five leagues, wee found twentie and five fadome water, and within one league twelve fadome, and very neere the shoare sixe fadome, rather more then lesse, and also good anckorage. But because wee would bee the better acquainted with this stonie and rockie ground, wee strooke our sailes lowe and athwart. The next day being the last of the moneth save one, the winde blewe South and by East. Wee sailed Westward untill Tuesday morning at Sunne rising, being the last of the moneth, without any sight or knowledge of any lande except in the evening toward Sunne set, that wee discovered a lande

---

[1] Deadman's Island. [2] Southwest Cape.

which seemed to be two Ilands, that were beyond us West southwest, about nine or tenne leagues. All the next day till the next morning at sunne rising wee sailed Westward about fourtie leagues, and by the way we perceived that the land we had seene like Ilands, was firme land, lying South southeast, and North northwest, to a very good Cape of land called Cape Orleans.[1] Al the said land is low and plaine, and the fairest that may possibly be seene, full of goodly medowes and trees. True it is that we could finde no harborough there, because it is all full of shelves and sands. We with our boates went on shore in many places, and among the rest wee entred into a goodly river, but very shallow, which we named The river of boates,[2] because that there wee saw boates full of wild men that were crossing the river. We had no other notice of the said wild men: for the wind came from the sea, and so beat us against the shore, that wee were constrained to retire our selves with our boates toward our ships. Till the next day morning at Sunne rising, being the first of July we sailed Northeast, in which time there rose great mistes and stormes, and therefore wee strucke our sailes till two of the clocke in the afternoone, that the weather became cleare, and there we had sight of Cape Orleans, and of another about seven leagues from us, lying North and by East, and that we called Wilde mens Cape.[3] On the Northside of this Cape about halfe a league, there is a very dangerous shelfe, and banke of stones. Whilst wee were at this Cape, we sawe a man running after our boates that were going along the coast, who made signes unto us that we should returne toward the said Cape againe. We seeing such signes, began to turne toward him, but he seeing us come, began to flee: so soone as we were come on shoare, we set a knife before him and a woollen girdle on a little staffe, and then came to our ships again. That day we trended the said land about 9. or 10. leagues, hoping to finde some good harborough, but it was not possible: for as I have said already, it is a very low land, and environed round about with great

---

[1] Cape Kildare. [2] The Narrows in Richmond Bay. [3] North Point.

shelves. Nevertheless we went that day on shore in foure places to see the goodly and sweete smelling trees that were there: we found them to be Cedars, ewetrees, Pines, white elmes, ashes, willowes, with many other sorts of trees to us unknowen, but without any fruit. The grounds where no wood is, are very faire, and all full of peason, white and red gooseberies, strawberies, blackeberies, and wilde corne, even like unto Rie, which seemed to have bene sowen and plowed. This countrey is of better temperature then any other that can be seene, and very hote. There are many thrushes, stockdoves, and other birds: to be short, there wanteth nothing but good harboroughs.

Of the Bay called S. Lunario, and other notable Bayes and Capes of land, and of the qualitie, and goodnesse of those grounds.

The next day being the second of July we discovered and had sight of land on the Northerne side toward us, that did joyne unto the land abovesaid, al compassed about, and we knew that it had about   in depth, and as much athwart, and we named it S. Lunarios Bay,[1] and with our boats we went to the Cape toward the North, and found the shore so shallow, that for the space of a league from land there was but a fadome water. On the Northeast side from the said Cape about 7. or 8. leagues there is another Cape of land, in the middst whereof there is a Bay[2] fashioned trianglewise, very deepe, and as farre off as we could ken from it the same lieth Northeast. The said Bay is compassed about with sands and shelves about 10. leagues from land, and there is but two fadome water: from the said Cape to the bank of the other, there is about 15. leagues. We being a crosse the said Capes, discovered another land and Cape,[3]

[1] Strait of Northumberland, which Cartier supposed to be a bay.
[2] Miramichi.   [3] Blackland Point.

and as farre as we could ken, it lay North and by East. All that night the weather was very ill, and great winds, so that wee were constrained to beare a smal saile until the next morning, being the thirde of July when the winde came from the West: and we sailed Northward to have a sight of the land that we had left on the Northeast side, above the low lands, among which high and low lands there is a gulfe [1] or breach in some places about 55. fadome deepe, and 15. leagues in bredth. By reason of the great depth and bredth of the gulfe, and change of the lands, we conceived hope that we should finde a passage, like unto the passage of The Castles. The said gulfe lieth East Northeast, and West southwest. The ground that lieth on the Southside of the said gulfe, is as good and easie to be manured, and full of as goodly fields and meadowes, as any that ever wee have seene, as plaine and smooth as any die: and that which lyeth on the North is a countrey altogether hilly, full of woods, and very high and great trees of sundry sorts: among the rest there are as goodly Cedars, and Firre trees, as possibly can be seene, able to make mastes for ships of three hundred Tunne: neither did we see any place that was not full of the saide trees, except two onely that were full of goodly medowes, with two very faire lakes. The middest of the said Bay is 47. degrees and halfe in latitude.

Of the Cape D'Esperance, or the Cape of Hope, and of S. Martins Creeke, and how seven boats full of wilde men, comming to our boat, would not retire themselves, but being terrified with our Culverins which we shot at them, and our lances, they fled with great hast.

The Cape of the said South land was called The Cape of Hope,[2] through the hope that there we had to finde some passage. The fourth of July we went along the coast of the said land on the Northerly side to find some harborough, where wee entred into a creeke altogether open toward the South,

---

[1] Bay of Chaleur.   [2] Point Miscou.

where there is no succour against the wind: we thought good to name it S. Martines Creeke. There we stayed from the fourth of July until the twelfth: while we were there, on Munday being the sixth of the moneth, Service being done, wee with one of our boates went to discover a Cape and point of land that on the Westerne side was about seven or eight leagues from us, to see which way it did bend, and being within halfe a league of it, wee sawe two companies of boates of wilde men going from one land to the other: their boates were in number about fourtie or fiftie. One part of the which came to the said point, and a great number of men went on shore making a great noise, beckening unto us that wee should come on land, shewing us certaine skinnes upon pieces of wood, but because we had but one onely boat, wee would not goe to them, but went to the other side lying in the See: they seeing us flee, prepared two of their boats to follow us, with which came also five more of them that were comming from the Sea side, all which approched neere unto our boate, dancing, and making many signes of joy and mirth, as it were desiring our friendship, saying in their tongue Napeu tondamen assurtah,[1] with many other words that we understood not. But because (as we have said) we had but one boat, wee would not stand to their courtesie, but made signes unto them that they should turne back, which they would not do, but with great furie came toward us: and suddenly with their boates compassed us about: and because they would not away from us by any signes that we could make, we shot off two pieces among them, which did so terrifie them, that they put themselves to flight toward the sayde point, making a great noise: and having staid a while, they began anew, even as at the first to come to us againe, and being come neere our boat wee strucke at them with two lances, which thing was so great a terrour unto them, that with great haste they beganne to flee, and would no more follow us.

[1] Belleforest translates, "We wish to have your friendship."

How the said wilde men comming to our ships, and our men going toward them, both parties went on land, and how the saide wilde men with great joy began to trafique with our men.

The next day part of the saide wilde men with nine of their boates came to the point and entrance of the Creeke, where we with our ships were at road. We being advertised of their comming, went to the point where they were with our boates: but so soone as they saw us, they began to flee, making signes that they came to trafique with us, shewing us such skinnes as they cloth themselves withall, which are of small value. We likewise made signes unto them, that we wished them no evill: and in signe thereof two of our men ventured to go on land to them, and carry them knives with other Iron wares, and a red hat to give unto their Captaine. Which when they saw, they also came on land, and brought some of their skinnes, and so began to deale with us, seeming to be very glad to have our iron ware and other things, stil dancing with many other ceremonies, as with their hands to cast Sea water on their heads. They gave us whatsoever they had, not keeping any thing, so that they were constrained to go back againe naked, and made signes that the next day they would come againe, and bring more skinnes with them.

How that we having sent two of our men on land with wares, there came about 300. wilde men with great gladnesse. Of the qualitie of the countrey, what it bringeth forth, and of the Bay called Baie du Chaleur, or The Bay of heat.

Upon Thursday being the eight of the moneth, because the winde was not good to go out with our ships, we set our boates in a readinesse to goe to discover the said Bay, and that day wee went 25. leagues within it. The next day the wind and weather being faire, we sailed until noone, in which time we had notice of a great part of the said Bay, and how that over the low lands, there were other lands with high mountaines: but seeing that there was no passage at all, wee began to turne back againe, taking our way along the coast: and sayling, we saw certaine wilde men that stood upon the shoare of a lake, that is among the low grounds, who were making fires and smokes: wee went thither, and found that there was a channel of the sea that did enter into the lake, and setting our boats at one of the banks of the chanell, the wilde men with one of their boates came unto us, and brought up pieces of Seales ready sodden, putting them upon pieces of wood: then retiring themselves, they would make signes unto us, that they did give them us. We sent two men unto them with hatchets, knives, beads, and other such like ware, whereat they were very glad, and by and by in clusters they came to the shore where wee were, with their boates, bringing with them skinnes and other such things as they had, to have of our wares. They were more than 300. men, women, and children: Some of the women which came not over, wee might see stand up to the knees in water, singing and dancing: the other that had passed the river where we were, came very friendly to us, rubbing our armes with their owne handes, then would they lift them up toward heaven, shewing many signes of gladnesse: and in such wise were wee assured one of another, that we very familiarly began to trafique for whatsoever they had, til they had nothing but their naked bodies; for they gave us all whatsoever they had, and that was but of small value. We perceived that this people might very easily be converted to our Religion. They goe from place to place. They live onely with fishing. They have an ordinarie time to fish for their provision. The countrey is hotter than the countrey of Spaine, and the fairest that can possibly be found, altogether smooth, and level. There is no place be it never so little, but it hath some trees (yea albeit it be sandie) or else is full of wilde corne, that hath an eare like unto Rie: the corne is like oates, and smal peason as thicke as if they had bene sowen and plowed, white and red gooseberies, strawberies, blackberies, white and red Roses, with many other floures of very sweet and pleasant smell. There be also many goodly medowes full of grasse, and lakes wherein great plentie of salmons be. They call a hatchet in their tongue Cochi, and a knife Bacon: we named it The bay of heat.

Of another nation of wilde men: of their manners, living and clothing.

Being certified that there was no passage through the said Bay, we hoised saile, and went from S. Martines Creeke upon Sunday being the 12. of July, to goe and discover further beyond the said Bay, and went along the sea coast Eastward about eighteene leagues, till we came to the Cape of Prato,[1] where we found the tide very great, but shallow ground, and the Sea stormie, so that we were constrained to draw toward shore, between the said Cape and an Iland lying Eastward, about a league from the said Cape, where we cast anker for that night. The next morning we hoised saile to trend the said coast about, which lyeth North Northeast. But there rose such a stormie and raging winde against us, that we were constrained to come to the place againe, from whence we were come: there did we stay all that day til the next that we hoised up saile, and came to the middest of a river five or sixe leagues from the Cape of Prato Northward, and being overthwart the said River, there arose againe a contrary winde, with great fogges and stormes. So that we were constrained upon Tuesday being the fourteenth of the moneth to enter into the river, and there did we stay till the sixteenth of the moneth looking for faire weather to come out of it: on which day being Thursday, the winde became so raging that one of our ships lost an anker; and we were constrained to goe up higher into the river seven or eight leagues, into a good harborough and ground that we with our boates found out, and through the evill weather, tempest, and darkenesse that was, wee stayed in the saide harborough till the five and twentieth of the moneth, not being able to put out: in the meane time wee sawe a great multitude of wilde men that were fishing for mackerels, whereof there is great store. Their

[1] White Head.

boates were about 40, and the persons what with men, women, and children two hundred, which after they had hanted our company a while, they came very familiarly with their boats to the sides of our ships. We gave them knives, combes, beads of glasse, and other trifles of small value, for which they made many signes of gladnesse, lifting their hands up to heaven dancing and singing in their boates. These men may very well and truely be called Wilde, because there is no poorer people in the world. For I thinke all that they had together, besides their boates and nets, was not worth five souce.[1] They goe altogether naked saving their privities, which are covered with a little skinne, and certaine olde skinnes that they cast upon them. Neither in nature nor in language, doe they any whit agree with them which we found first: their heads be altogether shaven, except one bush of haire which they suffer to grow upon the top of their crowne as long as a horse taile, and then with certaine leather strings binde it in a knot upon their heads. They have no other dwelling but their boates, which they turne upside downe, and under them they lay themselves all along upon the bare ground. They eate their flesh almost raw, save onely that they heat it a little upon imbers of coales, so doe they their fish. Upon Magdalens day we with our boates went to the bancke of the river, and freely went on shore among them, whereat they made many signs, and all their men in two or three companies began to sing and dance, seeming to be very glad of our comming. They had caused all the young women to flee into the wood, two or three excepted, that stayed with them, to ech of which we gave a combe, and a little bell made of Tinne, for which they were very glad, thanking our Captaine, rubbing his armes and breasts with their hands. When the men saw us give something unto those that had stayed, it caused al the rest to come out of the wood, to the end that that they should have as much as the others: These women are about twenty, who altogether in a knot fell upon our Captaine, touching and rubbing him with their hands, according to their manner of cherishing and making much of one, who gave

[1] Sous.

to each of them a little Tinne bell: then suddenly they began to dance, and sing many songs. There we found great store of mackrels, that they had taken upon the shore, with certaine nets that they made to fish, of a kinde of Hempe that groweth in that place where ordinarily they abide, for they never come to the sea, but onely in fishing time. As farre as I understand, there groweth likewise a kind of Millet as big as Peason, like unto that which groweth in Bresil, which they eate in stead of bread. They had great store of it. They call it in their tongue Kapaige. They have also Prunes (that is to say Damsins) which they dry for winter as we doe, they call them Honesta. They have also Figs,[1] Nuts, Apples, and other fruits, and Beans that they call Sahu, their nuts Cahehya. If we shewed them any thing that they have not, nor know not what it is, shaking their heads, they will say Nohda, which is as much to say, they have it not, nor they know it not. Of those things they have, they would with signes shew us how to dresse them, and how they grow. They eate nothing that hath any taste of salt. They are very great theeves, for they will filch and steale whatsoever they can lay hold of, and all is fish that commeth to net.

How our men set up a great Crosse upon the poynt of the sayd Porte, and the Captaine of those wild men, after a long Oration, was by our Captain appeased, and contented that two of his Children should goe with him.

Upon the 25 of the moneth, wee caused a faire high Crosse to be made of the height of thirty foote, which was made in the presence of many of them, upon the point of the entrance of the sayd haven,[2] in the middest whereof we hanged up a Shield with three Floure de Luces in it, and in the top was carved in the wood with Anticke letters this posie, Vive le Roy de France. Then before them all we set it upon the sayd point. They with great heed beheld both the making and setting of it up.

[1] Cartier has but one word for figs and plums. The reference evidently is to the common Canada plum.
[2] Gaspé Bay.

So soone as it was up, we altogether kneeled downe before them, with our hands toward Heaven, yeelding God thankes: and we made signes unto them, shewing them the Heavens, and that all our salvation dependeth onely on him which in them dwelleth: whereat they shewed a great admiration, looking first one at another, and then upon the Crosse. And after wee were returned to our ships, their Captaine clad with an old Beares skin, with three of his sonnes, and a brother of his with him, came unto us in one of their boates, but they came not so neere us as they were wont to doe: there he made a long Oration unto us, shewing us the crosse we had set up, and making a crosse with two fingers, then did he shew us all the Countrey about us, as if he would say that all was his, and that wee should not set up any crosse without his leave. His talke being ended, we shewed him an Axe, faining that we would give it him for his skin, to which he listned, for by little and little hee came neere our ships. One of our fellowes that was in our boate, tooke hold on theirs, and suddenly leapt into it, with two or three more, who enforced them to enter into our ships, whereat they were greatly astonished. But our Captain did straightwaies assure them, that they should have no harme, nor any injurie offred them at all, and entertained them very friendly, making them eate and drinke. Then did we shew them with signes, that the crosse was but onely set up to be as a light and leader which wayes to enter into the port, and that wee would shortly come againe, and bring good store of iron wares and other things, but that we would take two of his children with us, and afterward bring them to the sayd port againe: and so wee clothed two of them in shirts, and coloured coates, with red cappes, and put about every ones necke a copper chaine, whereat they were greatly contented: then gave they their old clothes to their fellowes that went backe againe, and we gave to each one of those three that went backe, a hatchet, and some knives, which made them very glad. After these were gone, and had told the newes unto their fellowes, in the afternoone there came to our ships six boates of them, with five or sixe men in every one, to take their farewels of those two we had detained to take with us,[1] and brought them some fish, uttering many words which we did not understand, making signes that they would not remove the crosse we had set up.

How after we were departed from the sayd porte, following our voyage along the sayd coast, we went to discover the land lying Southeast, and Northwest.

The next day, being the 25 of the moneth, we had faire weather, and went from the said port: and being out of the river, we sailed Eastnortheast, for after the entrance into the said river, the land is environed about, and maketh a bay in maner of halfe a circle, where being in our ships, we might see all the coast sayling behind, which we came to seeke, the land lying Southeast and Northwest, the course of which was distant from the river about twentie leagues.

Of the Cape S. Alvise, and Cape Memorancie, and certaine other lands, and how one of our Boates touched a Rocke and suddenly went over it.

On Munday being the 27 of the moneth, about sunne-set we went along the said land, as we have said, lying Southeast and Northwest, till Wednesday that we saw another Cape where the land beginneth to bend toward the East: we went along about 15 leagues, then doeth the land begin to turne Northward. About three leagues from the sayd Cape we sounded, and found 24 fadome water. The said lands are plaine, and the fairest and most without woods that we have seene, with goodly greene fields and medowes: we named the sayd Cape S. Alvise Cape,[2] because that was his day: it is 49

[1] Their names were Taignoagny and Domagaia. Both returned with Cartier in the following year.
[2] Loys in the French. Named for St. Louis, king of France. This is the present East Cape on the island of Anticosti. Cartier had failed to discover the broad opening to the St. Lawrence River.

degrees and an halfe in latitude, and in longitude On Wednesday morning we were on the East side of the Cape, and being almost night we went Northwestward for to approch neere to the sayd land, which trendeth North and South. From S. Alvise Cape to another called Cape Memorancie,[2] about fifteene leagues, the land beginneth to bend Northwest. About three leagues from the sayd Cape we would needes sound, but wee could finde no ground at 150 fadome, yet went we along the said land about tenne leagues, to the latitude of 50 degrees. The Saturday following, being the first of August, by Sunne rising, wee had certaine other landes, lying North and Northeast,[3] that were very high and craggie, and seemed to be mountaines: betweene which were other low lands with woods and rivers: wee went about the sayd lands, as well on the one side as on the other, still bending Northwest, to see if it were either a gulfe, or a passage, untill the fift of the moneth. The distance from one land to the other is about fifteene leagues. The middle betweene them both is 50 degrees and a terce in latitude. We had much adoe to go five miles farther, the winds were so great and the tide against us. And at five miles end, we might plainely see and perceive land on both sides, which there beginneth to spread it selfe, but because we rather fell, then got way against the wind, we went toward land, purposing to goe to another Cape of land,[4] lying Southward, which was the farthermost out into the sea that we could see, about five leagues from us, but so soone as we came thither, we found it to be naught else but Rockes, stones, and craggie cliffes, such as we had not found any where since we had sailed Southward from S. Johns Cape: and then was the tide with us, which caried us against the wind Westward, so that as we were sayling along the sayd coast, one of our boats touched a Rocke, and suddenly went over, but we were constrained to leape out for to direct it on according to the tide.

[1] Blank in the original. [2] Table Head.
[3] The Labrador coast.
[4] North Point, the northwestern point of Anticosti. Cartier was on the eve of discovering the St. Lawrence River, and missed it.

How after we had agreed and consulted what was best to be done, we purposed to returne: and of S Peters Streight, and of Cape Tiennot.

After we had sailed along the sayd coast, for the space of two houres, behold, the tide began to turne against us, with so swift and raging a course, that it was not possible for us with 13 oares to row or get one stones cast farther, so that we were constrained to leave our boates with some of our men to guard them, and 10 or 12 men went ashore to the sayd Cape, where we found that the land beginneth to bend Southwest, which having seene, we came to our boats againe, and so to our ships, which were stil ready under saile, hoping to go forward: but for all that, they were fallen more then foure leagues to leeward from the place where we had left them, where so soone as we came, wee assembled together all our Captaines, Masters, and Mariners, to have their advice and opinion what was best to be done: and after that every one had said, considering that the Easterly winds began to beare away, and blow, and that the flood was so great, that we did but fall, and that there was nothing to be gotten, and that stormes and tempests began to reigne in New-found land, and that we were so farre from home, not knowing the perils and dangers that were behind, for either we must agree to returne home againe, or els to stay there all the yeere. Moreover, we did consider, that if the Northerne winds did take us, it were not possible for us to depart thence. All which opinions being heard and considered, we altogether determined to addresse our selves homeward. Nowe because upon Saint Peters day wee entred into the sayd Streite, wee named it Saint Peters Streite.[1] Wee sounded it in many places, in some wee found 150 fadome water, in some 100, and neere the shoare sixtie, and cleere ground. From that day till Wednesday following, we had a good and prosperous gale of winde, so that we trended the said North shore East, Southeast, West North-

[1] The strait between Anticosti and Labrador.

west: for such is the situation of it, except one Cape of low lands that bendeth more toward the Southeast, about twenty five leagues from the Streight. In this place we saw certaine smokes, that the people of the countrey made upon the sayd cape: but because the wind blewe us toward the coast, we went not to them, which when they saw, they came with two boates and twelve men unto us, and as freely came unto our ships, as if they had bene French men, and gave us to understand, that they came from the great gulfe, and that Tiennot was their Captaine, who then was upon that Cape, making signes unto us, that they were going home to their Countreys whence we were come with our ships, and that they were laden with Fish. We named the sayd Cape, Cape Tiennot.[1] From the said Cape all the land trendeth Eastsoutheast, and Westnorthwest. All these lands lie low, very pleasant, environed with sand, where the sea is entermingled with marishes and shallowes, the space of twentie leagues: then doth the land begin to trend from West to Eastnortheast altogether environed with Islands two or three leagues from land, in which as farre as we could see, are many dangerous shelves more then foure or five leagues from land.

How that upon the ninth of August wee entred within White Sands, and upon the fift of September we came to the Port of S. Malo.

From the sayd Wednesday untill Saturday following, we had a great wind from the Southwest, which caused us to run Eastnortheast, on which day we came to the Easterly partes of Newfoundland, between the Granges and the Double Cape. There began great stormie windes comming from the East with great rage: wherefore we coasted the Cape Northnorthwest, to search the Northerne part, which is (as we have sayd) all environed with Islands, and being neere the said Islands and land, the wind turned into the South, which brought us within the

[1] Natashquan Point.

sayd gulfe, so that the next day being the 9 of August, we by the grace of God entred within the white Sands.[1] And this is so much as we have discovered. After that, upon the 15 of August, being the feast of the Assumption of our Lady, after that we had heard service, we altogether departed from the porte of White Sands, and with a happy and prosperous weather we came into the middle of the sea, that is between Newfoundland and Britanie, in which place we were tost and turmoyled three dayes long with great stormes and windy tempests comming from the East, which with the ayde and assistance of God we suffred: then had we faire weather, and upon the fift o' September, in the sayd yere, we came to the Port of S. Malo whence we departed.

The language that is spoken in the Land newly discovered, called New France.

God	———	a Hatchet	asogne
the Sunne	Isnez	a Cod fish	gadagoursere
the Heaven	camet	good to be eaten	guesande
the Day	———		
the Night	aiagla	Flesh	———
Water	ame	Almonds	anougaza
Sand	estogaz	Figs	asconda
a sayle	aganie	Gold	henyosco
the Head	agonaze	the privie members	assegnega
the Throate	conguedo		
the Nose	hehonguesto	an Arrow	cacta
the Teeth	hesangue	a greene Tree	haveda
the Nayles	agetascu	an earthen dish	undaco
the Feete	ochedasco		
the Legs	anoudasco	a Bow	———
a dead man	amocdaza	Brasse	aignetaze
a Skinne	aionasca	the Brow	ansce
that Man	yca	a Feather	yco

[1] It was two months from the time Cartier was at this place and entered the Gulf of St. Lawrence.

the Moone	casmogan	a sicke Man	alouedeche
the Earth	conda	Shooes	atta
the Wind	canut	a skinne to	
the Raine	onnoscon	cover a mans	ouscozon
Bread	cacacomy	privy mem-	vondico
the Sea	amet	bers	
a Ship	casaomy	red cloth	cahoneta
a Man	undo	a Knife	agoheda
the Haires	hoc hosco	a Mackrell	agedoneta
the Eyes	ygata	Nuttes	caheya
the Mouth	heche	Apples	honesta
the Eares	hontasco	Beanes	sahe
the Armes	agescu	a Sword	achesco
a Woman	enrasesco		

A SHORTE AND BRIEFE NARRATION
(CARTIER'S SECOND VOYAGE)
1535–1536

INTRODUCTION

CARTIER reached France after an absence of less than six months. What he had seen during the summer had wonderfully impressed him and those associated with him. The expedition had been without mishap of any kind. His report was an inspiration to the king, and to all interested in the voyage. The termination of the work of exploration — the land falling off to the southwest and open waters to the westward leading whither no one could say — called imperatively for added endeavor and a larger outlay. On the last day of October, 1535, the king, through the Admiral of France, gave to the explorer a new commission, in which Cartier was designated as "Captain and Pilot of the King"; three vessels, well-equipped and furnished with provisions for fifteen months, were provided; while with Cartier were associated in the expedition some of the younger nobility of France. A report of this second voyage was printed in France in 1545 under the title *Brief Récit et Succincte Narration de là Navigation faicte es ysles de Canada*. Only one copy of this printed report has been preserved, and is now in the British Museum. In 1863, a new edition of the *Brief Récit* was published in Paris by the bookseller Tross, under the direction of the distinguished French geographer, M. d'Avezac. An Italian translation by Ramusio appeared in his third volume, folio 441 *et seqq*. (Venice, 1556). There are three contemporary narratives of the second voyage in manuscript in the Bibliothèque Nationale in Paris, numbered 5589, 5644, and 5653. The first two were printed in Paris in 1841, the third in Quebec in 1843. Mr. Baxter (*Memoir of Jacques Cartier*, p. 4) is of the opinion that the manuscript numbered 5653 was probably used by the editor of the *Brief Récit*. Comparing these manuscripts with the printed copy, Mr. Baxter found so many errors and omissions that he decided to use in his *Memoir* the manuscript numbered 5589. The following account of the second voyage, a translation from Ramusio, is from Hakluyt's great work, edition of 1600.

H. S. B.

CARTIER'S SECOND VOYAGE

A shorte and briefe narration of the Navigation made by the commandement of the King of France, to the islands of Canada, Hochelaga, Saguenay, and divers others which now are called New France, with the particular customes, and maners of the inhabitants therein.

Chap. 1

IN the yeere of our Lord 1535, upon Whitsunday, being the 16. of May, by the commandement of our Captaine James Cartier, and with a common accord, in the Cathedrall Church of S. Malo we devoutly each one confessed our selves, and received the Sacrament: and all entring into the Quier of the sayd Church, wee presented our selves before the Reverend Father in Christ, the Lord Bishop of S. Malo,[1] who blessed us all, being in his Bishops roabes. The Wednesday following, being the 19. of May, there arose a good gale of wind, and therefore we hoysed sayle with three ships, that is to say, the great Hermina, being in burden about a hundreth, or a hundreth and twentie tunne, wherein the foresaid Captaine James Cartier was Generall, and master Thomas Frosmont chiefe Master, accompanied with master Claudius de Pont Briand, sonne to the Lorde of Montcevell, and Cup-bearer to the Dolphin of France, Charles of Pomeraies, John Powlet, and other Gentlemen. In the second ship called the little Hermina, being of threescore tunne burden, were Captaines under the sayd Cartier, Mace Salobert,[2] and Master William Marie. In the third ship called the Hermerillon, being of forty tunne in burden, were Captains M. William Britton, and M. James Maringare. So we sayled with a good

[1] Bishop Bohier, grandson of Cardinal Briçonnet.
[2] Marc Jalobert, Cartier's brother-in-law.

and prosperous wind, untill the 20 of the said moneth, at
which time the weather turned into stormes and tempests,
the which with contrary winds, and darkenesse, endured so
long that our ships being without any rest, suffered as much
as any ships that ever went on seas: so that the 25 of June,
by reason of that foule and foggie weather, all our ships lost
sight one of another againe till wee came to Newfoundland
where wee had appointed to meete. After we had lost one
another, wee in the Generals ship were with contrary winds tost
to and fro on the sea, until the seventh of July, upon which
day we arrived in Newe found land, and came to the Island
called The Island of Birds, which lyeth from the maine land
14 leagues. This Island is so full of birds, that all our
ships might easily have bene fraighted with them, and yet
for the great number that there is, it would not seeme that
any were taken away. We to victuall our selves filled two
boats of them. This Island hath the Pole elevated 49 degrees, and 40 minutes. Upon the eight of the sayd moneth
we sailed further, and with a prosperous weather, came to the
Port called The Port of white sands, that is in the Bay called
The Bay of Castels, where we had purposed to meete and stay
together the 15 of the said moneth. In this place therefore we
looked for our fellowes, that is to say, the other two ships, till
the 26 of the moneth, on which day both came together. So
soone as our fellowes were come, we set our ships in a readines,
taking in both water, wood, and other necessaries. And then
on the 29 of the sayd moneth, early in the morning we hoised
saile to passe on further, and sayling along the Northerne
coast that runneth Northeast and Southwest, til two houres
after Sun-set or thereabouts, then we crossed along two Islands,
which doe stretch further foorth then the others, which we
called S. Williams Islands,[1] being distant about 20 leagues or
more from the Port of Brest. All the coast from the Castels
to that place lieth East and West, Northeast and Southwest,
having betweene it sundry little Islands, altogether barren and

---

[1] Probably Treble Hill and Great Meccatina.

full of stones, without either earth or trees, except certain valleys only. The next day being the 30 of July, we sailed on Westward to find out other Islands which as yet we had not found 12 leagues and a halfe, among which there is a great Bay toward the North all full of Islands and great creekes, where many good harboroughs seeme to be: them we named S. Marthas Islands,[1] from which about a league and a halfe further into the sea there is a dangerous shallow, wherein are five rockes, which lie from Saint Marthas Islands about seven leagues as you passe into the sayd Islands, on the East and on the West side, to which we came the sayd day an houre after noone, and from that houre untill midnight we sailed about fifteene leagues athwart a cape of the lower Islands, which we named S. Germans Islands[2] Southeastward, from which place about three leagues, there is a very dangerous shallow. Likewise betweene S. Germans cape and Saint Marthas, about two leagues from the sayd Islands, there lyeth a banke of sand, upon which banke the water is but foure fadome deepe, and therefore seeing the danger of the coast, we strucke saile and went no further that night: The next day being the last of July, we went all along the coast that runneth East and West, and somewhat Southeasterly which is all environed about with Islands and drie sands, and in trueth it is very dangerous. The length from S. Germans Cape to the said Islands is about 17 leagues and a halfe, at the end of which there is a goodly plot of ground full of huge and high trees, albeit the rest of the coast be compassed about with sands without any signe or shew of harboroughs, till we came to Cape Thiennot,[3] which trendeth Northwest about seven leagues from the foresaid Islands, which Cape Thiennot we noted in our former voyage, and therefore we sailed on all that night West and Westnorthwest, till it was day, and then the wind turned against us, wherefore we went to seeke a haven wherein we might harbour our ships, and by

[1] Little Meccatina and the small peninsula opposite, which from the sea have the appearance of two islands.
[2] Cape Whittle Islands.
[3] By some identified as Mont Joli, but more probably the reference is to Natashquan Point.

good hap, found one fit for our purpose, about seven leagues
and a halfe beyond Cape Thiennot, and that we named S.
Nicholas Haven, it'lieth amidst 4 Islands that stretch into the
sea: Upon the neerest wee for a token set up a woodden crosse.
But note by the way, that this crosse must be brought Northeast, and then bending toward it, leave it on the left hand and
you shall find sixe fadome water, and within the haven foure.
Also you are to take heede of two shelves that leane outward
halfe a league. All this coast is full of shoulds and very dangerous, albeit in sight many good havens seeme to be there,
yet is there nought else but shelves and sands. We staied
and rested our selves in the sayd haven, until the seventh of
August being Sonday:[2] on which day we hoysed sayle, and
came toward land on the South side toward Cape Rabast,[3]
distant from the sayd haven about twentie leagues Northnortheast, and Southsouthwest: but the next day there rose
a stormie and a contrary winde, and because we could find no
haven there toward the South, thence we went coasting along
toward the North, beyond the abovesayd haven about ten
leagues, where we found a goodly great gulfe, full of Islands,
passages, and entrances toward what wind soever you please
to bend: for the knowledge of this gulfe there is a great Island
that is like to a Cape of lande, stretching somewhat further
foorth than the others, and about two leagues within the land,
there is an hill fashioned as it were an heape of corne.[4] We
named the sayd gulfe Saint Laurence his bay.[5] The twelfth of
the sayd moneth wee went from the sayd Saint Laurence
his Bay, or gulfe, sayling Westward, and discovered a Cape[6]
of land toward the South, that runneth West and by South,
distant from the sayd Saint Laurence his Bay, about five and
twenty leagues. And of the two wilde men which wee tooke
in our former voyage, it was tolde us, that this was part of the
Southerne coaste, and that there was an Island, on the South-

[1] Mushkoniatawee Bay.
[2] Manuscript 5589, in Baxter's *Memoir of Jacques Cartier*, says, "Sunday, the eighth day of August," which is correct.
[3] Cow Point on the island of Anticosti.   [4] Mount St. Genevieve.
[5] Pillage Bay.   [6] North Cape on Anticosti Island.

erly parte of which is the way to goe from Honguedo[1] (where the yeere before we had taken them) to Canada, and that two dayes journey from the sayd Cape and Island began the Kingdome of Saguenay, on the North shore extending toward Canada, and about three leagues athwart the sayd Cape, there is above a hundreth fadome water. Moreover I beleeve that there were never so many Whales seen as wee saw that day about the sayd Cape. The next day after being our Ladie day of August the fifteenth of the moneth,[2] having passed the Straight, we had notice of certaine lands that wee left toward the South, which landes are full of very great and high hills, and this Cape wee named The Island of the Assumption,[3] and one Cape of the said high countreys lyeth Eastnortheast, and Westsouthwest, the distance betweene which is abuot five and twenty leagues. The Countreys lying North may plainely be perceived to be higher then the Southerly, more then thirty leagues in length. We trended the sayd landes about toward the South: from the sayd day untill Tewesday noone following, the winde came West, and therefore wee bended toward the North, purposing to goe and see the land that we before had spied. Being arrived there, we found the sayd landes, as it were joyned together, and low toward the Sea. And the Northerly mountaines that are upon the sayd low lands stretch East, and West, and a quarter of the South.[4] Our wild men told us that there was the beginning of Saguenay,[5] and that it was land inhabited, and that thence commeth the red Copper, of them named Caignetdaze. There is betweene the Southerly lands and the Northerly about thirty leagues distance, and more then two hundreth fadome depth. The sayd men did moreover certifie unto us, that there was the way and beginning of the great river of Hochelaga[6] and ready way to Canada, which river the further it went the narrower it came, even unto Canada, and that then there was fresh water, which went so farre upwards, that they had never heard of any man

[1] Gaspe. [2] The feast of the Assumption of the Virgin Mary.
[3] Anticosti.
[4] High lands on the north side of the river near Cape des Monts.
[5] The country westward from the river of that name. [6] St. Lawrence.

who had gone to the head of it, and that there is no other passage but with small boates. Our Captaine hearing their talke, and how they did affirme no other passage to be there, would not at that time proceede any further, till he had seene and noted the other lands, and coast toward the North, which he had omitted to see from S. Laurence his gulfe, because he would know, if between the lands toward the North any passage might be discovered.[1]

How our Captaine caused the ships to returne backe againe, only to know if in Saint Laurence gulfe there were any passage toward the North.

Chap. 2

Upon the 18 of August being Wednesday, our Captaine caused his shippes to wind backe, and bend toward the other shore, so that we trended the said Northerly cost, which runneth Northeast and Southwest, being fashioned like unto halfe a bowe, and is a very high land, but yet not so high as that on the South parts. The Thursday following we came to seven very high Islands, which we named The round Islands.[2] These Islands are distant from the South shore about 40 leagues, and stretch out into the sea about 3 or 4 leagues. Against these there are goodly low grounds to be seene full of goodly trees, which we the Friday following, with our boats compassed about. Overthwart these lands there are divers sandy shelves more then two leagues into the sea, very dangerous, which at a low water remaine almost dry. At the furthest bounds of these lowe lands, that containe about ten leagues, there is a river of fresh water,[3] that with such swiftnesse runneth into the sea, that for the space of one league within it the water is as fresh as any fountaine water. We with our boates entred in the sayd river, at the entrance of which we found about one

---

[1] The northwest passage to the Indies Cartier seems to have had chiefly in mind in his work of discovery.
[2] The Seven Islands.
[3] Trout River.

fadome and a halfe of water. There are in this river many
fishes shaped like horses, which as our wild men told us, all the
day long lie in the water, and the night on land: of which we
saw therin a great number.[1] The next day being the 21 of
the moneth, by breake of day we hoysed saile, and sailed so
long along the said coast, that we had sight of the rest of the
sayd Northerne coast, which as yet we had not seene, and of the
Island of the Assumption which wee went to discover, departing from the sayd land: which thing so soone as we had done,
and that we were certified no other passage to be there, we
came to our ships againe, which we had left at the said Islands,
where is a good harborough, the water being about nine or ten
fadome. In the same place by occasion of contrary winds
and foggie mists, we were constrained to stay, not being either
able to come out of it, or hoise saile, till the 24 of the moneth:
On which day we departed and came to a haven on the Southerly coast about 80 leagues from the said Islands. This haven
is over against three flat Islands that lie amidst the river, because on the midway betweene those Islands, and the sayd
haven toward the North, there is a very great river that runneth betweene the high and low landes, and more then three
leagues into the sea it hath many shelves, and there is not altogether two fadome water, so that the place is very dangerous: and neere unto the said shelves, there is either fifteene or
20 fadomes from shore to shore. All the Northerly coaste runneth Northeast and by North, and Southwest and by South.
The said haven wherin we stayed on the South side, is as it
were but a sluce of the waters that rise by the flood, and but of
smal accompt: we named them S. Johns Islets,[2] because we
found them, and entred into them the day of the beheading of
that Saint. And before you come to the said haven, there is
an Island lying Eastward about 5 leagues distant from the
same: betweene which and the land there is no passage saving
only for smal boats. The haven of S. Johns Islets dryeth up
all the waters that rise by flowing, although they flow two fad-

[1] The walrus.   [2] Bic Islands.

ome at the least. The best place to harborough ships therein is on the South part of a little Island that is over against the said haven, whereby the bancke or shore of the Island riseth. Upon the first of September we departed out of the said haven, purposing to go toward Canada; and about 15 leagues from it toward the West, and Westsouthwest, amidst the river, there are three Islands, over against the which there is a river [1] which runneth swift, and is of a great depth, and it is that which leadeth, and runneth into the countrey and kingdome of Saguenay, as by the two wild men of Canada it was told us. This river passeth and runneth along very high and steepe hils of bare stone, where very little earth is, and notwithstanding there is great quantity of sundry sorts of trees that grow in the said bare stones, even as upon good and fertile ground, in such sort that we have seene some so great as wel would suffise to make a mast for a ship of 30 tunne burden, and as greene as possibly can be, growing in a stony rocke without any earth at all. At the entrance of the sayd river we met with 4 boats ful of wild men, which as far as we could perceive, very fearfully came toward us, so that some of them went backe againe, and the other came as neere us as easily they might heare and understand one of our wild men, who told them his name, and then tooke acquaintance of them, upon whose word they came to us. The next day being the 2 of September, we came out of the sayd river to go to Canada, and by reason of the seas flowing, the tide was very swift and dangerous, for that on the South part of it there lie two Islands, about which, more then three leagues compasse, lie many rocks and great stones, and but two fadome water: and the flowing amidst those Islands is very unconstant and doubtful, so that if it had not bene for our boats, we had been in great danger to lose our Pinnesse: and coasting along the said drie sands, there is more then 30 fadom water.

About five leagues beyond the river of Saguenay Southwest, there is another Iland [2] on the Northside, wherein are certaine

---

[1] Saguenay River.   [2] Hare Island.

high lands, and thereabouts we thought to have cast anker, on purpose to stay the next tide, but we could sound no ground in a 120 fadome, within a flight shoot from shore, so that we were constrained to winde backe to the said Iland, where wee sounded againe and found 35 fadome. The next morning we hoysed saile and went thence, sayling further on, where we had notice of a certaine kind of fish never before of any man seene or knowen. They are about the bignesse of a porpose, yet nothing like them, of body very well proportioned, headed like Grayhounds, altogither as white as snow without any spot, within which river there is great quantitie of them: they doe live altogither betweene the Sea and the fresh water. These people of the Countrey call them Adhothuys,[1] they tolde us that they be very savory and good to be eaten. Moreover they affirme none to be found elsewhere but in the mouth of that river. The sixth of the month, the weather being calme and faire, we went about 15 leagues more upward into the river, and there lighted on an Iland that looketh Northward, and it maketh a little haven or creeke wherein are many and innumerable great Tortoyzes, continually lying about that Iland. There are likewise great quantitie of the said Adhothuys taken by the inhabitours of the countrey, and there is as great a current in that place as is at Bordeux in France at every tide. This Iland is in length about three leagues, and in bredth two, and is a goodly and fertile plot of ground, replenished with many goodly and great trees of many sorts. Among the rest there are many Filberd-trees, which we found hanging full of them, somewhat bigger and better in savour then ours, but somewhat harder, and therefore we called it The Iland of Filberds.[2] The seventh of the moneth being our Ladies even,[3] after service we went from that Iland to goe up higher into the river, and came to 14 Ilands seven or eight leagues from the Iland of Filberds, where the countrey of Canada beginneth, one of which Ilands is ten leagues in length, and five in bredth, greatly inhabited of such men as onely live by fishing of such sorts of

---

[1] The narwhal.   [2] Hazelnuts
[3] The Nativity of the Virgin is celebrated on September 8.

fishes as the river affordeth, according to the season of them.
After we had cast anker betwene the said great Iland,[1] and
the Northerly coast, we went on land and tooke our two wild
men with us, meeting with many of these countrey people,
who would not at all approch unto us, but rather fled from us,
untill our two men began to speake unto them, telling them
that they were Taignoagny and Domagaia, who so soone as
they had taken acquaintance of them, beganne greatly to rejoyce, dancing and shewing many sorts of ceremonies: and
many of the chiefest of them came to our boats and brought
many Eeles and other sorts of fishes, with two or three burdens
of great Millet wherewith they make their bread, and many
great muske millions.[2] The same day came also many other
boates full of those countreymen and weomen, to see and
take acquaintance of our two men, all which were as courteously received and friendly entertained of our Captaine, as
possibly could be. And to have them the better acquainted
with him, and make them his friends, hee gave them many
small gifts, but of small value: neverthelesse they were greatly
contented with them. The next day following, the Lord of
Canada (whose proper name was Donnacona, but by the name
of Lord they call him Agouhanna) with twelve boats came to
our ships, accompanied with many people, who causing ten of
his boates to goe backe with the other two, approched unto us
with sixteene men. Then beganne the said Agouhanna over
against the smallest of our ships, according to their maner and
fashion, to frame a long Oration, mooving all his bodie and
members after a strange fashion, which thing is a ceremonie
and signe of gladnesse and securitie among them, and then
comming to the Generals ship, where Taignoagny and Domagaia were, he spake with them and they with him, where they
began to tell and shew unto him what they had seene in France,
and what good entertainement they had had: hearing which
things the said Lord seemed to be very glad thereof, and prayed
our Captaine to reach him his arme, that he might kisse it,

[1] Isle of Orleans. Cartier's estimate of its size is too large.
[2] Pumpkins.

which thing he did: their Lord taking it, laid it about his necke, for so they use to doe when they will make much of one. Then our Captaine entred into Agoùhannas boat, causing bread and wine to be brought to make the said Lord and his companie to eate and drinke, which thing they did, and were greatly thereby contented and satisfied. Our Captaine for that time gave them nothing, because he looked for a fitter opportunity. These things being done, ech one tooke leave of others, and the said Lord went with his boats againe to his place of abode. Our Captaine then caused our boates to be set in order, that with the next tide he might goe up higher into the river, to find some safe harborough for our ships: and we passed up the river against the streame about tenne leagues, coasting the said Iland, at the end whereof, we found a goodly and pleasant sound, where is a little river and haven, where by reason of the flood there is about three fadome water. This place seemed to us very fit and commodious to harbour our ships therein, and so we did very safely, we named it the holy Crosse,[1] for on that day [2] we came thither. Neere unto it, there is a village, whereof Donnacona is Lord, and there he keepeth his abode: it is called Stadacona,[3] as goodly a plot of ground as possibly may be seene, and therewithall very fruitfull, full of goodly trees even as in France, as Okes, Elmes, Ashes, Walnut trees, Maple tres, Cydrons, Vines, and white Thornes, that bring foorth fruit as bigge as any damsons, and many other sortes of trees, under which groweth as faire tall hempe, as any in France, without any seede or any mans worke or labour at all. Having considered the place, and finding it fit for our purpose, our Captaine withdrew himselfe on purpose to returne to our ships: but behold, as we were comming out of the river we met comming against us one of the Lords of the said village of Stadacona, accompanied with many others, as men, weomen, and children, who after the fashion of their country, in signe of mirth and joy, began to make a long Oration, the women still singing and dancing up to the knees in water. Our Captaine knowing

---

[1] St. Charles.   [2] *I.e.*, September 14.   [3] Present site of Quebec.

their good will and kindnesse toward us, caused the boat wherein they were, to come unto him, and gave them certaine trifles, as knives, and beades of glasse, whereat they were marvellous glad, for being gone about leagues from them, for the pleasure they conceived of our comming we might heare them sing, and see them dance for all they were so farre.

How our Captaine went to see and note the bignesse of the Iland, and the nature of it, and then returned to the ships, causing them to be brought to the river of The holy Crosse.

Chap. 3

After we were come with our boats unto our ships againe, our Captaine caused our barks to be made readie to goe on land in the said Iland, to note the trees that in shew seemed so faire, and to consider the nature and qualitie of it: which things we did, and found it full of goodly trees like to ours. Also we saw many goodly Vines, a thing not before of us seene in those countries, and therefore we named it Bacchus Iland.[1] It is in length about twelve leagues, in sight very pleasant, but full of woods, no part of it manured, unlesse it be in certaine places, where a few cottages be for Fishers dwellings as before we have said. The next day we departed with our ships to bring them to the place of the holy Crosse, and on the 14 of that moneth we came thither, and the Lord Donnacona, Taignoagny, and Domagaia, with 25 boats full of those people, came to meete us, comming from the place whence we were come, and going toward Stadacona, where their abiding is, and all came to our ships, shewing sundry and divers gestures of gladnesse and mirth, except those two that he had brought, to wit, Taignoagny, and Domagaia, who seemed to have altered and changed their mind, and purpose, for by no meanes they

[1] The Isle of Orleans. Cartier's estimate of its size, here as above, is too large.

would come unto our ships, albeit sundry times they were earnestly desired to doe it, whereupon we began to mistrust somewhat. Our Captaine asked them if according to promise they would go with him to Hochelaga? They answered yea, for so they had purposed, and then ech one withdrew himselfe. The next day being the fifteenth of the moneth, our Captaine went on shore, to cause certaine poles and piles to be driven into the water, and set up, that the better and safelier we might harbour our ships there: and many of those countrey people came to meete us there, among whom was Donnacona and our two men, with the rest of their company, who kept themselves aside under a point or nooke of land that is upon the shore of a certaine river, and no one of them came unto us as the other did that were not on their side. Our Captaine understanding that they were there commanded part of our men to follow him, and he went to the saide point where he found the said Donnacona, Taignoagny, Domagaia, and divers other: and after salutations given on ech side, Taignoagny setled himselfe formost to speake to our Captaine, saying that the Lord Donnacona did greatly grieve and sorrow that our Captaine and his men did weare warlike weapons, and they not. Our Captaine answered, that albeit it did greeve them yet would not he leave them off, and that (as he knew) it was the maner of France. But for all these words our Captaine and Donnacona left not off to speake one to another, and friendly to entertaine one another. Then did we perceive, that whatsoever Taignoagny spake, was onely long of himselfe and of his fellow for that before they departed thence our Captaine and Donnacona entred into a marvellous stedfast league of friendship, whereupon all his people at once with a loude voyce, cast out three great cryes, (a horrible thing to heare) and each one having taken leave of the other for that day, we went aboord againe. The day following we brought our two great shippes within the river and harborough, where the waters being at the highest, are three fadome deepe, and at the lowest, but halfe a fadome. We left our Pinnesse without the road to the end we might bring it to Hochelaga. So soone as we had safely placed our ships, behold we saw Donnacona, Taignoagny and Domagaia, with more then five hundred persons, men, women and children, and the said Lord with ten or twelve of the chiefest of the countrey came aboord of our ships, who were all courteously received, and friendly entertained both of our Captaine and of us all: and divers gifts of small value were given them. Then did Taignoagny tell our Captaine, that his Lord did greatly sorrow that he would go to Hochelaga, and that he would not by any meanes permit that any of them should goe with him, because the river was of no importance. Our Captaine answered him, that for all his saying, he would not leave off his going thither, if by any meanes it were possible, for that he was commanded by his king to goe as farre as possibly he could: and that if he (that is to say Taignoagny) would goe with him, as he had promised, he should be very well entertained, beside that, he should have such a gift given him, as he should well content himselfe: for he should doe nothing else but goe with him to Hochelaga and come againe. To whom Taignoagny answered, that he would not by any meanes goe, and thereupon they sodainly returned to their houses. The next day being the 17 of September, Donnacona and his company returned even as at the first, and brought with him many Eeles, with sundry sorts of other fishes, whereof they take great store in the said river, as more largely hereafter shall be shewed. And as soone as they were come to our ships, according to their wonted use they beganne to sing and dance. This done, Donnacona caused all his people to be set on the one side: then making a round circle upon the sand he caused our Captaine with all his people to enter thereinto, then he began to make a long Oration, holding in one of his hands a maiden child of ten or twelve yeeres old, which he presented unto our Captaine: then sodainly beganne all his people to make three great shreeks, or howles, in signe of joy and league of friendship: presently upon that he did present unto him two other young male children one after another, but younger then the other, at the giving of which even as before they gave out shreeks and howles very loud, with other cerimonies: for which presents, our Captaine, gave the saide Lorde great and hearty thankes. Then Taignoagny told our Captaine, that one of the children was his owne brother, and that the maiden child was daughter unto the said Lords owne sister, and the presents were only given him to the end he should not goe to Hochelaga at all: to whom our Captaine answered, that if they were only given him to that intent, if so he would, he should take them againe, for that by no meanes he would leave his going off, for as much as he was so commanded of his King. But concerning this, Domagaia told our Captaine that their Lord had given him those children as a signe and token of goodwill and security, and that he was contented to goe with him to Hochelaga, upon which talke great wordes arose betweene Taignoagny and Domagaia, by which we plainely perceived that Taignoagny was but a crafty knave, and that he intended but mischiefe and treason, as well by this deede as others that we by him had seene. After that our Captaine caused the said children to be put in our ships, and caused two Swords and two copper Basons, the one wrought, the other plaine, to be brought unto him, and them he gave to Donnacona, who was therewith greatly contented, yeelding most heartie thankes unto our Captaine for them, and presently upon that he commanded all his people to sing and dance, and desired our Captaine to cause a peece of artillerie to be shot off, because Taignoagny and Domagaia made great brags of it, and had told them marvellous things, and also, because they had never heard nor seene any before: to whom our Captaine answered, that he was content: and by and by he commanded his men to shoot off twelve cannons charged with bullets into the wood that was hard by those people and ships, at whose noyse they were greatly astonished and amazed, for they thought that heaven had fallen upon them, and put themselves to flight, howling, crying, and shreeking, so that it seemed hell was broken loose. But before we went thence, Taignoagny caused other men to tell us, that those men which we had left in our Pinnesse in the road, had slaine two men of their company, with a peece of ordinance that they had shot off, whereupon the rest had put themselves all to flight, as though they should all have bene slaine: which afterward we found untrue, because our men had not shot off any peece at all that day.

How Donnacona and Taignoagny with others, devised a prettie sleight or pollicie: for they caused three of their men to be attired like Divels, fayning themselves to be sent from their God Cudruaigny, onely to hinder our voyage to Hochelaga.

Chap. 4

The next day being the eighteenth of September, these men still endeavoured themselves to seeke all meanes possible to hinder and let our going to Hochelaga, and devised a prettie guile, as hereafter shalbe shewed. They went and dressed three men like Divels, being wrapped in dogges skinnes white and blacke, their faces besmeered as blacke as any coales, with hornes on their heads more then a yard long, and caused them secretly to be put in one of their boates, but came not neere our ships as they were wont to doe, for they lay hidden within the wood for the space of two houres, looking for the tide, to the end the boat wherein the Divels were, might approach and come neere us, which when time was, came, and all the rest issued out of the wood comming to us, but yet not so neere as they were wont to do. There began Taignoagny to salute our Captaine, who asked him if he would have the boate to come for him; he answered, not for that time, but after a while he would come unto our ships: then presently came that boat rushing out, wherein the three counterfeit Divels were with such long hornes on their heads, and the middlemost came making a long Oration and passed along our ships with out turning or looking toward us, but with the boat went toward the land. Then did Donnacona with all his people pursue them, and lay hold on the boat and Divels, who so soone as the men were come to them, fell prostrate in the boate, even as if they had beene dead: then were they taken up and carried into the wood, being but a stones cast off, then every one withdrew himselfe into the wood, not one staying behind with us, where being, they began to make a long discourse, so loud that we might heare them in our ships, which lasted about halfe an houre, and being ended we began to espie Taignoagny and Domagaia comming towards us, holding their hands upward joyned together, carying their hats under their upper garment, shewing a great admiration, and Taignoagny looking up to heaven, cryed three times Jesus, Jesus, Jesus, and Domagaia doing as his fellow had done before, cryed, Jesus Maria, James Cartier. Our Captaine hearing them, and seeing their gestures and ceremonies, asked of them what they ailed, and what was happened or chanced anew; they answered, that there were very ill tydings befallen, saying in French, Nenni est il bon, that is to say, it was not good: our Captaine asked them againe what it was, then answered they, that their God Cudruaigny had spoken in Hochelaga: and that he had sent those three men to shewe unto them that there was so much yce and snow in that countrey, that whosoever went thither should die, which wordes when we heard, we laughed and mocked them saying, that their God Cudruaigny was but a foole and a noddie, for he knew not what he did or said: then bade we them shew his messengers from us, that Christ would defend them from all colde, if they would beleeve in him. Then did they aske of our Captaine if he had spoken with Jesus: he answered no, but that his Priests had, and that he told them they should have faire weather: which wordes when they had heard, they thanked our Captaine, and departed toward the wood to tell those newes unto their felowes, who sodainly came all rushing out of the wood, seeming to be very glad for those words that our Captaine had spoken, and to shew that thereby they had had, and felt great joy, so soone as they were before our ships, they altogether gave out three great shreekes, and thereupon beganne to sing and dance, as they were wont to doe. But for a resolution of the matter Taignoagny and Domagaia tolde our Captaine, that their Lord **Donnacona** would by no meanes permit that any of them should goe with him to Hochelaga unlesse he would leave him some hostage to stay with him: our Captaine answered them, that if they would not goe with him with a good will, they should stay, and that for all them he would not leave off his journey thither.

How our Captaine with all his Gentlemen and fiftie Mariners departed with our Pinnesse, and the two boates from Canada to goe to Hochelaga: and also there is described, what was seene by the way upon the said river.

Chap. 5

The next day being the 19 of September we hoysed saile, and with our Pinnesse and two boates departed to goe up the river with the flood, where on both shores of it we beganne to see as goodly a countrey as possibly can with eye be seene, all replenished with very goodly trees, and Vines laden as full of grapes as could be all along the river, which rather seemed to have bin planted by mans hand than otherwise. True it is, that because they are not dressed and wrought as they should be, their bunches of grapes are not so great nor sweete as ours; also we sawe all along the river many houses inhabited of Fishers, which take all kindes of fishes, and they came with as great familiaritie and kindnesse unto us, as if we had beene their Countreymen, and brought us great store of fish, with other such things as they had, which we exchanged with them for other wares, who lifting up their hands toward heaven, gave many signes of joy: we stayed at a place called Hochelai,[1] about five and twentie leagues from Canada, where the river waxeth very narrow, and runneth very swift, wherefore it is very dangerous, not onely for that, but also for certaine great stones that are therein: Many boates and barkes came unto us, in one of which came one of the chiefe Lords of the countrey,

---

[1] Champlain says that this place was fifteen leagues from Quebec.

making a long discourse, who being come neere us, did by evident signes and gestures shew us, that the higher the river went, the more dangerous it was, and bade us take heede of our selves. The said Lord presented and gave unto our Captaine two of his owne children, of which our Captaine tooke one being a wench of 7 or 8 yeres old, the man child he gave him againe, because it was too yong, for it was but two or three yeeres old. Our Captaine as friendly and as courteously as he could did entertaine and receive the said Lord and his company, giving them certaine small trifles, and so they departed toward the shore againe. Afterwards the sayd Lord and his wife came unto Canada to visite his daughter, bringing unto our Captaine certaine small presents. From the nineteenth untill the eight and twentieth of September, we sailed up along the saide river, never losing one houre of time, all which time we saw as goodly and pleasant a countrey as possibly can be wished for, full (as we have said before) of all sorts of goodly trees, that is to say, Okes, Elmes, Walnut-trees, Cedars, Firres, Ashes, Boxe, Willowes, and great store of Vines, all as full of grapes as could be, so that if any of our fellowes went on shore, they came home laden with them: there are likewise many Cranes, Swannes, Geese, Duckes, Feasants, Partriges, Thrushes, Blackbirds, Turtles, Finches, Redbreasts, Nightingales, Sparrowes of diverse kindes, with many other sorts of Birds, even as in France, and great plentie and store. Upon the 28 of September we came to a great wide lake [1] in the middle of the river five or sixe leagues broad, and twelve long, all that day we went against the tide, having but two fadome water, still keeping the sayd scantling: being come to one of the heads of the lake, we could espie no passage or going out, nay, rather it seemed to have bene closed and shut up round about, and there was but a fadome and an halfe of water, little more or lesse. And therefore we were constrayned to cast anker, and to stay with our Pinnesse, and went with our two boates to seeke some going out, and in one place we found foure or five branches, which out of

[1] St. Peter's Lake. Hakluyt in the margin gives it the name of "The lake of Angolesme."

the river come into the lake, and they came from Hochelaga. But in the said branches, because of the great fiercenesse and swiftnesse wherewith they breake out, and the course of the water, they make certaine barres and shoulds, and at that time there was but a fadome water. Those Shouldes being passed, we found foure or five fadome, and as farre as we could perceive by the flood, it was that time of the yeere that the waters are lowest, for at other times they flowe higher by three fadomes. All these foure or five branches do compasse about five or sixe Ilands very pleasant, which make the head of the lake: about fifteene leagues beyond, they doe all come into one. That day we landed in one of the saide Islands, and met with five men that were hunting of wilde beastes, who as freely and familiarly came to our boates without any feare, as if we had ever bene brought up togither. Our boates being somewhat neere the shore, one of them tooke our Captaine in his armes, and caried him on shore, as lightly and as easily as if he had bene a child of five yeeres old: so strong and sturdie was this fellow. We found that they had a great heape of wild Rats[1] that live in the water, as bigge as a Conny, and very good to eate, which they gave unto our Captaine, who for a recompence gave them knives and glassen Beades. We asked them with signes if that was the way to Hochelaga, they answered yea, and that we had yet three dayes sayling thither.

How our Captaine caused our boates to be mended and dressed
 to goe to Hochelaga: and because the way was somewhat difficult and hard, we left our Pinnesse behinde:
 and how we came thither, and what entertainment
 we had of the people.

Chap. 6

The next day our Captaine seeing that for that time it was not possible for our Pinnesse to goe on any further, he caused

[1] Muskrats.

our boates to be made readie, and as much munition and victuals to be put in them, as they could well beare: he departed with them, accompanyed with many Gentlemen, that is to say, Claudius of Ponte Briand, Cup-bearer to the Lorde Dolphin of France, Charles of Pommeraye, John Gouion, John Powlet, with twentie and eight Mariners: and Mace Jallobert, and William Briton, who had the charge under the Captaine of the other two ships, to goe up as farre as they could into that river: we sayled with good and prosperous weather untill the second of October, on which day we came to the towne of Hochelaga, distant from the place where we had left our Pinnesse five and fortie leagues. In which place of Hochelaga, and all the way we went, we met with many of those countriemen, who brought us fish and such other victuals as they had, still dancing and greatly rejoycing at our comming. Our Captaine to lure them in, and to keepe them our friends, to recompence them, gave them knives, beades, and such small trifles, wherewith they were greatly satisfied. So soone as we were come neere Hochelaga, there came to meete us above a thousand persons, men, women and children, who afterward did as friendly and merily entertaine and receive us as any father would doe his child, which he had not of long time seene, the men dauncing on one side, the women on another, and likewise the children on another: after that they brought us great store of fish, and of their bread made of Millet,[1] casting them into our boates so thicke, that you would have thought it to fall from heaven. Which when our Captaine sawe, he with many of his company went on shore: so soone as ever we were aland they came clustring about us, making very much of us, bringing their young children in their armes, onely to have our Captaine and his company to touch them, making signes and shewes of great mirth and gladnesse, that lasted more than halfe an houre. Our Captaine seeing their loving kindnesse and entertainment of us, caused all the women orderly to be set in aray, and gave them Beades made of Tinne, and other such

[1] Indian corn.

small trifles, and to some of the men he gave knives: then he
returned to the boates to supper, and so passed that night, all
which while all those people stood on the shore as neere our
boates as they might, making great fires, and dauncing very
merily, still crying Aguiaze, which in their tonge signifieth
Mirth and Safetie.

How our Captaine with five gentlemen and twentie armed men
all well in order, went to see the towne of Hochelaga,
and the situation of it.

Chap. 7

Our Captaine the next day very earely in the morning, having very gorgeously attired himselfe, caused all his company
to be set in order to go to see the towne and habitation
of those people, and a certaine mountaine [1] that is somewhat
neere the citie: with whom went also five Gentlemen and
twentie Mariners, leaving the rest to keepe and looke to our
boates: we tooke with us three men of Hochelaga to bring us
to the place. All along as we went we found the way as well
beaten and frequented as can be, the fairest and best countrey
that possibly can be seene, full of as goodly great Okes as are
in any wood in France, under which the ground was all covered
over with faire Akornes. After we had gone about foure or
five miles,[2] we met by the way one of the chiefest Lords of the
citie, accompanied with many moe, who so soone as he sawe us
beckned and made signes upon us, that we must rest us in that
place where they had made a great fire, and so we did. After
that we had rested our selves there a while, the said Lord began
to make a long discourse, even as we have saide above, they are
accustomed to doe in signe of mirth and friendship, shewing
our Captaine and all his company a joyfull countenance, and

---

[1] Mont Royal as below, whence the name Montreal. Hochelaga stood near the present site of Montreal.
[2] The margin reads, "Hochelaga sixe miles from the river side." Manuscript 5589 says the distance marched was "about a league and a half."

good will, who gave him two hatchets, a paire of knives and a crosse which he made him to kisse, and then put it about his necke, for which he gave our Captaine heartie thankes. This done, we went along, and about a mile and a halfe farther, we began to finde goodly and large fieldes, full of such corne as the countrie yeeldieth. It is even as the Millet of Bresil, as great and somewhat bigger than small peason, wherewith they live even as we doe with ours. In the midst of those fields is the citie of Hochelaga, placed neere, and as it were joyned to a great mountaine that is tilled round about, very fertill, on the top of which you may see very farre, we named it Mount Roiall. The citie of Hochelaga is round, compassed about with timber, with three course of Rampires, one within another framed like a sharpe Spire, but laide acrosse above. The middlemost of them is made and built, as a direct line, but perpendicular. The Rampires are framed and fashioned with peeces of timber, layd along on the ground, very well and cunningly joyned togither after their fashion. This enclosure is in height about two rods. It hath but one gate or entrie thereat, which is shut with piles, stakes, and barres. Over it, and also in many places of the wall, there be places to runne along, and ladders to get up, all full of stones, for the defence of it. There are in the towne about fiftie houses, about fiftie paces long, and twelve, or fifteene broad, built all of wood, covered over with the barke of the wood as broad as any boord, very finely and cunning joyned together. Within the said houses, there are many roomes, lodgings and chambers. In the middest of every one there is a great Court, in the middle whereof they make their fire. They live in common togither: then doe the husbands, wives and children each one retire themselves to their chambers. They have also on the top of their houses certaine garrets, wherein they keepe their corne to make their bread withall: they call it Carraconny, which they make as hereafter shall follow. They have certaine peeces of wood, made hollow like those whereon we beat our hempe, and with certaine beetles of wood they beat their corne to powder: then they make paste of it, and of the paste, cakes or wreathes, then they lay them on a broad and hote stone, and then cover it with hote stones, and so they bake their bread in stead of Ovens. They make also sundry sorts of pottage with the said corne and also of pease and of beanes, whereof they have great store, as also with other fruits, as Muske-Millions, and very great Cowcumbers. They have also in their houses certaine vessels as bigge as any But or Tun, wherein they preserve and keepe their fish, causing the same in sommer to be dried in the sunne, and live therewith in winter, whereof they make great provision, as we by experience have seene. All their viands and meates are without any taste or savour of salt at all. They sleepe upon barkes of trees laide all along upon the ground being over-spread with the skinnes of certaine wilde Beastes, wherewith they also cloth and cover themselves. The thing most precious that they have in all the world they call Asurgny [1] : it is as white as any snow: they take it in the said river of Cornibotz, in the maner folowing. When any one hath deserved death, or that they take any of their enemies in Warres, first they kill him, then with certaine knives they give great slashes and strokes upon their buttocks, flankes, thighs, and shoulders: then they cast the same bodie so mangled downe to the bottome of the river, in a place where the said Esurgny is, and there leave it ten or 12 houres, then they take it up againe, and in the cuts find the said Esurgny or Cornibotz. Of them they make beads, and weare them about their necks, even as we doe chaines of gold and silver, accounting it the preciousest thing in the world. They have this vertue and propertie in them, they will stop or stanch bleeding at the nose, for we have prooved it. These people are given to no other exercise, but onely to husbandrie and fishing for their sustenance: they have no care of any other wealth or commoditie in this world, for they have no knowledge of it, and that is, because they never travell and go out of their countrey, as those of Canada and Saguenay doe, albeit the Canadians with eight or nine Villages more alongst the river be subjects unto them.

[1] Wampum.

How we came to the Towne of Hochelaga, and the entertainement which there we had, and of certaine gifts which our Captaine gave them, with divers other things.

Chap. 8

So soone as we were come neere the Towne, a great number of the inhabitants thereof came to present themselves before us after their fashion, making very much of us: we were by our guides brought into the middest of the towne. They have in the middlemost part of their houses a large square place, being from side to side a good stones cast, whither we were brought, and there with signes were commanded to stay: then suddenly all the women and maidens of the towne gathered themselves together, part of which had their armes full of young children, and as many as could came to rubbe our faces, our armes, and what part of the bodie soever they could touch, weeping for very joy that they saw us, shewing us the best countenance that possibly they could, desiring us with their signes, that it would please us to touch their children. That done, the men caused the women to withdraw themselves backe, then they every one sate downe on the ground round about us, as if they would have shewen and rehearsed some Comedie or other shew: then presently came the women againe, every one bringing a foure square Matte in manner of Carpets, and spreading them abroad on the ground in that place, they caused us to sit upon them. That done, the Lord and King of the countrey was brought upon 9 or 10 mens shoulders, (whom in their tongue they call Agouhanna) sitting upon a great Stagges skinne, and they laide him downe upon the foresaid mats neere to the Captaine, every one beckning unto us that hee was their Lord and King. This Agouhanna was a man about fiftie yeeres old: he was no whit better apparelled then any of the rest, onely excepted, that he had a certaine thing made of the skinnes of Hedgehogs like a red wreath, and that was in stead of his Crowne. He was full of the palsie, and his members shronke togither. After he had with certaine signes saluted our Captaine and all his companie, and by manifest tokens bid all welcome, he shewed his legges and armes to our Captaine, and with signes desired him to touch them, and so he did, rubbing them with his owne hands: then did Agouhanna take the wreath or crowne he had about his head, and gave it unto our Captaine: that done they brought before him divers diseased men, some blinde, some criple, some lame and impotent, and some so old that the haire of their eyelids came downe and covered their cheekes, and layd them all along before our Captaine, to the end they might of him be touched: for it seemed unto them that God was descended and come downe from heaven to heale them. Our Captaine seeing the misery and devotion of this poore people, recited the Gospel of Saint John, that is to say, In the beginning was the word; touching every one that were diseased, praying to God that it would please him to open the hearts of this poore people, and to make them know his holy word, and that they might receive Baptisme and Christendome: that done, he tooke a Service-booke in his hand, and with a loud voyce read all the passion of Christ, word by word that all the standers by might heare him: all which while this poore people kept silence, and were marvellously attentive, looking up to heaven, and imitating us in gestures. Then he caused the men all orderly to be set on one side, the women on another, and likewise the children on an other, and to the chiefest of them he gave hatchets, to the other knives, and to the women beads and such other small trifles. Then where the children were, he cast rings, counters, and brooches made of Tin, whereat they seemed to be very glad. That done, our Captaine commanded Trumpets and other musicall instruments to be sounded, which when they heard, they were very merie. Then we tooke our leave and went to our boate: the women seeing that, put themselves before to stay us, and brought us out of their meates that they had made readie for us, as fish, pottage beanes, and such other things, thinking to make us eate, and dine in that place: but because the meates had no savour at all of salt, we liked them not, but thanked them, and with signes gave them to understand that we had no neede to eate. When wee were out of the Towne, diverse of the men and women followed us, and brought us to the toppe of the foresaid mountaine, which we named Mount Roiall, it is about a league from the Towne. When as we were on the toppe of it, we might discerne and plainly see thirtie leagues about. On the Northside of it there are many hilles to be seene running West and East, and as many more on the South, amongst and betweene the which the Countrey is as faire and as pleasant as possibly can be seene, being levell, smooth, and very plaine, fit to be husbanded and tilled: and in the middest of those fieldes we saw the river further up a great way then where we had left our boates, where was the greatest and the swiftest fall of water that any where hath beene seene,[1] and as great, wide, and large as our sight might discerne, going Southwest along three faire and round mountaines that wee sawe, as we judged about fifteene leagues from us. Those which brought us thither tolde and shewed us, that in the sayd river there were three such falles of water more, as that was where we had left our boates: but because we could not understand their language, we could not knowe how farre they were from one another. Moreover they shewed us with signes, that the said three fals being past, a man might sayle the space of three monethes more alongst that River, and that along the hilles that are on the North side there is a great river,[2] which (even as the other) commeth from the West, we thought it to be the river that runneth through the Countrey of Saguenay: and without any signe or question mooved or asked of them, they tooke the chayne of our Captaines whistle, which was of silver, and the dagger-haft of one of our fellow Mariners, hanging on his side being of yellow copper guilt, and shewed us that such stuffe came from the said River, and that there be Agouionda, that is as much to say, as evill people, who goe all armed even to their finger ends. Also they shewed us the manner and making of their armour: they are made of cordes and wood,

---

[1] The Lachine Rapids.   [2] The Ottawa.

finely and cunningly wrought togither. They gave us also to understande that those Agouionda doe continually warre one against another, but because we did not understand them well, we could not perceive how farre it was to that Countrey. Our Captaine shewed them redde Copper, which in their language they call Caignetadze, and looking towarde that Countrey, with signes asked them if any came from thence, they shaking their heads answered no: but they shewed us that it came from Saguenay, and that lyeth cleane contrary to the other. After we had heard and seene these things of them, we drewe to our boates accompanied with a great multitude of those people: some of them when as they sawe any of our fellowes weary, would take them up on their shoulders, and carry them as on horsebacke. So soone as we came to our boates we hoysed saile to goe toward our Pinnesse, doubting of some mischance. Our departure grieved and displeased them very much, for they followed us along the river as farre as they could: we went so fast that on Munday being the fourth of October wee came where our Pinnesse was. The Tuesday following being the fift of the moneth, we hoysed saile, and with our Pinnesse and boates departed from thence toward the Province of Canada, to the port of the Holy Crosse, where we had left our ships. The seventh day we came against a river that commeth from the North, and entred into that river, at the entrance whereof are foure little Ilands full of faire and goodly trees: we named that river The river of Fouetz:[1] But because one of those Ilandes stretcheth it selfe a great way into the river, our Captaine at the point of it caused a goodly great Crosse to be set up, and commanded the boates to be made readie, that with the next tide he might goe up the saide river, and consider the qualitie of it, which wee did, and that day went up as farre as we could: but because we found it to be of no importance, and very shallow, we returned and sayled down the river.

[1] The St. Maurice.

How we came to the Port of the Holy Crosse, and in what state
we found our ships: and how the Lord of the Countrey
came to visit our Captaine, and our Captaine him:
and of certaine particular customes of the people.

Chap. 9

Upon Monday being the 11 of October we came to the Port
of the Holy Crosse, where our ships were, and found that the
Masters and Mariners we had left there, had made and reared
a trench before the ships, altogither closed with great peeces of
timber set upright and verywell fastened togither: then had
they beset the said trench about with peeces of Artillerie and
other nec' ssarie things to shield and defend themselves from
the powe. of all the countrey. So soone as the Lord of the
countrey heard of our comming, the next day being the
twelfth of October, he came to visite us, accompanied with
Taignoagny, Domagaia, and many others, fayning to be very
glad of our comming, making much of our Captaine, who as
friendly as he could, entertained them, albeit they had not
deserved it. Donnacona their Lord desired our Captaine the
next day to come and see Canada, which he promised to doe: for
the next day being the 13 of the moneth, he with all his Gentlemen and fiftie Mariners very well appointed, went to visite Donnacona and his people, about a league from our ships. The place
where they make their abode is called Stadacona. When we
were about a stones cast from their houses, many of the inhabitants came to meete us, being all set in a ranke, and (as
their custome is) the men all on one side, and the women on
the other, still dancing and singing without any ceasing: and after
we had saluted and received one another, our Captaine gave
them knives and such other sleight things: then he caused all
the women and children to passe along before him, giving each
one a ring of Tin, for which they gave him hearty thankes:
that done, our Captaine was by Donnacona and Taignoagny,
brought to see their houses, which (the qualitie considered)

F

were very well provided, and stored with such victuals as the countrey yeeldeth, to passe away the winter withall. Then they shewed us the skins of five mens heads spread upon boards as we do use parchment:[1] Donnacona told us that they were skins of Toudamani,[2] a people dwelling toward the South, who continually doe warre against them. Moreover they told us, that it was two yeeres past that those Toudamans came to assault them, yea even into the said river, in an Iland that lyeth over against Saguenay, where they had bin the night before, as they were going a warfaring in Hognedo, with 200 persons, men, women, and children, who being all asleepe in a Fort that they had made, they were assaulted by the said Toudamans, who put fire round about the Fort, and as they would have come out of it to save themselves, they were all slaine, only five excepted, who escaped. For which losse they yet sorrov ∋d, shewing with signes, that one day they would be revenged: that done, we came to our ships againe.

The maner how the people of that Countrey live: and of certaine conditions: of their faith, maners, and customes.

Chap. 10

This people beleeve no whit in God, but in one whom they call Cudruaigni: they say that often he speaketh with them and telleth them what weather shal follow, whether good or bad. Moreover they say, that when he is angry with them he casteth dust into their eyes: they beleeve that when they die they go into the stars, and thence by litle and little descend downe into the Horizon, even as the stars doe, and that then they goe into certaine greene fields full of goodly faire and precious trees, floures, and fruits. After that they had given us these things to understand, we shewed them their error, and

---

[1] Scalps.
[2] Baxter (*Memoir of Jacques Cartier*, p. 174) identifies the Toudamani with the ferocious Iroquois.

told that their Cudruaigni did but deceive them, for he is but a Divell and an evill spirit: affirming unto them, that there is but one onely God, who is in heaven, and who giveth us all necessaries, being the Creatour of all himselfe, and that onely we must beleeve in him: moreover, that it is necessarie for us to be baptised, otherwise wee are damned into hell. These and many other things concerning our faith and religion we shewed them, all which they did easily beleeve, calling their Cudruaigni, Agouiada, that is to say, nought, so that very earnestly they desired and prayed our Captaine that he would cause them to be baptised, and their Lorde, and Taignoagny, Domagaia, and all the people of the towne came unto us, hoping to be baptised: but because we did not throughly know their minde, and that there was no bodie could teach them our beliefe and religion, we excused our selves, desiring Taignoagny, and Domagaia, to tell the rest of their countreymen, that [we] would come againe another time, and bring Priests and chrisome with us, for without them they could not be baptised: which they did easily beleeve, for Domagaia and Taignoagny had seene many children baptised in Britain[1] whiles they were there. Which promise when they heard they seemed to be very glad. They live in common togither: and of such commodities as their countrey yeeldeth they are indifferently well stored, the inhabitants of the countrey cloth themselves with the skinnes of certaine wilde beasts, but very miserably. In winter they weare hosen and shoes made of wilde beasts skins, and in Sommer they goe barefooted. They keepe and observe the rites of matrimonie saving that every one weddeth 2 or 3 wives, which (their husbands being dead) do never marrie againe, but for the death of their husbands weare a certaine blacke weede all the daies of their life, besmearing al their faces with cole dust and grease mingled togither as thicke as the backe of a knife, and by that they are knowen to be widdowes. They have a filthy and detestable use in marrying of their maidens, and that is this, they put them

---

[1] Brittany.

all (after they are of lawfull age to marry) in a common place, as harlots free for every man that will have to doe with them, untill such time as they find a match. This I say, because I have seene by experience many housen full of those Damosels, even as our schooles are full of children in France to learne to reade. Moreover, the misrule and riot that they keepe in those houses is very great, for very wantonly they sport and dally togither, shewing whatsoever God hath sent them. They are no men of great labour. They digge their grounds with certaine peeces of wood, as bigge as halfe a sword, on which ground groweth their corne, which they call Offici:[1] it is as bigge as our small peason: there is great quantitie of it growing in Bresill. They have also great store of Muske-milions, Pompions, Gourds, Cucumbers, Peason and Beanes of every colour, yet differing from ours. There groweth also a certaine kind of herbe,[2] whereof in Sommer they make great provision for all the yeere, making great account of it, and onely men use of it, and first they cause it to be dried in the Sunne, then weare it about their neckes wrapped in a little beasts skinne made like a little bagge, with a hollow peece of stone or wood like a pipe: then when they please they make pouder of it, and then put it in one of the ends of the said Cornet or pipe, and laying a cole of fire upon it, at the other ende sucke so long, that they fill their bodies full of smoke, till that it commeth out of their mouth and nostrils, even as out of the Tonnell of a chimney. They say that this doth keepe them warme and in health: they never goe without some of it about them. We ourselves have tryed the same smoke, and having put it in our mouthes, it seemed almost as hot as Pepper. The women of that countrey doe labour much more then the men, as well in fishing (whereto they are greatly given) as in tilling and husbanding their grounds, and other things: as well the men as women and children, are very much more able to resist cold then savage beastes, for wee with our owne eyes have seene some of them, when it was coldest (which cold was extreme raw and

---

[1] Maize, according to a gloss in the margin.   [2] Tobacco.

bitter) come to our ships starke naked going upon snow and yce, which thing seemeth incredible to them that have not seene it. When as the snow and yce lyeth on the ground, they take great store of wilde beasts, as Faunes, Stags, Beares, Marterns, Hares and Foxes, with divers other sorts whose flesh they eate raw, having first dried it in the sunne or smoke, and so they doe their fish. As farre foorth as we could perceive and understand by these people, it were a very easie thing to bring them to some familiaritie and civility, and make them learne what one would. The Lord God for his mercies sake set thereunto his helping hand when he seeth cause. Amen.

Of the greatnesse and depth of the said river, and of the sorts of beasts, birdes, fishes, and other things that we have seene, with the situation of the place.

Chap. 11

The said river beginneth beyond the Iland of the Assumption, over against the high mountaines of Hognedo, and of the seven Ilands. The distance over from one side to the other is about 35 or 40 leagues. In the middest it is above 200 fadome deepe. The surest way to sayle upon it is on the South side. And toward the North, that is to say, from the said 7 Ilands, from side to side, there is seven leagues distance, where are also two great rivers that come downe from the hils of Saguenay,[1] and make divers very dangerous shelves in the Sea. At the entrance of those two rivers we saw many and great store of Whales and Sea horses. Overthwart the said Ilands there is another little river that runneth along those marrish grounds about 3 or 4 leagues, wherein there is great store of water foules. From the entrance of that river to Hochelaga there is about 300 leagues distance:[2] the originall beginning of it is in the river that commeth from Saguenay, which riseth and

[1] Moisie and St. Margaret.
[2] Hakluyt says in the margin, "It is now found to be but 200 leagues."

springeth among high and steepe hils: it entreth into that river before it commeth to the Province of Canada on the North side. That river is very deepe, high, and streight, wherefore it is very dangerous for any vessell to goe upon it. After that river followeth the Province of Canada, wherein are many people dwelling in open boroughes and villages. There are also in the circuit and territorie of Canada, along, and within the said river, many other Ilands, some great, and some small, among which there is one that containeth above ten leagues in length, full of goodly and high trees, and also many Vines. You may goe into it from both sides, but yet the surest passage is on the South side. On the shore or banke of that river Westward, there is a goodly, faire, and delectable bay or creeke, convenient and fit for to harborough ships. Hard by there is in that river one place very narrow, deepe, and swift running, but it is not passing the third part of a league, over against the which there is a goodly high piece of land, with a towne therein: and the countrey about it is very well tilled and wrought, and as good as possibly can be seene. That is the place and abode of Donnacona, and of our two men we tooke in our first voyage. It is called Stadacona. But before we come to it, there are 4 other peopled townes, that is to say, Ayraste, Starnatan, Tailla, which standeth upon a hill, Scitadin, and then Stadagona, under which towne toward the North the river and port of the holy crosse is, where we staied from the 15 of September, until the 16 of May 1536, and there our ships remained dry, as we have said before. That place being past, we found the habitation of the people called Teguenondahi, standing upon an high mountaine, and the valley of Hochelay, which standeth in a Champaigne countrey. All the said countrey on both sides of the river as farre as Hochelay and beyond, is as faire and plaine as ever was seene. There are certain mountaines farre distant from the said river, which are to be seene above the foresaid townes, from which mountaines divers rivers descend, which fall into the said river. All that countrey is full of sundry sorts of wood and many Vines, unless it be about the places that are inhabited, where they have pulled

up the trees to till and labour the ground, and to build their
houses and lodgings. There is great store of Stags, Deere,
Beares, and other such like sorts of beasts, as Connies, Hares,
Marterns, Foxes, Otters, Bevers, Weasels, Badgers, and Rats
exceeding great and divers other sortes of wilde beasts.
They cloth themselves with the skinnes of those beasts,
because they have nothing else to make them apparell withall.
There are also many sorts of birdes, as Cranes, Swannes,
Bustards, wild Geese white and gray, Duckes, Thrushes,
Blackbirdes, Turtles, wilde Pigeons, Lenites, Finches, Redbreasts, Stares, Nightingales, Sparrowes, and other Birdes,
even as in France. Also, as we have said before, the said river
is the plentifullest of fish that ever hath of any man bene seene
or heard of, because that from the mouth to the end of it, according to their seasons, you shall finde all sorts of fresh
water fish and salt. There are also many Whales, Porposes,
Seahorses, and Adhothuis, which is a kind of fish that we had
never seene or heard of before. They are as great as Porposes,
as white as any snow, their bodie and head fashioned as a
grayhound, they are wont alwaies to abide betwene the fresh
and salt water, which beginneth betweene the river of Saguenay
and Canada.

Of certaine advertisements and notes given unto us by those
countreymen, after our returne from Hochelaga

Chap. 12

After our returne from Hochelaga, we dealt, traffickt, and
with great familiaritie and love were conversant with those that
dwelt neerest unto our ships, except that sometimes we had
strife and contention with certaine naughtie people, full sore
against the will of the others. Wee understood of Donnacona
and of others, that the said river is called the river of Saguenay,
and goeth to Saguenay, being somewhat more then a league
farther Westnorthwest, and that 8 or 9 dayes journeys beyond,
it will beare but small boats. But the right and readie way

to Saguenay is up that river to Hochelaga, and then into another that commeth from Saguenay, and then entreth into the foresaid river, and that there is yet one moneths sayling thither. Moreover, they told us and gave us to understand, that there are people clad with cloth as we are, very honest, and many inhabited townes, and that they have great store of Gold and red Copper: and that about the land beyond the said first river to Hochelaga and Saguenay, is an Iland environed round about with that and other rivers, and that beyond Saguenay the said river entereth into two or 3 great lakes, and that there is a Sea of fresh water [1] found, and as they have heard say of those of Saguenay, there was never man heard of that found out the end thereof: for, as they told us, they themselves were never there. Moreover they told us, that where we had left our Pinnesse when wee went to Hochelaga, there is a river that goeth Southwest, from whence there is a whole moneths sayling to goe to a certaine land,[2] where there is neither yce nor snow seene, where the inhabitants doe continually warre one against another, where there is great store of Oranges, Almonds, Nuts, and Apples, with many other sorts of fruits, and that the men and women are clad with beasts skinnes even as they: we asked them if there were any gold or red copper, they answered no. I take this place to be toward Florida, as farre as I could perceive and understand by their signes and tokens.

Of a strange and cruell disease that came to the people of Stadacona, wherewith because we did haunt their company, we were so infected, that there died 25 of our company.

Chap. 13

In the moneth of December, wee understood that the pestilence was come among the people of Stadacona, in such

[1] Probably Lake Ontario.
[2] A reference to a way southward by Lake Champlain and the Hudson River, or by waterways farther west. The river alluded to is further designated by Hakluyt in the margin as "The river of Irrouacas [Iroquois] falling into the lake of Angolesme"; *i.e.*, the Richelieu River.

sort, that before we knew of it, according to their confession, there were dead above 50: whereupon we charged them neither to come neere our Fort, nor about our ships, or us. And albeit we had driven them from us, the said unknowen sicknes began to spread itselfe amongst us after the strangest sort that ever was eyther heard of or seene, insomuch as some did lose all their strength, and could not stand on their feete, then did their legges swel, their sinnowes shrinke as blacke as any cole. Others also had all their skins spotted with spots of blood of a purple coulour: then did it ascend up to their ankels, knees, thighes, shoulders, armes and necke: their mouth became stincking, their gummes so rotten, that all the flesh did fall off, even to the rootes of the teeth, which did also almost all fall out. With such infection did this sicknesse [1] spread itselfe in our three ships, that about the middle of February, of a hundreth and tenne persons that we were, there were not ten whole, so that one could not help the other, a most horrible and pitifull case, considering the place we were in, forsomuch as the people of the countrey would dayly come before our fort, and saw but few of us. There were alreadie eight dead, and more then fifty sicke, and as we thought, past all hope of recovery. Our Captaine seeing this our misery, and that the sicknesse was gone so farre, ordained and commanded, that every one should devoutly prepare himselfe to prayer, and in remembrance of Christ, caused his Image to be set upon a tree, about a flight shot from the fort amidst the yce and snow, giving all men to understand, that on the Sunday following, service should be said there, and that whosoever could goe, sicke or whole, should goe thither in Procession, singing the seven Psalmes of David, with other Letanies, praying most heartily that it would please the said our Christ to have compassion upon us. Service being done, and as well celebrated as we could, our Captaine there made a vow, that if it would please God to give him leave to returne into France, he would go on Pilgrimage to our Ladie of Rocquemado. That day Philip Rougemont,

---

[1] The scurvy.

borne in Amboise, died, being 22 yeeres olde, and because the sicknesse was to us unknowen, our Captaine caused him to be ripped to see if by any meanes possible we might know what it was, and so seeke meanes to save and preserve the rest of the company: he was found to have his heart white, but rotten, and more then a quart of red water about it: his liver was indifferent faire, but his lungs blacke and mortified, his blood was altogither shrunke about the heart, so that when he was opened great quantitie of rotten blood issued out from about his heart: his milt toward the backe was somewhat perished, rough as it had bene rubbed against a stone. Moreover, because one of his thighs was very blacke without, it was opened, but within it was whole and sound: that done, as well as we could he was buried. In such sort did the sicknesse continue and increase, that there were not above three sound men in the ships, and none was able to goe under hatches to draw drinke for himselfe nor for his fellowes. Sometimes we were constrained to bury some of the dead under the snow, because we were not able to digge any graves for them the ground was so hard frozen, and we so weake. Besides this, we did greatly feare that the people of the countrey would perceive our weaknesse and miserie, which to hide, our Captaine, whom it pleased God always to keepe in health, would go out with two or three of the company, some sicke and some whole, whom when he saw out of the Fort, he would throw stones at them and chide them, faigning that so soone as he came againe, he would beate them, and then with signes shewe the people of the countrey that hee caused all his men to worke and labour in the ships, some in calking them, some in beating of chalke, some in one thing, and some in another, and that he would not have them come foorth till their worke was done. And to make his tale seeme true and likely, he would make all his men whole and sound to make a great noyse with knocking stickes, stones, hammers, and other things togither, at which time we were so oppressed and grieved with that sicknesse, that we had lost all hope ever to see France againe, if God of his infinite goodnesse and mercie had not with his pitifull eye looked upon us, and revealed a singular and excellent remedie against all diseases unto us, the best that ever was found upon earth, as hereafter shall follow.

How long we stayed in the Port of the holy Crosse amidst the snow and yce, and how many died of the said disease, from the beginning of it to the midst of March

Chap. 14

From the midst of November untill the midst of March, we were kept in amidst the yce above two fadomes thicke, and snow above foure foot high and more, higher then the sides of our ships, which lasted till that time, in such sort, that all our drinkes were frozen in the Vessels, and the yce through all the ships was above a hand-breadth thicke, as well above hatches as beneath, and so much of the river as was fresh, even to Hochelaga, was frozen, in which space there died five and twentie of our best and chiefest men, and all the rest were so sicke, that wee thought they should never recover againe, only three or foure excepted. Then it pleased God to cast his pitiful eye upon us, and sent us the knowledge of remedie of our healthes and recoverie, in such maner as in the next Chapter shall be shewed.

How by the grace of God we had notice of a certaine tree, whereby we all recovered our health: and the maner how to use it.

Chap. 15

Our Captaine considering our estate (and how that sicknesse was encreased and hot amongst us) one day went foorth of the Forte, and walking upon the yce, hee saw a troupe of those Countreymen comming from Stadacona, among which was Domagaia, who not passing ten or twelve dayes afore, had bene very sicke with that disease, and had his knees swolne as bigge as a childe of two yeres old, all his sinews shrunke together, his teeth spoyled, his gummes rotten, and stinking. Our Captaine seeing him whole and sound, was thereat marvellous glad, hoping to understand and know of him how he had healed himselfe, to the end he might ease and help his men. So soone as they were come neere him, he asked Domagaia how he had done to heale himselfe: he answered, that he had taken the juice and sappe of the leaves of a certain Tree, and therewith had healed himselfe: For it is a singular remedy against that disease. Then our Captaine asked of him if any were to be had thereabout, desiring him to shew him, for to heale a servant of his, who whilest he was in Canada with Donnacona, was striken with that disease: That he did because he would not shew the number of his sicke men. Domagaia straight sent two women to fetch some of it, which brought ten or twelve branches of it, and therewithall shewed the way how to use it, and that is thus, to take the barke and leaves of the sayd tree, and boile them togither, then to drinke of the sayd decoction every other day, and to put the dregs of it upon his legs that is sicke: moreover, they told us, that the vertue of that tree was, to heale any other disease: the tree is in their language called Ameda or Hanneda, this is thought to be the Sassafras tree. Our Captaine presently caused some of that drink to be made for his men to drink of it, but there was none durst tast of it, except one or two, who ventured the drinking of it, only to tast and prove it: the other seeing that did the like, and presently recovered their health, and were delivered of that sickenes, and what other disease soever, in such sorte, that there were some had bene diseased and troubled with the French Pockes foure or five yeres, and with this drinke were cleane healed. After this medicine was found and proved to be true, there was such strife about it, who should be first to take it, that they were ready to kill one another, so that a tree as big as any Oake in France was spoiled and lopped bare, and occupied all in five or sixe daies, and it wrought so wel, that if all the phisicians of Mountpelier and Lovaine had bene there with all the drugs of Alexandria, they would not have done so much in one yere, as that tree [1] did in sixe dayes, for it did so prevaile, that as many as used of it, by the grace of God recovered their health.

How the Lord Donnacona accompanied with Taignoagny and divers others, faining that they would goe to hunt Stags, and Deere, taried out two moneths, and at their returne brought a great multitude of people with them, that we were not wont to see before.

Chap. 16

While that disease lasted in our ships, the lord Donnacona, Taignoagny, with many others went from home, faining that they would goe to catch Stags and Deere, which are in their tongue called Aiounesta, and Asquenoudo, because the yce and snow was not so broken along the river that they could sayle: it was told us of Domagaia and others, that they would stay out but a fortnight, and we beleeved it, but they stayed above two moneths, which made us mistrust that they had bene gone to raise the countrey to come against us, and do us some displeasure, we seeing our selves so weake and faint. Albeit we had used such diligence and policie in our Fort, that if all the power of the countrey had bene about it, they could have done nothing but looke upon us: and whilest they were foorth, many of the people came dayly to our ships, and brought us fresh meat, as Stags, Deere, fishes, with divers other things, but held them at such an excessive price, that rather then they would sell them any thing cheape, many times they would carie them backe againe, because that yere the Winter was very long, and they had some scarcity and neede of them.

[1] The bark of the white pine is an antiscorbutic.

How Donnacona came to Stadacona againe with a great number of people, and because he would not come to visit our Captaine, fained himselfe to be sore sicke, which he did only to have the Captaine come see him.

Chap. 17

On the one and twentieth day of April Domagaia came to the shore side, accompanied with divers lusty and strong men, such as we were not wont to see, and tolde us that their lord Donnacona would the next day come and see us, and bring great store of Deeres flesh, and other things with him. The next day he came and brought a great number of men to Stadacona, to what end, and for what cause wee knew not, but (as the proverb sayth) hee that takes heede and shields himselfe from all men, may hap to scape from some: for we had need to looke about us, considering how in number we were diminished, and in strength greatly weakned, both by reason of our sicknesse and also of the number that were dead, so that we were constrained to leave one of our ships in the Port of the Holy Crosse. Our Captaine was warned of their comming, and how they had brought a great number of men with them, for Domagaia came to tell it us, and durst not passe the river that was betwixt Stadacona and us, as he was wont to doe, whereupon we mistrusted some treason. Our Captaine seeing this sent one of his servants to them, accompanied with John Poulet being best beloved of those people, to see who were there, and what they did. The sayd Poulet and the other fained themselves onely to be come to visit Donnacona, and bring him certaine presents, because they had beene together a good while in the sayd Donnaconas Towne. So soone as he heard of their comming, he got himselfe to bed, faining to bee very sicke. That done, they went to Taignoagny his house to see him, and wheresoever they went, they saw so many people, that in a maner one could not stirre for another, and such men as they were never wont to see. Taignoagny would not permit our men to enter into any other houses, but still kept them company, and brought them halfe way to their ships, and tolde them that if it would please our captaine to shew him so much favour as to take a Lord of the Countrey, whose name was Agonna, of whom hee had received some displeasure, and carie him with him into France, he should therefore for ever be bound unto him, and would doe for him whatsoever hee would command him, and bade the servant come againe the next day, and bring an answere. Our Captaine being advertised of so many people that were there, not knowing to what end, purposed to play a prettie prancke, that is to say, to take their Lord Donnacona, Taignoagny, Domagaia, and some more of the chiefest of them prisoners, in so much as before hee had purposed, to bring them into France, to shew unto our King what he had seene in those Westerne parts, and marvels of the world, for that Donnacona had told us, that he had bene in the Countrey of Saguenay, in which are infinite Rubies, Gold, and other riches, and that there are white men, who clothe themselves with woollen cloth even as we doe in France. Moreover he reported, that hee had bene in another countrey of a people called Picquemians, and other strange people. The sayd Lord was an olde man, and even from his childehood had never left off nor ceased from travailing into strange Countreys, as well by water and rivers, as by lande. The sayd Poulet and the other having tolde our Captaine their Embassage, and shewed him what Taignoagny his will was, the next day he sent his servant againe to bid Taignoagny come and see him, and shewe what hee should, for he should be very well entertained, and also part of his will should be accomplished. Taignoagny sent him word, that the next day hee would come and bring the Lord Donnacona with him, and him that had so offended him, which hee did not, but stayed two dayes, in which time none came from Stadacona to our shippes, as they were wont to doe, but rather fled from us, as if we would have slaine them, so that then wee plainely perceived their knavery.

But because they understood, that those of Sidatin did frequent our company, and that we had forsaken the bottome of a ship [1] which we would leave, to have the olde nailes out of it, the third day following they came from Stadacona, and most of them without difficulty did passe from one side of the river to the other with small Skiffes: but Donnacona would not come over: Taignoagny and Domagaia stood talking together about an houre before they would come over, at last they came to speake with our Captaine. There Taignoagny prayed him that hee would cause the foresayd man to be taken and caried into France. Our Captaine refused to doe it, saying that his King had forbidden him to bring any man or woman into France, onely that he might bring two or three yong boyes to learne the language, but that he would willingly cary him to Newfoundland, and there leave him in an Island. Our Captaine spake this, onely to assure them, that they should bring Donnacona with them, whom they had left on the other side: which wordes, when Taignoagny heard, hee was very glad, thinking hee should never returne into France againe, and therefore promised to come the next day, which was the day of the Holy Crosse, and to bring Donnacona and all the people with him.

How that upon Holyrood day our Captaine caused a Crosse to be set up in our Forte: and how the Lord Donnacona, Taignoagny, Domagaia, and others of their company came: and of the taking of the sayd Lord.

Chap. 18

The third of May being Holyroode day, our Captaine for the solemnitie of the day, caused a goodly fayre crosse of 35 foote in height to bee set up, under the crosset of which hee caused a

---

[1] The remains were discovered in 1843. A part was sent to the museum of the Historical Society at Quebec, and the rest to the museum at St.-Malo. The museum of the Historical Society at Quebec was destroyed by fire in 1854.

shield to be hanged, wherein were the Armes of France, and over them was written in antique letters, Franciscus primus Dei gratia Francorum Rex regnat. And upon that day about noone, there came a great number of the people of Stadacona, men, women and children, who told us that their Lord Donnacona, Taignoagny, and Domagaia were comming, whereof we were very glad, hoping to retaine them. About two of the clocke in the afternoone they came, and being come neere our ships, our Captaine went to salute Donnacona, who also shewed him a mery countenance, albeit very fearefully his eyes were still bent toward the wood. Shortly after came Taignoagny, who bade Donnacona that he should not enter into our Forte, and therefore fire was brought forth by one of our men, and kindled where their Lord was. Our Captaine prayed him to come into our ships to eate and drinke as hee was wont to do, and also Taignoagny, who promised, that after a while he would come, and so they did, and entred into our ships: but first it was told our Captain by Domagaia that Taignoagny had spoken ill of him, and that he had bid Donnacona hee should not come aboord our ships. Our Captaine perceiving that, came out of the Forte, and saw that onely by Taignoagny his warning the women ran away, and none but men stayed in great number, wherefore he straight commanded his men to lay hold on Donnacona, Taignoagny, and Domagaia, and two more of the chiefest whom he pointed unto: then he commanded them to make the other to retire. Presently after, the said lord entred into the Fort with the Captaine, but by and by Taignoagny came to make him come out againe. Our Captaine seeing that there was no other remedy, began to call unto them to take them, at whose crie and voice all his men came forth, and tooke the sayd Lord with the others, whom they had appointed to take. The Canadians seeing their Lord taken, began to run away, even as sheepe before the woolfe, some crossing over the river, some through the woods, each one seeking for his owne advantage. That done, we retired our selves, and laid up the prisoners under good guard and safety.

How the said Canadians the night following came before our ships to seeke their men, crying and howling all night like Woolves: of the talke and conclusion they agreed upon the next day: and of the gifts which they gave our Captaine.

Chap. 19

The night following they came before our ships, (the river being betwixt us) striking their breasts, and crying and howling like woolves, still calling Agouhanna, thinking to speake with him, which our Captaine for that time would not permit, neither all the next day till noone, whereupon they made signes unto us, that we had hanged or killed him. About noone, there came as great a number in a cluster, as ever we saw, who went to hide themselves in the Forest, except some, who with a loud voice would call and crie to Donnacona to speake unto them. Our Captaine then commanded Donnacona to be brought up on high to speake unto them, and bade him be merrie, for after he had spoken, and shewed unto the King of France what hee had seene in Saguenay and other countreys, after ten or twelve moneths, he should returne againe, and that the King of France would give him great rewards. Donnacona was very glad, and speaking to the others told it them, who in token of joy, gave out three great cryes, and then Donnacona and his people had great talke together, which for want of interpreters, cannot be described. Our Captaine bade Donnacona that hee should cause them to come to the other side of the river, to the end they might better talke together without any feare, and that he should assure them: which Donnacona did, and there came a boate full of the chiefest of them to the ships, and there anew began to talke together, giving great praise to our captaine, and gave him a present of foure and twenty chaines of Esurgny, for that is the greatest and preciousest riches they have in this world, for they esteeme more of that, then of any gold or silver. After they had long talked together, and that their Lord sawe that there was no remedy to avoide his going into France, hee commanded his people the next day, to bring him some victuals to serve him by the way. Our Captaine gave Donnacona, as a great present, two Frying pannes of copper, eight Hatchets, and other small trifles, as Knives, and Beades, whereof hee seemed to be very glad, who sent them to his wives and children. Likewise, he gave to them that came to speake with Donnacona, they thanked him greatly for them, and then went to their lodgings.

How the next day, being the fift of May, the same people came againe to speake unto their Lord, and how foure women came to the shore to bring him victuals.

Chap. 20

Upon the fift of May, very early in the morning, a great number of the sayd people came againe to speake unto their Lord, and sent a boate, which in their tongue they call Casnoni, wherein were onely foure women, without any man, for feare their men should be retained.

These women brought great store of victuals, as great Millet, which is their corne that they live withall, flesh, fish, and other things, after their fashion.

These women being come to our shippes, our Captaine did very friendly entertaine them. Then Donnacona prayed our Captaine to tell these women that hee should come againe after ten or twelve moneths, and bring Donnacona to Canada with him: this hee sayd only to appease them, which our Captaine did: wherefore the women, as well by words as signes, seemed to be very glad, giving our Captaine thanks, and told him, if he came againe, and brought Donnacona with him, they would give him many things: in signe whereof, each one gave our Captaine a chaine of Esurgny, and then passed to the other side of the river againe, where stood all the people of Stadacona, who taking all leave of their Lord, went home againe. On Satur-

day following, being the sixt of the moneth, we departed out
of the sayd Port of Santa Croix, and came to harborough a
little beneath the Island of Orleans, about twelve leagues from
the Port of the Holy Crosse, and upon Sonday we came to the
Island of Filberds, where we stayed until the sixteenth of that
moneth, till the fiercenesse of the waters were past, which at
that time ranne too swift a course, and were too dangerous
to come downe along the river, and therefore we stayed till
faire weather came. In the meane while many of Donnaconas
subjects came from the river of Saguenay to him, but being by
Domagaia advertised, that their Lord was taken to bee caryed
into France they were all amazed: yet for all that they would
not leave to come to our ships, to speake to Donnacona, who
told them that after twelve moneths he should come againe,
and that he was very well used by the Captaine, Gentlemen,
and Mariners. Which when they heard, they greatly thanked
our Captaine and gave their Lord three bundles of Beavers,
and Sea Woolves skinnes, with a great knife of red copper that
commeth from Saguenay, and other things. They gave also
to our Captaine a chaine of Esurgny, for which our Captaine
gave them ten or twelve Hatchets, and they gave him hearty
thankes, and were very well contented. The next day, being
the sixteenth of May, we hoysed sayle, and came from the
said Island of Filberds, to another about fifteene leagues from it,
which is about five leagues in length, and there, to the end we
might take some rest the night following, we stayed that day,
in hope the next day we might passe and avoide the dangers
of the river of Saguenay, which are great. That evening we
went a land and found great store of Hares, of which we tooke
a great many, and therefore we called it the Island of Hares:
in the night there arose a contrary winde, with such stormes
and tempest, that wee were constrained to returne to the Island
of Filberds againe, from whence wee were come, because there
was none other passage among the sayde Islandes, and there
we stayed till the one and twentieth of that moneth, till faire
weather and good winde came againe: and then wee sayled
againe, and that so prosperously, that we passed to Honguedo,

which passage untill that time had not bene discovered: wee caused our ships to course athwart Cape Prat which is the beginning of the Port of Chaleur: and because the winde was good and convenient, we sayled all day and all night without staying, and the next day we came to the middle of Brions Island, which we were not minded to doe, to the end wee might shorten our way. These two lands lie Northwest, and Southeast, and are about fiftie leagues one from another. The sayd Island is in latitude 47 degrees and a halfe. Upon Thursday being the twenty sixe of the moneth, and the feast of the Ascension of our Lord, we coasted over to a land and shallow of lowe sandes, which are about eight leagues Southwest from Brions Island, above which are large Champaines, full of trees and also an enclosed sea, whereas we could neither see, nor perceive any gappe or way to enter thereinto. On Friday following, being the 27 of the moneth, because the wind did change on the coast, we came to Brions Island againe, where we stayed till the beginning of June, and toward the Southeast of this Island, wee sawe a lande, seeming unto us an Island, we coasted it about two leagues and a halfe, and by the way we had notice of three other high Islands, lying toward the Sands: after wee had knowen these things we returned to the Cape of the sayd land, which doeth devide it selfe into two or three very high Capes: the waters there are very deepe, and the flood of the sea runneth so swift, that it cannot possibly be swifter. That day we came to Cape Loreine,[1] which is in forty seven degrees and a halfe toward the South: on which cape there is a low land, and it seemeth that there is some entrance of a river, but there is no haven of any worth. Above these lands we saw another cape toward the South, we named it Saint Paules Cape,[2] it is at 47 degrees and a quarter.

The Sonday following, being the fourth of June, and Whitsonday, wee had notice of the coast lying Eastsoutheast, distant from the Newfoundland about two and twenty leagues: and because the wind was against us, we went to a Haven, which

[1] Cape St. Lawrence.
[2] Cheticamp, on the western coast of Cape Breton.

wee named S. Spiritus Porte,[1] where we stayed till Tewesday that we departed thence, sayling along that coast untill we came to Saint Peters Islands.[2] Wee found along the sayd coast many very dangerous Islands and shelves, which lye all in the Eastsoutheast and Westnorthwest, about three and twenty leagues into the sea. Whilest we were in the sayd Saint Peters Islands we met with many ships of France and of Britaine,[3] wee stayed there from Saint Barnabas day, being the eleventh of the moneth, until the sixteenth that we departed thence and came to Cape Rase, and entred into a Port called Rognoso, where we took in fresh water, and wood to passe the sea: there wee left one of our boates. Then upon Monday, being the nineteenth of June, we went from that Port, and with such good and prosperous weather we sailed along the sea, in such sorte, that upon the sixt of July 1536 we came to the Porte of S. Malo, by the grace of God, to whom we pray, here ending our Navigation, that of his infinite mercy he will grant us his grace and favour, and in the end bring us to the place of everlasting felicitie. Amen.

Here followeth the language of the countrey, and kingdomes of Hochelaga and Canada, of us called New France: But first the names of their numbers.

Secada	1	Indahir	6
Tigneni	2	Aiaga	7
Hasche	3	Addigue	8
Hannaion	4	Madellon	9
Oviscon	5	Assem	10

[1] Le Poil Bay, on the southern coast of Newfoundland.
[2] St. Pierre, off the southern coast of Newfoundland.
[3] Brittany.

Here follow the names the chiefest partes of men, and other words necessary to be knowen.

the Head	aggonzi	leaves of	hoga
the Browe	hegueniascon	Trees	
the Eyes	higata	God	cudragny
the Eares	abontascon	give me some	quazahoa-
the Mouth	esahe	drink	quea
the Teeth	esgongay	give me to	quaso hoa
the Tongue	osnache	breakfast	quascaboa
the Throat	agonhon	give me my	quaza hoa
the Beard	hebelim	supper	quatfriam
the Face	hegouascon	let us goe to	casigno agny-
the Haires	aganiscon	bed	dahoa
the Armes	aiayascon	a Man	aguehum
the Flanckes	aissonne	a woman	agruaste
the Stomacke	aggruascon	a Boy	addegesta
the Bellie	eschehenda	a Wench	agniaquesta
the Thighes	hetnegradascon	a Child	exiasta
the Knees	agochinegodas-con	a Gowne	cabata
		a Doublet	caioza
the Legges	agouguene-honde	Hosen	hemondoha
		Shooes	atha
the Feete	onchidascon	a Shirt	amgoua
the Hands	aignoascon	a Cappe	castrua
the Fingers	agenoga	Corne	osizi
the Nailes	agedascon	Bread	carraconny
a Mans member	ainoascon	Water	ame
		Flesh	quahouascon
a Womans member	castaigne	Reisins	queion
		Damsons	honnesta
an Eele	esgueny	Figges	absconda
a Snaile	undeguezi	Grapes	ozoba
a Tortois	heuleuxima	Nuttes	quahoya
Woods	conda	a Hen	sahomgahoa

a Lamprey	zisto	a Bow	ahenca
a Salmon	ondacon	a Darte	quahetan
a Whale	ainne honne	let us goe a	Casigno don-
a Goose	sadeguenda	hunting	nascat
a Streete	adde	a Stagge	aionnesta
Cucumber	casconda	a Sheepe	asquenondo
seede		a Hare	Sourhanda
to Morrowe	achide	a Dogge	agaya
the Heaven	quenhia	a Towne	canada
the Earth	damga	the Sea	agogasy
the Sunne	ysmay	the waves of	coda
the Moone	assomaha	the sea	
the Starres	stagnehoham	an Island	cohena
the Winde	cohoha	an Hill	agacha
good morrow	aignag	the yce	honnesca
let us go to	casigno caudy	Snow	camsa
play		Colde	athau
come and	assigniquad-	Hotte	odazani
speak with	dadia	Fier	azista
me		Smoke	quea
looke upon me	quagathoma	a House	canoca
hold your	aista	Beanes	sahe
peace		Cinnamom	adhotathny
let us go with	casigno casnovy	my Father	addathy
the boat		my Mother	adanahoe
give me a	buazahca ago-	my Brother	addagrim
knife	heda	my Sister	adhoasseve
a Hatchet	adogne		

They of Canada say, that it is a moneths sayling to goe to a lande where Cinnamom and Cloves are gathered.

Here endeth the Relation of James Cartiers discovery and Navigation to the Newfoundlands, by him named **New France**.

THE THIRD VOYAGE OF DISCOVERY MADE BY CAPTAINE JAQUES CARTIER
1541

INTRODUCTION

CARTIER had discovered a great river, bordered by fertile lands. The terrible sufferings through which the explorers passed during their long winter at St. Croix, however, made a deep impression upon them, and their sufferings very naturally found expression in the reports of the expedition made by the survivors on their return to France. Not much was said about gold in these reports, and it was gold with other valuable commodities which the Spaniards were bringing from their New World possessions. The king accordingly hesitated to encourage Cartier in his wish to return, and take possession of the country he had discovered. The invasion of his kingdom by the king of Spain, moreover, now occupied his attention. At length, however, he was persuaded by an influential nobleman in the small district of Vimeux in the province of Picardy, — Jean François de la Rocque de Roberval, — who was not only deeply interested in the undertaking, but was ready to embark in it personally. By letters patent, dated January 15, 1540, Roberval as "Lord of Norumbega, Viceroy and Lieutenant-general of Canada, Hochelaga, Saguenay, Newfoundland, Belle Isle, Carpunt, Labrador, the Great Bay and Baccalaos," to all which was given the name of New France — considered by Francis to be the northeastern end of Asia — was placed at the head of the expedition, while Cartier retained his title of Captain-general and Chief Pilot of the king's ships. Roberval was to establish a colony in the new possessions, which included all the territory north of 40°. Sailing from St.-Malo in May, 1541 (probably),[1] Cartier spent the winter of 1541–1542 at

See p. 95, note 1, below.

Charlesbourg Royal, about four leagues beyond the harbor of St. Croix, and at the end of May, 1542, not hearing from Roberval, and having an insufficient supply of provisions, the Indians also appearing unfriendly, he concluded to return to France. On his way, in the harbor of St. John's, Newfoundland, Cartier found Roberval with his three ships and two hundred colonists; but he could not be induced to turn back, and continued his voyage homeward. Roberval located his colony at Charlesbourg Royal, and in the autumn sent two of his vessels back to France for supplies. After a winter of hardship and suffering, Roberval explored the Saguenay, and later returned to France, Cartier, some think, leading a relief expedition. If so, this was Cartier's last voyage to the New World. He died September 1, 1557, either at St.-Malo, or at his summer seat called Limoïlou. The following report of Cartier's third voyage is a translation made by Hakluyt of the official French report. Unfortunately it is a fragment, the last date mentioned in the narrative being September 11, and as we have no other source of information concerning the third voyage, the original narrative of the expedition in French not having been found, we have no account of Cartier's second-winter experiences in Canada.

H. S. B.

THE THIRD VOYAGE OF DISCOVERY MADE BY CAPTAINE JAQUES CARTIER
1541

The third voyage of discovery made by Captaine Jaques Cartier, 1540. [1541] unto the Countreys of Canada, Hochelaga, and Saguenay.

KING FRANCIS the first having heard the report of Captaine Cartier his Pilot generall in his two former Voyages of discovery, as well by writing as by word of mouth, touching that which hee had found and seene in the Westerne partes discovered by him in the parts of Canada and Hochelaga, and having also seene and talked with the people, which the sayd Cartier had brought out of those Countreys, whereof one was king of Canada, whose name was Donnacona, and others: which after that they had bene a long time in France and Britaine,[1] were baptized at their owne desire and request, and died in the sayd countrey of Britaine. And albeit his Majestie was advertized by the sayd Cartier of the death and decease of all the people which were brought over by him (which were tenne in number) saving one little girle about tenne yeeres old, yet he resolved to send the sayd Cartier his Pilot thither againe, with John Francis de la Roche, Knight, Lord of Roberval,[2] whome hee appointed his Lieutenant and Governour in the Countreys of Canada and Hochelaga, and the sayd Cartier Captaine Generall and leader of the shippes that they might discover more then was done before in the former voyages, and attaine (if it were possible) unto the knowledge of the Countrey of Saguenay, whereof the people brought by Cartier, as is declared, made mention unto the King, that there were great riches, and very good countreys.

[1] Brittany.   [2] Near Boulogne, between that town and Calais.

And the King caused a certaine summe of money to be delivered to furnish out the sayd voyage with five shippes: which thing was perfourmed by the sayd Monsieur Roberval and Cartier. After that they had agreed together to rigge the sayd five ships at Saint Malo in Britaine, where the two former voyages had beene prepared and set forth, And the said Monsieur Roberval sent Cartier thither for the same purpose, And after that Cartier had caused the said five ships to be built and furnished and set in good order, Monsieur Roberval came downe to S. Malo and found the ships fallen downe to the roade, with their yards acrosse full ready to depart and set saile, staying for nothing else but the comming of the Generall, and the payment of the furniture. And because Monsieur Roberval the kings lieutenant had not as yet his artillery, powder and munitions, and other things necessary come downe, which he had provided for the voyage, in the Countreys of Champaigne and Normandie: and because the said things were very necessary, and that hee was loth to depart without them, he determined to depart from S. Malo to Roan,[1] and to prepare a ship or two at Honfleur, whither he thought his things were come: And that the said Cartier shoulde depart with the five shippes which he had furnished, and should goe before. Considering also that the said Cartier had received letters from the king, whereby hee did expresly charge him to depart and set sayle immediatly upon the sight and receit thereof, on payne of incurring his displeasure, and to lay all the fault on him. And after the conclusion of these things, and the said Monsieur Roberval had taken muster and view of the gentlemen, souldiers, and mariners which were retained and chosen for the performance of the sayd voyage, hee gave unto Captain Cartier full authoritie to depart and goe before, and to governe all things as if he had bene there in person: and himselfe departed to Honfleur to make his farther preparation. After these things thus dispatched, the winde comming faire, the foresayd five ships set sayle together

[1] Rouen.

well furnished and victualled for two yeere, the 23. of May, 1540.[1] And we sailed so long with contrary winds and continuall torments, which fell out by reason of our late departure, that wee were on the sea with our sayd five ships full three moneths before wee could arrive at the Port and Haven of Canada, without ever having in all that time 30 houres of good wind to serve us to keepe our right course: so that our five shippes through those stormes lost company one of another, all save two that kept together, to wit that wherein the Captaine was, and the other wherein went the Vicount of Beaupre, untill at length at the end of one moneth wee met all together at the Haven of Carpont[2] in Newfoundland. But the length of time which we were in passing betweene Britayne and Newfoundland was the cause that we stood in great neede of water, because of the cattell, as well Goates, Hogges, as other beastes which we caried for breede in the Countrey, which wee were constrained to water with Sider and other drinke. Now therefore because we were the space of three moneths in sayling on the sea, and staying in Newfoundland, wayting for Monsieur Roberval, and taking in of fresh water and other things necessary, wee arrived not before the Haven of Saincte Croix in Canada, (where in the former voyage we had remayned eight moneths) untill the 23. day of August. In which place the people of the Countrey came to our shippes, making shew of joy for our arrivall, and namely he came thither which had the rule and government of the Countrey of Canada, named Agona, which was appointed king there by Donacona, when in the former

---

[1] Baxter, in his *Memoir of Jacques Cartier*, p. 44, gives May 23, 1541, as the date of Cartier's sailing from St.-Malo. This is necessary in order to bring the narrative into harmony with the dates given in the relation of Roberval's voyage, which followed in the succeeding year. If Cartier left France May 23, 1540, and returned to France in the summer of 1541, he could not have met Roberval in the harbor of St. John's, Newfoundland, in June, 1542, as is stated in the relation of Roberval's voyage in Hakluyt. The difficulty is relieved by supposing an error in Hakluyt, and making the date of Cartier's sailing from France on his third voyage May 23, 1541, instead of May 23, 1540.

[2] Island off the northeastern extremity of Newfoundland.

voyage we carried him into France. And hee came to the
Captaines ship with 6. or 7. boates, and with many women
and children. And after the sayd Agona had inquired of the
Captaine where Donacona and the rest were, the Captaine answered him, That Donacona was dead in France, and that his
body rested in the earth, and that the rest stayed there as great
Lords, and were maried, and would not returne backe into
their Countrey: the said Agona made no shewe of anger at all
these speeches: and I thinke he tooke it so well because he
remained Lord and Governour of the countrey by the death of
the said Donacona. After which conference the said Agona
tooke a piece of tanned leather of a yellow skin edged about
with Esnoguy (which is their riches and the thing which they
esteeme most precious, as wee esteeme gold) which was upon
his head in stead of a crowne, and he put the same on the head
of our Captaine, and tooke from his wrists two bracelets of
Esnoguy, and put them upon the Captaines armes, colling him
about the necke, and shewing unto him great signes of joy:
which was all dissimulation, as afterward it wel appeared.
The captaine tooke his said crowne of leather and put it againe
upon his head, and gave him and his wives certaine smal
presents, signifying unto him that he had brought certaine
new things, which afterward he would bestow upon him: for
which the sayd Agona thanked the Captaine. And after that
he had made him and his company eat and drinke, they departed and returned to the shore with their boates. After
which things the sayd Captaine went with two of his boates up
the river, beyond Canada and the Port of Saincte Croix, to
view a Haven and a small river,[1] which is about 4. leagues
higher: which he found better and more commodious to ride
in and lay his ships, then the former. And therefore he returned and caused all his ships to be brought before the sayd
river, and at a lowe water he caused his Ordinance to bee
planted to place his ships in more safetie, which he meant to
keepe and stay in the Countrey, which were three: which hee

---

[1] Cape Rouge River.

did the day following, and the rest remayned in the roade in the middest of the river (In which place the victuals and other furniture were discharged, which they had brought) from the 26. of August untill the second of September, what time they departed to returne for S. Malo, in which ships he sent backe Mace Jolloberte[1] his brother in lawe, and Steven Noel his Nephew, skilfull and excellent pilots, with letters unto the king, and to advertise him what had bene done and found: and how Monsieur de Roberval was not yet come, and that hee feared that by occasion of contrary winds and tempests he was driven backe againe into France.

The description of the aforesaid River and Haven.

The sayd River is small, not past 50. pases broad, and shippes drawing three fathoms water may enter in at a full sea: and at a low water there is nothing but a chanell of a foote deepe or thereabout. On both sides of the said River there are very good and faire grounds, full of as faire and mightie trees as any be in the world, and divers sorts, which are above tenne fathoms higher then the rest, and there is one kind of tree above three fathoms about, which they in the Countrey call Hanneda, which hath the most excellent vertue of all the trees in the world, whereof I will make mention hereafter. Moreover there are great store of Okes the most excellent that ever I saw in my life, which were so laden with Mast that they cracked againe: besides this there are fairer Arables,[2] Cedars, Beeches, and other trees, then grow in France: and hard unto this wood on the South side the ground is all covered with Vines, which we found laden with grapes as blacke as Mulberies, but they be not so kind as those of France because the Vines bee not tilled, and because they grow of their owne accord. Moreover there are many white Thornes, which beare leaves as bigge as oken leaves, and fruit like unto Medlers.[3]

[1] Marc Jalobert.   [2] Sugar-maples.
[3] A fruit resembling a small apple.

To bee short, it is as good a Countrey to plow and mannure as a man should find or desire. We sowed seedes here of our Countrey, as Cabages, Naveaus,[1] Lettises and others, which grew and sprong up out of the ground in eight dayes. The mouth of the river is toward the South, and it windeth Northward like unto a snake: and at the mouth of it toward the East there is a high and steepe cliffe, where we made a way in maner of a payre of staires, and aloft we made a Fort[2] to keepe the nether Fort and the ships, and all things that might passe aswell by the great as by this small river. Moreover a man may behold a great extension of ground apt for tillage, straite and handsome, and somewhat enclining toward the South, as easie to be brought to tillage as I would desire, and very well replenished with faire Okes and other trees of great beauty, no thicker then the Forrests of France. Here we set twenty men to worke, which in one day had laboured about an acre and an halfe of the said ground, and sowed it part with Naveaus or small Turneps, which at the ende of eight dayes, as I said before, sprang out of the earth. And upon that high cliffe wee found a faire fountaine very neere the sayd Fort: adjoyning whereunto we found good store of stones, which we esteemed to be Diamants. On the other side of the said mountaine and at the foote thereof, which is towards the great River is all along a goodly Myne of the best yron in the world, and it reacheth even hard unto our Fort, and the sand which we tread on is perfect refined Myne, ready to be put into the fornace. And on the waters side we found certaine leaves of fine gold as thicke as a mans nayle. And Westward of the said River there are, as hath bene sayd, many faire trees: and toward the water a goodly Medow full of as faire and goodly grasse as ever I sawe in any Medowe in France: and betweene the said Medow and the Wood are great store of Vines: and beyond the said Vines the land groweth full of Hempe which groweth of it selfe, which is as good as possibly may be seene,

[1] Turnips, as below.
[2] The river is the Cape Rouge River and the fort was built on the high ground now known as Redclyffe.

and as strong. And at the ende of the sayd Medow within an hundred pases there is a rising ground, which is of a kind of slate stone blacke and thicke, wherein are veines of mynerall matter, which shewe like gold and silver: and throughout all that stone there are great graines of the sayd Myne. And in some places we have found stones like Diamants, the most faire, pollished and excellently cut that it is possible for a man to see, when the Sunne shineth upon them, they glister as it were sparkles of fire.[1]

How after the departure of the two shippes which were sent backe into Britaine, and that the Fort was begun to be builded, the Captaine prepared two boates to go up the great River to discover the passage of the three Saults or falles of the River.

The sayd Captaine having dispatched two ships to returne to carry newes, according as hee had in charge from the king, and that the Fort was begun to be builded, for preservation of their victuals and other things, determined with the Vicount of Beaupre, and other Gentlemen, Masters, and Pilots chosen for counsayle, to make a voyage with two boates furnished with men and victuals to goe as farre as Hochelaga, of purpose to view and understand the fashion of the Saults of water, which are to be passed to goe to Saguenay, that hee might be the readier in the spring to passe farther, and in the Winter time to make all things needefull in a readinesse for their businesse. The foresaid boates being made ready, the Captaine and Martine de Painpont, with other Gentlemen and the remnant of the Mariners departed from the sayd place of Charlesburg Royal the seventh day of September in the yeere aforesayd 1540. And the Vicount of Beaupre stayed behind for the garding and governement of all things in the Fort. And as they went up the river, the Captaine went to see the Lord of Hochelay, which dwelleth betweene Canada and Hochelaga: which in the former voyage had given unto the said Captaine

[1] One may still find the shining crystals at this place.

a little girle, and had oftentimes enformed him of the treasons which Taignoagny and Domagaya (whom the Captaine in his former voyage had caried into France) would have wrought against him. In regard of which his curtesie the said Captaine would not passe by without visiting of him, and to let him understand that the Captaine thought himselfe beholding unto him, hee gave unto him two yong boyes, and left them with him to learne their language, and bestowed upon him a cloake of Paris red, which cloake was set with yealow and white buttons of Tinne, and small belles. And withall hee gave him two Basons of Laton,[1] and certaine hachets and knives: whereat the sayde Lord seemed highly to rejoyce, and thanked the Captaine. This done, the Captaine and his company departed from that place: And wee sailed with so prosperous a wind, that we arrived the eleventh day of the moneth at the first Sault[2] of water, which is two leagues distant from the Towne of Tutonaguy. And after wee were arrived there, wee determined to goe and passe as farre up as it was possible with one of the boates, and that the other should stay there till it returned: and wee double manned her to rowe up against the course or streame of the sayde Sault. And after wee had passed some part of the way from our other boate, wee found badde ground and great rockes, and so great a current,[3] that wee could not possibly passe any further with our Boate. And the Captaine resolved to goe by land to see the nature and fashion of the Sault.[4] And after that we were come on shore, wee founde hard by the water side a way and beaten path going toward the sayde Saultes, by which wee tooke our way. And on the sayd way, and soone after we found an habitation of people which made us great cheere, and entertained us very friendly. And after that he had signified unto them, that wee were going toward the Saults, and that wee desired to goe to Saguenay, foure yong men went along with us to shewe us the way, and they brought us so farre that wee came to another village or habitation of good people, which dwell over against

---

[1] An alloy of copper and zinc.
[2] The Lachine Rapids.
[3] Courant de Ste. Marie.
[4] Sault de St. Louis.

the second Sault, which came and brought us of their victuals, as Pottage and Fish, and offered us of the same. After that the Captaine had enquired of them as well by signes as wordes, how many more Saults we had to passe to goe to Saguenay, and what distance and way it was thither, this people shewed us and gave us to understand, that wee were at the second Sault, and that there was but one more to passe, that the River was not navigable to goe to Saguenay, and that the sayd Sault was but a third part farther then we had travailed, shewing us the same with certaine little stickes, which they layd upon the ground in a certaine distance, and afterward layde other small branches betweene both, representing the Saults. And by the sayde marke, if their saying be true, it can be but sixe leagues by land to passe the sayd Saults.

[Here after followeth the figure of the three Saults.]

After that we had bene advertised by the sayde people, of the things abovementioned, both because the day was farre spent, and we had neither drunke nor eaten the same day, we concluded to returne unto our boats, and we came thither, where we found great store of people to the number of 400 persons or thereabout, which seemed to give us very good entertainment and to rejoyce of our comming: And therefore our Captaine gave eche of them certaine small trifles, as combs, brooches of tynne and copper, and other smal toyes, and unto the chiefe men every one his litle hatchet and hooke, whereat they made certaine cries and ceremonies of joy. But a man must not trust them for all their faire ceremonies and signes of joy, for if they had thought they had bene too strong for us, then would they have done their best to have killed us, as we understood afterward. This being done, we returned with our boats, and passed by the dwelling of the Lord of Hochelay, with whom the Captaine had left the two youths as he came up the river, thinking to have found him: But hee coulde find no body save one of his sonnes, who tolde the Captaine that hee was gone to Maisouna, as our boyes also told us, saying that it was two dayes since he departed. But in truth hee was gone to Canada to conclude with Agona what they should doe against us. And when we were arrived at our Fort, wee understoode by our people, that the Savages of the Countrey came not any more about our Fort as they were accustomed, to bring us fish, and that they were in a wonderful doubt and feare of us. Wherefore our Captaine, having bene advertised by some of our men which had bene at Stadacona to visite them, that there were a wonderfull number of the Countrey people assembled together, caused all things in our fortresse to bee set in good order: etc.

The rest is wanting.

THE VOYAGE OF M. HORE, 1536

INTRODUCTION

REPORTS of Cartier's discoveries soon reached England. Prominent among those who studied those reports, and by them was stirred to activity in behalf of English enterprise, was Mr. Robert Hore of London. Hakluyt's narrative of Hore's voyage, written long after the return of the expedition and as the result of painstaking investigations, included facts communicated by Hakluyt's cousin, Mr. Richard Hakluyt of the Middle Temple. It is very probable that Mr. Hore had devoted considerable attention to the project of the Cabots with reference to a northwest passage to the East Indies. His study of "cosmographie" had doubtless convinced him that such a passage, if it could be found, would prove a much shorter route to those far-away regions than that by way of the Cape of Good Hope. Hore reached Newfoundland, as the account of the voyage clearly shows; but how far he penetrated into the regions higher up the American coast, it is impossible to conjecture from Hakluyt's fragmentary narrative. The great distress which befell the members of the expedition evidently made a deep impression upon the survivors. Because of the reports of their sufferings and of the ill success attending their quest, it was a long time, very naturally, before other Englishmen made their way to the northern part of the American coast.

H. S. B.

THE VOYAGE OF M. HORE

The voyage of M. Hore and divers other gentlemen, to Newfoundland, and Cape Briton, in the yeere 1536 and in the 28 yere of King Henry the 8.

ONE master Hore of London, a man of goodly stature and of great courage, and given to the studie of Cosmographie, in the 28 yere of king Henry the 8 and in the yere of our Lord 1536 encouraged divers Gentlemen and others, being assisted by the kings favour and good countenance, to accompany him in a voyage of discoverie upon the Northwest parts of America: wherein his perswasions tooke such effect, that within short space many gentlemen of the Innes of court, and of the Chancerie, and divers others of good worship, desirous to see the strange things of the world, very willingly entered into the action with him, some of whose names were as followeth: M. Weekes a gentleman of the West countrey of five hundred markes by the yeere living. M. Tucke a gentleman of Kent. M. Tuckfield. M. Thomas Buts the sonne of Sir William Buts [1] knight, of Norfolke, which was lately living, and from whose mouth I wrote most of this relation. M. Hardie, M. Biron, M. Carter, M. Wright, M. Rastall Serjeant Rastals brother, M. Ridley, and divers other, which all were in the Admyrall called the Trinitie, a ship of seven score tunnes, wherein M. Hore himselfe was imbarked. In the other ship whose name was the Minion, went a very learned and vertuous gentleman one M. Armigil Wade,[2] Afterwards Clerke of the Counsailes of king Henry the 8 and king Edward the sixth, father to the

[1] Physician to Henry VIII., and one of the founders of the College of Physicians.
[2] Afterward clerk of the privy council, and a member of Parliament for Chipping Wycombe, 1547–1553. He died June 20, 1568.

worshipfull M. William Wade[1] now Clerke of the privie Counsell, M. Oliver Dawbeney marchant of London, M. Joy afterward gentleman of the Kings Chappel, with divers other of good account. The whole number that went in the two tall ships aforesaid, to wit, the Trinitie and the Minion, were about sixe score persons, whereof thirty were gentlemen, which all were mustered in warlike maner at Gravesend, and after the receiving of the Sacrament, they embarked themselves in the ende of Aprill. 1536.

From the time of their setting out from Gravesend,[2] they were very long at sea, to witte, above two moneths, and never touched any land untill they came to part of the West Indies about Cape Briton,[3] shaping their course thence Northeastwardes, untill they came to the Island of Penguin,[4] which is very full of rockes and stones, whereon they went and found it full of great foules white and gray, as big as geese, and they saw infinite numbers of their egges. They drave a great number of the foules into their boates upon their sayles, and tooke up many of their egges, the foules they flead and their skinnes were very like hony combes full of holes being flead[5] off: they dressed and eate them and found them to be very good and nourishing meat. They saw also store of beares both blacke and white, of whome they killed some, and tooke them for no bad foode.

M. Oliver Dawbeny, which (as it is before mentioned) was in this voyage, and in the Minion, told M. Richard Hakluyt of the middle Temple these things following: to wit, That after their arrivall in Newfoundland, and having bene there certaine dayes at ancre, and not having yet seene any of the naturall

[1] Afterward successively ambassador to Spain, Scotland, and France. He was a member of Parliament in 1588, 1601, and 1604–1611, was knighted May 20, 1603, and was lieutenant of the Tower under James I. He died October 21, 1623.
[2] A village on the right bank of the Thames, twenty-one miles below London.
[3] An island belonging to the province of Nova Scotia, from which it is separated by the Strait of Canso. Its name is derived from that of its east cape, which was probably named by Breton fishermen.
[4] On the eastern coast of Newfoundland.   [5] Flayed.

people of the countrey, the same Dawbeney walking one day on the hatches, spied a boate with Savages of those parts, rowing downe the Bay toward them, to gaze upon the ship and our people, and taking viewe of their comming aloofe, hee called to such as were under the hatches, and willed them to come up if they would see the natural people of the countrey, that they had so long and so much desired to see: whereupon they came up, and tooke viewe of the Savages rowing toward them and their ship, and upon the viewe they manned out a shipboat to meet them and to take them. But they spying our ship-boat making towards them, returned with maine force and fled into an Island that lay up in the Bay or river there, and our men pursued them into the Island, and the Savages fledde and escaped: but our men found a fire, and the side of a beare on a wooden spit left at the same by the Savages that were fled.

There in the same place they found a boote of leather garnished on the outward side of the calfe with certaine brave trailes, as it were of rawe silke, and also found a certaine great warme mitten: And these caryed with them, they returned to their shippe, not finding the Savages, nor seeing any thing else besides the soyle, and the things growing in the same, which chiefely were store of firre and pine trees.

And further, the said M. Dawbeney told him, that lying there they grew into great want of victuals, and that there they found small reliefe, more then that they had from the nest of an Osprey, that brought hourely to her yong great plentie of divers sorts of fishes. But such was the famine that increased amongst them from day to day, that they were forced to seeke to relieve themselves of raw herbes and rootes that they sought on the maine: but the famine increasing, and the reliefe of herbes being to little purpose to satisfie their insatiable hunger, in the fieldes and deserts here and there, the fellowe killed his mate while he stooped to take up a roote for his reliefe, and cutting out pieces of his bodie whom he had murthered, broyled the same on the coles and greedily devoured them.

By this meane the company decreased, and the officers knew not what was become of them; And it fortuned that one of the company driven with hunger to seeke abroade for reliefe found out in the fieldes the savour of broyled flesh, and fell out with one for that he would suffer him and his fellowes to sterve, enjoying plentie as he thought: and this matter growing to cruell speaches, he that had the broyled meate, burst out into these wordes: If thou wouldest needes know, the broyled meate that I had was a piece of such a mans buttocke. The report of this brought to the ship, the Captaine found what became of those that were missing, and was perswaded that some of them were neither devoured with wilde beastes, nor yet destroyed by Savages: And hereupon hee stood up and made a notable Oration, containing, Howe much these dealings offended the Almightie, and vouched the Scriptures from first to last, what God had in cases of distresse done for them that called upon him, and told them that the power of the Almighty was then no lesse, then in al former time it had bene. And added, that if it had not pleased God to have holpen them in that distresse, that it had bene better to have perished in body, and to have lived everlastingly, then to have relieved for a poore time their mortal bodyes, and to bee condemned everlastingly, both body and soule to the unquenchable fire of hell. And thus having ended to that effect, he began to exhort to repentance, and besought all the company to pray, that it might please God to looke upon their miserable present state and for his owne mercie to relieve the same. The famine increasing, and the inconvenience of the men that were missing being found, they agreed amongst themselves rather then all should perish, to cast lots who should be killed: And such was the mercie of God, that the same night there arrived a French ship [1] in that port, well furnished with vittaile, and such was the policie of the English, that they became masters

---

[1] Fishing vessels from France early found their way to Newfoundland. English fishing vessels came thither not long after Cabot's discovery, and so important had English interests in this vicinity become in 1583 that English merchants and fishermen were "at the head of all the other nations," according to Sir Humphrey Gilbert.

of the same, and changing ships and vittailing them, they set sayle to come into England.

In their journey they were so farre Northwards, that they sawe mighty Islands of yce [1] in the sommer season, on which were haukes and other foules to rest themselves being weary of flying over farre from the maine. They sawe also certaine great white foules with red bils and red legs, somewhat bigger then Herons, which they supposed to be Storkes. They arrived at S. Ives [2] in Cornewall about the ende of October. From thence they departed unto a certaine castle belonging to sir John Luttrell, where M. Thomas Buts, and M. Rastall and other Gentlemen of the voyage were very friendly entertained: after that they came to the Earle of Bathe at Bathe, and thence to Bristoll, so to London. M. Buts was so changed in the voyage with hunger and miserie, that sir William his father and my Lady his mother knew him not to be their sonne, untill they found a secret marke which was a wart upon one of his knees, as hee told me Richard Hakluyt of Oxford himselfe, to whom I rode 200. miles onely to learne the whole trueth of this voyage from his own mouth, as being the onely man now alive that was in this discoverie.

Certaine moneths after, those Frenchmen came into England and made complaint to king Henry the 8: the king causing the matter to be examined, and finding the great distresse of his subjects, and the causes of the dealing so with the French, was so mooved with pitie, that he punished not his subjects, but of his owne purse made full and royall recompence unto the French.

In this distresse of famine, the English did somewhat relieve their vitall spirits, by drinking at the springs the fresh water out of certaine wooden cups, out of which they had drunke their Aqua composita before.

[1] From the west coast of Greenland icebergs in large numbers are carried past Newfoundland by the great polar currents. Some of them are of vast dimensions.

[2] On the northern side of the southwest extremity of England, and about fifteen miles from Land's End.

THE VOYAGE MADE BY
M. JOHN HAWKINS ESQUIRE
1565

INTRODUCTION

JOHN HAWKINS, a native of Plymouth, England, was a son of William Hawkins, the pioneer in the African slave trade so far as England is concerned, and "the first Englishman who sailed a ship into the Southern Seas." Having "armed out a tall and goodly ship of his own," the elder Hawkins three times visited the west coast of Africa for slaves, and found a market for them in Brazil. John inherited the adventurous spirit of his father. About 1551 he entered the maritime service, and is said to have made voyages to Spain, Portugal, and other places. In 1556 he was admitted a freeman of Plymouth, and in 1558 he invented the chain pump for ships. In 1562, on his first voyage as commander, he proceeded to the coast of Guinea, where, by the sword and other means, he procured about three hundred slaves, whom he carried to the West Indies, and sold at various ports of Hispaniola. He then loaded not only his three vessels with hides, ginger, sugar, "and some quantitie of pearles," but two other vessels, despatching the latter to Spain. Hawkins safely reached home with his own vessels, but the Spanish government confiscated the cargoes of the two vessels sent to Spain. With the profits of this expedition, notwithstanding his losses, Hawkins fitted out another and larger expedition in the following year, a record of which, written by "John Sparke the younger," who accompanied the expedition and became its historian, is given herewith. After the first paragraph of the narration, there is in the following reprint an omission of Hawkins's experiences on the African coast, and of most of his experiences in the West Indies. What follows is of especial interest, as it brought to the English people their first knowledge of Florida. The Hakluyt Society reprinted the Hawkins voyages in 1878.

H. S. B.

THE VOYAGE MADE BY M. JOHN HAWKINS ESQUIRE, 1565

The voyage made by M. John Hawkins Esquire, and afterward knight, Captaine of the Jesus of Lubek, one of her Majesties shippes, and Generall of the Salomon, and other two barkes going in his companie, to the coast of Guinea, and the Indies of Nova Hispania, begun in An. Dom. 1564.

MASTER JOHN HAWKINS with the Jesus of Lubek, a shippe of 700. and the Salomon a shippe of 140. the Tiger a barke of 50. and the Swallow of 30. tunnes, being all well furnished with men to the number of one hundreth threescore and tenne, as also with ordinance and victuall requisite for such a voyage, departed out of Plymmouth the 18. day of October, in the yeere of our Lord 1564. with a prosperous winde.

* * * * * * * * *

Thus the 17. of June, we departed and on the 20. wee fell with the West end of Cuba, called Cape S. Antony,[1] where for the space of three dayes wee doubled along, till wee came beyond the shoales, which are 20. leagues beyond S. Anthony. And the ordinary Brise taking us, which is the Northeast winde, put us the 24. from the shoare, and therefore we went to the Northwest to fetch wind, and also to the coast of Florida to have the helpe of the current, which was judged to have set to the Eastward: so the 29. wee found our selves in 27. degrees, and in the soundings of Florida, where we kept our selves the space of foure dayes, sailing along the coast as neere as we could, in tenne or twelve fadome water, having all the while no sight of land.

[1] San Antonio.

The fift of July we had sight of certeine Islands of sand, called the Tortugas [1] (which is lowe land) where the captaine went in with his pinnesse, and found such a number of birds, that in halfe an houre he laded her with them; and if they had beene ten boats more, they might have done the like. These Islands beare the name of Tortoises, because of the number of them, which there do breed, whose nature is to live both in the water and upon land also, but breed onely upon the shore, in making a great pit wherein they lay egges, to the number of three or foure hundred, and covering them with sand, they are hatched by the heat of the Sunne; and by this meanes commeth the great increase. Of these we tooke very great ones, which have both backe and belly all of bone, of the thicknes of an inch: the fish whereof we proved, eating much like veale; and finding a number of egges in them, tasted also of them, but they did eat very sweetly. Heere wee ankered sixe houres, and then a fair gale of winde springing, we weyed anker, and made saile toward Cuba, whither we came the sixt day, and weathered as farre as the Table,[2] being a hill so called because of the forme thereof: here we lay off and on all night to keepe that we had gotten to windward, intending to have watered in the morning, if we could have done it, or els if the winde had come larger, to have plied to wind-ward to Havana, which is an harborow whereunto all the fleet of the Spanyards come, and doe there tary to have one the company of another. This hill we thinking to have beene the Table, made account (as it was indeed) that Havana was but eight leagues to wind-ward, but by the perswasion of a French man, who made the captaine beleeve he

[1] A group of small islands at the western extremity of the Florida Keys, one hundred and twenty miles west southwest of Cape Sable. They received their name from a Spanish word meaning a tortoise.

[2] Vessels still, in making the port of Havana from the northward or westward, look for the Table, or "Mesa de Mariel" (*mesa* being the Spanish for table). The sailing directions are as follows: "Port Mariel is 21 miles west of Havana and is a snug little harbor. A short distance inland to the eastward of the port is a remarkable long flat ridge of moderate height with a notch or step at its east end called the Mesa de Mariel, which cannot be mistaken."

knew the Table very well, and had beene at Havana, sayd that it was not the Table, and that the Table was much higher, and neerer to the sea side, and that there was no plaine ground to the Eastward, nor hilles to the Westward, but all was contrary, and that behind the hilles to the Westward was Havana. To which persuasion credit being given by some, and they not of the woorst, the captaine was persuaded to goe to leeward, and so sailed along the seventh and eight dayes, finding no habitation nor no other Table; and then perceiving his folly to give eare to such praters, was not a little sory, both because he did consider what time he should spend yer he could get so far to wind-ward againe, which would have bene, with the weathering which we had, ten or twelve dayes worke, and what it would have bene longer he knew not, and (that which was woorst) he had not above a dayes water, and therfore knew not what shift to make: but in fine, because the want was such, that his men could not live with it, he determined to seeke water, and to goe further to leeward, to a place (as it is set in the card) called Rio de los puercos,[1] which he was in doubt of, both whether it were inhabited, and whether there were water or not, and whether for the shoalds he might have accesse with his ships, that he might conveniently take in the same. And while we were in these troubles, and kept our way to the place aforesayd, almighty God our guide (who would not suffer us to run into any further danger, which we had bene like to have incurred, if we had ranged the coast of Florida along as we did before, which is so dangerous (by reports) that no ship escapeth which commeth thither, as the Spanyards have very wel proved the same) sent us the eight day at night a faire Westerly winde, whereupon the captaine and company consulted, determining not to refuse Gods gift, but every man was contented to pinch his owne bellie, whatsoever had happened; and taking the sayd winde, the ninth day of July got to the Table, and sailing the same night, unawares overshot Havana; at which place wee thought to have

[1] Rio de Puercos, a suburb in the municipal district of Consolacion del Norte, province of Pinar del Rio.

watered: but the next day, not knowing that wee had overshot the same, sailed along the coast, seeking it, and the eleventh day in the morning, by certaine knowen marks, we understood that we had overshot it 20 leagues: in which coast ranging, we found no convenient watering place, whereby there was no remedy but to disemboque, and to water upon the coast of Florida: for, to go further to the Eastward, we could not for the shoalds, which are very dangerous; and because the current [1] shooteth to the Northeast, we doubted by the force thereof to be set upon them, and therefore durst not approch them: so making but reasonable way the day aforesayd, and all the night, the twelfth day in the morning we fell with the Islands upon the cape of Florida, which we could scant double by the meanes that fearing the shoalds to the Eastwards, and doubting the current comming out of the West, which was not of that force we made account of; for we felt little or none till we fell with the cape, and then felt such a current, that bearing all sailes against the same, yet were driven backe againe a great pace: the experience whereof we had by the Jesus pinnesse, and the Salomons boat, which were sent the same day in the afternoone, whiles the ships were becalmed, to see if they could finde any water upon the Islands aforesaid; who spent a great part of the day in rowing thither, being further off then they deemed it to be, and in the meane time a faire gale of winde springing at sea, the ships departed, making a signe to them to come away, who although they saw them depart, because they were so neere the shore, would not lose all the labour they had taken, but determined to keepe their way, and see if there were any water to be had, making no account but to finde the shippes well enough: but they spent so much time in filling the water which they had found, that the night was come before they could make an end. And having lost the sight of the ships, they rowed what they could, but were wholly ignorant which way they should seeke them againe; as indeed there was a more doubt then they knew of:

---

[1] The Gulf Stream.

for when they departed, the shippes were in no current; and sailing but a mile further, they found one so strong, that bearing all sailes, it could not prevaile against the same, but were driven backe: whereupon the captaine sent the Salomon, with the other two barks, to beare neere the shore all night, because the current was lesse there a great deale,[1] and to beare light, with shooting off a piece now and then, to the intent the boats might better know how to come to them.

The Jesus also bare a light in her toppe gallant, and shot off a piece also now and then, but the night passed, and the morning was come, being the thirteenth day, and no newes could be heard of them, but the ships and barkes ceased not to looke still for them, yet they thought it was all in vaine, by the meanes they heard not of them all the night past; and therefore determined to tary no longer, seeking for them till noone, and if they heard no newes, then they would depart to the Jesus, who perforce (by the vehemency of the current) was caried almost out of sight; but as God would have it, [noone] time being come, and they having tacked about in the pinnesses top, had sight of them, and tooke them up: they in the boats, being to the number of one and twenty, having sight of the ships, and seeing them tacking about; whereas before at the first sight of them they did greatly rejoyce, were now in a greater perplexitie then ever they were: for by this they thought themselves utterly forsaken, whereas before they were in some hope to have found them. Truly God wrought marvellously for them, for they themselves having no victuals but water, and being sore oppressed with hunger, were not of opinion to bestow any further time in seeking the shippes then that present noone time: so that if they had not at that instant espied them, they had gone to the shore to have made provision for victuals, and with such things as they could have gotten, either to have gone for that part of Florida where the French men were planted (which would have bene very hard for them to have done, because they wanted victuals to

[1] Ponce de Leon had a like experience with these currents and countercurrents in 1513.

bring them thither, being an hundred and twenty leagues off) or els to have remained amongst the Floridians; at whose hands they were put in comfort by a French man, who was with them, that had remained in Florida, at the first finding thereof, a whole yeere together, to receive victuals sufficient, and gentle entertainment, if need were, for a yeere or two, untill which time God might have provided for them. But how contrary this would have fallen out to their expectations, it is hard to judge, seeing those people of the cape of Florida are of more savage and fierce nature, and more valiant then any of the rest; which the Spanyards well prooved, who being five hundred men, who intended there to land, returned few or none of them, but were inforced to forsake the same: and of their cruelty mention is made in the booke of the Decades,[1] of a frier, who taking upon him to persuade the people to subjection, was by them taken, and his skin cruelly pulled over his eares, and his flesh eaten.

In these Islands they being a shore, found a dead man, dried in a maner whole, with other heads and bodies of men: so that these sorts of men are eaters of the flesh of men, aswel as the Canibals. But to returne to our purpose.

The foureteenth day the shippe and barks came to the Jesus, bringing them newes of the recovery of the men, which was not a little to the rejoycing of the captaine, and the whole company: and so then altogether they kept on their way along the coast of Florida, and the fifteenth day come to an anker, and so from sixe and twenty degrees to thirty degrees and a halfe, where the French men abode, ranging all the coast along, seeking for fresh water, ankering every night, because we would overshoot no place of fresh water, and in the day time the captaine in the ships pinnesse sailed along the shore, went into every creeke, speaking with divers of the Floridians, because hee would understand where the French men inhabited; and

[1] Peter Martyr of Anghiera, *De Rebus Oceanicis et Orbe Novo Decades Tres* (Alcalá, 1530), the primary general book on the earliest explorations of America; known to Englishmen through Richard Eden's translation published in London in 1555.

not finding them in eight and twentie degrees, as it was declared unto him, marvelled thereat, and never left sailing along the coast till he found them, who inhabited in a river, by them called the river of May,[1] and standing in thirty degrees and better. In ranging this coast along, the captaine found it to be all an Island,[2] and therefore it is all lowe land, and very scant of fresh water, but the countrey was marvellously sweet, with both marish and medow ground, and goodly woods among. There they found sorell to grow as abundantly as grasse, and where their houses were, great store of maiz and mill, and grapes of great bignesse, but of taste much like our English grapes. Also Deere great plentie, which came upon the sands before them. Their houses are not many together, for in one house an hundred of them do lodge; they being made much like a great barne, and in strength not inferiour to ours, for they have stanchions and rafters of whole trees, and are covered with palmito-leaves, having no place divided, but one small roome for their king and queene. In the middest of this house is a hearth, where they make great fires all night, and they sleepe upon certeine pieces of wood hewin in for the bowing of their backs, and another place made high for their heads, which they put one by another all along the walles on both sides. In their houses they remaine onely in the nights, and in the day they desire the fields, where they dresse their meat, and make provision for victuals, which they provide onely for a meale from hand to mouth. There is one thing to be marvelled at, for the making of their fire, and not onely they but also the Negros doe the same, which is made onely by two stickes, rubbing them one against another: and this they may doe in any place they come, where they finde sticks sufficient for the purpose. In their apparell the men onely use deere skinnes, wherewith some onely cover their privy members, other some use the same as garments to cover them

---

[1] The St. John River. Hawkins's attention was called to it by his French pilot, Martin Atinas.

[2] The explorers regarded Florida as an island, as appears elsewhere in the narrative.

before and behind; which skinnes are painted, some yellow and red, some blacke and russet, and every man according to his owne fancy. They do not omit to paint their bodies also with curious knots, or antike worke, as every man in his owne fancy deviseth, which painting, to make it continue the better, they use with a thorne to pricke their flesh, and dent in the same, whereby the painting may have better hold. In their warres they use a sleighter colour of painting their faces, whereby to make themselves shew the more fierce; which after their warres ended, they wash away againe. In their warres they use bowes and arrowes, whereof their bowes are made of a kind of Yew, but blacker then ours, and for the most part passing the strength of the Negros or Indians, for it is not greatly inferior to ours: their arrowes are also of a great length, but yet of reeds like other Indians, but varying in two points, both in length and also for nocks and feathers, which the other lacke, whereby they shoot very stedy: the heads of the same are vipers teeth, bones of fishes, flint stones, piked points of knives, which they having gotten of the French men, broke the same, and put the points of them in their arrowes heads: some of them have their heads of silver, othersome that have want of these, put in a kinde of hard wood, notched, which pierceth as farre as any of the rest. In their fight, being in the woods, they use a marvellous pollicie for their owne safegard, which is by clasping a tree in their armes, and yet shooting notwithstanding: this policy they used with the French men in their fight, whereby it appeareth that they are people of some policy: and although they are called by the Spanyards Gente triste, that is to say, Bad people, meaning thereby, that they are not men of capacity: yet have the French men found them so witty in their answeres, that by the captaines owne report, a counseller with us could not give a more profound reason.

The women also for their apparell use painted skinnes, but most of them gownes of mosse, somewhat longer then our mosse, which they sowe together artificially, and make the same surplesse wise, wearing their haire down to their shoulders, like the Indians. In this river of May aforesayd, the captaine entring with his pinnesse, found a French ship of fourescore tun, and two pinnesses of fifteene tun a piece, by her, and speaking with the keepers thereof, they tolde him of a fort two leagues up, which they had built, in which their captaine Monsieur Laudonniere [1] was, with certeine souldiers therein. To whom our captaine sending to understand of a watering place, where he might conveniently take it in, and to have licence for the same, he straight, because there was no convenient place but up the river five leagues, where the water was fresh, did send him a pilot for the more expedition thereof, to bring in one of his barks, which going in with other boats provided for the same purpose, ankered before the fort, into the which our captaine went; where hee was by the Generall, with other captaines and souldiers, very gently enterteined, who declared unto him the time of their being there, which was fourteene moneths, with the extremity they were driven to for want of victuals, having brought very little with them; in which place they being two hundred men at their first comming, had in short space eaten all the maiz they could buy of the inhabitants about them, and therefore were driven certeine of them to serve a king of the Floridians against other

[1] A French Huguenot expedition, under Jean Ribault, was on the coast of South Carolina in 1562. A second expedition, also of Huguenot origin, was sent out in 1564, under René de Laudonnière, who was on the American coast with Ribault in 1562. Laudonnière located his colony on the St. John River. The vessels Hawkins found in the river evidently were those of the French colonists. After Hawkins's departure, Laudonnière was superseded by Ribault, who had sailed from France May 22, 1565, with orders from Coligny to relieve Laudonnière. Shortly after Ribault's arrival, Don Pedro Menendez, sent by Philip II. to destroy the French colonists who had presumed to settle on what he claimed to be Spanish territory, appeared on the coast of Florida, the French fort was captured and most of the colonists were massacred. Laudonnière and a few others escaped, and fled to the coast, where they were picked up by a French vessel, which landed Laudonnière and his companions at Swansea in Wales, whence they made their way to London. Ribault, who had withdrawn to his ships before the massacre, was at length shipwrecked, and he and his men, in their effort to reach the French fort, unaware of its fate, were discovered by the Spaniards and with a few exceptions were put to death.

his enemies, for mill and other victuals: which having gotten
could not serve them, being so many, so long a time: but
want came upon them in such sort, that they were faine to
gather acorns, which being stamped small, and often washed,
to take away the bitternesse of them, they did use for bread,
eating withall sundry times, roots, whereof they found many
good and holesome, and such as serve rather for medecines
then for meates alone. But this hardnesse not contenting
some of them, who would not take the paines so much as to
fish in the river before their doores, but would have all things
put in their mouthes, they did rebell against the captaine,
taking away first his armour, and afterward imprisoning him:
and so to the number of fourescore of them, departed with a
barke and a pinnesse, spoiling their store of victuall, and taking
away a great part thereof with them, and so went to the
Islands of Hispaniola [1] and Jamaica a roving, where they
spoiled and pilled the Spanyards; and having taken two
caravels laden with wine and casavi, which is a bread made of
roots, and much other victuals and treasure, had not the grace
to depart therewith, but were of such haughty stomacks, that
they thought their force to be such that no man durst meddle
with them, and so kept harborow in Jamaica, going dayly
ashore at their pleasure. But God which would not suffer
such evill doers unpunished, did indurate their hearts in such
sort, that they lingered the time so long, that a ship and
galliasse [2] being made out of Santa Domingo came thither into
the harborow, and tooke twenty of them, whereof the most part
were hanged, and the rest caried into Spaine, and some (to the
number of five and twenty) escaped in the pinnesse, and came
to Florida; where at their landing they were put in prison,
and incontinent foure of the chiefest being condemned, at the
request of the souldiers, did passe the harquebuzers, and then
were hanged upon a gibbet. This lacke of threescore men
was a great discourage and weakening to the rest, for they
were the best souldiers that they had: for they had now

---

[1] Santo Domingo.   [2] A large galley.

made the inhabitants weary of them by their dayly craving of maiz, having no wares left to content them withall, and therefore were inforced to rob them, and to take away their victual perforce, which was the occasion that the Floridians (not well contented therewith) did take certeine of their company in the woods, and slew them; whereby there grew great warres betwixt them and the Frenchmen: and therefore they being but a few in number durst not venture abroad, but at such times as they were inforced thereunto for want of food to do the same: and going twenty harquebuzers in a company, were set upon by eighteene kings, having seven or eight hundred men, which with one of their bowes slew one of their men, and hurt a dozen, and drove them all downe to their boats; whose pollicy in fight was to be marvelled at: for having shot at divers of their bodies which were armed, and perceiving that their arrowes did not prevaile against the same, they shot at their faces and legs, which were the places that the Frenchmen were hurt in. Thus the Frenchmen returned, being in ill case by the hurt of their men, having not above forty souldiers left unhurt, whereby they might ill make any more invasions upon the Floridians, and keepe their fort withall: which they must have beene driven unto, had not God sent us thither for their succour; for they had not above ten dayes victuall left before we came. In which perplexity our captaine seeing them, spared them out of his ship twenty barrels of meale, and foure pipes of beanes, with divers other victuals and necessaries which he might conveniently spare: and to helpe them the better homewardes, whither they were bound before our comming, at their request we spared them one of our barks of fifty tun. Notwithstanding the great want that the Frenchmen had, the ground doth yeeld victuals sufficient, if they would have taken paines to get the same; but they being souldiers desired to live by the sweat of other mens browes: for while they had peace with the Floridians, they had fish sufficient, by weares which they made to catch the same: but when they grew to warres, the Floridians tooke away the same againe, and then would not the Frenchmen take the paines to make any more. The ground yeeldeth naturally grapes in great store, for in the time that the Frenchmen were there, they made 20 hogsheads of wine.[1] Also it yeeldeth roots passing good, Deere marvellous store, with divers other beasts, and fowle, serviceable to the use of man. These be things wherewith a man may live, having corne or maiz wherewith to make bread: for maiz maketh good savory bread, and cakes as fine as flowre. Also it maketh good meale, beaten and sodden with water, and eateth like pap wherewith we feed children. It maketh also good beverage, sodden in water, and nourishable; which the Frenchmen did use to drinke of in the morning, and it assuageth their thirst, so that they had no need to drinke all the day after. And this maiz was the greatest lacke they had, because they had no labourers to sowe the same, and therefore to them that should inhabit the land it were requisit to have labourers to till and sowe the ground: for they having victuals of their owne, whereby they neither rob nor spoile the inhabitants, may live not onely quietly with them, who naturally are more desirous of peace then of warres, but also shall have abundance of victuals profered them for nothing: for it is with them as it is with one of us, when we see another man ever taking away from us, although we have enough besides, yet then we thinke all too little for our selves: for surely we have heard the Frenchmen report, and I know it by the Indians, that a very little contenteth them: for the Indians with the head of maiz rosted, will travell a whole day, and when they are at the Spanyards finding, they give them nothing but sodden herbs and maiz: and in this order I saw threescore of them feed, who were laden with wares, and came fifty leagues off. The Floridians when they travell, have a kinde of herbe dried,[2] who with a cane and an earthen cup in the end, with fire, and the dried herbs put together, doe sucke thorow the cane the smoke

---

[1] "Like to the wine of Orleans," says the margin.

[2] "Tobacco," says the margin. This was twenty years before tobacco was introduced into England by Ralph Lane. It had been used in southern Europe before.

thereof, which smoke satisfieth their hunger, and therwith they live foure or five dayes without meat or drinke, and this all the Frenchmen used for this purpose: yet do they holde opinion withall, that it causeth water and fleame to void from their stomacks. The commodities of this land are more then are yet knowen to any man: for besides the land it selfe, whereof there is more then any Christian king is able to inhabit, it flourisheth with medow, pasture ground, with woods of Cedar and Cypres, and other sorts, as better can not be in the world. They have for apothecary herbs, trees, roots and gummes great store, as Storax liquida, Turpintine, Gumme, Myrrhe, and Frankinsence, with many others, whereof I know not the names. Colours both red, blacke, yellow, and russet, very perfect, wherewith they so paint their bodies, and Deere skinnes which they weare about them, that with water it neither fadeth away, nor altereth colour. Golde and silver they want not: for at the Frenchmens first comming thither they had the same offered them for little or nothing, for they received for a hatchet two pound weight of golde, because they knew not the estimation thereof: but the souldiers being greedy of the same, did take it from them, giving them nothing for it: the which they perceiving, that both the Frenchmen did greatly esteeme it, and also did rigorously deale with them, by taking the same away from them, at last would not be knowen they had any more, neither durst they weare the same for feare of being taken away: so that saving at their first comming, they could get none of them: and how they came by this golde and silver the French men know not as yet, but by gesse, who having travelled to the Southwest of the cape, having found the same dangerous, by means of sundry banks, as we also have found the same: and there finding masts which were wracks of Spaniards comming from Mexico, judged that they had gotten treasure by them. For it is most true that divers wracks have beene made of Spaniards, having much treasure: for the Frenchmen having travelled to the capeward an hundred and fiftie miles, did finde two Spanyards with the Floridians, which they brought afterward to their fort, whereof one was in a caravel comming from the Indies, which was cast away fourteene yeeres ago, and the other twelve yeeres; of whose fellowes some escaped, othersome were slain by the inhabitants. It seemeth they had estimation of their golde and silver, for it is wrought flat and graven, which they weare about their neckes; othersome made round like a pancake, with a hole in the midst, to boulster up their breasts withall, because they thinke it a deformity to have great breasts. As for mines either of gold or silver, the Frenchmen can heare of none they have upon the Island, but of copper, whereof as yet also they have not made the proofe, because they were but few men:[1] but it is not unlike, but that in the maine where are high hilles, may be golde and silver as well as in Mexico, because it is all one maine. The Frenchmen obtained pearles of them of great bignesse, but they were blacke, by meanes of rosting of them, for they do not fish for them as the Spanyards doe, but for their meat: for the Spanyards use to keepe dayly afishing some two or three hundred Indians, some of them that be of choise a thousand: and their order is to go in canoas, or rather great pinnesses, with thirty men in a piece, whereof the one halfe, or most part be divers, the rest doe open the same for the pearles: for it is not suffered that they should use dragging, for that would bring them out of estimation, and marre the beds of them. The oisters which have the smallest sort of pearles are found in seven or eight fadome water, but the greatest in eleven or twelve fadome.

The Floridians have pieces of unicornes hornes which they weare about their necks, whereof the Frenchmen obteined many pieces. Of those unicornes[2] they have many: for that they doe affirme it to be a beast with one horne, which comming to the river to drinke, putteth the same into the water before he drinketh. Of this unicornes horne there are of our company, that having gotten the same of the Frenchmen brought home thereof to shew. It is therefore to be presupposed that

[1] " This copper," says the margin, " was found perfect golde, called by the Savages Sycroa phyra."
[2] According to the margin, the native name was Souannamma.

there are more commodities as well as that, which for want
of time, and people sufficient to inhabit the same, can not yet
come to light: but I trust God will reveale the same before
it be long, to the great profit of them that shal take it in hand.
Of beasts in this countrey besides deere, foxes, hares, polcats,
conies, ownces, and leopards, I am not able certeinly to say:
but it is thought that there are lions and tygres as well as
unicornes; lions especially; if it be true that is sayd, of the
enmity betweene them and the unicornes; for there is no
beast but hath his enemy, as the cony the polcat, a sheepe
the woolfe, the elephant the rinoceros; and so of other beasts
the like: insomuch, that whereas the one is, the other can not
be missing. And seeing I have made mention of the beasts of
this countrey, it shall not be from my purpose to speake also
of the venimous beasts, as crocodiles, whereof there is great
abundance, adders of great bignesse, whereof our men killed some
of a yard and halfe long. Also I heard a miracle of one of these
adders, upon the which a faulcon seizing, the sayd adder did
claspe her tail about her; which the French captain seeing,
came to the rescue of the falcon, and tooke her slaying the
adder; and this faulcon being wilde, he did reclaim her, and
kept her for the space of two moneths, at which time for very
want of meat he was faine to cast her off. On these adders
the Frenchmen did feed, to no little admiration of us, and
affirmed the same to be a delicate meat. And the captaine of
the Frenchmen saw also a serpent with three heads and foure
feet, of the bignesse of a great spaniell, which for want of a
harquebuz he durst not attempt to slay. Of fish also they
have in the river, pike, roch, salmon, trout, and divers other
small fishes, and of great fish, some of the length of a man and
longer, being of bignesse accordingly, having a snout much
like a sword of a yard long. There be also of sea fishes, which
we saw coming along the coast flying, which are of the bignesse
of a smelt, the biggest sort whereof have foure wings, but the
other have but two: of these wee sawe comming out of Guinea
a hundred in a company, which being chased by the gilt heads,
otherwise called the bonitos, do to avoid them the better, take

their flight out of the water, but yet are they not able to fly
farre, because of the drying of their wings, which serve them
not to flie but when they are moist, and therefore when they
can flie no further, they fall into the water, and having wet
their wings, take a new flight againe. These bonitos be of
bignesse like a carpe, and in colour like a makarell, but it is
the swiftest fish in swimming that is, and followeth her prey
very fiercely, not only in the water, but also out of the water:
for as the flying fish taketh her flight, so doeth this bonito
leape after them, and taketh them sometimes above the water.
There were some of those bonitos, which being galled by a
fishgig, did follow our shippe comming out of Guinea 500
leagues. There is a sea-fowle also that chaseth this flying
fish aswell as the bonito: for as the flying fish taketh her
flight, so doth this fowle pursue to take her, which to beholde
is a greater pleasure then hawking, for both the flights are as
pleasant, and also more often then an hundred times: for the
fowle can flie no way, but one or other lighteth in her pawes,
the number of them are so abundant. There is an innumerable yoong frie of these flying fishes, which commonly
keepe about the ship, and are not so big as butter-flies, and
yet by flying do avoid the unsatiablenesse of the bonito. Of
the bigger sort of these fishes wee tooke many, which both
night and day flew into the sailes of our ship, and there was
not one of them which was not woorth a bonito: for being
put upon a hooke drabling in the water, the bonito would
leape thereat, and so was taken. Also, we tooke many with
a white cloth made fast to a hooke, which being tied so short
in the water, that it might leape out and in, the greedie bonito
thinking it to be a flying fish leapeth thereat, and so is deceived.
We tooke also dolphins which are of very goodly colour and
proportion to behold, and no less delicate in taste. Fowles
also there be many, both upon land and upon sea: but concerning them on the land I am not able to name them, because my abode was there so short. But for the fowle of the
fresh rivers, these two I noted to be the chiefe, whereof the
Flemengo is one, having all red feathers, and long red legs like

a herne, a necke according to the bill, red, whereof the upper neb hangeth an inch over the nether; and an egript,[1] which is all white as the swanne, with legs like to an hearn-shaw, and of bignesse accordingly, but it hath in her taile feathers of so fine a plume,[2] that it passeth the estridge[3] his feather. Of the sea-fowle above all other not common in England, I noted the pellicane, which is fained to be the lovingst bird that is; which rather then her yong should want, wil spare her heart bloud out of her belly: but for all this lovingnesse she is very deformed to beholde; for she is of colour russet: notwithstanding in Guinea I have seene of them as white as a swan, having legs like the same, and a body like a hearne, with a long necke, and a thick long beak, from the nether jaw whereof downe to the breast passeth a skinne of such a bignesse, as is able to receive a fish as big as ones thigh, and this her big throat and long bill doeth make her seem so ougly.

Here I have declared the estate of Florida, and the commodities therein to this day knowen, which although it may seeme unto some, by the meanes that the plenty of golde and silver, is not so abundant as in other places, that the cost bestowed upon the same will not be able to quit the charges: yet am I of the opinion, that by that which I have seene in other Islands of the Indians, where such increase of cattell hath bene, that of twelve head of beasts in five and twenty yeeres, did in the hides of them raise a thousand pound profit yerely, that the increase of cattel only would raise profit sufficient for the same: for wee may consider, if so small a portion did raise so much gaines in such short time, what would a greater do in many yeres? and surely I may this affirme, that the ground of the Indians for the breed of cattell, is not in any point to be compared to this of Florida, which all the yeere long is so greene, as any time in the Summer with us: which surely is not to be marvelled at, seeing the countrey standeth in so watery a climate: for once a day without faile they have a shower of raine; which by meanes of the countrey

---

[1] Egret.   [2] Aigrettes.   [3] Ostrich.

it selfe, which is drie, and more fervent hot then ours, doeth make all things to flourish therein. And because there is not the thing we all seeke for, being rather desirous of present gaines, I doe therefore affirme the attempt thereof to be more requisit for a prince, who is of power able to go thorow with the same, rather then for any subject.

From thence wee departed the 28 of July, upon our voyage homewards, having there all things as might be most convenient for our purpose: and tooke leave of the Frenchmen that there still remained, who with diligence determined to make as great speede after, as they could. Thus by meanes of contrary windes oftentimes, wee prolonged our voyage in such manner that victuals scanted with us, so that we were divers times (or rather the most part) in despaire of ever comming home, had not God in his goodnesse better provided for us, then our deserving.[1] In which state of great miserie, wee were provoked to call upon him by fervent prayer, which mooved him to heare us, so that we had a prosperous winde, which did set us so farre shot, as to be upon the banke of Newfound land, on Saint Bartholomews eve,[2] and we sounded therupon, finding ground at an hundred and thirty fadoms, being that day somewhat becalmed, and tooke a great number of fresh codde-fish, which greatly relieved us: and being very glad thereof, the next day we departed, and had lingring little gales for the space of foure and five dayes, at the ende of which we sawe a couple of French shippes, and had of them so much fish as would serve us plentifully for all the rest of the way, the Captaine paying for the same both golde and silver, to the just value thereof, unto the chiefe owners of the saide shippes, but they not looking for any thing at all, were glad in themselves to meete with such good intertainement at sea, as they had at our handes. After which departure from them, with a good large winde, the twentieth of September we came to Padstow[3] in Cornewall, God be thanked, in safetie, with

[1] Hawkins was the first English navigator to make his way up the American coast. Cabot had sailed down the coast. [2] *I.e.*, on August 23.
[3] On Padstow Bay, on the northern coast of Cornwall.

the losse of twentie persons in all the voyage, and with great profit to the venturers of the said voyage, as also to the whole realme, in bringing home both golde, silver, pearles and other jewels great store. His name therefore be praised for evermore. Amen.

The names of certaine Gentlemen that were in this voyage.

M. John Hawkins.
M. John Chester, sir William Chesters sonne.
M. Anthony Parkhurst
M. Fitzwilliam.
M. Thomas Woorley.
M. Edward Lacie, with divers others.

The Register and true accounts of all herein expressed hath beene approoved by me John Sparke the younger, who went upon the same voyage, and wrote the same.

THE THIRD TROUBLESOME VOYAGE MADE WITH THE JESUS OF LUBEC
1567–1568

INTRODUCTION

HAWKINS reached England in September, 1565, bringing with him much treasure in gold, silver, and various commodities, and valuable information concerning that part of the New World which he had visited. With such results as a return for his outlay, Hawkins had no difficulty in enlisting the interest of his countrymen in a new and larger expedition, having commercial gains principally in view. The record of this third "troublesome" voyage was written by Hawkins himself. It was reprinted by the Hakluyt Society in its Hawkins volume in 1868. Francis Drake, afterward Sir Francis Drake, commanded one of the vessels connected with the expedition. The African coast was again visited, and a large number of slaves were secured and afterward sold in the Spanish settlements of the New World. Neither in the relation of the second voyage by Sparke, nor in this by Hawkins, is there any intimation whatever that at that time the slightest disgrace attached to slave-stealing and slave-selling. The authorities for the voyage are best discussed by Mr. Julian S. Corbett, *Drake and the Tudor Navy*, I. 414–420. Hawkins was a member of Parliament for Plymouth from 1571 to 1583. Deceiving both the Queen of Scots and Philip as to his loyalty, Hawkins was made a grandee of Spain in 1571, and received as a reward for his pretended treachery a considerable sum of money, which he used in equipping a large number of vessels for operations against Spain in the summer of 1572. He was made treasurer of the navy in 1573, succeeding his father-in-law, Ben Gonson. He was "the man to whom is due all the credit of preparing the royal fleet to meet the Armada," in 1588, served with distinction as rear-admiral in the naval conflict that ensued, and was knighted July 25, 1588. With Frobisher, Hawkins undertook a voyage in 1590 for the purpose of harassing Spanish commerce. In 1592 he founded, at Chatham, "Sir John Hawkins's Hospital" for needy mariners and shipwrights. In 1595, in company with Drake, he was connected with an expedition against the Spanish settlements in the West Indies; and he died at sea November 12, 1595, "neere the Easternmost end of Saint Juan de Puerto Rico."

H. S B.

THE THIRD VOYAGE BY M. JOHN HAWKINS, 1567–1568

The third troublesome voyage made with the Jesus of Lubec, the Minion, and foure other ships, to the parts of Guinea, and the West Indies, in the yeeres 1567 and 1568 by M. John Hawkins.

THE ships departed from Plimmouth, the second day of October, Anno 1567 and had reasonable weather untill the seventh day, at which time fortie leagues North from Cape Finister,[1] there arose an extreme storme, which continued foure dayes, in such sort, that the fleete was dispersed, and all our great boats lost, and the Jesus our chiefe shippe, in such case, as not thought able to serve the voyage: whereupon in the same storme we set our course homeward, determining to give over the voyage: but the eleventh day of the same moneth, the winde changed with faire weather, whereby we were animated to followe our enterprise, and so did, directing our course with the Islands of the Canaries, where according to an order before prescribed, all our shippes before dispersed, met at one of those Ilands, called Gomera, where we tooke water, and departed from thence the fourth day of November, towards the coast of Guinea, and arrived at Cape Verde, the eighteenth of November: where we landed 150 men, hoping to obtain some Negros, where we got but fewe, and those with great hurt and damage to our men, which chiefly proceeded of their envenomed arrowes: and although in the beginning they seemed to be but small hurts, yet there hardly escaped any that had blood drawen of them, but died in strange sort, with

[1] On the northwestern coast of Spain.

their mouthes shut some tenne dayes before they died, and after
their wounds were whole;[1] where I my selfe had one of the
greatest woundes, yet thanks be to God, escaped. From
thence we passed the time upon the coast of Guinea, searching with all diligence the rivers from Rio grande, unto Sierra
Leona, till the twelfth of Januarie, in which time we had not
gotten together a hundreth and fiftie Negros: yet nothwith-
standing the sicknesse of our men, and the late time of the
yeere commanded us away: and thus having nothing wherewith to seeke the coast of the West Indies, I was with the
rest of our company in consultation to goe to the coast of the
Mine,[2] hoping there to have obtained some golde for our wares,
and thereby to have defraied our charge. But even in that
present instant, there came to us a Negro, sent from a king
oppressed by other Kings his neighbours, desiring our aide,
with promise that as many Negros as by these warres might
be obtained, aswell of his part as of ours, should be at our
pleasure: whereupon we concluded to give aide, and sent 120
of our men, which the 15 of Januarie, assaulted a towne of
the Negros of our Allies adversaries, which had in it 8000
Inhabitants, being very strongly impaled and fenced after
their manner, but it was so well defended that our men prevailed not, but lost sixe men and fortie hurt: so that our men
sent forthwith to me for more helpe: whereupon considering
that the good successe of this enterprise might highly further
the commoditie of our voyage, I went my selfe, and with the
helpe of the king of our side, assaulted the towne, both by
land and sea, and very hardly with fire (their houses being
covered with dry Palme leaves) obtained the towne, and put
the inhabitants to flight, where we tooke 250 persons, men,
women, and children, and by our friend the king of our side,
there were taken 600 prisoners, whereof we hoped to have had
our choise: but the Negro (in which nation is seldome or never
found truth) meant nothing lesse: for that night he remooved

[1] The West African negroes poisoned their arrows; the wounds produced
by them tended to result in something resembling lockjaw.
[2] El Mina, or the Gold Coast.

his campe and prisoners, so that we were faine to content us with those fewe which we had gotten ourselves.

Now had we obtained between foure and five hundred Negros, wherewith we thought it somewhat reasonable to seeke the coast of the West Indies, and there, for our Negros, and other our merchandize, we hoped to obtaine, whereof to countervaile our charges with some gaines, wherunto we proceeded with all diligence, furnished our watering, tooke fuell, and departed the coast of Guinea the third of Februarie, continuing at the sea with a passage more hard, then before had bene accustomed till the 27 day of March, which day we had sight of an Iland, called Dominica, upon the coast of the West Indies, in fourteene degrees: from thence we coasted from place to place, making our traffike with the Spaniards as we might, somewhat hardly, because the king had straightly commanded all his Governours in those parts, by no meanes to suffer any trade to be made with us: notwithstanding we had reasonable trade, and courteous entertainement, from the Ile of Margarita [1] unto Cartagena,[2] without any thing greatly worth the noting, saving at Capo de la Vela,[3] in a towne called Rio de la Hacha [4] (from whence come all the pearles) the treasurer who had the charge there, would by no meanes agree to any trade, or suffer us to take water, he had fortified his towne with divers bulwarkes in all places where it might be entered, and furnished himselfe with an hundred Hargabuziers,[5] so that he thought by famine to have inforced us to have put a land our Negros: of which purpose he had not greatly failed, unlesse we had by force entred the towne: which (after we could by no meanes obtaine his favour) we were inforced to doe, and so with two hundred men brake in upon their bulwarkes, and entred the towne with the losse onely of two men

[1] In the Caribbean Sea, off the coast of Venezuela.
[2] A city on the northern coast of Colombia, capital of a province of the same name and of the state of Bolivar.
[3] On the coast of Magdalena, one of the states of Colombia.
[4] West of Capo de la Vela.
[5] Men armed with the arquebus, a firearm of the period; written also harquebus.

of our partes, and no hurt done to the Spaniards because after their voley of shot discharged, they all fled.

Thus having the town with some circumstance, as partly by the Spaniards desire of Negros, and partly by friendship of the Treasurer, we obtained a secret trade: whereupon the Spaniards resorted to us by night, and bought of us to the number of 200 Negros: in all other places where we traded the Spaniards inhabitants were glad of us, and traded willingly.

At Cartagena the last towne we thought to have seene on the coast, we could by no meanes obtaine to deale with any Spaniard, the governor was so straight, and because our trade was so neere finished we thought not good either to adventure any landing, or to detract further time, but in peace departed from thence the 24 of July, hoping to have escaped the time of their stormes which then soone after began to reigne, the which they called Furicanos, but passing by the West end of Cuba, towards the coast of Florida, there happened to us the 12 day of August an extreme storme which continued by the space of foure dayes, which so beat the Jesus, that we cut downe all her higher buildings, her rudder also was sore shaken, and withall was in so extreme a leake, that we were rather upon the point to leave her then to keepe her any longer, yet hoping to bring all to good passe, we sought the coast of Florida, where we found no place nor Haven for our ships, because of the shalownesse of the coast: thus being in greater dispaire, and taken with a newe storme which continued other 3 dayes, we were inforced to take for our succour the Port which serveth the citie of Mexico called Saint John de Ullua,[1] which standeth in 19 degrees: in seeking of which Port we tooke in our way 3 ships which carried passengers to the number of an hundred, which passengers we hoped should be a meane to us the better to obtaine victuals for our money, and a quiet place for the repairing of our fleete. Shortly after this the 16 of September we entered the Port of Saint John de Ullua and in our entrie the Spaniardes thinking us to be the fleete of Spaine, the

[1] San Juan de Ulua, a small island on the Mexican coast opposite Vera Cruz, on which is a castle of the same name.

chiefe officers of the Countrey came aboord us, which being deceived of their expectation were greatly dismayed: but immediatly when they sawe our demand was nothing but victuals, were recomforted. I found also in the same Port twelve ships which had in them by the report two hundred thousand pound in gold and silver, all which (being in my possession, with the kings Iland as also the passengers before in my way thitherward stayed) I set at libertie, without the taking from them the waight of a groat: onely because I would not be delayed of my dispatch, I stayed two men of estimation and sent post immediatly to Mexico, which was two hundred miles from us, to the Presidentes and Councell there, shewing them of our arrivall there by the force of weather, and the necessitie of the repaire of our shippes and victuals, which wantes we required as friends to king Philip to be furnished of for our money: and that the Presidents and Councell there should with all convenient speede take order, that at the arrivall of the Spanish fleete, which was dayly looked for, there might no cause of quarrell rise betweene us and them, but for the better maintenance of amitie, their commandement might be had in that behalfe. This message being sent away the sixteenth day of September at night, being the very day of our arrivall, in the next morning which was the seventeenth day of the same moneth, we sawe open of the Haven thirteene great shippes, and understanding them to bee the fleete of Spaine, I sent immediatly to advertise the Generall of the fleete of my being there, doing him to understand, that before I would suffer them to enter the Port, there should some order of conditions passe betweene us for our safe being there, and maintenance of peace. Now it is to be understood that this Port is made by a little Iland of stones not three foote above the water in the highest place, and but a bow-shoot of length any way, this Iland standeth from the maine land two bow shootes or more, also it is to be understood that there is not in all this coast any other place for shippes to arrive in safety, because the North winde hath there such violence, that unlesse the shippes be very safely mored with their ankers fastened

upon this Iland, there is no remedie for these North windes but
death: also the place of the Haven was so little, that of necessitie the shippes must ride one aboord the other, so that we
could not give place to them, nor they to us: and here I
beganne to bewaile that which after followed, for now, said I,
I am in two dangers, and forced to receive the one of them.
That was, either I must have kept out the fleete from entering the Port, the which with Gods helpe I was very well able
to doe, or else suffer them to enter in with their accustomed
treason, which they never faile to execute, where they may
have opportunitie, to compasse it by any meanes: if I had
kept them out, then had there bene present shipwracke of all
the fleete which amounted in value to sixe Millions, which was
in value of our money 1800000. li. which I considered I was not
able to answere, fearing the Queenes Majesties indignation in
so waightie a matter. Thus with my selfe revolving the
doubts, I thought rather better to abide the Jutt of the un-
certainty, then the certaintie. The uncertaine doubt I account
was their treason which by good policie I hoped might be
prevented, and therefore as chusing the least mischiefe I proceeded to conditions. Now was our first messenger come and
returned from the fleete with report of the arrivall of a Viceroy,
so that hee had authoritie, both in all this Province of Mexico
(otherwise called Neuva Espanna) and in the sea, who sent
us word that we should send our conditions, which of his part
should (for the better maintenance of amitie betweene the
Princes) be both favourably granted, and faithfully performed
with many faire wordes how passing the coast of the Indies
he had understood of our honest behaviour towardes the inhabitants where we had to doe, aswell elsewhere as in the
same Port, the which I let passe: thus following our demand,
we required victuals for our money, and licence to sell as
much ware as might furnish our wants, and that there might
be of either part twelve gentlemen as hostages for the maintenance of peace: and that the Iland for our better safetie
might be in our owne possession, during our abode there, and
such ordinance as was planted in the same Iland which were

eleven peeces of brasse: and that no Spaniard might land in
the Iland with any kind of weapon: these conditions at the
first he somewhat misliked, chiefly the guard of the Iland to
be in our owne keeping, which if they had had, we had soone
knowen our fare: for with the first North winde they had cut
our cables and our ships had gone ashore: but in the ende he
concluded to our request, bringing the twelve hostages to ten,
which with all speede of either part were received, with a
writing from the Viceroy signed with his hande and sealed
with his seale of all the conditions concluded, and forthwith a
trumpet blowen with commandement that none of either part
should be meane to violate the peace upon paine of death:
and further it was concluded that the two Generals of the
fleetes should meete, and give faith ech to other for the performance of the premisses which was so done. Thus at the
end of 3 dayes all was concluded and the fleete entered the
port, saluting one another as the maner of the sea doth require. Thus as I said before, Thursday we entred the port,
Friday we saw the fleete, and on Munday at night they entered
the Port: then we laboured 2. daies placing the English ships
by themselves, and the Spanish ships by themselves, the captaines of ech part and inferiour men of their parts promising
great amity of al sides: which even as with all fidelitie it was
ment on our part, so the Spaniards ment nothing lesse on
their parts, but from the maine land had furnished themselves with a supply of men to the number of 1000, and ment
the next Thursday being the 23 of September at dinner time,
to set upon us on all sides. The same Thursday in the morning the treason being at hand, some appearance shewed, as
shifting of weapon from ship to ship, planting and bending of
ordinance from the ships to the Iland where our men warded,
passing too and fro of companies of men more then required
for their necessary busines, and many other ill likelihoods,
which caused us to have a vehement suspition, and therewithall sent to the Viceroy to enquire what was ment by it,
which sent immediatly straight commandement to unplant all
things suspicious, and also sent word that he in the faith of a

Viceroy would be our defence from all villanies. Yet we being not satisfied with this answere, because we suspected a great number of men to be hid in a great ship of 900 tunnes, which was mored next unto the Minion, sent againe to the Viceroy the master of the Jesus which had the Spanish tongue, and required to be satisfied if any such thing were or not. The Viceroy now seeing that the treason must be discovered, foorthwith stayed our master, blew the Trumpet, and of all sides set upon us: our men which warded a shore being stricken with sudden feare, gave place, fled, and sought to recover succour of the ships; the Spaniardes being before provided for the purpose landed in all places in multitudes from their ships which they might easily doe without boates, and slewe all our men ashore without mercie, a fewe of them escaped aboord the Jesus. The great ship which had by the estimation three hundred men placed in her secretly, immediatly fell aboord the Minion, but by Gods appointment, in the time of the suspicion we had, which was onely one halfe houre, the Minion was made readie to avoide, and so leesing her hedfasts, and hayling away by the sternefastes she was gotten out: thus with Gods helpe she defended the violence of the first brunt of these three hundred men. The Minion being past out, they came aboord the Jesus, which also with very much a doe and the losse of manie of our men were defended and kept out. Then there were also two other ships that assaulted the Jesus at the same instant, so that she had hard getting loose, but yet with some time we had cut our head-fastes, and gotten out by the stern-fastes. Nowe when the Jesus and the Minion were gotten about two shippes length from the Spanish fleete, the fight beganne so hotte on all sides that within one houre the Admirall of the Spaniards was supposed to be sunke, their Viceadmirall burned, and one other of their principall ships supposed to be sunke, so that the shippes were little able to annoy us.

Then it is to be understood, that all the Ordinance upon the Ilande was in the Spaniardes handes, which did us so great annoyance, that it cut all the mastes and yardes of the Jesus in such sort that there was no hope to carrie her away: also it sunke our small shippes, whereupon we determined to place the Jesus on that side of the Minion, that she might abide all the batterie from the land, and so be a defence for the Minion till night, and then to take such reliefe of victuall and other necessaries from the Jesus, as the time would suffer us, and to leave her. As we were thus determining, and had placed the Minion from the shot of the land, suddenly the Spaniards had fired two great shippes which were comming directly with us, and having no meanes to avoide the fire, it bredde among our men a marvellous feare, so that some sayd, let us depart with the Minion, other said, let us see whether the winde will carrie the fire from us. But to be short, the Minions men which had alwayes their sayles in a readinesse, thought to make sure worke, and so without either consent of the Captaine or Master cut their saile, so that very hardly I was received into the Minion.

The most part of the men that were left alive in the Jesus, made shift and followed the Minion in a small boat, the rest which the little boate was not able to receive, were inforced to abide the mercie of the Spaniards (which I doubt was very little) so with the Minion only and the Judith (a small barke of 50 tunne) we escaped, which barke the same night forsooke us in our great miserie: we were now remooved with the Minion from the Spanish ships two bow-shootes, and there rode all that night: the next morning we recovered an Iland a mile from the Spaniardes, where there tooke us a North winde, and being left onely with two ankers and two cables (for in this conflict we lost three cables and two ankers) we thought always upon death which ever was present, but God preserved us to a longer time.

The weather waxed reasonable, and the Saturday we set saile, and having a great number of men and little victuals our hope of life waxed lesse and lesse: some desired to yeeld to the Spaniards, some rather desired to obtain a place where they might give themselves to the Infidels, and some had rather abide with a little pittance the mercie of God at Sea:

so thus with many sorowful hearts we wandred in an unknowen Sea by the space of 14 dayes, till hunger inforced us to seek the land, for hides were thought very good meat, rats, cats, mice and dogs, none escaped that might be gotten, parrats and monkeyes that were had in great price, were thought there very profitable if they served the turne one dinner: thus in the end the 8 day of October we came to the land in the botome of the same bay of Mexico in 23 degrees and a halfe, where we hoped to have found inhabitants of the Spaniards, reliefe of victuals, and place for the repaire of our ship, which was so sore beaten with shot from our enemies and brused with shooting off our owne ordinance, that our wearie and weake armes were scarce able to defende and keepe out water. But all things happened to the contrary, for we found neither people, victuall, nor haven of reliefe, but a place where having faire weather with some perill we might land a boat; our people being forced with hunger desired to be set on land, whereunto I consented.

And such as were willing to land I put them apart, and such as were desirous to goe homewardes, I put apart, so that they were indifferently parted a hundred of one side and a hundred of the other side: these hundred men we set a land with all diligence in this little place beforesaid,[1] which being landed, we determined there to take in fresh water, and so with our little remaine of victuals to take the sea.

The next day having a land with me fiftie of our hundreth men that remained for the speedier preparing of our water

[1] The number was one hundred and fourteen. David Ingram, Richard Brown and Richard Twide made their way northward, and about fifty leagues from Cape Breton found a French vessel, on which they were carried to England. About seventy of the others, including Miles Phillips and Job Hortop, marched westward into Mexico. Of this number sixty-eight suffered punishment and imprisonment in the galleys, and three were burned to death. Narratives written by Miles Phillips and Job Hortop are preserved in Hakluyt's *Voyages*, IX. 398–465, of the Hakluyt Society's edition. David Ingram's narrative, printed by Hakluyt in his edition of 1589, was omitted in the edition of 1600 on account of "some incredibilities." In his *Westward Ho*, Charles Kingsley made extensive use of the material furnished by these relations, as well as of that found in Hawkins's own narrative.

aboord, there arose an extreame storme, so that in three dayes we could by no meanes repaire aboord our ship: the ship also was in such perill that every houre we looked for shipwracke.

But yet God againe had mercie on us, and sent faire weather, we had aboord our water, and departed the sixteenth day of October, after which day we had faire and prosperous weather till the sixteenth day of November, which day God be praysed we were cleere from the coast of the Indies, and out of the chanell and gulfe of Bahama, which is betweene the Cape of Florida, and the Ilandes of Lucayo.[1] After this growing neere to the colde countrey, our men being oppressed with famine, died continually, and they that were left, grew into such weakenesse that we were scantly able to manage our shippe, and the winde being always ill for us to recover England, we determined to goe with Galicia[2] in Spaine, with intent there to relieve our companie and other extreame wantes. And being arrived the last day of December in a place neere unto Vigo called Ponte Vedra,[3] our men with excesse of fresh meate grew into miserable disscases, and died a great part of them. This matter was borne out as long as it might be, but in the end although there were none of our men suffered to goe a land, yet by accesse of the Spaniards, our feeblenesse was knowen to them. Whereupon they ceased not to seeke by all meanes to betray us, but with all speede possible we departed to Vigo, where we had some helpe of certaine English ships and twelve fresh men, wherewith we repaired our wants as we might, and departing the 20 day of January 1568[4] arrived in Mounts bay[5] in Cornewall the 25 of the same moneth, praised be God therefore.

If all the miseries and troublesome affaires of this sorowfull

---

[1] Hawkins was familiar with this route, as he passed the same way in his previous voyage.
[2] Northwest province of Spain.
[3] In the southern part of the province of Galicia.
[4] Old style. By new style, 1569.
[5] On the southern coast of Cornwall, between the Lizard and Land's End.

voyage should be perfectly and throughly written, there should neede a painefull man with his pen, and as great a time as he had that wrote the lives and deathes of the Martyrs.

JOHN HAWKINS.

THE WORLD ENCOMPASSED BY SIR FRANCIS DRAKE, (CALIFORNIA) 1579

INTRODUCTION

FRANCIS DRAKE, a native of Tavistock, Devonshire, early entered upon a sea life. In Hawkins's expedition of 1567 he commanded the *Judith*. The treatment he and others received at San Juan de Ulua so greatly embittered him against the Spaniards that for several years he ravaged the Spanish main. It was on one of these expeditions that Drake crossed the Isthmus of Panama, and obtained a view of the Pacific Ocean, which later he was to navigate and explore. He sailed from Plymouth, on his celebrated voyage around the world, November 15, 1577, his fleet consisting of five vessels. In sailing down the South American coast, Drake paused to refit here and there. Two months, from June 19, 1578, to August 17, were spent at Port St. Julian. The Straits of Magellan were reached August 20, and, after entering the waters of the Pacific, several months were passed in preying upon various Spanish interests on the west coast of South America, Drake enriching himself here and there with Spanish plunder. In March, 1579, having become separated from his consorts, Drake was at Cape San Francisco, a little north of the equator. April 15 he reached the harbor of Guatulco, or Aguatulco, with a reference to which the following extract from the *World Encompassed* begins.

After the events there narrated, Drake, leaving the American coast, crossed the Pacific to the Philippines, and then made his way home by way of the Cape of Good Hope, thus encompassing the world. He reached Plymouth September 26, 1580. The earliest relation of the voyage in print is the one ascribed to Francis Pretty, entitled *The Famous Voyage of Sir Francis Drake into the South Sea . . . begun in the yeare of our*

Lord 1577. Hakluyt had a copy, but in the introduction of his edition of 1589 he says that the friends of Drake, who did not wish to have their publications forestalled, asked him to omit it. He seems to have printed it privately, however, and the six pages, without pagination, were inserted after page 643 in some, if not all, of the copies of the edition. The John Carter Brown Library at Brown University and the Library of Harvard University have copies. Pretty's narrative found a place in the third volume of the edition of 1598–1600. The authoritative account of the expedition is to be found in *The World Encompassed by Sir Francis Drake, carefully Collected out of the notes of Master Francis Fletcher, Preacher in this Imployment, and divers others his followers* (London, 1628). A reprint, edited by W. S. W. Vaux, was published by the Hakluyt Society (London, 1854). A portion has been reprinted in the *Old South Leaflets*, No. 116. The best discussion of the materials for the history of Drake's voyage of circumnavigation will be found in Mr. Julian S. Corbett's *Drake and the Tudor Navy*, I. 421–429.

Drake was rewarded by Elizabeth with the honor of knighthood. In 1587, when the Spanish Armada was in preparation, Drake, with his fleet, entered the harbor of Cadiz and destroyed nearly a hundred vessels. In the following year, at the destruction of the Armada, Drake was present as vice-admiral. In 1592 he was made a member of Parliament. He died December 27, 1595, while leading an expedition against Spanish interests in the West Indies, and was buried at sea. Of the voyage of 1595–1596 there is a manuscript account by Thomas Maynarde in the British Museum. This, with a Spanish account, was printed by the Hakluyt Society in 1849.

H. S. B.

SIR FRANCIS DRAKE ON THE CALIFORNIA COAST, 1579

From Guatulco [1] we departed the day following, viz., Aprill 16, [1579] setting our course directly into the sea, whereon we sayled 500 leagues in longitude, to get a winde: and betweene that and June 3, 1400 leagues in all, till we came into 42 deg. of North latitude, where in the night following we found such alteration of heate, into extreame and nipping cold, that our men in generall did grievously complaine thereof, some of them feeling their healths much impaired thereby; neither was it that this chanced in the night alone, but the day following carried with it not onely the markes, but the stings and force of the night going before, to the great admiration of us all; for besides that the pinching and biting aire was nothing altered, the very roapes of our ship were stiffe, and the raine which fell was an unnatural congealed and frozen substance, so that we seemed rather to be in the frozen Zone then any way so neere unto the sun, or these hotter climates.

Neither did this happen for the time onely, or by some sudden accident, but rather seemes indeed to proceed from some ordinary cause, against the which the heate of the sun prevailes not; for it came to that extremity in sayling but 2 deg. farther to the Northward in our course, that though sea-men lack not good stomaches, yet it seemed a question to many amongst us, whether their hands should feed their mouthes, or rather keepe themselves within their coverts from the pinching cold that did benumme them. Neither could we impute it to the tendernesse of our bodies, though we came lately from the extremitie of heate, by reason whereof we might be more sensible of the present cold: insomuch as the dead and sencelesse creatures

[1] A small port of Guatemala.

were as well affected with it as ourselves: our meate, as soone as it was remooved from the fire, would presently in a manner be frozen up, and our ropes and tackling in few dayes were growne to that stiffnesse, that what 3 men afore were able with them to performe, now 6 men, with their best strength and uttermost endeavour, were hardly able to accomplish: whereby a sudden and great discouragement seased upon the mindes of our men, and they were possessed with a great mislike and doubting of any good to be done that way; yet would not our General be discouraged, but as wel by comfortable speeches, of the divine providence, and of God's loving care over his children, out of the Scriptures, as also by other good and profitable perswasions, adding thereto his own cheerfull example, he so stirred them up to put on a good courage, and to quite themselves like men, to indure some short extremity to have the speedier comfort, and a little trouble to obtaine the greater glory, that every man was throughly armed with willingnesse and resolved to see the uttermost, if it were possible, of what good was to be done that way.

The land in that part of America, bearing farther out into the West then we before imagined, we were neerer on it than wee were aware; and yet the neerer still wee came unto it, the more extremitie of cold did sease upon us. The 5 day of June wee were forced by contrary windes to runne in with the shoare, which we then first descried, and to cast anchor in a bad bay, the best roade we could for the present meete with, where wee were not without some danger by reason of the many extreme gusts and flawes that beate upon us, which if they ceased and were still at any time, immediately upon their intermission there followed most vile, thicke, and stinking fogges, against which the sea prevailed nothing, till the gusts of wind againe removed them, which brought with them such extremity and violence when they came, that there was no dealing or resisting against them.

In this place was no abiding for us; and to go further North, the extremity of the cold (which had now utterly discouraged our men) would not permit us; and the winds directly bent against us, having once gotten us under sayle againe, commanded us to the Southward whether we would or no.

From the height of 48 deg., in which now we were, to 38, we found the land, by coasting alongst it, to bee but low and reasonable plaine; every hill (whereof we saw many, but none verie high), though it were in June, and the sunne in his neerest approch unto them, being covered with snow.

In 38 deg. 30 min. we fell with a convenient and fit harborough,[1] and June 17 came to anchor therein, where we continued till the 23 day of July following. During all which time, notwithstanding it was in the height of summer, and so neere the sunne, yet were wee continually visited with like nipping colds as we had felt before; insomuch that if violent exercises of our bodies, and busie employment about our necessarie labours, had not sometimes compeld us to the contrary, we could very well have been contented to have kept about us still our winter clothes; yea (had our necessities suffered us) to

[1] Professor George Davidson, of the United States Coast and Geodetic Survey, after a careful study of the *Narrative* and the coast (*Voyages of Discovery and Exploration on the Northwest Coast of America from 1539 to 1603*, Washington, Government Printing-office, 1887, pp. 214–218), identifies the harbor entered by Drake with Drake's Bay, under Point Reyes, about thirty miles north of San Francisco. "Drake's Bay," he says, "is a capital harbor in northwest winds, such as Drake encountered. It is easily entered, sheltered by high lands, and a vessel may anchor in three fathoms close under the shore in good holding ground. . . . If he had been inside the Estero Limantour, of which he could not have detected the entrance from his vessel, he would necessarily have been very close to either shore. And had he seen it, he would not have dared to enter it without sounding it out. It has only thirteen feet of water on the bar at the highest tides, and he would not have hazarded his vessel in entering such a doubtful anchorage. Nor would he have risked the possibility of attack from the Indians in such a contracted place. He doubtless anchored in Drake's Bay, and the reef in his plan represents in a crude manner the reef of the easternmost point of Point Reyes Head. In a rough sketch of his anchorage it is called Portus Novae Albionis." On the other hand Edward Everett Hale, in his "Critical Essay on Drake's Bay," in Winsor's *Narrative and Critical History of America*, III. 74–78, identifies the "convenient and fit harbor," which Drake entered, with San Francisco Bay. The consensus of opinion among scholars on the Pacific coast at the present time, however, is said to be in favor of Drake's Bay, and such is also the view expressed by Mr. Corbett in his *Drake and the Tudor Navy*.

have kept our beds; neither could we at any time, in whole fourteene dayes together, find the aire so cleare as to be able to take the height of sunne or starre.

And here, having so fit occasion (notwithstanding it may seeme to be besides the purpose of writing the history of this our voyage), we will a little more diligently inquire into the causes of the continuance of the extreame cold in these parts, as also into the probabilities or unlikelihoods of a passage to be found that way. Neither was it (as hath formerly beene touched) the tendernesse of our bodies, comming so lately out of the heate, whereby the poores were opened, that made us so sensible of the colds we here felt: in this respect, as in many others, we found our God a provident Father and carefull Physitian for us. We lacked no outward helpes nor inward comforts to restore and fortifie nature, had it beene decayed or weakened in us; neither was there wanting to us the great experience of our Generall, who had often himselfe proved the force of the burning Zone, whose advice alwayes prevailed much to the preserving of a moderate temper in our constitutions; so that even after our departure from the heate wee alwayes found our bodies, not as sponges, but strong and hardned, more able to beare out cold, though we came out of excesse of heate, then a number of chamber champions could have beene, who lye on their feather beds till they go to sea, or rather, whose teeth in a temperate aire do beate in their heads at a cup of cold sack and sugar by the fire.

And that it was not our tendernes, but the very extremitie of the cold itselfe that caused this sensiblenes in us, may the rather appeare, in that the naturall inhabitants of the place (with whom we had for a long season familiar intercourse, as is to be related), who had never beene acquainted with such heate, to whom the countrey, ayre, and climate was proper, and in whom custome of cold was as it were a second nature; yet used to come shivering to us in their warme furres, crowding close together, body to body, to receive heate one of another, and sheltring themselves under a lee bancke, if it were possible, and as often as they could labouring to shroude themselves under our garments also to keepe them warme. Besides, how unhandsome and deformed appeared the face of the earth it selfe! shewing trees without leaves, and the ground without greennes in those moneths of June and July. The poore birds and foules not daring (as we had great experience to observe it), not daring so much as once to arise from their nests after the first egge layed, till it, with all the rest, be hatched and brought to some strength of nature, able to helpe itselfe. Onely this recompence hath nature affoorded them, that the heate of their owne bodies being exceeding great, it perfecteth the creature with greater expedition, and in shorter time then is to be found in many places.

As for the causes of this extremity, they seeme not to be so deeply hidden but that they may, at least in part, be guessed at. The chiefest of which we conceive to be the large spreading of the Asian and American continent, which (somewhat Northward of these parts), if they be not fully joined, yet seeme they to come very neere one to the other. From whose high and snow-covered mountaines, the North and North-west winds (the constant visitants of those coasts) send abroad their frozen nimphes, to the infecting the whole aire with this insufferable sharpnesse: not permitting the Sunne, no, not in the pride of his heate, to dissolve that congealed matter and snow, which they have breathed out so nigh the Sunne, and so many degrees distant from themselves. And that the North and North-west winds are here constant in June and July, as the North wind alone is in August and September, we not onely found it by our owne experience, but were fully confirmed in the opinion thereof, by the continued observations of the Spaniards. Hence comes the generall squalidnesse and barrennesse of the countrie; hence comes it, that in the middest of their summer, the snow hardly departeth even from their very doores, but is never taken away from their hils at all; hence come those thicke mists and most stinking fogges, which increase so much the more, by how much higher the pole is raised: wherein a blind pilot is as good as the best director of a course. For the Sunne striving to perform his naturall office, in elevating the vapors out of these inferior bodies, draweth necessarily abundance of moisture out of the sea; but the nipping cold (from the former causes) meeting and opposing the sunnes indevour, forces him to give over his worke imperfect; and instead of higher elevation, to leave in the lowest region, wandring upon the face of the earth and waters as it were a second sea, through which its owne beames cannot possibly pierce, unlesse sometimes when the sudden violence of the winds doth helpe to scatter and breake through it; which thing happeneth very seldome, and when it happeneth is of no continuance. Some of our mariners in this voyage had formerely beene at Wardhouse,[1] in 72 deg. of North latitude, who yet affirmed that they felt no such nipping cold there in the end of the summer, when they departed thence, as they did here in those hottest moneths of June and July.[2]

And also from these reasons we conjecture, that either there is no passage at all through these Northerne coasts (which is most likely), or if there be, that yet it is unnavigable. Adde hereunto, that though we searched the coast diligently, even unto the 48 deg., yet found we not the land to trend so much as one point in any place towards the East, but rather running on continually North-west, as if it went directly to meet with Asia; and even in that height, when we had a franke winde to have carried us through, had there beene a passage, yet we had a smoothe and calme sea, with ordinary flowing and reflowing, which could not have beene had there beene a frete;[3] of which we rather infallibly concluded, then conjectured, that there was none. But to returne.

The next day, after our comming to anchor in the aforesaid harbour, the people of the countrey shewed themselves, send-

---

[1] Vardöhuus, in northern Norway.

[2] It was the unfavorable season for a visit to that part of the coast. The winters there are warm and the summers cool. Great changes occur in the temperature within twenty-four hours, the mercury varying from twenty to thirty degrees. Especially are the nights cool. For eight months in the year the wind pours in from the sea toward noon, and increases in chilliness till late at night. Heavy fogs occur during June, July, and August.

[3] Strait; Lat., *fretum*.

ing off a man with great expedition to us in a canow. Who being yet but a little from the shoare, and a great way from our ship, spake to us continually as he came rowing on. And at last at a reasonable distance staying himselfe, he began more solemnely a long and tedious oration, after his manner: using in the deliverie thereof many gestures and signes, moving his hands, turning his head and body many wayes; and after his oration ended, with great shew of reverence and submission returned backe to shoare againe. He shortly came againe the second time in like manner, and so the third time, when he brought with him (as a present from the rest) a bunch of feathers, much like the feathers of a blacke crow, very neatly and artificially gathered upon a string, and drawne together into a round bundle; being verie cleane and finely cut, and bearing in length an equall proportion one with another; a speciall cognizance (as wee afterwards observed) which they that guard their kings person weare on their heads. With this also he brought a little basket made of rushes, and filled with an herbe which they called *Tabâh*.[1] Both which being tyed to a short rodde, he cast into our boate. Our Generall intended to have recompenced him immediatly with many good things he would have bestowed on him; but entring into the boate to deliver the same, he could not be drawne to receive them by any meanes, save one hat, which being cast into the water out of the ship, he tooke up (refusing utterly to meddle with any other thing, though it were upon a board put off unto him) and so presently made his returne. After which time our boate could row no way, but wondring at us as at gods, they would follow the same with admiration.

The 3 day following, viz., the 21, our ship having received a leake at sea, was brought to anchor neerer the shoare, that, her goods being landed, she might be repaired; but for that we were to prevent any danger that might chance against our

---

[1] Possibly tobacco. That Drake and his men should not have recognized it as something known to them is not strange, as tobacco seems not to have been known in England until introduced by Ralph Lane and his colonists on their return from Roanoke Island in 1586.

safety, our Generall first of all landed his men, with all necessary provision, to build tents and make a fort for the defence of our selves and goods: and that wee might under the shelter of it with more safety (what ever should befall) end our businesse; which when the people of the countrey perceived us doing, as men set on fire to war in defence of their countrie, in great hast and companies, with such weapons as they had, they came downe unto us, and yet with no hostile meaning or intent to hurt us: standing, when they drew neere, as men ravished in their mindes, with the sight of such things as they never had seene or heard of before that time: their errand being rather with submission and feare to worship us as Gods, then to have any warre with us as with mortall men. Which thing, as it did partly shew itselfe at that instant, so did it more and more manifest itself afterwards, during the whole time of our abode amongst them. At this time, being willed by signes to lay from them their bowes and arrowes, they did as they were directed, and so did all the rest, as they came more and more by companies unto them, growing in a little while to a great number, both of men and women.

To the intent, therefore, that this peace which they themselves so willingly sought might, without any cause of the breach thereof on our part given, be continued, and that wee might with more safety and expedition end our businesses in quiet, our Generall, with all his company, used all meanes possible gently to intreate them, bestowing upon each of them liberally good and necessary things to cover their nakednesse; withall signifying unto them we were no Gods, but men, and had neede of such things to cover our owne shame; teaching them to use them to the same ends, for which cause also wee did eate and drinke in their presence, giving them to understand that without that wee could not live, and therefore were but men as well as they.

Notwithstanding nothing could perswade them, nor remove that opinion which they had conceived of us, that wee should be Gods.

In recompence of those things which they had received of

us, as shirts, linnen cloth, etc., they bestowed upon our Generall, and diverse of our company, diverse things, as feathers, cawles of networke, the quivers of their arrowes, made of fawne skins, and the very skins of beasts that their women wore upon their bodies. Having thus had their fill of this times visiting and beholding of us, they departed with joy to their houses, which houses are digged round within the earth, and have from the uppermost brimmes of the circle clefts of wood set up, and joined close together at the top, like our spires on the steeple of a Church; which being covered with earth, suffer no water to enter, and are very warme; the doore in the most part of them performes the office also of a chimney to let out the smoake: its made in bignesse and fashion like to an ordinary scuttle in a ship, and standing slopewise: their beds are the hard ground, onely with rushes strewed upon it, and lying round about the house, have their fire in the middest, which by reason that the house is but low vaulted, round, and close, giveth a marvelous reflexion to their bodies to heate the same.

Their men for the most part goe naked; the women take a kinde of bulrushes, and kembing it after the manner of hemp, make themselves thereof a loose garment, which being knitte about their middles, hanges downe about their hippes, and so affordes to them a covering of that which nature teaches should be hidden; about their shoulders they weare also the skin of a deere, with the haire upon it. They are very obedient to their husbands, and exceeding ready in all services; yet of themselves offring to do nothing, without the consents or being called of the men.

As soone as they were returned to their houses, they began amongst themselves a kind of most lamentable weeping and crying out; which they continued also a great while together, in such sort that in the place where they left us (being neere about 3 quarters of an English mile distant from them) we very plainely, with wonder and admiration, did heare the same, the women especially extending their voices in a most miserable and dolefull manner of shreeking.

Notwithstanding this humble manner of presenting them-

M

selves, and awfull demeanour used towards us, we thought it no wisedome too farre to trust them (our experience of former Infidels dealing with us before, made us carefull to provide against an alteration of their affections or breach of peace if it should happen), and therefore with all expedition we set up our tents, and intrenched ourselves with walls of stone; that so being fortified within ourselves, we might be able to keepe off the enemie (if they should so prove) from comming amongst us without our good wills: this being quickly finished, we went the more cheerefully and securely afterward about our other businesse.

Against the end of two daies (during which time they had not againe beene with us), there was gathered together a great assembly of men, women, and children (invited by the report of them which first saw us, who, as it seems, had in that time of purpose dispersed themselves into the country, to make knowne the newes), who came now the second time unto us, bringing with them, as before had beene done, feathers and bagges of *Tobàh* for presents, or rather indeed for sacrifices, upon this perswasion that we were gods.

When they came to the top of the hill, at the bottom whereof wee had built our fort, they made a stand; where one (appointed as their chiefe speaker) wearied both us his hearers, and himselfe too, with a long and tedious oration; delivered with strange and violent gestures, his voice being extended to the uttermost strength of nature, and his wordes falling so thicke one in the necke of another, that he could hardly fetch his breath againe: as soone as he had concluded, all the rest, with a reverend bowing of their bodies (in a dreaming manner, and long producing of the same) cryed *Oh:* thereby giving their consents that all was very true which he had spoken, and that they had uttered their minde by his mouth unto us; which done, the men laying downe their bowes upon the hill, and leaving their women and children behinde them, came downe with their presents; in such sort as if they had appeared before a God indeed, thinking themselves happy that they might have access unto our Generall, but much more happy when they sawe that he would receive at their hands those things which they so willingly had presented: and no doubt they thought themselves neerest unto God when they sate or stood next to him. In the meane time the women, as if they had beene desperate, used unnatural violence against themselves, crying and shrieking piteously, tearing their flesh with their nailes from their cheekes in a monstrous manner, the blood streaming downe along their brests, besides despoiling the upper parts of their bodies of those single coverings they formerly had, and holding their hands above their heads that they might not rescue their brests from harme, they would with furie cast themselves upon the ground, never respecting whether it were cleane or soft, but dashed themselves in this manner on hard stones, knobby hillocks, stocks of wood, and pricking bushes, or whatever else lay in their way, itterating the same course againe and againe, yea women great with child, some nine or ten times each, and others holding out till 15 or 16 times (till their strengths failed them) exercised this cruelty against themselves: a thing more grievous for us to see or suffer, could we have holpe it, then trouble to them (as it seemed) to do it. This bloudie sacrifice (against our wils) beeing thus performed, our Generall, with his companie, in the presence of those strangers, fell to prayers; and by signes in lifting up our eyes and hands to heaven, signified unto them that that God whom we did serve, and whom they ought to worship, was above: beseeching God, if it were his good pleasure, to open by some meanes their blinded eyes, that they might in due time be called to the knowledge of him, the true and everliving God, and of Jesus Christ whom he hath sent, the salvation of the Gentiles. In the time of which prayers, singing of Psalmes, and reading of certaine Chapters in the Bible, they sate very attentively: and observing the end at every pause, with one voice still cried, Oh, greatly rejoycing in our exercises. Yea they tooke such pleasure in our singing of Psalmes, that whensoever they resorted to us, their first request was commonly this, *Gnaáh*, by which they intreated that we would sing.

Our Generall having now bestowed upon them divers things, at their departure they restored them all againe, none carrying with him anything of whatsoever hee had received, thinking themselves sufficiently enriched and happie that they had found so free accesse to see us.

Against the end of three daies more (the newes having the while spread itselfe farther, and as it seemed a great way up into the countrie), were assembled the greatest number of people which wee could reasonably imagine to dwell within any convenient distance round about. Amongst the rest the king himselfe, a man of a goodly stature and comely personage, attended with his guard of about 100 tall and warlike men, this day, viz., June 26, came downe to see us.

Before his comming, were sent two embassadors or messengers to our Generall, to signifie that their *Hióh*, that is, their king, was comming and at hand. They in the delivery of their message, the one spake with a soft and low voice, prompting his fellow; the other pronounced the same, word by word, after him with a voice more audible, continuing their proclamation (for such it was) about halfe an houre. Which being ended, they by signes made request to our Generall, to send something by their hands to their *Hióh* or king, as a token that his comming might be in peace. Our Generall willingly satisfied their desire; and they, glad men, made speedy returne to their *Hióh*. Neither was it long before their king (making as princely a shew as possibly he could) with all his traine came forward.

In their comming forwards they cryed continually after a singing manner, with a lustie courage. And as they drew neerer and neerer towards us, so did they more and more strive to behave themselves with a certaine comelinesse and gravity in all their actions.

In the forefront came a man of a large body and goodly aspect, bearing the Septer or royall mace, made of a certaine kind of blacke wood, and in length about a yard and a halfe, before the king. Whereupon hanged two crownes, a bigger and a lesse, with three chaines of a marvellous length, and often doubled, besides a bagge of the herbe *Tabâh*. The crownes were made of knitworke, wrought upon most curiously with feathers of divers colours, very artificially placed, and of a formall fashion. The chaines seemed of a bony substance, every linke or part thereof being very little, thinne, most finely burnished, with a hole pierced through the middest. The number of linkes going to make one chaine, is in a manner infinite; but of such estimation it is amongst them, that few be the persons that are admitted to weare the same; and even they to whom its lawfull to use them, yet are stinted what number they shall use, as some ten, some twelve, some twentie, and as they exceed in number of chaines, so thereby are they knowne to be the more honorable personages.

Next unto him that bare this Scepter, was the king himselfe with his guard about him; his attire upon his head was a cawle of knitworke, wrought upon somewhat like the crownes, but differing much both in fashion and perfectnesse of worke; upon his shoulders he had on a coate of the skins of conies, reaching to his wast; his guard also had each coats of the same shape, but of other skins; some having cawles likewise stucke with feathers, or covered over with a certaine downe, which groweth up in the countrey upon an herbe much like our lectuce, which exceeds any other downe in the world for finenesse, and beeing layed upon their cawles, by no winds can be removed. Of such estimation is this herbe amongst them, that the downe thereof is not lawfull to be worne, but of such persons as are about the king (to whom also it is permitted to weare a plume of feathers on their heads, in signe of honour), and the seeds are not used but onely in sacrifice to their gods. After these, in their order, did follow the naked sort of common people, whose haire being long, was gathered into a bunch behind, in which stucke plumes of feathers; but in the forepart onely single feathers like hornes, every one pleasing himselfe in his owne device.

This one thing was observed to bee generall amongst them all, that every one had his face painted, some with white, some blacke, and some with other colours, every man also bringing in his hand one thing or other for a gift or present. Their traine or last part of their company consisted of women and children, each woman bearing against her breast a round basket or two, having within them divers things, as bagges of *Tobâh*, a roote which they call *Petâh*, whereof they make a kind of meale, and either bake it into bread, or eate it rawe; broyled fishes, like a pilchard; the seede and downe aforenamed, with such like.

Their baskets were made in fashion like a deep boale, and though the matter were rushes, or such other kind of stuffe, yet was it so cunningly handled, that the most part of them would hold water: about the brimmes they were hanged with peeces of the shels of pearles, and in some places with two or three linkes at a place, of the chaines forenamed: thereby signifying that they were vessels wholly dedicated to the onely use of the gods they worshipped; and besides this, they were wrought upon with the matted downe of red feathers, distinguished into divers workes and formes.

In the meane time, our Generall having assembled his men together (as forecasting the danger and worst that might fall out) prepared himselfe to stand upon sure ground, that wee might at all times be ready in our owne defence, if any thing should chance otherwise than was looked for or expected.

Wherefore every man being in a warlike readinesse, he marched within his fenced place, making against their approach a most warlike shew (as he did also at all other times of their resort), whereby if they had beene desperate enemies, they could not have chosen but have conceived terrour and fear, with discouragement to attempt anything against us, in beholding of the same.

When they were come somewhat neere unto us, trooping together, they gave us a common or generall salutation, observing in the meane time a generall silence. Whereupon, he who bare the Scepter before the king, being prompted by another whom the king assigned to that office, pronounced with an audible and manly voice what the other spake to him in secret, continuing, whether it were his oration or proclamation, at the least halfe an houre. At the close whereof there was a common *Amen*, in signe of approbation, given by every person: and the king himselfe, with the whole number of men and women (the little children onely remaining behind) came further downe the hill, and as they came set themselves againe in their former order.

And beeing now come to the foot of the hill and neere our fort, the Scepter bearer, with a composed countenance and stately carriage began a song, and answerable thereunto observed a kind of measures in a dance: whom the king with his guard and every other sort of person following, did in like manner sing and daunce, saving onely the women, who danced but kept silence. As they danced they still came on: and our Generall perceiving their plaine and simple meaning, gave order that they might freely enter without interruption within our bulwarke. Where, after they had entred, they yet continued their song and dance a reasonable time, their women also following them with their wassaile boales in their hands, their bodies bruised, their faces torne, their dugges, breasts, and other parts bespotted with bloud, trickling downe from the wounds, which with their nailes they had made before their comming.

After that they had satisfied, or rather tired themselves in this manner, they made signes to our Generall to have him sit down; unto whom both the king and divers others made severall orations, or rather, indeed, if wee had understood them, supplications, that hee would take the Province and kingdome into his hand, and become their king and patron: making signes that they would resigne unto him their right and title in the whole land, and become his vassals in themselves and their posterities: which that they might make us indeed beleeve that it was their true meaning and intent, the king himselfe, with all the rest, with one consent and with great reverence, joyfully singing a song, set the crowne upon his head, inriched his necke with all their chaines, and offering unto him many other things, honoured him by the name of *Hyóh*. Adding thereunto (as it might seeme) a song and dance of triumph; because they were not onely visited of the gods (for so they still judged us to be), but the great and chiefe God was now become their God, their king and patron, and themselves were become the onely happie and blessed people in the world.

These things being so freely offered, our Generall thought not meet to reject or refuse the same, both for that he would not give them any cause of mistrust or disliking of him (that being the onely place, wherein at this present, we were of necessitie inforced to seeke reliefe of many things), and chiefely for that he knew not to what good end God had brought this to passe, or what honour and profit it might bring to our countrie in time to come.

Wherefore, in the name and to the use of her most excellent majesty, he tooke the scepter, crowne, and dignity of the sayd countrie into his hand; wishing nothing more than that it had layen so fitly for her majesty to enjoy, as it was now her proper owne, and that the riches and treasures thereof[1] (wherewith in the upland countries it abounds) might with as great conveniency be transported, to the enriching of her kingdome here at home, as it is in plenty to be attained there; and especially that so tractable and loving a people as they shewed themselves to be, might have meanes to have manifested their most willing obedience the more unto her, and by her meanes, as a mother and nurse of the Church of *Christ*, might by the preaching of the Gospell, be brought to the right knowledge and obedience of the true and everliving God.

The ceremonies of this resigning and receiving of the kingdome being thus performed, the common sort, both of men and women, leaving the king and his guard about him, with our Generall, dispersed themselves among our people, taking a diligent view or survey of every man; and finding such as pleased their fancies (which commonly were the youngest of us), they presently enclosing them about offred their sacrifices unto them, crying out with lamentable shreekes and moanes, weep-

---

[1] Drake little even dreamed of the treasures of gold and silver in those upland countries, as well as in the beds of the streams flowing from the highlands.

ing and scratching and tearing their very flesh off their faces with their nailes; neither were it the women alone which did this, but even old men, roaring and crying out, were as violent as the women were.

We groaned in spirit to see the power of Sathan so farre prevaile in seducing these so harmlesse soules, and laboured by all meanes, both by shewing our great dislike, and when that served not, by violent withholding of their hands from that madnesse, directing them (by our eyes and hands lift up towards heaven) to the living God whom they ought to serve; but so mad were they upon their Idolatry, that forcible withholding them would not prevaile (for as soone as they could get liberty to their hands againe, they would be as violent as they were before) till such time, as they whom they worshipped were conveyed from them into the tents, whom yet as men besides themselves, they would with fury and outrage seeke to have againe.

After that time had a little qualified their madnes, they then began to shew and make knowne unto us their griefes and diseases which they carried about them; some of them having old aches, some shruncke sinewes, some old soares and canchred ulcers, some wounds more lately received, and the like; in most lamentable manner craving helpe and cure thereof from us; making signes, that if we did but blowe upon their griefes, or but touched the diseased places, they would be whole.

Their griefes we could not but take pitty on them, and to our power desire to helpe them: but that (if it pleased God to open their eyes) they might understand we were but men and no gods, we used ordinary meanes, as lotions, emplaisters, and unguents, most fitly (as farre as our skills could guesse) agreeing to the natures of their griefes, beseeching God, if it made for his glory, to give cure to their diseases by these meanes. The like we did from time to time as they resorted to us.

Few were the dayes, wherein they were absent from us, during the whole time of our abode in that place; and ordinarily every third day they brought their sacrifices, till such time as they certainely understood our meaning, that we tooke no pleasure, but were displeased with them; whereupon their zeale abated, and their sacrificing, for a season, to our good liking ceased; notwithstanding they continued still to make their resort unto us in great abundance, and in such sort, that they oft-time forgate to provide meate for their owne sustenance; so that our Generall (of whom they made account as of a father) was faine to performe the office of a father to them, relieving them with such victualls as we had provided for our selves, as Muscles, Seales, and such like, wherein they tooke exceeding much content; and seeing that their sacrifices were displeasing to us, yet (hating ingratitude) they sought to recompence us with such things as they had, which they willingly inforced upon us, though it were never so necessarie or needfull for themselves to keepe.

They are a people of a tractable, free, and loving nature, without guile or treachery; their bowes and arrowes (their only weapons, and almost all their wealth) they use very skillfully, but yet not to do any great harme with them, being by reason of their weaknesse more fit for children then for men, sending the arrowes neither farre off nor with any great force: and yet are the men commonly so strong of body, that that which 2 or 3 of our men could hardly beare, one of them would take upon his backe, and without grudging carrie it easily away, up hill and downe hill an English mile together: they are also exceeding swift in running, and of long continuance, the use whereof is so familiar with them, that they seldome goe, but for the most part runne. One thing we observed in them with admiration, that if at any time they chanced to see a fish so neere the shoare that they might reach the place without swimming, they would never, or very seldome, misse to take it.

After that our necessary businesses were well dispatched, our Generall, with his gentlemen and many of his company, made a journy up into the land, to see the manner of their dwelling, and to be the better acquainted with the nature and commodities of the country. There houses were all such as we have formerly described, and being many of them in one place, made severall villages here and there. The inland we found to be farre different from the shoare, a goodly country, and fruitfull soyle, stored with many blessings fit for the use of man: infinite was the company of very large and fat Deere which there we sawe by thousands, as we supposed, in a heard; besides a multitude of a strange kinde of Conies, by farre exceeding them in number: their heads and bodies, in which they resemble other Conies, are but small; his tayle, like the tayle of a Rat, exceeding long; and his feet like the pawes of a Want or moale; under his chinne, on either side, he hath a bagge, into which he gathereth his meate, when he hath filled his belly abroade, that he may with it, either feed his young, or feed himselfe when he lists not to travaile from his burrough; the people eate their bodies, and make great account of their skinnes, for their kings holidaies coate was made of them.

This country our Generall named *Albion*, and that for two causes; the one in respect of the white bancks and cliffes, which lie toward the sea; the other, that it might have some affinity, even in name also, with our own country, which was sometimes so called.

Before we went from thence, our Generall caused to be set up a monument[1] of our being there, as also of her majesties and successors right and title to that kingdome; namely, a plate of brasse, fast nailed to a great and firme poste; whereon is engraven her graces name, and the day and yeare of our arrivall there, and of the free giving up of the province and kingdome, both by the king and people, into her majesties hands: together with her highnesse picture and armes, in a piece of sixpence currant English monie, shewing itselfe by a hole made of purpose through the plate; underneath was likewise engraven the name of our Generall, etc.

[1] In giving a name to the country, and in setting up a monument in token of discovery, Drake laid the foundation of a claim to English sovereignty.

The Spaniards never had any dealing, or so much as set a foote in this country, the utmost of their discoveries reaching onely to many degrees Southward of this place.

And now, as the time of our departure was perceived by them to draw nigh, so did the sorrowes and miseries of this people seeme to themselves to increase upon them, and the more certaine they were of our going away, the more doubtful they shewed themselves what they might doe; so that we might easily judge that that joy (being exceeding great) wherewith they received us at our first arrivall, was cleane drowned in their excessive sorrow for our departing. For they did not onely loose on a sudden all mirth, joy, glad countenance, pleasant speeches, agility of body, familiar rejoycing one with another, and all pleasure what ever flesh and blood might bee delighted in, but with sighes and sorrowings, with heavy hearts and grieved minds, they powred out wofull complaints and moanes, with bitter teares and wringing of their hands, tormenting themselves. And as men refusing all comfort, they onely accounted themselves as cast-awayes, and those whom the gods were about to forsake: so that nothing we could say or do, was able to ease them of their so heavy a burthen, or to deliver them from so desperate a straite, as our leaving of them did seeme to them that it would cast them into.

Howbeit, seeing they could not still enjoy our presence, they (supposing us to be gods indeed) thought it their duties to intreate us that, being absent, we would yet be mindfull of them, and making signes of their desires that in time to come wee would see them againe, they stole upon us a sacrifice, and set it on fire erre we were aware, burning therein a chaine and a bunch of feathers. We laboured by all meanes possible to withhold or withdraw them, but could not prevaile, till at last we fell to prayers and singing of Psalmes, whereby they were allured immediatly to forget their folly, and leave their sacrifice unconsumed, suffering the fire to go out; and imitating us in all our actions, they fell a lifting of their eyes and hands to heaven, as they saw us do.

The 23 of July they tooke a sorrowfull farewell of us, but being loath to leave us, they presently ranne to the top of the hils to keepe us in their sight as long as they could, making fires before and behind, and on each side of them, burning therein (as is to be supposed) sacrifices at our departure.

A REPORT OF THE VOYAGE OF SIR HUMFREY GILBERT, KNIGHT, 1583, BY MASTER EDWARD HAIES

INTRODUCTION

HUMPHREY GILBERT, a son of Sir Otho Gilbert, and a half-brother of Sir Walter Ralegh, studied at Eton and Oxford, and in his youth was a servitor of Queen Elizabeth, whose favor he won, and retained throughout his career. Entering the military service at an early age, he served as a captain in Ireland under Sir Henry Sidney in 1566, and in 1569 he was made governor of Munster. For his services in Ireland he was knighted in 1570. In 1571 he entered Parliament, and in the following year he was in the Netherlands fighting against Spain. For a long time he had been interested in western discovery. As early as 1566 he petitioned Queen Elizabeth for permission to seek a northwest passage to the Indies, and wrote a tract, *A Discourse of Discovery for a new Passage to Cataia*, which was published ten years afterward. From time to time he appealed to the queen for service in exploration, and on June 11, 1578, she responded by bestowing upon him a royal patent which gave him authority to discover and possess lands in America, with the proviso, however, that there should be no robbery "by sea or by land." Preparation for an expedition, in which Ralegh was associated with him, was at once made. With a fleet of seven ships, Gilbert left England in November; but he soon met with disaster, and returned, Ralegh's vessel being the last to reach England.

Gilbert's ardor for discovery, however, was not lessened by ill success. He at once began to make preparations for another voyage, and on June 11, 1583, with only one year remaining before his patent would expire, he left England with five vessels and two hundred and sixty men. The expedition proved a failure, and Gilbert, on the return voyage, perished in the foundering of his vessel in a storm. This was another sad blow to a great undertaking. Gilbert has the honor, however, of having been the first leader of an English expedition "that caried people to erect an habitation and government in these Northerly countreys of America." The writer of the story of the expedition, Mr. Edward Hayes, was the author of *A Treatise . . . conteining important inducements for the planting of these parts and finding a passage that way to the South sea and China*, which was annexed to the second edition of Brereton's *Briefe and true Relation*, published in 1602. Hayes's narrative has been reprinted in the Prince Society's volume entitled *Sir Humphrey Gylberte*. The volume also contains a memoir of Gilbert by Rev. Carlos Slafter.

H. S. B.

VOYAGE OF SIR HUMFREY GILBERT KNIGHT, 1583

A report of the voyage and successe thereof, attempted in the yeere of our Lord 1583 by sir Humfrey Gilbert knight, with other gentlemen assisting him in that action, intended to discover and to plant Christian inhabitants in place convenient, upon those large and ample countreys extended Northward from the cape of Florida, lying under very temperate Climes, esteemed fertile and rich in Minerals, yet not in the actuall possession of any Christian prince, written by M. Edward Haies gentleman, and principall actour in the same voyage, who alone continued unto the end, and by Gods speciall assistance returned home with his retinue safe and entire.

MANY voyages have bene pretended, yet hitherto never any thorowly accomplished by our nation of exact discovery into the bowels of those maine, ample and vast countreys, extended infinitely into the North from 30 degrees, or rather from 25 degrees of Septentrionall latitude, neither hath a right way bene taken of planting a Christian habitation and regiment upon the same, as well may appeare both by the little we yet do actually possesse therein, and by our ignorance of the riches and secrets within those lands, which unto this day we know chiefly by the travell and report of other nations, and most of the French, who albeit they can not challenge such right and interest unto the sayd countreys as we, neither these many yeeres have had opportunity nor meanes so great to discover and to plant (being vexed with the calamnities of intestine warres) as we have had by the inestimable benefit of our long and happy peace: yet have they both waies performed more, and had long since attained a sure possession and setled government of many provinces in those Northerly parts of America, if their many attempts into those forren and remote lands had not bene impeached by their garboils at home.

The first discovery of these coasts (never heard of before) was well begun by John Cabot the father, and Sebastian his sonne, an Englishman borne, who were the first finders out of all that great tract of land stretching from the cape of Florida unto those Islands which we now call the Newfoundland: all which they brought and annexed unto the crowne of England.[1] Since when, if with like diligence the search of inland countreys had bene followed, as the discovery upon the coast, and out-parts therof was performed by those two men: no doubt her Majesties territories and revenue had bene mightily inlarged and advanced by this day. And which is more: the seed of Christian religion had bene sowed amongst those pagans, which by this time might have brought foorth a most plentifull harvest and copious congregation of Christians; which must be the chiefe intent of such as shall make any attempt that way: or els whatsoever is builded upon other foundation shall never obtaine happy successe nor continuance.

And although we can not precisely judge (which onely belongeth to God) what have bene the humours of men stirred up to great attempts of discovering and planting in those remote countreys, yet the events do shew that either Gods cause hath not bene chiefly preferred by them, or els God hath not permitted so abundant grace as the light of his word and

[1] It is thought that John Cabot, in the interest of Bristol merchants, may have been engaged in voyages to the American coast as early as 1491. In 1495 he presented a petition to Henry VII., requesting permission for himself and his three sons to discover and possess new lands in the New World. The patent was granted on March 5, 1496, and on May 2, 1497, Cabot, accompanied by his son Sebastian, sailed from Bristol. In this voyage, Cabot discovered land on the coast of Labrador, and after some exploration of the coast he returned to England with the news of his discovery. Sebastian Cabot accompanied his father to the American coast in the voyage of 1498. After a period of service under the English crown he entered the service of Spain. Subsequent to the death of Henry VIII. (January 25, 1547), he returned to England, where he remained until his death.

knowledge of him to be yet revealed unto those infidels before the appointed time.

But most assuredly, the only cause of religion hitherto hath kept backe, and will also bring forward at the time assigned by God, an effectuall and compleat discovery and possession by Christians both of those ample countreys and the riches within them hitherto concealed: whereof notwithstanding God in his wisdome hath permitted to be revealed from time to time a certaine obscure and misty knowledge, by little and little to allure the mindes of men that way (which els will be dull enough in the zeale of his cause) and thereby to prepare us unto a readinesse for the execution of his will against the due time ordeined, of calling those pagans unto Christianity.

In the meane while, it behooveth every man of great calling, in whom is any instinct of inclination unto this attempt, to examine his owne motions: which if the same proceed of ambition or avarice, he may assure himselfe it commeth not of God, and therefore can not have confidence of Gods protection and assistance against the violence (els irresistable) both of sea, and infinite perils upon the land; whom God yet may use an instrument to further his cause and glory some way, but not to build upon so bad a foundation.

Otherwise, if his motives be derived from a vertuous and heroycall minde, preferring chiefly the honour of God, compassion of poore infidels captived by the devill, tyrannizing in most woonderfull and dreadfull maner over their bodies and soules; advancement of his honest and well disposed countreymen, willing to accompany him in such honourable actions: reliefe of sundry people within this realme distressed: all these be honourable purposes, imitating the nature of the munificent God, wherwith he is well pleased, who will assist such an actour beyond expectation of man. And the same, who feeleth this inclination in himselfe, by all likelihood may hope, or rather confidently repose in the preordinance of God, that in this last age of the world (or likely never) the time is compleat of receiving also these Gentiles into his mercy, and that God will raise him an instrument to effect the same: it seeming prob-

able by event of precedent attempts made by the Spanyards
and French sundry times, that the countreys lying North of
Florida, God hath reserved the same to be reduced unto Christian civility by the English nation. For not long after that
Christopher Columbus had discovered the Islands and continent
of the West Indies for Spaine, John and Sebastian Cabot made
discovery also of the rest from Florida Northwards[1] to the
behoofe of England.

And whensoever afterwards the Spanyards (very prosperous
in all their Southerne discoveries) did attempt any thing into
Florida and those regions inclining towards the North they
proved most unhappy, and were at length discouraged utterly
by the hard and lamentable successe of many both religious
and valiant in armes, endevouring to bring those Northerly
regions also under the Spanish jurisdiction; as if God had prescribed limits unto the Spanish nation which they might not
exceed; as by their owne gests recorded may be aptly gathered.

The French, as they can pretend lesse title unto these
Northerne parts then the Spanyard, by how much the Spanyard made the first discovery of the same continent so far
Northward as unto Florida, and the French did but review
that before discovered by the English nation, usurping upon
our right, and imposing names upon countreys, rivers, bayes,
capes, or head lands, as if they had bene the first finders of those
coasts: which injury we offered not unto the Spanyards, but
left off to discover when we approached the Spanish limits:
even so God hath not hitherto permitted them to establish a
possession permanent upon anothers right, notwithstanding
their manifolde attempts, in which the issue hath bene no lesse
tragicall then that of the Spanyards, as by their owne reports
is extant.

Then seeing the English nation onely hath right unto these
countreys of America from the cape of Florida Northward by

[1] The extent of the discoveries of the Cabots is a matter of controversy.
John Cabot certainly did not reach the coast of the United States. Sebastian Cabot proceeded south as far as the latitude of the Strait of Gibraltar,
according to a statement made by him to Peter Martyr — that is, as far as
Cape Hatteras.

the privilege of first discovery, unto which Cabot was authorised by regall authority, and set forth by the expense of our late famous king Henry the seventh: which right also seemeth strongly defended on our behalfe by the powerfull hand of almighty God, withstanding the enterprises of other nations: it may greatly incourage us upon so just ground, as is our right, and upon so sacred an intent, as to plant religion (our right and intent being meet foundations for the same) to prosecute effectually the full possession of those so ample and pleasant countreys apperteining unto the crowne of England: the same (as is to be conjectured by infallible arguments of the worlds end approching) being now arrived unto the time by God prescribed of their vocation, if ever their calling unto the knowledge of God may be expected. Which also is very probable by the revolution and course of Gods word and religion, which from the beginning hath moved from the East, towards, and at last unto the West, where it is like to end, unlesse the same begin againe where it did in the East, which were to expect a like world againe. But we are assured of the contrary by the prophesie of Christ, whereby we gather, that after his word preached thorowout the world shalbe the end. And as the Gospel when it descended Westward began in the South, and afterward spread into the North of Europe: even so, as the same hath begunne in the South countreys of America, no lesse hope may be gathered that it will also spread into the North.

These considerations may helpe to suppresse all dreads rising of hard events in attempts made this way by other nations, as also of the heavy successe and issue in the late enterprise made by a worthy gentleman our countryman sir Humfrey Gilbert knight, who was the first of our nation that caried people to erect an habitation and government in those Northerly countreys of America. About which, albeit he had consumed much substance, and lost his life at last, his people also perishing for the most part: yet the mystery thereof we must leave unto God, and judge charitably both of the cause (which was just in all pretence) and of the person, who was very zealous in prosecuting the same, deserving honourable remembrance for his good minde, and expense of life in so vertuous an enterprise. Whereby neverthelesse, least any man should be dismayd by example of other folks calamity, and misdeeme that God doth resist all attempts intended that way: I thought good, so farre as my selfe was an eye witnesse, to deliver the circumstance and maner of our proceedings in that action: in which the gentleman was so incumbred with wants, and woorse matched with many ill disposed people, that his rare judgement and regiment premeditated for those affaires, was subjected to tolerate abuses, and in sundry extremities to holde on a course, more to upholde credite, then likely in his owne conceit happily to succeed.

The issue of such actions, being always miserable, not guided by God, who abhorreth confusion and disorder, hath left this for admonition (being the first attempt by our nation to plant) unto such as shall take the same cause in hand hereafter not to be discouraged from it: but to make men well advised how they handle his so high and excellent matters, as the cariage of his word into those very mighty and vast countreys. An action doubtlesse not to be intermedled with base purposes; as many have made the same but a colour to shadow actions otherwise scarse justifiable: which doth excite Gods heavy judgements in the end, to the terrifying of weake mindes from the cause, without pondering his just proceedings: and doth also incense forren princes against our attempts how just soever, who can not but deeme the sequele very dangerous unto their state (if in those parts we should grow to strength) seeing the very beginnings are entred with spoile.

And with this admonition denounced upon zeale towards Gods cause, also towards those in whom appeareth disposition honourable unto this action of planting Christian people and religion in those remote and barbarous nations of America (unto whom I wish all happinesse) I will now proceed to make relation briefly, yet particularly, of our voyage undertaken with sir Humfrey Gilbert, begun, continued, and ended adversly.

When first sir Humfrey Gilbert undertooke the Westerne discovery of America, and had procured from her Majesty a very large commission to inhabit and possesse at his choice all remote and heathen lands not in the actuall possession of any Christian prince, the same commission exemplified with many privileges, such as in his discretion he might demand, very many gentlemen of good estimation drew unto him, to associate him in so commendable an enterprise, so that the preparation was expected to grow unto a puissant fleet, able to encounter a kings power by sea: neverthelesse, amongst a multitude of voluntary men, their dispositions were divers, which bred a jarre, and made a division in the end, to the confusion of that attempt even before the same was begun. And when the shipping was in a maner prepared, and men ready upon the coast to go aboord: at that time some brake consort, and followed courses degenerating from the voyage before pretended: Others failed of their promises contracted, and the greater number were dispersed, leaving the Generall[1] with few of his assured friends, with whom he adventured to sea: where having tasted of no lesse misfortune, he was shortly driven to retire home with the losse of a tall ship, and (more to his griefe) of a valiant gentleman Miles Morgan.[2]

Having buried onely in a preparation a great masse of substance, wherby his estate was impaired, his minde yet not dismaid he continued his former designment and purpose to revive this enterprise, good occasion serving. Upon which determination standing long, without meanes to satisfy his desire; at last he granted certaine assignments out of his commission to sundry persons of meane ability, desiring the privilege of his grant, to plant and fortifie in the North parts of America about the river of Canada,[3] to whom if God gave good successe in the North parts (where then no matter of moment was expected) the same (he thought) would greatly

---

[1] At that time the designation of the head of an expedition.
[2] The reference is to Gilbert's first voyage in 1578. Queen Elizabeth's patent of that year to Gilbert is printed in Hakluyt, edition of 1903, VIII 17-23.   [3] The St. Lawrence.

advance the hope of the South, and be a furtherance unto his determination that way. And the worst that might happen in that course might be excused without prejudice unto him by the former supposition, that those North regions were of no regard: but chiefly a possession taken in any parcell of those heathen countreys, by vertue of his grant, did invest him of territories extending every way two hundred leagues: which induced sir Humfry Gilbert to make those assignments, desiring greatly their expedition, because his commission did expire after six yeres, if in that space he had not gotten actuall possession.

Time went away without any thing done by his assignes: insomuch that at last he must resolve himselfe to take a voyage in person, for more assurance to keepe his patent in force, which then almost was expired, or within two yeres.

In furtherance of his determination, amongst others, sir George Peckam [1] knight shewed himselfe very zealous to the action, greatly aiding him both by his advice and in the charge. Other gentlemen to their ability joyned unto him, resolving to adventure their substance and lives in the same cause. Who beginning their preparation from that time, both of shipping, munition, victual, men, and things requisit, some of them continued the charge two yeres compleat without intermission. Such were the difficulties and crosse accidents opposing these proceedings, which tooke not end in lesse then two yeres: many of which circumstances I will omit.

The last place of our assembly, before we left the coast of England, was in Causet [2] bay neere unto Plimmouth: then resolved to put unto the sea with shipping and provision, such as we had, before our store yet remaining, but chiefly the time and season of the yeere, were too farre spent. Neverthelesse it seemed first very doubtfull by what way to shape our course, and to begin our intended discovery, either from the South Northward, or from the North Southward.

---

[1] Author of *True Report of the Late Discoveries*, etc., published in 1583. He was Gilbert's "chiefe adventurer and furtherer." See Hakluyt, Hakluyt Society edition, IX. 88.   [2] Causand.

The first, that is, beginning South, without all controversie was the likeliest, wherein we were assured to have commodity of the current, which from the cape of Florida setteth Northward, and would have furthered greatly our navigation, discovering from the foresayd cape along towards cape Briton, and all those lands lying to the North.

Also the yere being farre spent, and arrived to the moneth of June, we were not to spend time in Northerly courses, where we should be surprised with timely Winter, but to covet the South, which we had space enough then to have attained: and there might with lesse detriment have wintred that season, being more milde and short in the South then in the North where winter is both long and rigorous.

These and other like reasons alleged in favour of the Southerne course first to be taken, to the contrary was inferred: that forasmuch as both our victuals, and many other needfull provisions were diminished and left insufficient for so long a voyage, and for the wintering of so many men, we ought to shape a course most likely to minister supply; and that was to take the Newfoundland in our way, which was but seven hundred leagues from our English coast. Where being usually at that time of the yere, and untill the fine[1] of August, a multitude of ships repairing thither for fish,[2] we should be relieved abundantly with many necessaries, which after the fishing ended, they might well spare, and freely impart unto us.

Not staying long upon that Newland coast, we might proceed Southward, and follow still the Sunne, untill we arrived at places more temperate to our content.

By which reasons we were the rather induced to follow this Northerly course, obeying unto necessity, which must be supplied. Otherwise, we doubted that sudden approch of Winter, bringing with it continuall fogge, and thicke mists, tempest and rage of weather; also contrariety of currents descending

[1] End.
[2] European fishing vessels were on the American coast in the neighborhood of Newfoundland at an early period. Their number rapidly increased in the sixteenth century

from the cape of Florida unto cape Briton and cape Rase, would fall out to be great and irresistable impediments unto our further proceeding for that yeere, and compell us to Winter in those North and colde regions.

Wherefore suppressing all objections to the contrary, we resolved to begin our course Northward, and to follow directly as we might, the trade way unto Newfoundland: from whence after our refreshing and reparation of wants, we intended without delay (by Gods permission) to proceed into the South, not omitting any river or bay which in all that large tract of land appeared to our view worthy of search. Immediatly we agreed upon the maner of our course and orders to be observed in our voyage; which were delivered in writing unto the captaines and masters of every ship a copy in maner following.

Every shippe had delivered two bullets or scrowles, the one sealed up in waxe, the other left open: in both which were included severall watch-words. That open, serving upon our owne coast or the coast of Ireland: the other sealed was promised on all hands not to be broken up untill we should be cleere of the Irish coast; which from thencefoorth did serve untill we arrived and met altogether in such harbors of the Newfoundland as were agreed for our Rendez vouz. The sayd watch-words being requisite to know our consorts whensoever by night, either by fortune of weather, our fleet dispersed should come together againe: or one should hale another; or if by ill watch and steerage one ship should chance to fall aboord of another in the darke.

The reason of the bullet sealed was to keepe secret that watch-word while we were upon our owne coast, lest any of the company stealing from the fleet might bewray the same: which knowen to an enemy, he might boord us by night without mistrust, having our owne watch-word.

Orders agreed upon by the Captaines and Masters to be observed by the fleet of Sir Humfrey Gilbert.

First the Admirall to cary his flag by day, and his light by night.

2 Item, if the Admirall shall shorten his saile by night, then to shew two lights untill he be answered againe by every ship shewing one light for a short time.

3 Item, if the Admirall after his shortening of saile, as aforesayd, shall make more saile againe: then he to shew three lights one above another.

4 Item, if the Admirall shall happen to hull in the night, then to make a wavering light over his other light, wavering the light upon a pole.

5 Item, if the fleet should happen to be scattered by weather, or other mishap, then so soone as one shall descry another to hoise both toppe sailes twise, if the weather will serve, and to strike them twise againe; but if the weather serve not, then to hoise the maine top saile twise, and forthwith to strike it twise againe.

6 Item, if it shall happen a great fogge to fall, then presently every shippe to beare up with the admirall, if there be winde: but if it be a calme, then every ship to hull, and so to lie at hull till it be cleere. And if the fogge do continue long, then the Admirall to shoot off two pieces every evening, and every ship to answere it with one shot: and every man bearing to the ship, that is to leeward so neere as he may.

7 Item, every master to give charge unto the watch to looke out well, for laying aboord one of another in the night, and in fogges.

8 Item, every evening every ship to haile the admirall, and so to fall asterne him, sailing thorow the Ocean: and being on the coast, every ship to haile him both morning and evening.

9 Item, if any ship be in danger any way, by leake or otherwise, then she to shoot off a piece, and presently to hang out one light, whereupon every man to beare towards her, answer-

ing her with one light for a short time, and so to put it out againe; thereby to give knowledge that they have seene her token.

10 Item, whensoever the Admirall shall hang out her ensigne in the maine shrowds, then every man to come aboord her, as a token of counsell.

11 Item, if there happen any storme or contrary winde to the fleet after the discovery, whereby they are separated: then every ship to repair unto their last good port, there to meete againe.

Our course agreed upon.

The course first to be taken for the discovery is to beare directly to Cape Rase, the most Southerly cape of Newfound land; and there to harbour ourselves either in Rogneux[1] or Fermous,[2] being the first places appointed for our Rendez vous, and the next harbours unto the Northward of cape Rase: and therefore every ship separated from the fleete to repaire to that place so fast as God shall permit, whether you shall fall to the Southward or to the Northward of it, and there to stay for the meeting of the whole fleet the space of ten dayes: and when you shall depart, to leave marks.

A direction of our course unto the Newfound land.

Beginning our course from Silley,[3] the neerest is by West-southwest (if the winde serve) untill such time as we have brought our selves in the latitude of 43 or 44 degrees, because the Ocean is subject much to Southerly windes in June and July. Then to take traverse from 45 to 47 degrees of latitude, if we be inforced by contrary windes: and not to go to the Northward of the height of 47 degrees of Septentrionall latitude by no meanes; if God shall not inforce the contrary; but to do

---
[1] Renewse.   [2] Fermeuse.
[3] The Scilly Islands, at the entrance of the English Channel.

your indevour to keepe in the height of 46 degrees, so nere as you can possibly, because cape Rase lieth about that height.

Notes.

If by contrary windes we be driven backe upon the coast of England, then to repaire unto Silley for a place of our assembly or meeting.

If we be driven backe by contrary winds that we can not passe the coast of Ireland, then the place of our assembly to be at Beare haven or Baltimore haven.[1]

If we shall not happen to meete at cape Rase, then the place of Rendez vous to be at cape Briton, or the neerest harbour unto the Westward of cape Briton.

If by meanes of other shipping we may not safely stay there, then to rest at the very next safe port to the Westward; every ship leaving their marks behinde them for the more certainty of the after commers to know where to finde them.

The marks that every man ought to leave in such a case, were of the Generals private device written by himselfe, sealed also in close waxe, and delivered unto every shippe one scroule, which was not to be opened untill occasion required, whereby every man was certified what to leave for instruction of after commers: that every of us comming into any harbour or river might know who had bene there, or whether any were still there up higher into the river, or departed, and which way.

Orders thus determined, and promises mutually given to be observed, every man withdrew himselfe unto his charge, the ankers being already weyed, and our shippes under saile, having a soft gale of winde, we began our voyage upon Tuesday the eleventh day of June, in the yere of our Lord 1583, having in our fleet (at our departure from Causet bay) these shippes, whose names and burthens, with the names of the captaines and masters of them, I have also inserted, as followeth:

[1] Southern extremity of Ireland.

1 The Delight aliâs The George, of burthen 120 tunnes, was Admirall: in which went the Generall, and William Winter [1] captaine in her and part owner, and Richard Clearke [2] master.

2 The Barke Raleigh set forth by M. Walter Raleigh, of the burthen of 200 tunnes, was then Vice-admirall: in which went M. Butler captaine, and Robert Davis of Bristoll master.

3 The Golden hinde, of burthen 40 tunnes, was then Reare-admirall: in which went Edward Hayes [3] captaine and owner, and William Cox [4] of Limehouse master.

4 The Swallow, of burthen 40 tunnes: in her was captaine Maurice Browne.[5]

5 The Squirrill, of burthen 10 tunnes: in which went captaine William Andrewes,[6] and one Cade master.

We were in number in all about 260 men: among whom we had of every faculty good choice, as Shipwrights, Masons, Carpenters, Smithes, and such like, requisite to such an action: also Minerall men and Refiners. Besides, for solace of our people, and allurement of the Savages, we were provided of Musike in good variety: not omitting the least toyes, as Morris dancers, Hobby horses, and Maylike conceits to delight the Savage people, whom we intended to winne by all faire meanes possible. And to that end we were indifferently furnished of all petty haberdasherie wares to barter with those people.

In this maner we set forward, departing (as hath bene said) out of Causon bay the eleventh day of June being Tuesday, the weather and winde faire and good all day, but a great storme of thunder and winde fell the same night.

Thursday following, when we hailed one another in the

[1] Winter returned to England, and Browne, captain of the *Swallow*, was made captain of the *Delight*.

[2] Author of *The Voyage for the discovery of Norembega*, 1583. He belonged in Weymouth. His own account of the loss of the *Delight* and his controversy with Gilbert is in Hakluyt, VIII. 85-88.

[3] Author of this narrative of the voyage.

[4] Hayes, the author of the "report," elsewhere designates William Cox and John Paul, his mate, as "expert men."

[5] Drowned when the *Delight* was wrecked at Cape Breton, August 29.

[6] Andrewes returned to England from Newfoundland.

evening (according to the order before specified) they signified unto us out of the Vizadmirall, that both the Captaine, and very many of the men were fallen sicke, And about midnight the Vizeadmirall forsooke us, notwithstanding we had the winde East, faire and good. But it was after credibly reported, that they were infected with a contagious sicknesse, and arrived greatly distressed at Plimmoth: the reason I could never understand. Sure I am, no cost was spared by their owner Master Raleigh in setting them forth: Therefore I leave it unto God.

By this time we were in 48 degrees of latitude, not a little grieved with the losse of the most puissant ship in our fleete: after whose departure, the Golden Hind succeeded in the place of Vizadmirall, and remooved her flagge from the mizon unto the foretop.

From Saturday the 15 of June untill the 28, which was upon a Friday, we never had faire day without fogge or raine, and windes bad, much to the West northwest, whereby we were driven Southward unto 41 degrees scarse.

About this time of the yere the winds are commonly West towards the Newfound land, keeping ordinarily within two points of West to the South or to the North, whereby the course thither falleth out to be long and tedious after June, which in March, Apriell and May, hath bene performed out of England in 22 dayes and lesse. We had winde always so scant from West northwest, and from West southwest againe, that our traverse was great, running South unto 41 degrees almost, and afterward North into 51 degrees.

Also we were incombred with much fogge and mists in maner palpable, in which we could not keepe so well together, but were dissevered, losing the company of the Swallow and the Squirrill upon the 20 day of July, whom we met againe at severall places upon the Newfound land coast the third of August, as shalbe declared in place convenient.

Saturday the 27 of July, we might descry not farre from us, as it were mountaines of yce driven upon the sea, being then in 50 degrees, which were caried Southward to the weather of

o

us: whereby may be conjectured that some current doth set that way from the North.

Before we come to Newfound land about 50 leagues on this side, we passe the banke,[1] which are high grounds rising within the sea and under water, yet deepe enough and without danger, being commonly not lesse then 25 and 30 fadome water upon them: the same (as it were some vaine of mountaines within the sea) doe runne along, and from the Newfound land, beginning Northward about 52 or 53 degrees of latitude, and do extend into the South infinitly. The bredth of this banke is somewhere more, and somewhere lesse: but we found the same about 10 leagues over, having sounded both on this side thereof, and the other toward Newfound land, but found no ground with almost 200 fadome of line, both before and after we had passed the banke. The Portugals, and French chiefly, have a notable trade of fishing upon this banke, where are sometimes an hundred or more sailes of ships: who commonly beginne the fishing in Apriell, and have ended by July. That fish is large, alwayes wet, having no land neere to drie, and is called Corre fish.

During the time of fishing, a man shall know without sounding when he is upon the banke, by the incredible multitude of sea foule hovering over the same, to prey upon the offalles and garbish of fish throwen out by fishermen, and floting upon the sea.

Upon Tuesday the 11 of June, we forsooke the coast of England. So againe Tuesday the 30 of July (seven weekes after) we got sight of land, being immediatly embayed in the Grand bay, or some other great bay: the certainty whereof we could not judge, so great hase and fogge did hang upon the coast, as neither we might discerne the land well, nor take the sunnes height. But by our best computation we were then in the 51 degrees of latitude.

Forsaking this bay and uncomfortable coast (nothing appearing unto us but hideous rockes and mountaines, bare of

---

[1] The only shallow part of the Atlantic. The bottom is rocky, and is generally reached at from twenty-five to ninety-five fathoms.

trees, and voide of any greene herbe) we followed the coast to the South, with weather faire and cleare.

We had sight of an Iland named Penguin,[1] of a foule there breeding in abundance, almost incredible, which cannot flie, their wings not able to carry their body, being very large (not much lesse then a goose) and exceeding fat: which the French men use to take without difficulty upon that Iland, and to barrell them up with salt. But for lingering of time we had made us there the like provision.

Trending this coast, we came to the Iland called Baccalaos,[2] being not past two leagues from the maine: to the South thereof lieth Cape S. Francis,[3] 5. leagues distant from Baccalaos, between which goeth in a great bay, by the vulgar sort called the bay of Conception. Here we met with the Swallow againe, whom we had lost in the fogge, and all her men altered into other apparell: wherof it seemed their store was so amended, that for joy and congratulation of our meeting, they spared not to cast up into the aire and overboord, their caps and hats in good plenty. The Captaine albeit himselfe was very honest and religious, yet was he not appointed of men to his humor and desert: who for the most part were such as had bene by us surprised upon the narrow seas of England, being pirats and had taken at that instant certaine Frenchmen laden, one barke with wines, and another with salt. Both which we rescued, and tooke the man of warre with all her men, which was the same ship now called the Swallow, following still their kind so oft, as (being separated from the Generall) they found opportunitie to robbe and spoile. And because Gods justice did follow the same company, even to destruction, and to the overthrow also of the Captaine (though not consenting to their misdemeanor) I will not conceale any thing that maketh to the manifestation and approbation of his judgements, for examples of others, perswaded that God more sharpely tooke

[1] On the eastern coast of Newfoundland. The island is mentioned in Hore's narrative, p. 107, above.
[2] The ancient Basque name for codfish, attesting the early presence of Basque fishermen on the Newfoundland coast. The island is now known as Baccalieu Island. [3] At the southern entrance of Conception Bay.

revenge upon them, and hath tolerated longer as great outrage in others: by how much these went under protection of his cause and religion, which was then pretended.

Therefore upon further enquiry it was knowen, how this company met with a barke returning home after the fishing with his fraight: and because the men in the Swallow were very neere scanted of victuall, and chiefly of apparell, doubtful withall where or when to find and meete with their Admiral, they besought the captaine they might go aboord this Newlander, only to borrow what might be spared, the rather because the same was bound homeward. Leave given, not without charge to deale favorably, they came aboord the fisherman, whom they rifled of tackle, sailes, cables, victuals, and the men of their apparell: not sparing by torture (winding cords about their heads) to draw out else what they thought good. This done with expedition (like men skilfull in such mischiefe) as they tooke their cocke boate to go aboord their own ship, it was overwhelmed in the sea, and certaine of these men were drowned: the rest were preserved even by those silly soules whom they had before spoyled, who saved and delivered them aboord the Swallow. What became afterward of the poore Newlander, perhaps destitute of sayles and furniture sufficient to carry them home (whither they had not lesse to runne then 700 leagues) God alone knoweth, who tooke vengeance not long after of the rest that escaped at this instant: to reveale the fact, and justifie to the world Gods judgements inflicted upon them, as shalbe declared in place convenient.

Thus after we had met with the Swallow, we held on our course Southward, untill we came against the harbor called S. John, about 5 leagues from the former Cape of S. Francis: where before the entrance into the harbor, we found also the Frigate or Squirrill lying at anker. Whom the English marchants (that were and alwaies be Admirals[1] by turnes interchangeably over the fleetes of fishermen within the same

[1] The marginal note in Hakluyt is as follows, " English ships are the strongest and Admirals of other fleetes fishing upon the South parts of Newfound land."

harbor) would not permit to enter into the harbor. Glad of so happy meeting both of the Swallow and Frigate in one day (being Saturday the 3. of August) we made readie our fights, and prepared to enter the harbor, any resistance to the contrarie notwithstanding, there being within of all nations, to the number of 36 sailes. But first the Generall dispatched a boat to give them knowledge of his comming for no ill intent, having Commission from her Majestie for his voiage he had in hand. And immediatly we followed with a slacke gale, and in the very entrance (which is but narrow, not above 2 buts length) the Admirall fell upon a rocke on the larboord side by great oversight, in that the weather was faire, the rocke much above water fast by the shore, where neither went any sea gate. But we found such readinesse in the English Marchants to helpe us in that danger, that without delay there were brought a number of boats, which towed off the ship, and cleared her of danger.

Having taken place convenient in the road, we let fall ankers, the Captaines and Masters repairing aboord our Admirall: whither also came immediatly the Masters and owners of the fishing fleete of Englishmen, to understand the Generals intent and cause of our arrivall there. They were all satisfied when the General had shewed his commission, and purpose to take possession of those lands to the behalfe of the crowne of England, and the advancement of Christian religion in those Paganish regions, requiring but their lawfull ayde for repayring of his fleete, and supply of some necessaries, so farre as might conveniently be afforded him, both out of that and other harbors adjoyning. In lieu whereof, he made offer to gratifie them, with any favour and priviledge, which upon their better advise they should demand, the like being not to be obteyned hereafter for greater price. So craving expedition of his demand, minding to proceede further South without long detention in those partes, he dismissed them, after promise given of their best indevour to satisfie speedily his so reasonable request. The marchants with their Masters departed, they caused forthwith to be discharged all the great Ordinance of their fleete in token of our welcome.

It was further determined that every ship of our fleete should deliver unto the marchants and Masters of that harbour a note of all their wants: which done, the ships aswell English as strangers, were taxed at an easie rate to make supply. And besides, Commissioners were appointed, part of our owne companie and part of theirs, to go into other harbours adjoyning (for our English marchants command all there) to leavie our provision: whereunto the Portugals (above other nations) did most willingly and liberally contribute. Insomuch as we were presented (above our allowance) with wines, marmalads, most fine ruske or biskct, swcct oylcs and sundry dclicacics. Also we wanted not of fresh salmons, trouts, lobsters and other fresh fish brought daily unto us. Moreover as the maner is in their fishing, every weeke to choose their Admirall a new, or rather they succeede in orderly course, and have weekely their Admirals feast solemnized: even so the General, Captaines and masters of our fleete were continually invited and feasted. To grow short, in our abundance at home, the intertainment had bene delightfull, but after our wants and tedious passage through the Ocean, it seemed more acceptable and of greater contentation, by how much the same was unexpected in that desolate corner of the world: where at other times of the yeare, wilde beasts and birds have only the fruition of all those countries, which now seemed a place very populous and much frequented.

The next morning being Sunday and the 4 of August, the Generall and his company were brought on land by English marchants, who shewed unto us their accustomed walks unto a place they call the Garden. But nothing appeared more then Nature it selfe without art: who confusedly hath brought foorth roses abundantly, wilde, but odoriferous, and to sense very comfortable. Also the like plentie of raspis berries, which doe grow in every place.

Munday following, the Generall had his tent set up, who being accompanied with his own followers, summoned the marchants and masters, both English and strangers to be present at his taking possession of those Countries. Before whom openly was read and interpreted unto the strangers his Commission: by vertue whereof he tooke possession in the same harbour of S. John, and 200 leagues every way, invested the Queenes Majestie with the title and dignitie thereof, had delivered unto him (after the custome of England) a rod and a turffe of the same soile, entring possession also for him, his heires and assignes for ever: And signified unto al men, that from that time forward, they should take the same land as a territorie appertaining to the Queene of England, and himselfe authorised under her Majestie to possesse and enjoy it, And to ordaine lawes for the governement thereof, agreeable (so neere as conveniently might be) unto the lawes of England: under which all people coming thither hereafter, either to inhabite, or by way of traffique, should be subjected and governed. And especially at the same time for a beginning, he proposed and delivered three lawes to be in force immediatly. That is to say: the first for Religion, which in publique exercise should be according to the Church of England. The 2. for maintenance of her Majesties right and possession of those territories, against which if any thing were attempted prejudiciall the partie or parties offending should be adjudged and executed as in case of high treason, according to the lawes of England. The 3. if any person should utter words sounding to the dishonour of her Majestie, he should loose his eares, and have his ship and goods confiscate.

These contents published, obedience was promised by generall voyce and consent of the multitude aswell of Englishmen as strangers, praying for continuance of this possession and governement begun. After this, the assembly was dismissed. And afterward were erected not farre from that place the Armes of England ingraven in lead, and infixed upon a pillar of wood. Yet further and actually to establish this possession taken in the right of her Majestie, and to the behoofe of Sir Humfrey Gilbert knight, his heires and assignes for ever: the Generall granted in fee farme divers parcels of land lying by the water side, both in this harbor of S. John, and elsewhere, which was to the owners a great commoditie, being thereby assured (by their proper inheritance) of grounds convenient to dresse and to drie their fish, whereof many times before they did faile, being prevented by them that came first into the harbor. For which grounds they did covenant to pay a certaine rent and service unto sir Humfrey Gilbert, his heires or assignes for ever, and yeerely to maintaine possession of the same, by themselves or their assignes.

Now remained only to take in provision granted, according as every shippe was taxed, which did fish upon the coast adjoyning. In the meane while, the Generall appointed men unto their charge: some to repaire and trim the ships, others to attend in gathering togither our supply and provisions: others to search the commodities and singularities of the countrey, to be found by sea or land, and to make relation unto the Generall what eyther themselves could knowe by their owne travaile and experience, or by good intelligence of English men or strangers, who had longest frequented the same coast. Also some observed the elevation of the pole, and drewe plats of the countrey exactly graded. And by that I could gather by each mans severall relation, I have drawen a briefe description of the Newfoundland, with the commodities by sea or lande alreadie made, and such also as are in possibilitie and great likelihood to be made: Neverthelesse the Cardes and plats that were drawing, with the due gradation of the harbors, bayes, and capes, did perish with the Admirall: wherefore in the description following, I must omit the particulars of such things.

A briefe relation of the New found lande, and the commodities thereof.

That which we doe call the Newfound land, and the Frenchmen Bacalaos, is an Iland, or rather (after the opinion of some) it consisteth of sundry Ilands and broken lands, situate in the North regions of America, upon the gulfe and entrance of the great river called S. Laurence in Canada. Into the which, navigation may be made both on the South and North side of this Iland. The land lyeth South and North, containing in length betweene three and 400 miles, accounting from cape Race (which is 46 degrees 25 minuts) unto the Grand bay in 52 degrees of Septentrionall latitude. The Iland round about hath very many goodly bayes and harbors, safe roads for ships, the like not to be found in any part of the knowen world.

The common opinion that is had of intemperature and extreme cold that should be in this countrey, as of some part it may be verified, namely the North, where I grant it is more colde then in countries of Europe, which are under the same elevation: even so it cannot stand with reason and nature of the clime, that the South parts should be so intemperate as the brute [1] hath gone. For as the same doe lie under the climats of Briton, Anjou, Poictou in France, betweene 46 and 49 degrees, so can they not so much differ from the temperature of those countries: unlesse upon the outcoast lying open unto the Ocean and sharpe windes, it must in deede be subject to more colde, then further within the land, where the mountaines are interposed, as walles and bulwarkes, to defend and to resist the asperitie and rigor of the sea and weather. Some hold opinion, that the Newfound land might be the more subject to cold, by how much it lyeth high and neere unto the middle region. I grant that not in Newfound land alone, but in Germany Italy and Afrike, even under the Equinoctiall line, the mountaines are extreme cold, and seeldome uncovered of snow, in their culme and highest tops, which commeth to passe by the same reason that they are extended towards the middle region: yet in the countries lying beneth them, it is found quite contrary. Even so all hils having their discents, the valleis also and low grounds must be likewise hot or temperate, as the clime doeth give in Newfound land: though I am of opinion that the Sunnes reflection is much cooled, and cannot be so forcible in the Newfound land, nor generally throughout America, as

---

[1] Bruit, rumor.

in Europe or Afrike: by how much the Sunne in his diurnall course from East to West passeth over (for the most part) dry land and sandy countries, before he arriveth at the West of Europe or Afrike, whereby his motion increaseth heate, with little or no qualification by moyst vapours. Where, on the contrarie he passeth from Europe and Afrike unto America over the Ocean, from whence it draweth and carieth with him abundance of moyst vapours, which doe qualifie and infeeble greatly the Sunnes reverberation upon this countrey chiefly of Newfound land, being so much to the Northward. Neverthelesse (as I sayd before) the cold cannot be so intollerable under the latitude of 46 47 and 48 (especiall within land) that it should be unhabitable, as some do suppose, seeing also there are very many people more to the North by a great deale. And in these South parts there be certaine beastes, Ounces or Leopards, and birdes in like maner which in the Sommer we have seene, not heard of in countries of extreme and vehement coldnesse. Besides, as in the monethes of June, July, August and September, the heate is somewhat more then in England at those seasons: so men remaining upon the South parts neere unto Cape Race, untill after Hollandtide,[1] have not found the cold so extreme, nor much differing from the temperature of England. Those which have arrived there after November and December, have found the snow exceeding deepe, whereat no marvaile, considering the ground upon the coast, is rough and uneven, and the snow is driven into the places most declyning as the like is to be seene with us. The like depth of snow happily shall not be found within land upon the playner countries, which also are defended by the mountaines, breaking off the violence of winds and weather. But admitting extraordinary cold in those South parts, above that with us here: it can not be as great as in Swedland, much lesse in Moscovia or Russia: yet are the same countries very populous, and the rigor and cold is dispensed with by the commoditie of Stoves, warme clothing, meats and drinkes: all which neede

---

[1] All Hallow tide, *i.e.*, the period about All Saints' Day, November 1.

not to be wanting in the Newfound land, if we had intent there to inhabite.

In the South parts we found no inhabitants, which by all likelihood have abandoned those coastes, the same being so much frequented by Christians: But in the North are savages altogether harmlesse. Touching the commodities of this countrie, serving either for sustentation of inhabitants, or for maintenance of traffique, there are and may be made divers: so that it seemeth Nature hath recompenced that only defect and incommoditie of some sharpe cold, by many benefits: viz. With incredible quantitie, and no lesse varietie of kindes of fish in the sea and fresh waters, as Trouts, Salmons, and other fish to us unknowen: Also Cod, which alone draweth many nations thither, and is become the most famous fishing of the world. Abundance of Whales, for which also is a very great trade in the bayes of Placentia and the Grand bay, where is made Traine oiles of the Whale: [1] Herring the largest that have bene heard of, and exceeding the Malstrond [2] herring of Norway: but hitherto was never benefit taken of the herring fishing. There are sundry other fish very delicate, namely the Bonito, Lobsters, Turbut, with others infinite not sought after: Oysters having pearle but not orient in colour: I tooke it by reason they were not gathered in season.

Concerning the inland commodities, aswel to be drawen from this land, as from the exceeding large countries adjoyning: there is nothing which our East and Northerly countries of Europe doe yeelde, but the like also may be made in them as plentifully by time and industrie: Namely rosen, pitch, tarre, sopeashes, dealboord, mastes for ships, hides, furres, flaxe, hempe, corne, cordage, linnen-cloth, mettals and many more. All which the countries will aford, and the soyle is apt to yeelde.

The trees for the most in those South parts are Firretrees, Pine and Cypresse, all yeelding Gumme and Turpentine.

Cherrie trees bearing fruit no bigger than a small pease.

---

[1] Made from the blubber or fat of whales by boiling.   [2] Maelstrom.

Also peare trees but fruitlesse. Other trees of some sorts to us unknowen.

The soyle along the coast is not deepe of earth, bringing forth abundantly peason small, yet good feeding for cattel. Roses passing sweet, like unto our muske roses in forme, raspases, a berry which we call Hurts, good and holesome to eat. The grasse and herbe doth fat sheepe in very short space, proved by English marchants which have caried sheepe thither for fresh victuall and had them raised exceeding fat in lesse then three weekes. Peason which our countreymen have sowen in the time of May, have come up faire, and bene gathered in the beginning of August, of which our Generall had a present acceptable for the rarenesse, being the first fruits comming up by art and industrie in that desolate and dishabited land.

Lakes or pooles of fresh water, both on the tops of mountaines and in the vallies. In which are said to be muskles not unlike to have pearle, which I had put in triall, if by mischance falling unto me, I had not bene letted from that and other good experiments I was minded to make.

Foule both of water and land in great plentie and diversitie. All kind of greene foule: Others as bigge as Bustards, yet not the same. A great white foule called by some a Gaunt.

Upon the land divers sorts of haukes, as Faulcons, and others by report: Partridges most plentifull larger than ours, gray and white of colour, and rough footed like doves, which our men after one flight did kill with cudgels, they were so fat and unable to flie. Birds some like blackbirds, linnets, canary birds, and other very small. Beasts of sundry kindes, red deare, buffles or a beast, as it seemeth by the tract and foote very large in maner of an oxe. Beares, ounces or leopards, some greater and some lesser, wolves, foxes, which to the Northward a little further are black, whose furre is esteemed in some Countries of Europe very rich. Otters, bevers, and marternes: And in the opinion of most men that saw it, the Generall had brought unto him a Sable alive, which he sent unto his brother sir John Gilbert knight [1] of Devonshire: but it was never delivered, as after I understood. We could not observe the hundreth part of creatures in those unhabited lands: but these mentioned may induce us to glorifie the magnificent God, who hath superabundantly replenished the earth with creatures serving for the use of man, though man hath not used a fift part of the same, which the more doth aggravate the fault and foolish slouth in many of our nation, chusing rather to live indirectly, and very miserably to live and die within this realme pestered with inhabitants, then to adventure as becommeth men, to obtaine an habitation in those remote lands, in which Nature very prodigally doth minister unto mens endevours, and for art to worke upon.

For besides these alreadie recounted and infinite moe, the mountaines generally make shew of minerall substance: Iron very common, lead, and somewhere copper. I will not averre of richer mettals: albeit by the circumstances following, more then hope may be conceived thereof.

For amongst other charges given to inquire out the singularities of this countrey, the Generall was most curious in the search of mettals, commanding the minerall man and refiner, especially to be diligent. The same was a Saxon borne, honest and religious, named Daniel.[2] Who after search brought at first some sort of Ore, seeming rather to be yron then other mettal. The next time he found Ore, which with no small shew of contentment he delivered unto the General, using protestation, that if silver were the thing which might satisfie the Generall and his followers, there it was, advising him to seeke no further: the perill whereof he undertooke upon his life (as deare unto him as the Crowne of England unto her Majestie, that I may use his owne words) if it fell not out accordingly.

My selfe at this instant liker to die then to live, by a mischance, could not follow this confident opinion of our refiner to my owne satisfaction: but afterward demanding our Generals

[1] Eldest son of Sir Humphrey Gilbert the elder.
[2] Of Buda. He was drowned in the loss of the *Delight*, August 29.

opinion therein, and to have some part of the Ore, he replied: Content your selfe, I have seene ynough, and were it but to satisfie my private humor, I would proceede no further. The promise unto my friends, and necessitie to bring also the South countries within compasse of my Patent neere expired, as we have alreadie done these North parts, do only perswade me further. And touching the Ore, I have sent it aboord, whereof I would have no speech to be made so long as we remaine within harbor: here being both Portugals, Biscains, and Frenchmen not farre off, from whom must be kept any bruit or muttering of such matter. When we are at sea proofe shalbe made: if it be to our desire, we may returne the sooner hither againe. Whose answere I judged reasonable, and contenting me well: wherewith I will conclude this narration and description of the Newfound land, and proceede to the rest of our voyage, which ended tragically.

While the better sort of us were seriously occupied in repairing our wants, and contriving of matters for the commoditie of our voyage: others of another sort and disposition were plotting of mischiefe. Some casting to steale away our shipping by night, watching oportunitie by the Generals and Captaines lying on the shore: whose conspiracies discovered, they were prevented. Others drew together in company, and caried away out of the harbors adjoyning, a ship laden with fish, setting the poore men on shore. A great many more of our people stole into the woods to hide themselves, attending time and meanes to returne home by such shipping as daily departed from the coast. Some were sicke of fluxes, and many dead: and in briefe, by one meanes or other our company was diminished, and many by the Generall licensed to returne home. Insomuch as after we had reviewed our people, resolved to see an end of our voyage, we grewe scant of men to furnish all our shipping: it seemed good therefore unto the Generall to leave the Swallowe with such provision as might be spared for transporting home the sicke people.

The Captaine of the Delight or Admirall returned into England, in whose stead was appointed Captaine Maurice Browne, before Captaine of the Swallow: who also brought with him into the Delight all his men of the Swallow, which before have bene noted of outrage perpetrated and committed upon fishermen there met at sea.

The Generall made choise to goe in his frigate the Squirrell (whereof the Captaine also was amongst them that returned into England) the same Frigate being most convenient to discover upon the coast, and to search into every harbor or creeke, which a great ship could not doe. Therefore the Frigate was prepared with her nettings and fights, and overcharged with bases and such small Ordinance, more to give a shew, then with judgement to foresee unto the safetie of her and the men, which afterward was an occasion also of their overthrow.

Now having made readie our shipping, that is to say, the Delight, the golden Hinde, and the Squirrell, and put aboord our provision, which was wines, bread or ruske, fish wette and drie, sweete oiles: besides many other, as marmalades, figs, lymmons barrelled, and such like: Also we had other necessary provisions for trimming our ships, nets and lines to fish withall, boates or pinneses fit for discovery. In briefe, we were supplied of our wants commodiously, as if we had bene in a Countrey or some Citie populous and plentifull of all things.

We departed from this harbor of S. Johns upon Tuesday the twentieth of August, which we found by exact observation to be in 47 degrees 40 minutes. And the next day by night we were at Cape Race, 25 leagues from the same harborough.

This Cape lyeth South Southwest from S. Johns: it is a low land, being off from the Cape about halfe a league: within the sea riseth up a rocke against the point of the Cape, which thereby is easily knowen. It is in latitude 46 degrees 25 minutes.

Under this cape we were becalmed a small time, during which we layd out hookes and lines to take Codde, and drew in lesse then two houres, fish so large and in such abundance, that many dayes after we fed upon no other provision.

From hence we shaped our course unto the Island of Sablon,[1] if conveniently it would so fall out, also directly to Cape Briton.

Sablon lieth to the sea-ward of Cape Briton about 25 leagues, whither we were determined to goe upon intelligence we had of a Portugal, (during our abode in S. Johns) who was himselfe present, when the Portugals (above thirty yeeres past) did put into the same Island both Neat and Swine to breede, which were since exceedingly multiplied. This seemed unto us very happy tidings, to have in an Island lying so neere unto the maine, which we intended to plant upon, such store of cattell, whereby we might at all times conveniently be relieved of victuall, and served of store for breed.

In this course we trended along the coast, which from Cape Race stretched into the Northwest, making a bay which some called Trepassa. Then it goeth out againe toward the West, and maketh a point, which with Cape Race lieth in maner East and West. But this point inclineth to the North: to the West of which goeth in the bay of Placentia. We sent men on land to take view of the soyle along this coast, whereof they made good report, and some of them had wil to be planted there. They saw Pease growing in great abundance every where.

The distance betweene Cape Race and Cape Briton is 87 leagues. In which Navigation we spent 8 dayes, having many times the wind indifferent good; yet could we never attaine sight of any land all that time, seeing we were hindred by the current. At last we fell into such flats and dangers, that hardly any of us escaped: where neverthelesse we lost our Admiral with al the men and provision, not knowing certainly the place. Yet for inducing men of skill to make conjecture, by our course and way we held from Cape Race thither (that thereby the flats and dangers may be inserted in sea Cards, for warning

---

[1] Sable Island.

to others that may follow the same course hereafter) I have set downe the best reckonings that were kept by expert men, William Cox Master of the Hind, and John Paul his mate, both of Limehouse.

Reckonings kept in our course from Cape Race towards Cape Briton, and the Island of Sablon, to the time and place where we lost our Admirall.

August 22.	West,	14 leagues.
	West and by South,	25
	Westnorthwest,	25
	Westnorthwest,	9
	Southsouthwest,	10
	Southwest,	12
	Southsouthwest,	10
August 29.	Westnorthwest,	12. Here we lost our Admiral.

Summe of these leagues, 117.

The reckoning of John Paul Masters mate from Cape Race.

August 22.	West,	14 leagues.
23.	Northwest and by West,	9
24.	Southwest and by South,	5
25.	West and by South,	40
26.	West and by North,	7
27.	Southwest,	3
28.	Southwest,	9
	Southwest,	7
	Westsouthwest,	7
29.	Northwest and by West,	20. Here we lost our Admirall.

Summe of all these leagues, 121.

Our course we held in clearing us of these flats was Eastsoutheast, and Southeast, and South 14 leagues with a marveilous scant winde.

The maner how our Admirall was lost.

Upon Tewsday the 27 of August, toward the evening, our Generall caused them in his frigat to sound, who found white sande at 35 fadome, being then in latitude about 44 degrees.

Wednesday toward night the wind came South, and wee bare with the land all that night, Westnorthwest, contrary to the mind of master Cox: neverthelesse wee followed the Admirall deprived of power to prevent a mischiefe, which by no contradiction could be brought to hold other course, alleaging they could not make the ship to worke better, nor to lie otherwaies.

The evening was faire and pleasant, yet not without token of storme to ensue, and most part of this Wednesday night, like the Swanne that singeth before her death, they in the Admiral, or Delight, continued in sounding of Trumpets, with Drummes, and Fifes: also winding the Cornets, Haughtboyes: and in the end of their jolitie, left with the battell and ringing of doleful knels.

Towards the evening also we caught in the Golden Hinde a very mighty Porpose, with a harping yron, having first striken divers of them, and brought away part of their flesh, sticking upon the yron, but could recover onely that one. These also passing through the Ocean, in heardes, did portend storme. I omit to recite frivolous reportes by them in the Frigat, of strange voyces, the same night, which scarred some from the helme.

Thursday the 29 of August, the wind rose, and blew vehemently at South and by East, bringing withal raine, and thicke mist, so that we could not see a cable length before us. And betimes in the morning we were altogether runne and folded in amongst flats and sands, amongst which we found shoale and deepe in every three or foure shippes length, after wee began to sound: but first we were upon them unawares, untill master Cox looking out, discerned (in his judgement) white cliffes, crying (land) withall, though we could not afterward descrie any land, it being very likely the breaking of the sea white, which seemed to be white cliffes, through the haze and thicke weather.

Immediatly tokens were given unto the Delight, to cast about to seaward, which, being the greater ship, and of burden 120 tunnes, was yet formost upon the breach, keeping so ill watch, that they knew not the danger before they felt the same, too late to recover it: for presently the Admirall strooke a ground, and had soone after her sterne and hinder partes beaten in pieces:[1] whereupon the rest (that is to say, the Frigat in which was the Generall and the Golden Hinde) cast about Eastsoutheast, bearing to the South, even for our lives into the windes eye, because that way caried us to the seaward. Making out from this danger, wee sounded one while seven fadome, then five fadome, then foure fadome and lesse, againe deeper, immediatly foure fadome, then but three fadome, the sea going mightily and high. At last we recovered (God be thanked) in some despaire, to sea roome enough.

In this distresse, wee had vigilant eye unto the Admirall, whom wee sawe cast away, without power to give the men succour, neither could we espie any of the men that leaped overboord to save themselves, either in the same Pinnesse or Cocke, or upon rafters, and such like meanes, presenting themselves to men in those extremities: for we desired to save the men by every possible meanes. But all in vaine, sith God had determined their ruine: yet all that day, and part of the next, we beat up and downe as neere unto the wracke as was possible for us, looking out, if by good hap we might espie any of them.

This was a heavy and grievous event, to lose at one blow our chiefe shippe fraighted with great provision, gathered together with much travell, care, long time, and difficultie. But more was the losse of our men, which perished to the number almost of a hundreth soules. Amongst whom was drowned a learned man, an Hungarian, borne in the citie of Buda, called

[1] The scene of the wreck is best located on some point of the southeasterly part of the island of Cape Breton.

hereof Budæus,[1] who of pietie and zeale to good attempts, adventured in this action, minding to record in the Latine tongue, the gests and things worthy of remembrance, happening in this discoverie, to the honour of our nation, the same being adorned with the eloquent stile of this Orator, and rare Poet of our time.

Here also perished our Saxon Refiner and discoverer of inestimable riches, as it was left amongst some of us in undoubted hope.

No lesse heavy was the losse of the Captaine Maurice Browne, a vertuous, honest, and discreete Gentleman, overseene onely in liberty given late before to men, that ought to have bene restrained, who shewed himselfe a man resolved, and never unprepared for death, as by his last act of this tragedie appeared, by report of them that escaped this wracke miraculously, as shall bee hereafter declared. For when all hope was past of recovering the ship, and that men began to give over, and to save themselves, the Captaine was advised before to shift also for his life, by the Pinnesse at the sterne of the ship: but refusing that counsell, he would not give example with the first to leave the shippe, but used all meanes to exhort his people not to despaire, nor so to leave off their labour, choosing rather to die, then to incurre infamie, by forsaking his charge, which then might be thought to have perished through his default, shewing an ill president unto his men, by leaving the ship first himselfe. With this mind hee mounted upon the highest decke, where hee attended imminent death, and unavoidable; how long, I leave it to God, who withdraweth not his comfort from his servants at such times.

In the meane season, certaine, to the number of fourteene persons, leaped into a small Pinnesse (the bignes of a Thames barge, which was made in the New found land) cut off the rope

[1] Stephen Parmenius, a learned Hungarian. He was a room-mate of Hakluyt while at Oxford. Hakluyt prints, on the pages preceding Hayes's narrative, a Latin poem written by Parmenius in honor of the expedition, and, on the pages succeeding it, a letter addressed by him to Hakluyt in Latin with an English translation. Hakluyt Society edition, VIII. 23-33, 77-84.

wherewith it was towed, and committed themselves to Gods mercy, amiddest the storme, and rage of sea and windes, destitute of foode, not so much as a droppe of fresh water. The boate seeming overcharged in foule weather with company, Edward Headly a valiant souldier, and well reputed of his companie, preferring the greater to the lesser, thought better that some of them perished then all, made this motion to cast lots, and them to bee throwen overboord upon whom the lots fell, thereby to lighten the boate, which otherwayes seemed impossible to live, offred himselfe with the first, content to take his adventure gladly: which neverthelesse Richard Clarke, that was Master of the Admirall, and one of this number, refused, advising to abide Gods pleasure, who was able to save all, as well as a few.

The boate was caried before the wind, continuing sixe dayes and nights in the Ocean, and arrived at last with the men (alive, but weake) upon the New found land, saving that the foresayd Headly, (who had bene late sicke) and another called of us Brasile, of his travell into those Countreys, died by the way, famished, and lesse able to holde out, then those of better health. For such was these poore mens extremitie, in cold and wet, to have no better sustenance then their own urine, for sixe dayes together.

Thus whom God delivered from drowning, hee appointed to bee famished, who doth give limits to mans times, and ordaineth the manner and circumstance of dying: whom againe he will preserve, neither Sea nor famine can confound. For those that arrived upon the Newe found land, were brought into France by certaine French men, then being upon that coast.

After this heavie chance, wee continued in beating the sea up and downe, expecting when the weather would cleere up, that we might yet beare in with the land, which we judged not farre off, either the continent or some Island. For we many times, and in sundry places found ground at 50, 45, 40 fadomes, and lesse. The ground comming upon our lead, being sometimes oazie sand, and otherwhile a broad shell, with a little sand about it.

Our people lost courage dayly after this ill successe, the weather continuing thicke and blustering, with increase of cold, Winter drawing on, which tooke from them all hope of amendment, setling an assurance of worse weather to growe upon us every day. The Leeside of us lay full of flats and dangers inevitable, if the wind blew hard at South. Some againe doubted we were ingulphed in the Bay of S. Laurence, the coast full of dangers, and unto us unknowen. But above all, provision waxed scant, and hope of supply was gone, with losse of our Admirall.

Those in the Frigat were already pinched with spare allowance, and want of clothes chiefly: Whereupon they besought the Generall to returne for England, before they all perished. And to them of the Golden Hinde, they made signes of their distresse, pointing to their mouthes, and to their clothes thinne and ragged: then immediately they also of the Golden Hinde, grew to be of the same opinion and desire to returne home.

The former reasons having also moved the Generall to have compassion of his poore men, in whom he saw no want of good will, but of meanes fit to performe the action they came for, resolved upon retire: and calling the Captaine and Master of the Hinde, he yeelded them many reasons, inforcing this unexpected returne, withall protesting himselfe greatly satisfied with that hee had seene, and knew already.

Reiterating these words, Be content, we have seene enough, and take no care of expence past: I will set you foorth royally the next Spring, if God send us safe home. Therefore I pray you let us no longer strive here, where we fight against the elements.

Omitting circumstance, how unwillingly the Captaine and Master of the Hinde condescended to this motion, his owne company can testifie: yet comforted with the Generals promises of a speedie returne at Spring, and induced by other apparant reasons, proving an impossibilitie, to accomplish the action at that time, it was concluded on all hands to retire.

So upon Saturday in the afternoone the 31 of August, we

changed our course, and returned backe for England, at which very instant, even in winding about, there passed along betweene us and towards the land which we now forsooke a very lion to our seeming, in shape, hair and colour, not swimming after the maner of a beast by mooving of his feete, but rather sliding upon the water with his whole body (excepting the legs) in sight, neither yet diving under, and againe rising above the water, as the maner is, of Whales, Dolphins, Tunise, Porposes, and all other fish: but confidently shewing himselfe above water without hiding: Notwithstanding, we presented our selves in open view and gesture to amase him, as all creatures will be commonly at a sudden gaze and sight of men. Thus he passed along turning his head to and fro, yawning and gaping wide, with ougly demonstration of long teeth, and glaring eies, and to bidde us a farewell (comming right against the Hinde) he sent forth a horrible voyce, roaring or bellowing as doeth a lion, which spectacle wee all beheld so farre as we were able to discerne the same, as men prone to wonder at every strange thing, as this doubtlesse was, to see a lion in the Ocean sea, or fish in shape of a lion. What opinion others had thereof, and chiefly the Generall himselfe, I forbeare to deliver: But he tooke it for Bonum Omen, rejoycing that he was to warre against such an enemie, if it were the devill.

The wind was large for England at our returne, but very high, and the sea rough, insomuch as the Frigat wherein the Generall went was almost swalowed up.

Munday in the afternoone we passed in the sight of Cape Race, having made as much way in little more then two dayes and nights backe againe, as before wee had done in eight dayes from Cape Race, unto the place where our ship perished. Which hindrance thitherward, and speed back againe, is to be imputed unto the swift current, as well as to the winds, which we had more large in our returne.

This munday the Generall came aboord the Hind to have the Surgeon of the Hind to dresse his foote, which he hurt by treading upon a naile: At what time we comforted ech other with hope of hard successe to be all past, and of the good to come. So agreeing to cary out lights alwayes by night, that we might keepe together, he departed into his Frigat, being by no meanes to be intreated to tarie in the Hind, which had bene more for his security. Immediatly after followed a sharpe storme, which we overpassed for that time. Praysed be God.

The weather faire, the Generall came aboord the Hind againe, to make merrie together with the Captaine, Master and company, which was the last meeting, and continued there from morning untill night. During which time there passed sundry discourses, touching affaires past, and to come, lamenting greatly the losse of his great ship, more of the men, but most of all of his bookes and notes, and what els I know not, for which hee was out of measure grieved, the same doubtles being some matter of more importance then his bookes, which I could not draw from him: yet by circumstance I gathered, the same to be the Ore[1] which Daniel the Saxon had brought unto him in the New found land. Whatsoever it was, the remembrance touched him so deepe, as not able to containe himselfe, he beat his boy in great rage, even at the same time, so long after the miscarying of the great ship, because upon a faire day, when wee were becalmed upon the coast of the New found land, neere unto Cape Race, he sent his boy aboord the Admirall, to fetch certaine things: amongst which, this being chiefe, was yet forgotten and left behind. After which time he could never conveniently send againe aboord the great ship, much lesse hee doubted her ruine so neere at hand.

Herein my opinion was better confirmed diversly, and by sundry conjectures, which maketh me have the greater hope of this rich Mine. For where as the Generall had never before good conceit of these North parts of the world: now his mind was wholly fixed upon the New found land. And as before he refused not to grant assignements liberally to them that required the same into these North parts, now he became contrarily affected, refusing to make any so large grants, especially

[1] Gilbert was in such a state of mind as Frobisher was when he loaded his vessel with worthless, shining dirt.

of S. Johns, which certaine English merchants made suite for, offering to imploy their money and travell upon the same: yet neither by their owne suite, nor of others of his owne company, whom he seemed willing to pleasure, it could be obtained.

Also laying downe his determination in the Spring following, for disposing of his voyage then to be reattempted: he assigned the Captaine and Master of the Golden Hind, unto the South discovery, and reserved unto himselfe the North, affirming that this voyage had wonne his heart from the South, and that he was now become a Northerne man altogether.

Last, being demanded what means he had at his arrivall in England, to compasse the charges of so great preparation as he intended to make the next Spring: having determined upon two fleetes, one for the South, another for the North: Leave that to mee (hee replied) I will aske a pennie of no man. I will bring good tidings unto her Majesty, who wil be so gracious, to lend me 10000 pounds, willing us therefore to be of good cheere: for he did thanke God (he sayd) with al his heart, for that he had seene, the same being enough for us all, and that we needed not to seeke any further. And these last words he would often repeate, with demonstration of great fervencie of mind, being himselfe very confident, and setled in beliefe of inestimable good by this voyage: which the greater number of his followers nevertheles mistrusted altogether, not being made partakers of those secrets, which the Generall kept unto himselfe. Yet all of them that are living, may be witnesses of his words and protestations, which sparingly I have delivered.

Leaving the issue of this good hope unto God, who knoweth the trueth only, and can at his good pleasure bring the same to light: I will hasten to the end of this tragedie, which must be knit up in the person of our Generall. And as it was Gods ordinance upon him, even so the vehement perswasion and intreatie of his friends could nothing availe, to divert him from a wilfull resolution of going through in his Frigat, which was overcharged upon their deckes, with fights, nettings, and small artillerie, too cumbersome for so small a boate, that was to passe through the Ocean sea at that season of the yere, when by course we might expect much storme of foule weather, whereof indeed we had enough.

But when he was intreated by the Captaine, Master, and other his well willers of the Hinde, not to venture in the Frigat, this was his answere: I will not forsake my little company going homeward, with whom I have passed so many stormes and perils. And in very trueth, hee was urged to be so over hard, by hard reports given of him, that he was afraid of the sea, albeit this was rather rashnes, then advised resolution, to preferre the wind of a vaine report to the weight of his owne life.

Seeing he would not bend to reason, he had provision out of the Hinde, such as was wanting aboord his Frigat. And so we committed him to Gods protection, and set him aboord his Pinnesse, we being more then 300 leagues onward of our way home.

By that time we had brought the Islands of Açores South of us, yet wee then keeping much to the North, untill we had got into the height and elevation of England: we met with very foule weather, and terrible seas, breaking short and high Pyramid wise. The reason whereof seemed to proceede either of hilly grounds high and low within the sea, (as we see hilles and dales upon the land) upon which the seas doe mount and fall: or else the cause proceedeth of diversitie of winds, shifting often in sundry points: al which having power to move the great Ocean, which againe is not presently setled, so many seas do encounter together, as there had bene diversitie of windes. Howsoever it commeth to passe, men which all their life time had occupied the Sea, never saw more outragious Seas. We had also upon our maine yard, an apparition of a little fire by night, which seamen doe call Castor and Pollux. But we had onely one, which they take an evill signe of more tempest: the same is usuall in stormes.

Munday the ninth of September, in the afternoone, the Frigat was neere cast away, oppressed by waves, yet at that time recovered: and giving foorth signes of joy, the Generall sitting abaft with a booke in his hand, cried out unto us in the Hind (so oft as we did approch within hearing) We are as neere to heaven by sea as by land. Reiterating the same speech, well beseeming a souldier, resolute in Jesus Christ, as I can testifie he was.

The same Monday night, about twelve of the clocke, or not long after, the Frigat being ahead of us in the Golden Hinde, suddenly her lights were out, whereof as it were in a moment, we lost the sight, and withall our watch cryed, the Generall was cast away, which was too true. For in that moment, the Frigat was devoured and swallowed up of the Sea. Yet still we looked out all that night, and ever after, untill wee arrived upon the coast of England: Omitting no small saile at sea, unto which we gave not the tokens betweene us, agreed upon, to have perfect knowledge of each other, if we should at any time be separated.

In great torment of weather, and perill of drowning, it pleased God to send safe home the Golden Hinde, which arrived in Falmouth, the 22 day of September, being Sonday, not without as great danger escaped in a flaw, comming from the Southeast, with such thicke mist, that we could not discerne land, to put in right with the Haven.

From Falmouth we went to Dartmouth, and lay there at anker before the Range, while the captaine went aland, to enquire if there had bene any newes of the Frigat, which sayling well, might happily have bene there before us. Also to certifie Sir John Gilbert, brother unto the Generall of our hard successe, whom the Captaine desired (while his men were yet aboord him, and were witnesses of all occurrents in that voyage,) It might please him to take the examination of every person particularly, in discharge of his and their faithfull endevour. Sir John Gilbert refused so to doe, holding himselfe satisfied with report made by the Captaine: and not altogether dispairing of his brothers safetie, offered friendship and curtesie to the Captaine and his company, requiring to have his Barke brought into the harbour: in furtherance whereof, a boate was sent to helpe to tow her in.

Neverthelesse, when the Captaine returned aboord his ship, he found his men bent to depart, every man to his home: and then the winde serving to proceede higher upon the coast: they demanded monie to carie them home, some to London, others to Harwich, and elsewhere, (if the barke should be caried into Dartmouth, and they discharged, so farre from home) or else to take benefite of the wind, then serving to draw neerer home, which should be a lesse charge unto the Captaine, and great ease unto the men, having els farre to goe.

Reason accompanied with necessitie perswaded the Captaine, who sent his lawfull excuse and cause of his sudden departure unto Sir John Gilbert, by the boate of Dartmouth,[1] and from thence the Golden Hind departed, and tooke harbour at Waimouth. Al the men tired with the tediousnes of so unprofitable a voyage to their seeming: in which their long expence of time, much toyle and labour, hard diet and continuall hazard of life was unrecompensed: their Captaine neverthelesse by his great charges, impaired greatly thereby, yet comforted in the goodnes of God, and his undoubted providence following him in all that voyage, as it doth alwaies those at other times, whosoever have confidence in him alone. Yet have we more neere feeling and perseverance of his powerfull hand and protection, when God doth bring us together with others into one same peril, in which he leaveth them, and delivereth us, making us thereby the beholders, but not partakers of their ruine.

Even so, amongst very many difficulties, discontentments, mutinies, conspiracies, sicknesses, mortalitie, spoylings, and wracks by sea, which were afflictions, more then in so small a Fleete, or so short a time may be supposed, albeit true in every particularitie, as partly by the former relation may be collected, and some I suppressed with silence for their sakes living, it pleased God to support this company, (of which onely one man died of a maladie inveterate, and long infested): the rest kept

[1] This port and "Waimouth" below are seaports on the southern coast of England, Dartmouth being on the Devon coast and Weymouth on that of Dorset.

together in reasonable contentment and concord, beginning, continuing, and ending the voyage, which none els did accomplish either not pleased with the action, or impatient of wants, or prevented by death.

Thus have I delivered the contents of the enterprise and last action of sir Humfrey Gilbert knight, faithfully, for so much as I thought meete to be published: wherein may alwaies appeare, (though he be extinguished) some sparkes of his vertues, he remaining firme and resolute in a purpose by all pretence honest and godly, as was this, to discover, possesse, and to reduce unto the service of God, and Christian pietie, those remote and heathen Countreys of America, not actually possessed by Christians, and most rightly appertaining unto the Crowne of England: unto the which, as his zeale deserveth high commendation: even so, he may justly be taxed of temeritie and presumption (rather) in two respects.

First, when yet there was onely probabilitie, not a certaine and determinate place of habitation selected, neither any demonstration of commoditie there in esse, to induce his followers: nevertheles, he both was too prodigall of his owne patrimony, and too careles of other mens expences, to imploy both his and their substance upon a ground imagined good. The which falling, very like his associates were promised, and made it their best reckoning to bee salved some other way, which pleased not God to prosper in his first and great preparation.

Secondly, when by his former preparation he was enfeebled of abilitie and credit, to performe his designements, as it were impatient to abide in expectation better opportunitie and meanes, which God might raise, he thrust himselfe againe into the action, for which he was not fit, presuming the cause pretended on Gods behalfe, would carie him to the desired ende. Into which, having thus made reentrie, he could not yeeld againe to withdraw though hee sawe no encouragement to proceed, lest his credite, foyled in his first attempt, in a second should utterly be disgraced. Betweene extremities, hee made a right adventure, putting all to God and good fortune, and which was worst, refused not to entertaine every person and meanes whatsoever, to furnish out this expedition, the successe whereof hath bene declared.

But such is the infinite bountie of God, who from every evill deriveth good. For besides that fruite may growe in time of our travelling into those Northwest lands, the crosses, turmoiles, and afflictions, both in the preparation and execution of this voyage, did correct the intemperate humors, which before we noted to bee in this Gentleman, and made unsavorie, and lesse delightful his other manifold vertues.

Then as he was refined, and made neerer drawing unto the image of God: so it pleased the divine will to resume him unto himselfe, whither both his, and every other high and noble minde, have always aspired.

THE FIRST VOYAGE MADE TO THE COASTS OF AMERICA, 1584, BY CAPTAIN ARTHUR BARLOWE

INTRODUCTION

SIR WALTER RALEGH, a native of Devon, studied at Oxford, but soon left the university to serve with the Huguenots in France, and later against Spain in the Low Countries. He was in command of the *Falcon* when, in 1578, his half-brother, Sir Humphrey Gilbert, sailed from England for the American coast on a voyage of discovery. Disaster befell the expedition, and Gilbert was compelled to return without achieving his aim. Ralegh, however, who remained at sea, went in search of Spanish treasure-ships, and had a severe fight off the Cape Verde Islands. After his return, Ralegh assisted in putting down an insurrection in Ireland. He next furnished a vessel for Gilbert's ill-fated expedition of 1583. The disaster attending that expedition did not in the least lessen his ardor in western exploration and colonization. On March 25, 1584, he obtained a patent by which he was empowered to "discover, search, finde out and view such remote, heathen and barbarous lands, countreis, and territories, not actually possessed of any Christian prince, nor inhabited by Christian people," the colonists "to have all the priviledge of Denizens, and persons native of England . . . in such like ample maner and forme, as if they were borne and personally resident within our said Realme of England, any law, custome, or usage to the contrary notwithstanding." The text of this charter is given in Hakluyt, edition of 1903, VIII. 288–296, in Poore's *Charters and Constitutions*, and elsewhere.

Two vessels were at once fitted out for preliminary exploration; and the following narrative, written by Captain Arthur Barlowe, master of one of the vessels, has come down to us in a report addressed to Sir Walter Ralegh. When this expedition was in progress, Hakluyt was writing his "particular discourse concerning the great necessitie and manifolde comodyties that are like to growe to this Realme of Englande by the Westerne discoveries lately attempted." In the title of the "discourse," Hakluyt tells us it was written at the request of Sir Walter Ralegh. Several manuscript copies of this "discourse" were made by Hakluyt, but it was not printed until 1877, when a manuscript copy, found in England by the late Dr. Leonard Woods, was published by the Maine Historical Society as the second volume of its *Documentary Series*, edited by the late Charles Deane, LL.D. It has also a place in Goldsmid's Hakluyt, II. 169–358.

H. S. B.

CAPTAIN ARTHUR BARLOWE'S NARRATIVE OF THE FIRST VOYAGE TO THE COASTS OF AMERICA

The first voyage made to the coasts of America, with two barks, wherein were Captaines M. Philip Amadas, and M. Arthur Barlowe, who discovered part of the Countrey now called Virginia Anno 1584. Written by one of the said Captaines, and sent to sir Walter Ralegh knight, at whose charge and direction, the said voyage was set forth.

THE 27 day of Aprill, in the yeere of our redemption 1584, we departed the West of England, with two barkes well furnished with men and victuals, having received our last and perfect directions by your letters, confirming the former instructions, and commandements delivered by your selfe at our leaving the river of Thames. And I thinke it a matter both unnecessary, for the manifest discoverie of the Countrey, as also for tediousnesse sake, to remember unto you the diurnall of our course, sayling thither and returning: onely I have presumed to present unto you this briefe discourse, by which you may judge how profitable this land is likely to succeede, as well to your selfe, (by whose direction and charge, and by whose servantes this our discoverie hath beene performed) as also to her Highnesse, and the Common wealth, in which we hope your wisedome wilbe satisfied, considering that as much by us hath bene brought to light, as by those smal meanes, and number of men we had, could any way have bene expected, or hoped for.

The tenth of May we arrived at the Canaries, and the tenth of June in this present yeere, we were fallen with the Islands of the West Indies, keeping a more Southeasterly course then was needefull, because wee doubted that the current of the Bay of Mexico, disbogging betweene the Cape of Florida and Havana, had bene of greater force then afterwardes we found it to bee. At which Islands we found the ayre very unwholsome, and our men grew for the most part ill disposed: so that having refreshed our selves with sweet water, and fresh victuall, we departed the twelfth day of our arrivall there. These Islands, with the rest adjoyning, are so well knowen to your selfe, and to many others, as I will not trouble you with the remembrance of them.

The second of July, we found shole water, wher we smelt so sweet, and so strong a smel, as if we had bene in the midst of some delicate garden abounding with all kinde of odoriferous flowers, by which we were assured, that the land could not be farre distant: and keeping good watch, and bearing but slacke saile, the fourth of the same moneth we arrived upon the coast, which we supposed to be a continent and firme lande, and we sayled along the same a hundred and twentie English miles before we could finde any entrance, or river issuing into the Sea. The first [1] that appeared unto us, we entred, though not without some difficultie, and cast anker about three harquebuz-shot within the havens mouth, on the left hand of the same: and after thankes given to God for our safe arrivall thither, we manned our boats, and went to view the land next adjoyning, and to take possession of the same, in the right of the Queenes most excellent Majestie, as rightfull Queene, and Princesse of the same, and after delivered the same over to your use, according to her Majesties grant, and letters patents, under her Highnesse great seale.[2] Which being performed, according to the ceremonies used in such enterprises, we viewed the land about us, being, whereas we first landed, very sandie and low towards the waters side, but so full of grapes, as the very beating and surge of the sea overflowed them, of which we found such plentie, as well there as in all places else, both on the sand and on the greene soile on the hils, as in the plaines, as well on every little shrubbe, as also climing towardes the

---

[1] Identification of the inlet is difficult or impossible. The inlets which break the long sandy barrier of North Carolina are far from occupying the same places as those of three hundred years ago.

[2] In the margin against this passage Hakluyt gives the date "July 13, possession taken."

tops of high Cedars, that I thinke in all the world the like abundance is not to be found: and my selfe having seene those parts of Europe that most abound, find such difference as were incredible to be written.

We passed from the Sea side towardes the toppes of those hilles next adjoyning, being but of meane higth, and from thence wee behelde the Sea on both sides to the North, and to the South, finding no ende any of both wayes. This lande lay stretching it selfe to the West, which after wee found to bee but an Island of twentie miles long, and not above sixe miles broade.[1] Under the banke or hill whereon we stoode, we behelde the vallyes replenished with goodly Cedar trees, and having discharged our harquebuz-shot, such a flocke of Cranes (the most part white) arose under us, with such a cry redoubled by many ecchoes, as if an armie of men had showted all together.

This Island had many goodly woodes full of Deere, Conies, Hares, and Fowle, even in the middest of Summer in incredible abundance. The woodes are not such as you finde in Bohemia, Moscovia, or Hercynia, barren and fruitles, but the highest and reddest Cedars of the world, farre bettering the Ceders of the Açores, of the Indies, or Lybanus, Pynes, Cypres, Sassaphras, the Lentisk, or the tree that beareth the Masticke, the tree that beareth the rine of blacke Sinamon, of which Master Winter [2] brought from the streights of Magellan, and many other of excellent smell and qualitie. We remained by the side of this Island two whole dayes before we saw any people of the Countrey: the third day we espied one small boate rowing towardes us having in it three persons: this boat came to the Island side, foure harquebuz-shot from our shippes, and there two of the people remaining, the third came along

[1] In the margin of the Relation are the words, "The Isle of Wokokon." This was one of the more southerly of the islands enclosing Pamlico Sound, as appears from the two contemporary charts made by John White, our best authorities on the cartography of the Ralegh voyages. Of these two charts, one is reproduced in the present volume; both, in the Hakluyt Society's Hakluyt, VIII. 320, 400.

[2] John Winter, who was with Drake in his voyage round the world.

the shoreside towards us, and wee being then all within boord, he walked up and downe upon the point of the land next unto us: then the Master and the Pilot of the Admirall, Simon Ferdinando,[1] and the Captaine Philip Amadas,[2] my selfe, and others rowed to the land, whose comming this fellow attended, never making any shewe of feare or doubt. And after he had spoken of many things not understood by us, we brought him with his owne good liking, aboord the ships, and gave him a shirt, a hat and some other things, and made him taste of our wine, and our meat, which he liked very wel: and after having viewed both barks, he departed, and went to his owne boat againe, which hee had left in a little Cove or Creeke adjoyning: assoone as hee was two bow shoot into the water, he fell to fishing, and in lesse then halfe an houre, he had laden his boate as deepe, as it could swimme, with which hee came againe to the point of the lande, and there he divided his fish into two parts, pointing one part to the ship, and the other to the pinnesse; which, after he had (as much as he might) requited the former benefites received, departed out of our sight.

The next day there came unto us divers boates, and in one of them the Kings brother, accompanied with fortie or fiftie men, very handsome and goodly people, and in their behaviour as mannerly and civill as any of Europe. His name was Granganimeo,[3] and the king is called Wingina, the countrey Wingandacoa[4] and now by her Majestie Virginia.[5] The maner of

[1] In 1587 he was placed in charge of the three ships sent out by Sir Walter Ralegh to take the Roanoke colonists to Chesapeake Bay. A Spaniard by birth, he proved faithless, and the colony was left on Roanoke Island. Various hindrances prevented the sending of relief to the colonists, who later mingled with the natives, and finally were massacred at the instigation of Powhatan. See the ensuing narratives.

[2] This statement discloses the fact that that "one of the said captaines" who wrote the narrative was Arthur Barlowe.

[3] He remained faithful to the English, and died shortly after the arrival of the colony brought over by Sir Richard Grenville in 1585.

[4] Not understanding the language of the natives, Barlowe and his companions could hardly be expected to escape blunders in their interpretation of what was said to them by the Indians. Wingandacoa signifies, "You wear fine clothes," a polite remark, which could hardly be applied to the country.

[5] When Elizabeth, in commemoration of her maiden life, designated the

his comming was in this sort: hee left his boates altogether as the first man did a little from the shippes by the shore, and came along to the place over against the ships, followed with fortie men. When he came to the place his servants spread a long matte upon the ground, on which he sate downe, and at the other ende of the matte foure others of his companie did the like, the rest of his men stood round about him, somewhat a farre off: when we came to the shore to him with our weapons, hee never mooved from his place, nor any of the other foure, nor never mistrusted any harme to be offred from us, but sitting still he beckoned us to come and sit by him, which we performed: and being set hee made all signes of joy and welcome, striking on his head and his breast, and afterwardes on ours, to shew wee were all one, smiling and making shewe the best he could of all love, and familiaritie. After hee had made a long speech unto us, wee presented him with divers things, which hee received very joyfully, and thankefully. None of the companie durst speake one worde all the time: only the foure which were at the other ende, spake one in the others eare very softly.

The King is greatly obeyed, and his brothers and children reverenced: the King himselfe in person was at our being there, sore wounded in a fight which hee had with the King of the next countrey, called Wingina, and was shot in two places through the body, and once cleane through the thigh, but yet he recovered: by reason whereof and for that hee lay at the chiefe towne of the countrey, being sixe dayes journey off, we saw him not at all.

After we had presented this his brother with such things as we thought he liked, wee likewise gave somewhat to the other that satte with him on the matte: but presently he arose and tooke all from them and put it into his owne basket, making signes and tokens, that all things ought to bee delivered unto

newly discovered land Virginia, she conferred upon Ralegh the honor of knighthood. On his new seal he placed the legend, "Propria insignia Walteri Ralegh, militis, Domini et Gubernatoris Virginiae."

him, and the rest were but his servants, and followers. A day or two after this, we fell to trading with them, exchanging some things that we had, for Chamoys, Buffe, and Deere skinnes: when we shewed him all our packet of merchandize, of all things that he sawe, a bright tinne dish most pleased him, which hee presently tooke up and clapt it before his breast, and after made a hole in the brimme thereof and hung it about his necke, making signes that it would defende him against his enemies arrowes: for those people maintaine a deadly and terrible warre, with the people and King adjoyning. We exchanged our tinne dish for twentie skinnes, woorth twentie Crownes, or twentie Nobles: and a copper kettle for fiftie skins woorth fiftie Crownes. They offered us good exchange for our hatchets, and axes, and for knives and would have given any thing for swordes: but wee would not depart with any. After two or three dayes the Kings brother came aboord the shippes, and dranke wine, and eat of our meat and of our bread, and liked exceedingly thereof: and after a fewe days overpassed, he brought his wife with him to the ships, his daughter and two or three children: his wife was very well favoured, of meane stature, and very bashfull: shee had on her backe a long cloake of leather, with the furre side next to her body, and before her a piece of the same: about her forehead shee had a bande of white Corall, and so had her husband many times: in her eares shee had bracelets of pearles hanging downe to her middle, (whereof wee delivered your worship a little bracelet) and those were of the bignes of good pease. The rest of her women of the better sort had pendants of copper hanging in either eare, and some of the children of the kings brother and other noble men, have five or sixe in either eare: he himselfe had upon his head a broad plate of golde, or copper, for being unpolished we knew not what mettall it should be, neither would he by any meanes suffer us to take it off his head, but feeling it, it would bow very easily. His apparell was as his wives, onely the women weare their haire long on both sides, and the men but on one. They are of colour yellowish, and their hair black for the most part, and yet we saw children that had very fine aburne and chestnut coloured haire.[1]

After that these women had bene there, there came downe from all parts great store of people, bringing with them leather, corall, divers kindes of dies, very excellent, and exchanged with us: but when Granganimeo the kings brother was present, none durst trade but himselfe: except such as weare red pieces of copper on their heads like himselfe: for that is the difference betweene the noble men, and the governours of countreys, and the meaner sort. And we both noted there, and you have understood since by these men, which we brought home, that no people in the worlde cary more respect to their King, Nobilitie, and Governours, then these doe. The Kings brothers wife, when she came to us (as she did many times) was followed with forty or fifty women alwayes: and when she came into the shippe, she left them all on land, saving her two daughters, her nurse and one or two more. The Kings brother always kept this order, as many boates as he would come withall to the shippes, so many fires would hee make on the shore a farre off, to the end we might understand with what strength and company he approched. Their boates are made of one tree, either of Pine or of Pitch trees: a wood not commenly knowen to our people, nor found growing in England. They have no edge-tooles to make them withall; if they have any they are very fewe, and those it seemes they had twentie yeres since, which, as those two men declared, was out of a wracke which happened upon their coast of some Christian ship, being beaten that way by some storme and outragious weather, whereof none of the people were saved, but only the ship, or some part of her being cast upon the sand, out of whose sides they drew

[1] Hon. William Wirt Henry (Winsor's *Narrative and Critical History of America*, III. 110) says: "The phenomenon of auburn and chestnut-colored hair may be accounted for by the fact, related by the natives, that some years before a ship, manned by whites, had been wrecked on the coast; and that some of the people had been saved, and had lived with them for several weeks before leaving in their boats, in which, however, they were lost. It was the descendants of these men, doubtless, who were found by the English having hair unlike the other Indians."

the nayles and the spikes, and with those they made their best instruments. The manner of making their boates is thus: they burne downe some great tree, or take such as are winde fallen, and putting gumme and rosen upon one side thereof, they set fire into it, and when it hath burnt it hollow, they cut out the coale with their shels, and ever where they would burne it deeper or wider they lay on gummes, which burne away the timber, and by this meanes they fashion very fine boates, and such as will transport twentie men. Their oares are like scoopes, and many times they set with long poles, as the depth serveth.

The Kings brother had great liking of our armour, a sword, and divers other things which we had: and offered to lay a great box of pearl in gage for them: but we refused it for this time, because we would not make them knowe, that we esteemed thereof, untill we had understoode in what places of the countrey the pearle grew: which now your Worshippe doeth very well understand.

He was very just of his promise: for many times we delivered him merchandize upon his word, but ever he came within the day and performed his promise. He sent us every day a brase or two of fat Bucks, Conies, Hares, Fish the best of the world. He sent us divers kindes of fruites, Melons, Walnuts, Cucumbers, Gourdes, Pease, and divers rootes, and fruites very excellent good, and of their Countrey corne, which is very white, faire and well tasted, and groweth three times in five moneths: in May they sow, in July they reape, in June they sow, in August they reape: in July they sow, in September they reape: onely they cast the corne into the ground, breaking a little of the soft turfe with a wodden mattock, or pickeaxe: our selves prooved the soile, and put some of our Pease in the ground, and in tenne dayes they were of fourteene ynches high: they have also Beanes very faire of divers colours and wonderfull plentie: some growing naturally, and some in their gardens, and so have they wheat and oates.

The soile is the most plentifull, sweete, fruitfull and wholsome of all the worlde: there were above fourteene severall sweete smelling timber trees, and the most part of their underwoods are Bayes and such like: they have those Okes that we have, but farre greater and better. After they had bene divers times aboord our shippes, my selfe, with seven more went twentie mile into the River, that runneth towarde the Citie of Skicoak,[1] which River they call Occam:[2] and the evening following, wee came to an Island which they call Raonoak,[3] distant from the harbour by which we entered, seven leagues: and at the north end thereof was a village of nine houses, built of Cedar, and fortified round about with sharpe trees, to keepe out their enemies, and the entrance into it made like a turne pike very artificially; when wee came towardes it, standing neere unto the waters side, the wife of Granganimeo the kings brother came running out to meete us very cheerefully and friendly, her husband was not then in the village: some of her people shee commanded to drawe our boate on shore for the beating of the billoe: others she appointed to cary us on their backes to the dry ground, and others to bring our oares into the house for feare of stealing. When we were come into the utter roome, having five roomes in her house, she caused us to sit downe by a great fire, and after tooke off our clothes and washed them, and dryed them againe: some of the women plucked off our stockings and washed them, some washed our feete in warme water, and shee her selfe tooke great paines to see all thinges ordered in the best maner shee could, making great haste to dress some meate for us to eate.

After we had thus dryed ourselves, she brought us into the inner roome, where shee set on the boord standing along the house, some wheate like furmentie, sodden Venison, and roasted, fish sodden, boyled and roasted, Melons rawe, and sodden,

---

[1] Shown on White's charts as about where Portsmouth, Virginia, now is.
[2] Probably the north part of Pamlico Sound, plus Currituck Sound.
[3] A corruption, it may be, of the Indian name Ohanoak. The margin has "Roanoak," which is on subsequent pages the prevailing spelling. Roanoke Island, and the remains of English colonization there, are described by Mr. Talcott Williams in the *Annual Report of the American Historical Association* for 1895, pp. 57–61.

rootes of divers kindes and divers fruites: their drinke is commonly water, but while the grape lasteth, they drinke wine, and for want of caskes to keepe it, all the yere after they drink water, but it is sodden with Ginger in it, and black Sinamon, and sometimes Sassaphras, and divers others wholesome, and medicinable hearbes and trees. We were entertained with all love and kindnesse, and with as much bountie (after their maner) as they could possibly devise. We found the people most gentle, loving, and faithfull, voide of all guile and treason, and such as live after the maner of the golden age. The people onely care howe to defende them selves from the cold in their short winter, and to feed themselves with such meat as the soile affoordeth: there meat is very well sodden and they make broth very sweet and savorie: their vessels are earthen pots, very large, white and sweete, their dishes are wodden platters of sweet timber: within the place where they feede was their lodging, and within that their Idoll, which they worship, of whome they speake incredible things. While we were at meate, there came in at the gates two or three men with their bowes and arrowes from hunting, whom when wee espied, we beganne to looke one towardes another, and offered to reach our weapons: but assoone as shee espied our mistrust, shee was very much mooved, and caused some of her men to runne out, and take away their bowes and arrowes and breake them, and withall beate the poore fellowes out of the gate againe. When we departed in the evening and would not tary all night she was very sory, and gave us into our boate our supper halfe dressed, pottes and all, and brought us to our boate side, in which wee lay all night, remooving the same a prettie distance from the shoare: shee perceiving our jelousie, was much grieved, and sent divers men and thirtie women, to sit all night on the banke side by us, and sent us into our boates five mattes to cover us from the raine, using very many wordes to entreate us to rest in their houses: but because wee were fewe men, and if wee had miscaried, the voyage had bene in very great danger, wee durst not adventure any thing, although there was no cause of doubt: for a more kinde and loving people there can not be found in the worlde, as farre as we have hitherto had triall.

Beyond this Island there is the maine lande, and over against this Island falleth into this spacious water, the great river called Occam by the inhabitants on which standeth a towne called Pomeiock,[1] and sixe dayes journey from the same is situate their greatest citie, called Skicoak, which this people affirme to be very greate: but the Savages were never at it, only they speake of it by the report of their fathers and other men, whom they have heard affirme it to bee above one houres journey about.

Into this river falleth another great river, called Cipo, in which there is found great store of Muskles in which there are pearles: likewise there descendeth into this Occam, another river, called Nomopana, on the one side whereof standeth a great towne called Chawanook,[2] and the Lord of that towne and countrey is called Pooneno: this Pooneno is not subject to the king of Wingandacoa, but is a free Lord: beyond this country is there another king, whom they cal Menatonon, and these three kings are in league with each other. Towards the Southwest, foure dayes journey is situate a towne called Sequotan,[3] which is the Southermost towne of Wingandacoa, neere unto which, sixe and twentie yeres past there was a ship cast away, whereof some of the people were saved, and those were white people, whom the countrey people preserved.

And after ten dayes remaining in an out Island unhabited, called Wocokon,[4] they with the help of some of the dwellers of Sequotan, fastened two boates of the countrey

---

[1] On White's two charts (see that reproduced in this volume), Pomeyooc stands back from the sound, west of the present site of Engelhard, N.C.

[2] It is probable that the name Occam is extended to cover Albemarle Sound. Cipo may be the Alligator River. Nomopana is the Chowan. White's two charts show Chawanoac or Chawanooc as occupying a site well up that river.

[3] Shown on White's charts as occupying a position on the south side of the Pamlico River, apparently near Blount Bay.

[4] See p. 229, note 1.

together and made mastes unto them and sailes of their shirtes, and having taken into them such victuals as the countrey yeelded, they departed after they had remained in this out Island 3 weekes: but shortly after it seemed they were cast away, for the boates were found upon the coast, cast a land in another Island adjoyning: other then these, there was never any people apparelled, or white of colour, either seene or heard of amongst these people, and these aforesaid were seene onely of the inhabitantes of Secotan, which appeared to be very true, for they wondred marvelously when we were amongst them at the whitenes of our skins, ever coveting to touch our breasts, and to view the same. Besides they had our ships in marvelous admiration, and all things els were so strange unto them, as it appeared that none of them had ever seene the like. When we discharged any piece, were it but an hargubuz, they would tremble thereat for very feare, and for the strangenesse of the same: for the weapons which themselves use are bowes and arrowes: the arrowes are but of small canes, headed with a sharpe shell or tooth of a fish sufficient ynough to kill a naked man. Their swordes be of wood hardened: likewise they use wooden breastplates for their defence. They have besides a kinde of club, in the end whereof they fasten the sharpe hornes of a stagge, or other beast. When they goe to warres they cary about with them their idol, of whom they aske counsel, as the Romans were woont of the Oracle of Apollo. They sing songs as they march towardes the battell in stead of drummes and trumpets: their warres are very cruell and bloody, by reason whereof, and of their civill dissentions which have happened of late yeeres amongst them, the people are marvelously wasted, and in some places the countrey left desolate.

Adjoyning to this countrey aforesaid called Secotan beginneth a countrey called Pomooik,[1] belonging to another king whom they call Piamacum, and this king is in league with the

[1] In the margin an alternative form is given: "Or Pananuaioc," which name is found on the De Bry map, "Auctore Joanne With," reproduced in Winsor's *America*, III. 125.

next king adjoyning towards the setting of the Sunne, and the countrey Newsiok, situate upon a goodly river called Neus:[1] these kings have mortall warre with Wingina king of Wingandacoa: but about two yeeres past there was a peace made betweene the King Piemacum, and the Lord of Secotan, as these men which we have brought with us to England, have given us to understand: but there remaineth a mortall malice in the Secotanes, for many injuries and slaughters done upon them by this Piemacum. They invited divers men, and thirtie women of the best of his countrey to their towne to a feast: and when they were altogether merry, and praying before their Idol, (which is nothing els but a meer illusion of the devill) the captaine or Lord of the town came suddenly upon them, and slewe them every one, reserving the women and children: and these two have oftentimes since perswaded us to surprize Piemacum his towne, having promised and assured us, that there will be found in it great store of commodities. But whether their perswasion be to the ende they may be revenged of their enemies, or for the love they beare to us, we leave that to the tryall hereafter.

Beyond this Island called Roanoak, are maine Islands very plentifull of fruits and other naturall increases, together with many townes, and villages, along the side of the continent, some bounding upon the Islands, and some stretching up further into the land.

When we first had sight of this countrey, some thought the first land we saw to bee the continent; but after we entred into the Haven, we saw before us another mighty long Sea: for there lyeth along the coast a tracte of Islands, two hundreth miles in length, adjoyning to the Ocean sea, and betweene the Islands, two or three entrances: when you are entred betweene them (these Islands being very narrow for the most part, as in most places sixe miles broad, in some places lesse, in fewe more) then there appeareth another great

---

[1] Neuse. On White's chart Newasiwac occupies a position on the south side of the estuary of that river, near the sound.

Sea, containing in bredth in some places, forty, and in some
fifty, in some twenty miles over, before you come unto the
continent: and in this inclosed Sea there are above an hundreth Islands of divers bignesses, whereof one is sixteene miles
long,[1] at which we were, finding it a most pleasant and fertile
ground, replenished with goodly Cedars, and divers other
sweete woods, full of Corrants, of flaxe, and many other
notable commodities, which we at that time had no leasure to
view. Besides this Island there are many, as I have sayd,
some of two, or three, of foure, of five miles, some more, some
lesse, most beautifull and pleasant to behold, replenished with
Deere, Conies, Hares, and divers beasts, and about them the
goodliest and best fish in the world, and in greatest abundance.

Thus Sir, we have acquainted you with the particulars of
our discovery made this present voyage, as farre foorth as the
shortnesse of the time we there continued would affoord us to
take viewe of: and so contenting our selves with this service at
this time, which wee hope hereafter to inlarge, as occasion and
assistance shalbe given, we resolved to leave the countrey, and
to apply ourselves to returne for England, which we did accordingly, and arrived safely in the West of England about
the middest of September.

And whereas wee have above certified you of the countrey
taken in possession by us, to her Majesties use, and so to yours
by her Majesties grant, wee thought good for the better assurance thereof to record some of the particular Gentlemen,
and men of accompt, who then were present, as witnesses of
the same, that thereby all occasion of cavill to the title of the
countrey, in her Majesties behalfe may be prevented, which
otherwise, such as like not the action may use and pretend,
whose names are:

Master Philip Amadas, } Captaines.
Master Arthur Barlow,

---

[1] Roanoke Island is now about twelve miles long and three broad.

William Greenevile,
John Wood,
James Browewich,
Henry Greene,
Benjamin Wood,
Simon Ferdinando,
Nicholas Petman,
John Hewes,
} Of the companie.

We brought home also two of the Savages being lustie men, whose names were Wanchese and Manteo.[1]

[1] Manteo was a native of Croatoan (Hakluyt, edition of 1903, VIII. 418). He returned with Sir Richard Grenville in 1585 (Hakluyt, VIII. 315), and so probably did Wanchese. August 13, 1587, by order of Sir Walter Ralegh, Manteo "was christened at Roanoak, and called Lord thereof and of Dasamonguepeuk, in reward of his faithfull services." Hakluyt, VIII. 397, and p. 293, *post*.

ACCOUNT OF THE PARTICULARITIES OF THE IMPLOYMENTS OF THE ENGLISHMEN LEFT IN VIRGINIA, 1585–1586, BY MASTER RALPH LANE

INTRODUCTION

ENCOURAGED by Barlowe's report, Ralegh at once commenced preparations for sending out a colony to Virginia. Seven vessels were made ready, and the expedition sailed from Plymouth, April 9, 1585, under the command of Ralegh's cousin, Sir Richard Grenville. Grenville was born in the west of England about 1541. In early life he served in the imperial army in Hungary. Returning to England, he received an appointment to a command in Ireland. In 1571 he entered Parliament. By reason of his relationship to Ralegh, doubtless, he became interested in western colonization. In 1584 he aided in sending Amadas and Barlowe to the American coast. In 1591, as vice-admiral, in the *Revenge*, he encountered a large Spanish fleet off the Azores; and early in the unequal action, having been severely wounded, he was taken on board a Spanish vessel, where, three days after, he died. Ralph Lane, who was in charge of the colonists conveyed by Grenville to America, was in a government position in Ireland when he received his appointment, and was relieved "in consideration of his ready undertaking the Voyage to Virginia for Sir Walter Ralegh at her majesty's commandment." He was "a projecting man," and was knighted in 1593 for valued services. Captain Philip Amadas, master of one of the two vessels sent to America in 1584, was Lane's deputy. In Hakluyt, VIII. 310–318, there is a relation of Grenville's voyage of 1585, also a list containing "the names of those, as well Gentlemen as others, that remained one whole yeere in Virginia, under the Governement of Master Ralph Lane."

H. S. B.

LANE'S ACCOUNT OF THE ENGLISHMEN LEFT IN VIRGINIA

An account of the particularities of the imployments of the English men left in Virginia by Richard Greenevill under the charge of Master Ralph Lane Generall of the same, from the 17. of August 1585. until the 18. of June 1586.[1] at which time they departed the Countrey; sent and directed to Sir Walter Ralegh.

THAT I may proceede with order in this discourse, I thinke it requisite to divide it into two parts. The first shall declare the particularities of such partes of the Countrey within the maine, as our weake number, and supply of things necessarie did inable us to enter into the discovery of.

The second part shall set downe the reasons generally moving us to resolve on our departure at the instant with the Generall Sir Francis Drake, and our common request for passage with him, when the barkes, pinnesses, and boates with the Masters and Mariners meant by him to bee left in the Countrey, for the supply of such, as for a further time meant to have stayed there, were caryed away with tempest and foule weather: In the beginning whereof shall bee declared the conspiracie of Pemisapan, with the Savages of the maine to have cut us off, &c.

The first part declaring the particularities of the Countrey of Virginia.

First therefore touching the particularities of the Countrey, you shall understand that our discoverie of the same hath

[1] Sir Richard Grenville's fleet came to anchor June 26 at Wocokon, which is marked on John White's charts, Hakluyt, VIII. 320 and 400 (see above, p. 229, note 1), as a town on the island north of what is now known

beene extended from the Iland of Roanoak, (the same having bene the place of our settlement or inhabitation) into the South, into the North, into the Northwest, and into the West.

The uttermost place to the Southward of any discovery was Secotan,[1] being by estimation fourescore miles distant from Roanoak. The passage from thence was through a broad sound within the mayne, the same being without kenning of lande, and yet full of flats and shoalds: we had but one boate with four oares to passe through the same, which boate could not carry above fifteene men with their furniture, baggage, and victuall for seven dayes at the most: and as for our pinnesse, besides that she drew too deep water for that shallow sound, she would not stirre for an oare: for these and other reasons (winter also being at hand) we thought good wholly to leeve the discovery of those parts untill our stronger supply.

To the Northward our furthest discovery was to the Chesepians[2] distant from Roanoak about 130. miles, the passage to it was very shallow and most dangerous, by reason of the bredth of the sound, and the little succour that upon any flawe was there to be had.

But the Territorie and soyle of the Chesepians (being distant fifteene miles from the shoare) was for pleasantnes of seate, for temperature of Climate, for fertilitie of soyle and for the commoditie of the Sea, besides multitude of Beares (being an excellent good victuall) with great woods of Sassafras, and Wallnut trees, is not to be excelled by any other whatsoever.

There be sundry Kings, whom they call Weroances, and Countreys of great fertility adjoyning to the same, as the Man-

as Ocracoke Inlet. July 11 he crossed the southern part of Pamlico Sound, and visited the Indian towns, Pomeiok, Aquascogoc, and Secotan. Later he landed one hundred and seven colonists at Roanoke Island under Lane, and August 25 he set sail on the return voyage to England.

[1] Sequotan in Barlowe's narrative. A drawing representing it, by White, is reproduced in the recent edition of Hakluyt, VIII. 336. Many of the drawings made by John White, the artist of this expedition, are still preserved in the British Museum.

[2] Indians living on Chesapeake Bay. Their town is mentioned in a marginal note as Chesepiook.

doages, Tripanicks, and Opossians, which all came to visite the Colonie of the English, which I had for a time appointed to be resident there.

To the Northwest the farthest place of our discovery was to Chawanook distant from Roanoak about 130 miles. Our passage thither lyeth through a broad sound,[1] but all fresh water, and the chanell of a great depth, navigable for good shipping, but out of the chanell full of shoalds.

The Townes about the waters side situated by the way are these following: Passaquenoke The womans Towne, Chepanoc, Weapomeiok, Muscamunge,[2] and Metackwem: all these being under the jurisdiction of the king of Weopomeiok, called Okisco: from Muscamunge we enter into the River,[3] and jurisdiction of Chawanook: There the River beginneth to straighten until it come to Chawanook, and then groweth to be as narrow as the Thames betweene Westminster and Lambeth.

Betwene Muscamunge and Chawanook upon the left hand as wee passe thither, is a goodly high land, and there is a Towne which we called The blinde Towne, but the Savages called it Ohanoak,[4] and hath a very goodly corne field belonging unto it: it is subject to Chawanook.

Chawanook it selfe is the greatest Province and Seigniorie lying upon that River, and the very Towne it selfe is able to put 700. fighting men into the fielde, besides the force of the Province it selfe.

The King of the sayd Province is called Menatonon, a man impotent in his lims, but otherwise for a Savage, a very grave and wise man, and of a very singular good discourse in matters concerning the state, not onely of his owne Countrey, and the disposition of his owne men, but also of his neighbours round about him as well farre as neere, and of the commodities that eache Countrey yeeldeth. When I had him prisoner with me,

[1] Albemarle Sound.
[2] On White's charts Weapemeoc and Mascomenge are placed about where Edenton now stands. On the De Bry map Pasquenoke and Chepanum stand farther east, on the north side of the sound.
[3] Chowan River.
[4] Ohaunoock appears on the De Bry map.

for two dayes that we were together, he gave mee more understanding and light of the Countrey then I had received by all the searches and Savages that before I or any of my companie had had conference with: it was in March last past 1586. Amongst other things he tolde me, that going three dayes journey in a Canoa up his River of Chawanook, and then descending to the land, you are within foure dayes journey to passe over land Northeast to a certaine Kings countrey, whose Province lyeth upon the Sea, but his place of greatest strength is an Island[1] situate, as he described unto mee, in a Bay, the water round about the Island very deepe.

Out of this Bay hee signified unto mee, that this King had so greate quantitie of Pearle, and doeth so ordinarily take the same, as that not onely his owne skinnes that hee weareth, and the better sort of his gentlemen and followers are full set with the sayd Pearle, but also his beds, and houses are garnished with them, and that hee hath such quantitie of them, that it is a wonder to see.

He shewed me that the sayd King was with him at Chawanook two yeeres before, and brought him certaine Pearle, but the same of the worst sort, yet was he faine to buy them of him for copper at a deere rate, as he thought. Hee gave mee a rope of the same pearle, but they were blacke, and naught, yet many of them were very great, and a few amongst a number very orient and round, all which I lost with other things of mine, comming aboord Sir Francis Drake his Fleete;[2] yet he tolde me that the sayd King had great store of Pearle that were white, great, and round, and that his blacke Pearle his

[1] Identified by some as Craney Island in Chesapeake Bay.
[2] Sir Francis Drake left England in September, 1585, bearing a commission from the queen; and the Spanish settlements and shipping in the New World suffered not a little at his hands. "In his prosperous returne from the sacking of Sant Domingo, Cartagena, and Saint Augustine," Drake determined to visit his countrymen at Roanoke Island. He arrived off the English settlement June 8, 1586. As supplies promised by Easter had not then been received, the colonists devised several plans for relief after Drake's arrival; but these failing, they availed themselves of the opportunity afforded by Drake's presence on the coast, and made their way back to England in his ships.

men did take out of shallow water, but the white Pearle his men fished for in very deepe water.

It seemed to me by his speach, that the sayd King had traffique with white men that had clothes as we have, for these white Pearle, and that was the reason that hee would not depart with other then with blacke Pearles, to those of the same countrey.

The king of Chawanook promised to give me guids to go over land into that kings countrey whensoever I would: but he advised me to take good store of men with me, and good store of victuall, for he said, that king would be loth to suffer any strangers to enter into his Countrey, and especially to meddle with the fishing for any Pearle there, and that hee was able to make a great many of men into the field, which he sayd would fight very well.

Hereupon I resolved with my selfe, that if your supplie had come before the ende of Aprill, and that you had sent any store of boates or men, to have had them made in any reasonable time, with a sufficient number of men and victuals to have found us untill the newe corne were come in, I would have sent a small barke with two pinnesses about by Sea to the Northward to have found out the Bay he spake of, and to have sounded the barre if there were any, which should have ridden there in the sayd Bay about that Iland, while I with all the small boates I could make, and with two hundred men would have gone up to the head of the river of Chawanook with the guids that Menatonon would have given me, which I would have bene assured should have beene of his best men, (for I had his best beloved sonne prisoner with me) who also should have kept me companie in an handlocke with the rest, foote by foote, all the voyage over land.

My meaning was further at the head of the River in the place of my descent where I would have left my boates, to have raised a sconse with a small trench, and a pallisado upon the top of it, in the which, and in the guard of my boates I would have left five and twentie, or thirtie men, with the rest would I have marched with as much victuall as every man could have caried, with their furniture, mattocks, spades and axes, two dayes journey. In the ende of my march upon some convenient plot would I have raised another sconse according to the former, where I would have left fifteene or twentie. And if it would have fallen out conveniently, in the way I would have raised my saide sconse upon some Corne fielde, that my company might have lived upon it.

And so I would have holden this course of insconsing every two dayes march, untill I had bene arrived at the Bay or Port hee spake of: which finding to bee worth the possession, I would there have raised a maine fort, both for the defence of the harborough, and our shipping also, and would have reduced our whole habitation from Roanoak and from the harborough and port there (which by proofe is very naught) unto this other beforementioned, from whence, in the foure dayes march before specified, could I at al times returne with my company back unto my boates riding under my sconse, very neere whereunto directly from the West runneth a most notable River, and in all those parts most famous, called the River of Moratoc.[1] This River openeth into the broad Sound of Weapomeiok.[2] And whereas the River of Chawanook, and all the other Sounds, and Bayes, salt and fresh, shewe no current in the world in calme weather, but are mooved altogether with the winde: This River of Moratoc hath so violent a current from the West and Southwest, that it made me almost of opinion that with oares it would scarse be navigable: it passeth with many creekes and turnings, and for the space of thirtie miles rowing, and more, it is as broad as the Thames betwixt Green-wich and the Isle of dogges, in some place more, and in some lesse: the current runneth as strong, being entred so high into the River, as at London bridge upon a vale water.

And for that not onely Menatonon, but also the Savages of Moratoc themselves doe report strange things of the head of that River, and that from Moratoc it selfe which is a principall Towne upon that River, it is thirtie dayes as some of them

[1] Roanoke River.   [2] Albemarle Sound.

say, and some say fourtie dayes voyage to the head thereof, which head they say springeth out of a maine rocke in that abundance, that forthwith it maketh a most violent streame: and further, that this huge rock standeth so neere unto a Sea, that many times in stormes (the winde comming outwardly from the sea) the waves thereof are beaten into the said fresh streame, so that the fresh water for a certaine space, groweth salt and brackish: I tooke a resolution with my selfe, having dismissed Menatonon upon a ransome agreed for, and sent his sonne into the Pinnesse to Roanoak, to enter presently so farre into that River with two double whirries, and fourtie persons one or other, as I could have victuall to cary us, until we could meete with more either of the Moratoks, or of the Mangoaks, which is another kinde of Savages, dwelling more to the Westward of the said River: but the hope of recovering more victuall from the Savages made mee and my company as narrowly to escape starving in that discoverie before our returne, as ever men did, that missed the same.

For Pemisapan, who had changed his name of Wingina upon the death of his brother Granganimo, had given both the Choanists, and Mangoaks worde of my purpose towarde them, I having bene inforced to make him privie to the same, to bee served by him of a guide to the Mangoaks, and yet hee did never rest to solicite continually my going upon them, certifying mee of a generall assembly even at that time made by Menatonon at Chawanook of all his Weroances, and allies to the number of three thousand bowes, preparing to come upon us at Roanoak, and that the Mangoaks also were joyned in the same confederacie, who were able of themselves to bring as many more to the enterprise: And true it was that at that time the assembly was holden at Chawanook about us, as I found at my comming thither, which being unlooked for did so dismay them, as it made us have the better hand at them. But this confederacie against us of the Choanists and Mangoaks was altogether and wholly procured by Pemisapan himselfe, as Menatonon confessed unto me, who sent them continual word, that our purpose was fully bent to destroy them: on the other side he told me, that they had the like meaning towards us.

Hee in like sort having sent worde to the Mangoaks of mine intention to passe up into their River, and to kill them (as he saide) both they and the Moratoks, with whom before wee were entred into a league, and they had ever dealt kindly with us, abandoned their Townes along the River, and retired themselves with their Crenepos,[1] and their Corne within the maine: insomuch as having passed three dayes voyage up the River, wee could not meete a man, nor finde a graine of Corne in any of their Townes: whereupon considering with my selfe that wee had but two dayes victuall left, and that wee were then 160. miles from home, besides casualtie of contrarie windes or stormes, and suspecting treason of our owne Savages in the discoverie of our voyage intended, though wee had no intention to bee hurtfull to any of them, otherwise then for our copper to have had corne of them: I at night upon the Corps of guard, before the putting foorth of Centinels, advertised the whole company of the case wee stoode in for victuall, and of mine opinion that we were betrayed by our owne Savages, and of purpose drawen foorth by them upon vaine hope to be in the ende starved, seeing all the Countrey fled before us, and therefore while wee had those two dayes victual left, I thought it good for us to make our returne homeward, and that it were necessary for us to get the other side of the Sound of Weopomeiok in time, where wee might be relieved upon the weares of Chypanum, and the womens Towne, although the people were fled.

Thus much I signified unto them, as the safest way: neverthelesse I did referre it to the greatest number of voyces, whether wee should adventure the spending of our whole victuall in some further viewe of that most goodly River in hope to meete with some better happe, or otherwise to retire our selves backe againe. And for that they might be the better advised, I willed them to deliberate all night upon the matter,

---

[1] Women.

and in the morning at our going aborde to set our course according to the desires of the greatest part. Their resolution fully and wholy was (and not three founde to bee of the contrary opinion) that whiles there was lefte but one halfe pinte of Corne for a man, wee should not leave the search of that River, and that there were in the companie two Mastives, upon the pottage of which with Sassafras leaves (if the worst fell out) the company would make shift to live two dayes, which time would bring them downe the current to the mouth of the River, and to the entrie of the Sound, and in two dayes more at the farthest they hoped to crosse the Sound and to bee relieved by the weares, which two dayes they would fast rather then be drawen backe a foote till they had seene the Mangoaks, either as friendes or foes. This resolution of theirs did not a little please mee, since it came of themselves, although for mistrust of that which afterwards did happen, I pretended to have bene rather of the contrary opinion.

And that which made me most desirous to have some doings with the Mangoaks either in friendship or otherwise to have had one or two of them prisoners, was, for that it is a thing most notorious to all the countrey, that there is a Province to the which the said Mangoaks have recourse and trafique up that River of Moratoc, which hath a marveilous and most strange Minerall. This Mine is so notorious amongst them, as not onely to the Savages dwelling up the said river, and also to the Savages of Chawanook, and all them to the Westward, but also to all them of the maine: the Countreis name is of fame, and is called Chaunis Temoatan.

The Minerall they say is Wassador, which is copper, but they call by the name of Wassador every mettall whatsoever: they say it is of the colour of our copper, but our copper is better than theirs: and the reason is for that it is redder and harder, whereas that of Chaunis Temoatan is very soft, and pale: they say that they take the saide mettall out of a river that falleth very swift from hie rockes and hils, and they take it in shallow water: the maner is this. They take a great bowle by their description as great as one of our targets, and wrappe a skinne over the hollow parte thereof, leaving one part open to receive in the minerall: that done, they watch the comming downe of the current, and the change of the colour of the water, and then suddenly chop downe the said bowle with the skinne, and receive into the same as much oare as will come in, which is ever as much as their bowle will holde, which presently they cast into a fire, and foorthwith it melteth, and doeth yeelde in five parts at the first melting, two parts of mettall for three partes of oare. Of this mettall the Mangoaks have so great store, by report of all the Savages adjoyning, that they beautify their houses with greate plates of the same: and this to be true, I received by report of all the countrey, and particularly by yong Skiko, the King of Chawanooks sonne of my prisoner, who also him selfe had bene prisoner with the Mangoaks, and set downe all the particularities to me before mentioned: but hee had not bene at Chawnis Temoatan himselfe: for hee said it was twentie dayes journey overland from the Mangoaks, to the said Mineral Countrey, and that they passed through certaine other territories betweene them and the Mangoaks, before they came to the said Countrey.[1]

Upon report of the premisses, which I was very inquisitive in all places where I came to take very particular information of by all the Savages that dwelt towardes these parts, and especially of Menatonon himselfe, who in every thing did very particularly informe mee, and promised me guides of his owne men, who should passe over with me, even to the said Country of Chaunis Temoatan (for overland from Chawanook to the Mangoaks is but one dayes journey from Sunne rising to Sunne setting, whereas by water it is seven dayes with the soonest): These things, I say, made me very desirous by all meanes possible to recover the Mangoaks, and to get some of that their copper for an assay, and therefore I willingly yeelded to their resolution: But it fell out very contrary to all expectation, and likelyhood: for after two dayes travell, and our whole victuall spent, lying on shoare all night, wee could never

[1] It is probable that these reports had reference to the gold of the southern Appalachians.

see man, onely fires we might perceive made alongst the shoare where we were to passe, and up into the Countrey, untill the very last day. In the evening whereof, about three of the clocke wee heard certaine Savages call as we thought, Manteo, who was also at that time with me in the boat, whereof we all being very glad, hoping of some friendly conference with them, and making him to answere them, they presently began a song, as we thought, in token of our welcome to them: but Manteo presently betooke him to his piece, and tolde mee that they meant to fight with us: which worde was not so soone spoken by him, and the light horseman[1] ready to put to shoare, but there lighted a vollie of their arrowes amongst them in the boat, but did no hurt (God be thanked) to any man. Immediatly, the other boate lying ready with their shot to skoure the place for our hand weapons to lande upon, which was presently done, although the land was very high and steepe, the Savages forthwith quitted the shoare, and betooke themselves to flight: wee landed, and having faire and easily followed for a smal time after them, who had wooded themselves we know not where: the Sunne drawing then towards the setting, and being then assured that the next day if wee would pursue them, though we might happen to meete with them, yet wee should be assured to meete with none of their victuall, which we then had good cause to thinke of: therefore choosing for the company a convenient ground in safetie to lodge in for the night, making a strong Corps of guard, and putting out good Centinels, I determined the next morning before the rising of the Sunne to be going back againe, if possibly we might recover the mouth of the river, into the broad sound, which at my first motion I found my whole company ready to assent unto: for they were nowe come to their Dogges porredge, that they had bespoken for themselves if that befell them which did, and I before did mistrust we should hardly escape. The ende was, we came the next day by night to the Rivers mouth within foure or five miles of the

---

[1] An old name for the light boat since called a gig.

same, having rowed in one day downe the current, as much
as in foure dayes wee had done against the same: we lodged
upon an Iland, where we had nothing in the world to eate but
pottage of Sassafras leaves, the like whereof for a meate was
never used before as I thinke. The broad sound wee had to
passe the next day all fresh and fasting: that day the winde
blew so strongly and the billow so great, that there was no
possibilitie of passage without sinking of our boates. This was
upon Easter eve, which was fasted very truely. Upon Easter
day in the morning the winde comming very calme, we entred
the sound, and by foure of the clocke we were at Chipanum,
whence all the Savages that we had left there were fled, but
their weares did yeelde us some fish, as God was pleased not
utterly to suffer us to be lost: for some of our company of
the light horsemen were farre spent. The next morning wee
arrived at our home Roanoak.

I have set downe this Voyage somewhat particularly, to
the ende it may appeare unto you, (as true it is) that there
wanted no great good will from the most to the least amongst
us, to have perfited this discoverie of the Mine: for that the
discovery of a good Mine, by the goodnesse of God, or a passage to the South-sea, or some way to it, and nothing els can
bring this Countrey in request to be inhabited by our nation.
And with the discovery of either of the two above shewed, it
will bee the most sweete and healthfullest climate, and therewithall the most fertile soyle (being manured) in the world:
and then will Sassafras, and many other rootes and gummes
there found make good marchandise and lading for shipping,
which otherwise of themselves will not be worth the fetching.

Provided also, that there be found out a better harborough
then yet there is, which must be to the Northward, if any there
bee, which was mine intention to have spent this Summer in
the search of, and of the Mine of Chawnis Temoatan: the one
I would have done, if the barkes that I should have had of
Sir Francis Drake, by his honourable courtesie, had not bene
driven away by storme: the other if your supply of more men,
and some other necessaries had come to us in any convenient

sufficiencie. For this river of Moratico promiseth great things, and by the opinion of M. Hariots[1] the head of it by the description of the Countrey, either riseth from the Bay of Mexico, or els from very neere unto the same, that openeth out into the South sea.

And touching the Minerall, thus doeth M. Youghan affirme, that though it be but copper, seeing the Savages are able to melt it, it is one of the richest Minerals in the world.

Wherefore a good harborough found to the Northward, as before is saide, and from thence foure dayes overland, to the River of Choanoak sconses being raised, from whence againe overland through the province of Choanoak one dayes voyage to the first towne of the Mangoaks up the river of Moratico by the way, as also upon the said River for the defence of our boats like sconses being set, in this course of proceeding you shall cleare your selfe from al those dangers and broad shallow sounds before mentioned, and gaine within foure dayes travell into the heart of the maine 200. miles at the least, and so passe your discovery into that most notable countrey, and to the likeliest parts of the maine, with farre greater felicitie then otherwise can bee performed.

Thus Sir, I have though simply, yet truely set downe unto you, what my labour with the rest of the gentlemen, and poore men of our company (not without both paine and perill, which the Lord in his mercy many wayes delivered us from) could yeeld unto you, which might have bene performed in some more perfection, if the Lord had bene pleased that onely that which you had provided for us had at the first bene left with us, or that hee had not in his eternall providence now at the

---

[1] His name appears in the list of colonists as "Master Hariot." Thomas Harriot, afterward highly distinguished as a mathematician and an astronomer, published in 1588 *A briefe and true report of the new found land of Virginia: of the commodities there found and to be raysed, as well marchantable as others: . . . by Thomas Hariot, servant to the above named Sir Walter* [Ralegh], *a member of the Colony, and there imployed in discouvering*, with an introduction by Ralph Lane. This was reprinted in 1600 in Hakluyt's *Voyages* (see last edition, VIII. 348–386), and separately in 1869 and in 1900, the last issue being edited by Henry Stevens of Vermont.

last set some other course in these things, than the wisedome of man coulde looke into, which truely the carying away by a most strange and unlooked for storme of all our provision, with Barks, Master, Mariners, and sundry also of mine owne company, al having bene so courteously supplied by the generall Sir Francis Drake, the same having bene most sufficient to have performed the greatest part of the premisses, must ever make me to thinke the hand of God onely (for some his good purpose to my selfe yet unknowen) to have bene in the matter.

The second part touching the conspiracie of Pemisapan, the discovery of the same, and at the last, of our request to depart with Sir Francis Drake for England.

Ensenore a Savage father to Pemisapan being the onely friend to our nation that we had amongest them, and about the King, died the 20. of April 1586. He alone had before opposed himselfe in their consultations against all matters proposed against us, which both the King and all the rest of them after Grangemoes death, were very willing to have preferred. And he was not onely by the meere providence of God during his life, a meane to save us from hurt, as poysonings and such like, but also to doe us very great good, and singularly in this.

The King was advised and of himselfe disposed, as a ready meane to have assuredly brought us to ruine in the moneth of March 1586. himselfe also with all his Savages to have runne away from us, and to have left his ground in the Iland unsowed: which if hee had done, there had bene no possibilitie in common reason, (but by the immediate hande of God) that wee coulde have bene preserved from starving out of hande. For at that time wee had no weares for fish, neither coulde our men skill of the making of them, neither had wee one graine of Corne for seede to put into the ground.

In mine absence on my voyage that I had made against the

Chaonists, and Mangoaks, they had raised a brute[1] among themselves, that I and my company were part slaine, and part starved by the Chaonists, and Mangoaks. One part of this tale was too true, that I and mine were like to be starved, but the other false.

Neverthelesse untill my returne it tooke such effect in Pemisapans breast, and in those against us, that they grew not onely into contempt of us, but also (contrary to their former reverend opinion in shew, of the Almightie God of heaven, and Jesus Christ whom wee serve and worship, whom before they would acknowledge and confesse the onely God) now they began to blaspheme, and flatly to say, that our Lorde God was not God, since hee suffered us to sustaine much hunger, and also to be killed of the Renapoaks, for so they call by that generall name all the inhabitants of the whole maine, of what province soever. Insomuch as olde Ensenore, neither any of his fellowes, could for his sake have no more credite for us: and it came so farre that the king was resolved to have presently gone away as is aforesaid.

But even in the beginning of this bruite I returned, which when hee sawe contrary to his expectation, and the advertisement that hee had received: that not onely my selfe, and my company were all safe, but also by report of his owne 3. Savages which had bene with mee besides Manteo in that voyage, that is to say Tetepano, his sisters husband Eracano, and Cossine, that the Chanoists and Mangoaks (whose name and multitude besides their valour is terrible to all the rest of the provinces) durst not for the most part of them abide us, and that those that did abide us were killed, and that we had taken Menatonon prisoner, and brought his sonne that he best loved to Roanoak with mee, it did not a little asswage all devises against us: on the other side, it made Ensenores opinions to be received againe with greater respects. For he had often before tolde them, and then renewed those his former speeches, both to the king and the rest, that wee were the servants of

---

[1] Obsolete for "report." In the first line of the next paragraph but one it is printed "bruite."

God, and that wee were not subject to bee destroyed by them: but contrarywise, that they amongst them that sought our destruction, shoulde finde their owne, and not bee able to worke ours, and that we being dead men were able to doe them more hurt, then now we could do being alive: an opinion very confidently at this day holden by the wisest amongst them, and of their old men, as also, that they have bene in the night, being 100. miles from any of us, in the aire shot at, and stroken by some men of ours, that by sicknesse had died among them: and many of them holde opinion, that we be dead men returned into the world againe, and that wee doe not remaine dead but for a certaine time, and that then we returne againe.

All these speeches then againe grewe in ful credite with them, the King, and all, touching us, when hee sawe the small troupe returned againe, and in that sort from those whose very names were terrible unto them: But that which made up the matter on our side for that time was an accident, yea rather (as all the rest was) the good providence of the Almightie for the saving of us, which was this.

Within certaine dayes after my returne from the sayd journey, Menatonon sent a messenger to visite his sonne the prisoner with me, and sent me certaine pearle for a present, or rather, as Pemisapan tolde mee, for the ransome of his sonne, and therefore I refused them: but the greatest cause of his sending then, was to signifie unto mee, that hee had commaunded Okisko King of Weopomiok, to yeelde himselfe servant, and homager, to the great Weroanza of England, and after her to Sir Walter Raleigh: to perfourme which commandement received from Menatonon, the sayde Okiosko joyntly with this Menatonons messenger sent foure and twentie of his principallest men to Roanoak to Pemisapan, to signifie that they were ready to perfourme the same, and so had sent those his men to let mee knowe that from that time forwarde, hee, and his successours were to acknowledge her Majestie their onely Soveraigne, and next unto her, as is aforesayd.

All which being done, and acknowledged by them all, in the presence of Pemisapan his father, and all his Savages in counsell then with him, it did for the time thorowly (as it seemed) change him in disposition toward us: Insomuch as forthwith Ensenore wanne this resolution of him, that out of hand he should goe about, and withall, to cause his men to set up weares foorthwith for us: both which he at that present went in hande withall, and did so labour the expedition of it, that in the end of April he had sowed a good quantitie of ground, so much as had bene sufficient, to have fed our whole company (God blessing the grouth) and that by the belly, for a whole yere: besides that he gave us a certaine plot of ground for our selves to sowe. All which put us in marveilous comfort, if we could passe from Aprill untill the beginning of July, (which was to have bene the beginning of their harvest,) that then a newe supply out of England or else our owne store would well ynough maintaine us: All our feare was of the two monethes betwixt, in which meane space if the Savages should not helpe us with Chassavi, and Chyna, and that our weares should faile us, (as often they did) we might very well starve, notwithstanding the growing corne, like the starving horse in the stable, with the growing grasse, as the proverbe is: which wee very hardly had escaped, but onely by the hand of God, as it pleased him to try us. For within few dayes after, as before is saide, Ensenore our friend died, who was no sooner dead, but certaine of our great enemies about Pemisapan, as Osacan a Weroance, Tanaquiny and Wanchese[1] most principally, were in hand againe to put their old practises in ure against us, which were readily imbraced, and all their former devises against us, reneued, and new brought in question. But that of starving us, by their forbearing to sow, was broken by Ensenore in his life, by having made the King all at one instant to sow his ground, not onely in the Iland, but also at Dasamonquepeio in the maine, within two leagues over against us.[2] Neverthelesse there wanted no store of mischievous practises among them, and of all they resolved principally of this following.

[1] One of the two savages taken to England by Amadas and Barlowe on their return to England in the autumn of 1584.
[2] Immediately opposite Roanoke Island.

First that Okisko king of Weopomeiok with the Mandoages should bee mooved, and with great quantitie of copper intertained to the number of 7. or 8. hundreth bowes, to enterprise the matter thus to be ordered. They of Weopomeiok should be invited to a certaine kind of moneths minde which they doe use to solemnise in their Savage maner for any great personage dead, and should have bene for Ensenore. At this instant also should the Mandoaks, who were a great people, with the Chesepians and their friends to the number of 700. of them, be armed at a day appointed to the maine of Dasamonquepeio, and there lying close at the signe of fiers, which should interchangeably be made on both sides, when Pemisapan with his troupe above named should have executed me, and some of our Weroances (as they called all our principall officers,) the maine forces of the rest should have come over into the Iland, where they ment to have dispatched the rest of the company, whom they did imagine to finde both dismayed and dispersed abroad in the Island, seeking of crabs and fish to live withall. The maner of their enterprise was this.

Tarraquine and Andacon two principall men about Pemisapan, and very lustie fellowes, with twentie more appointed to them had the charge of my person to see an order taken for the same, which they ment should in this sort have bene executed. In the dead time of the night they would have beset my house, and put fire in the reedes that the same was covered with: meaning (as it was likely) that my selfe would have come running out of a sudden amazed in my shirt without armes, upon the instant whereof they would have knocked out my braines.

The same order was given to certaine of his fellowes, for M. Heriots: so for all the rest of our better sort, all our houses at one instant being set on fire as afore is saide, and that as well for them of the fort, as for us at the towne. Now to the ende that we might be the fewer in number together, and so bee the more easily dealt withall (for in deed tenne of us with our armes prepared, were a terrour to a hundred of the best sort of them,) they agreed and did immediatly put it in practise, that they should not for any copper sell us any victuals whatsoever: besides that in the night they should sende to have our weares robbed, and also to cause them to bee broken, and once being broken never to bee repaired againe by them. By this meanes the King stood assured, that I must bee enforced for lacke of sustenance there, to disband my company into sundry places to live upon shell fish, for so the Savages themselves doe, going to Hatorask, Croatoan,[1] and other places, fishing and hunting, while their grounds be in sowing, and their corne growing: which failed not his expectation. For the famine grew so extreeme among us, our weares failing us of fish, that I was enforced to sende Captaine Stafford with 20. with him to Croatoan my Lord Admirals Iland to serve two turnes in one, that is to say, to feede himselfe and his company, and also to keepe watch if any shipping came upon the coast to warne us of the same. I sent M. Pridiox with the pinnesse to Hatorask, and ten with him, with the Provost Marshal to live there, and also to wait for shipping: also I sent every weeke 16. or 20. of the rest of the company to the maine over against us, to live of Casada and oysters.

In the meane while Pemisapan went of purpose to Dasamonquepeio for three causes: The one to see his grounds there broken up, and sowed for a second crop: the other to withdrawe himselfe from my dayly sending to him for supply of victuall for my company, for hee was afraid to deny me any thing, neither durst hee in my presence but by colour and with excuses, which I was content to accept for the time, meaning in the ende as I had reason to give him the jumpe once for all: but in the meane whiles, as I had ever done before, I and mine bare all wrongs, and accepted of all excuses.

My purpose was to have relied my selfe with Menatonon, and the Chaonists, who in trueth as they are more valiant people and in greater number then the rest, so are they more

[1] Doubtless the geography of these sandy islands enclosing Pamlico Sound has been largely altered by storms since Lane's day. Judging by White's chart, Hatorask indicates, not the region of the present Cape Hatteras, but that of New Inlet, while Croatoan was an island extending approximately from Cape Hatteras to the present Hatteras Inlet.

faithfull in their promises, and since my late being there had given many tokens of earnest desire they had to joyne in perfect league with us, and therefore were greatly offended with Pemisapan and Weopomeiok for making him beleeve such tales of us.

The third cause of his going to Dasamonquepeio was to dispatch his messengers to Weopomeiok, and to the Mandoages, as aforesaid: all which he did with great imprest of copper in hand, making large promises to them of greater spoile.

The answere within few dayes after came from Weopomeiok, which was devided into two parts. First for the King Okisko, who denied to be of the partie for himselfe, or any of his especiall followers, and therefore did immediatly retire himselfe with his force into the maine: the other was concerning the rest of the province who accepted of it: and in like sort the Mandoags received the imprest.

The day of their assembly aforesaid at Roanoak was appointed the 10. of June: all which the premises were discovered by Skyco, the King Menatonon his sonne my prisoner, who having once attempted to run away, I laid him in the bylboes,[1] threatning to cut off his head, whom I remitted at Pemisapans request: whereupon hee being perswaded that hee was our enemie to the death, he did not onely feed him with himselfe, but also made him acquainted with all his practises. On the other side, the yong man finding himselfe as well used at my hande, as I had meanes to shew, and that all my company made much of him, he flatly discovered al unto me, which also afterwards was reveiled unto me by one of Pemisapans owne men, that night before he was slaine.

These mischiefes being all instantly upon me and my company to be put in execution, it stood mee in hand to study how to prevent them, and also to save all others, which were at that time as aforesaid so farre from me: whereupon I sent to Pemisapan to put suspition out of his head, that I meant

[1] Fetters for confinement of offenders on shipboard, and also, as here, the place of such confinement.

presently to go to Croatoan, for that I had heard of the arrivall of our fleete, (though I in trueth had neither heard nor hoped for so good adventure,) and that I meant to come by him, to borrow of his men to fish for my company, and to hunt for me at Croatoan, as also to buy some foure dayes provision to serve for my voyage.

He sent me word that he would himselfe come over to Roanoak, but from day to day he deferred, onely to bring the Weopomeioks with him and the Mandoags, whose time appointed was within eight dayes after. It was the last of May 1586 when all his owne Savages began to make their assembly at Roanoak, at his commandement sent abroad unto them, and I resolved not to stay longer upon his comming over, since he meant to come with so good company, but thought good to go and visit him with such as I had, which I resolved to do the next day: but that night I meant to give them in the Iland a camisado,[1] and at the instant to seize upon all the canoas about the Island, to keepe him from advertisements.

But the towne tooke the alarme before I meant it to them: the occasion was this, I had sent the Master of the light horseman, with a few with him, to gather up all the canoas in the setting of the Sun, and to take as many as were going from us to Dasamonquepeio, but to suffer any that came from thence, to land. He met with a Canoa, going from the shore, and overthrew the Canoa, and cut off two Savages heads: this was not done so secretly but he was discovered from the shore; whereupon the cry arose: for in trueth they, privy to their owne villanous purposes against us, held as good espial upon us, both day and night, as we did upon them.

The allarme given, they tooke themselves to their bowes, and we to our armes: some three or foure of them at the first were slaine with our shot; the rest fled into the woods. The next morning with the light horsman and one Canoa taking 25 with the Colonel of the Chesepians, and the Sergeant major,

---

[1] Night surprise. The origin of the term is to be found in the custom among horsemen of wearing white shirts over the armor, so as to recognize one another in the darkness.

I went to Dasamonquepeio: and being landed, sent Pemisapan word by one of his owne Savages that met me at the shore, that I was going to Croatoan, and meant to take him in the way to complaine unto him of Osocon, who the night past was conveying away my prisoner, whom I had there present tied in an handlocke. Heereupon the king did abide my comming to him, and finding myselfe amidst seven or eight of his principall Weroances and followers, (not regarding any of the common sort) I gave the watch-word agreed upon, (which was, Christ our victory) and immediatly those his chiefe men and himselfe had by the mercy of God for our deliverance, that which they had purposed for us. The king himselfe being shot thorow by the Colonell with a pistoll, lying on the ground for dead, and I looking as watchfully for the saving of Manteos friends, as others were busie that none of the rest should escape, suddenly he started up, and ran away as though he had not bene touched, insomuch as he overran all the company, being by the way shot thwart the buttocks by mine Irish boy with my petronell. In the end an Irish man serving me, one Nugent, and the deputy provost, undertooke him; and following him in the woods, overtooke him: and I in some doubt least we had lost both the king and my man by our owne negligence to have beene intercepted by the Savages, wee met him returning out of the woods with Pemisapans head in his hand.

This fell out the first of June 1586, and the eight of the same came advertisement to me from captaine Stafford, lying at my lord Admirals Island, that he had discovered a great fleet of three and twentie sailes: but whether they were friends or foes, he could not yet discerne. He advised me to stand upon as good guard as I could.

The ninth of the sayd moneth he himselfe came unto me, having that night before, and that same day travelled by land twenty miles: and I must truely report of him from the first to the last; hee was the gentleman that never spared labour or perill either by land or water, faire weather or foule, to performe any service committed unto him.

He brought me a letter from the Generall Sir Francis Drake, with a most bountifull and honourable offer for the supply of our necessities to the performance of the action wee were entred into; and that not only of victuals, munition, and clothing, but also of barks, pinnesses, and boats; they also by him to be victualled, manned and furnished to my contentation.

The tenth day he arrived in the road of our bad harborow: and comming there to an anker, the eleventh day I came to him, whom I found in deeds most honourably to performe that which in writing and message he had most curteously offered, he having aforehand propounded the matter to all the captaines of his fleet, and got their liking and consent thereto.

With such thanks unto him and his captaines for his care both of us and of our action, not as the matter deserved, but as I could both for my company and myselfe, I (being aforehand prepared what I would desire) craved at his hands that it would please him to take with him into England a number of weake and unfit men for any good action, which I would deliver to him; and in place of them to supply me of his company with oare-men, artificers, and others.

That he would leave us so much shipping and victuall, as about August then next following would cary me and all my company into England, when we had discovered somewhat, that for lacke of needfull provision in time left with us as yet remained undone.

That it woulde please him withall to leave some sufficient Masters not onely to cary us into England, when time should be, but also to search the coast for some better harborow, if there were any, and especially to helpe us to some small boats and oare-men.

Also for a supply of calievers, hand weapons, match and lead, tooles, apparell, and such like.

He having received these my requests, according to his usuall commendable maner of government (as it was told me) calling his captaines to counsell; the resolution was that I should send such of my officers of my company as I used in such matters, with their notes, to goe aboord with him; which were the Master of the victuals, the Keeper of the store, and the Vicetreasurer: to whom he appointed forthwith for me The Francis, being a very proper barke of 70 tun, and tooke present order for bringing of victual aboord her for 100 men for foure moneths, with all my other demands whatsoever, to the uttermost.

And further, he appointed for me two pinnesses, and foure small boats: and that which was to performe all his former liberality towards us, was that he had gotten the full assents of two of as sufficient experimented Masters as were any in his fleet, by judgement of them that knew them, with very sufficient gings[1] to tary with me, and to employ themselves most earnestly in the action, as I should appoint them, untill the terme which I promised of our returne into England againe. The names of one of those Masters was Abraham Kendall, the other Griffith Herne.

While these things were in hand, the provision aforesayd being brought, and in bringing aboord, my sayd Masters being also gone aboord, my sayd barks having accepted of their charge, and mine owne officers, with others in like sort of my company with them (all which was dispatched by the sayd Generall the 12 of the sayde moneth) the 13 of the same there arose such an unwoonted storme, and continued foure dayes, that had like to have driven all on shore, if the Lord had not held his holy hand over them, and the Generall very providently foreseene the woorst himselfe, then about my dispatch putting himselfe aboord: but in the end having driven sundry of the fleet to put to Sea the Francis also with all my provisions, my two Masters, and my company aboord, she was seene to be free from the same, and to put cleere to Sea.

This storme having continued from the 13 to the 16 of the moneth, and thus my barke put away as aforesayd, the Generall comming ashore made a new proffer unto me; which was a ship of 170 tunne, called The barke Bonner, with a sufficient Master and guide to tary with me the time appointed, and

---

[1] Gangs.

victualled sufficiently to cary me and my company into England, with all provisions as before: but he tolde me that he would not for any thing undertake to have her brought into our harbour, and therefore he was to leave her in the road, and to leave the care of the rest unto my selfe, and advised me to consider with my company of our case, and to deliver presently unto him in writing what I would require him to doe for us; which being within his power, he did assure me aswell for his Captaines as for himselfe, shoulde be most willingly performed.

Heereupon calling such Captaines and gentlemen of my company as then were at hand, who were all as privy as my selfe to the Generals offer; their whole request was to me, that considering the case that we stood in, the weaknesse of our company, the small number of the same, the carying away of our first appointed barke, with those two especiall Masters, with our principall provisions in the same, by the very hand of God as it seemed, stretched out to take us from thence; considering also, that his second offer, though most honourable of his part, yet of ours not to be taken, insomuch as there was no possibility for her with any safety to be brought into the harbour: seeing furthermore, our hope for supply with Sir Richard Greenvill, so undoubtedly promised us before Easter, not yet come, neither then likely to come this yeere, considering the doings in England for Flanders, and also for America, that therefore I would resolve my selfe with my company to goe into England in that fleet, and accordingly to make request to the Generall in all our names, that he would be pleased to give us present passage with him. Which request of ours by my selfe delivered unto him, hee most readily assented unto: and so he sending immediatly his pinnesses unto our Island for the fetching away of a few that there were left with our baggage, the weather was so boisterous, and the pinnesses so often on ground, that the most of all we had, with all our Cards, Books and writings were by the Sailers cast overboord, the greater number of the fleet being much agrieved with their long and dangerous abode in that miserable road.

From whence the Generall in the name of the Almighty, weying his ankers (having bestowed us among his fleet) for the reliefe of whom hee had in that storme susteined more perill of wracke then in all his former most honourable actions against the Spanyards, with praises unto God for all, set saile the nineteenth of June 1586, and arrived in Portsmouth the seven and twentieth of July the same yeere.

THE THIRD VOYAGE TO VIRGINIA, 1586

INTRODUCTION

LANE, in returning to England with his company of colonists, supposed that Ralegh had been prevented from fulfilling his promise to send supplies before Easter by "the doings in England for Flanders," England at that time supporting the Netherlands in their conflict with Spain. But Ralegh, though unable to send supplies as early as he had promised, had not forgotten Lane and his associates. Not only was a vessel despatched to the American coast with supplies for the colony, at the sole charge of Sir Walter Ralegh, but Sir Richard Grenville, with three ships, a little later, made a second voyage across the Atlantic, in the interest of English colonization in the New World; and though disappointed in not finding the colonists whom he had conveyed to Roanoke Island the year before, he instituted measures for maintaining his country's claim to the possession of the territory, and then returned to England. The following brief narrative is from Hakluyt.

H. S. B.

THE THIRD VOYAGE TO VIRGINIA, 1586

The third voyage made by a ship sent in the yeere 1586, to the reliefe of the Colony planted in Virginia, at the sole charges of Sir Walter Ralegh.

IN the yeere of our Lord 1586 Sir Walter Ralegh at his owne charge prepared a ship of an hundred tunne, fraighted with all maner of things in most plentifull maner, for the supply and reliefe of his Colony then remaining in Virginia: but before they set saile from England it was after Easter, so that our Colony halfe despaired of the comming of any supply: wherefore every man prepared for himselfe, determining resolutely to spend the residue of their life time in that countrey. And for the better performance of this their determination, they sowed, planted, and set such things as were necessary for their reliefe in so plentifull a maner as might have sufficed them two yeeres without any further labour. Thus trusting to their owne harvest, they passed the Summer till the tenth of June: at which time their corne which they had sowed was within one fortnight of reaping: but then it happened that Sir Francis Drake in his prosperous returne from the sacking of Sant Domingo, Cartagena, and Saint Augustine, determined in his way homeward to visit his countreymen the English Colony then remaining in Virginia. So passing along the coasts of Florida, he fell with the parts where our English Colony inhabited: and having espied some of that company, there he ankered and went aland, where hee conferred with them of their state and welfare, and how things had passed with them. They answered him that they lived all; but hitherto in some scarsity: and as yet could heare of no supply out of England: therefore they requested him that hee would leave with them some two or three ships, that if in some reasonable time they heard not out of England, they might then returne themselves. Which hee agreed to. Whilest some were then writing their letters to send into England, and some others making reports of the accidents of their travels ech to other, some on land, some on boord, a great storme arose, and drove the most of their fleet from their ankers to Sea, in which ships at that instant were the chiefest of the English Colony: the rest on land perceiving this, hasted to those three sailes which were appointed to be left there; and for feare they should be left behinde they left all things confusedly, as if they had bene chased from thence by a mighty army: and no doubt so they were; for the hand of God came upon them for the cruelty and outrages committed by some of them against the native inhabitants of that countrey.[1]

Immediatly after the departing of our English Colony out of this paradise of the world, the ship abovementioned sent and set forth at the charges of Sir Walter Ralegh and his direction, arrived at Hatorask;[2] who after some time spent in seeking our Colony up in the countrey, and not finding them, returned with all the aforesayd provision into England.

About fourteene or fifteene dayes after the departure of the aforesayd shippe, Sir Richard Grinvile Generall of Virginia, accompanied with three shippes[3] well appointed for the same voyage, arrived there; who not finding the aforesayd shippe according to his expectation, nor hearing any newes of our English Colony there seated, and left by him anno 1585, himselfe travelling up into divers places of the countrey, aswell to see if he could heare any newes of the Colony left there by

[1] See the different account given above by one of the colonists.
[2] See p. 264, note 1, above.
[3] In the margin the statement is made, "Sir Richard Grinvils third voyage." Grenville aided in sending out Amadas and Barlowe in 1584, but he did not accompany the expedition. This accordingly was his second voyage, not the third. In his *Sketches of the Literary History of Barnstaple*, Chanter has this item: "April 16, 1586. Sir Richard Greynville sailed over the barr at Barnstaple with his flee boat and frigot; but for want of sufficient water on the barr, being neare upon neape, he left his ship. This Sir Richard Greynville intended his goinge to Wyngandecora where he was last year."

him the yeere before, under the charge of Master Lane his deputy, as also to discover some places of the countrey; but after some time spent therein, not hearing any newes of them, and finding the places which they inhabited desolate, yet unwilling to loose the possession of the countrey which Englishmen had so long held: after good deliberation, hee determined to leave some men behinde to reteine possession of the Countrey: whereupon he landed fifteene men in the Isle of Roanoak, furnished plentifully with all maner of provision for two yeeres, and so departed for England.

Not long after he fell with the Isles of Açores, on some of which Islands he landed, and spoiled the townes of all such thinges as were woorth cariage, where also he tooke divers Spanyards. With these and many other exploits done him in this voyadge, as well outward as homeward, he returned into England.

THE FOURTH VOYAGE MADE TO VIRGINIA IN THE YERE 1587, BY GOVERNOR JOHN WHITE

INTRODUCTION

SIR WALTER RALEGH still maintained his interest in his schemes of American colonization, notwithstanding many discouragements. By an indenture, dated January 7, 1587, he granted to John White and others certain privileges for planting a colony in Virginia. First of all, White was to bring relief to the fifteen men left at Roanoke Island by Grenville the year before, and then he was to seek a new location for his colony on the shores of Chesapeake Bay. Of the thirty-two incorporators, nineteen were London merchants, of whom ten later were subscribers to the Virginia Company which settled at Jamestown. Stevens, *Bibliotheca Historica*, 1870, p. 222, identifies John White, the artist of the expedition of 1585, with Governor White of the expedition of 1587. The following journal was evidently written by White. The arrangement under month-headings is the same as in the account of the fifth voyage, which in Hakluyt follows this account of the fourth voyage.

H. S. B.

THE FOURTH VOYAGE MADE TO VIRGINIA, IN THE YERE 1587, BY GOVERNOR JOHN WHITE

The fourth voyage made to Virginia with three ships, in the yere 1587. Wherein was transported the second Colonie.

IN the yeere of our Lord 1587. Sir Walter Ralegh intending to persevere in the planting of his Countrey of Virginia, prepared a newe Colonie of one hundred and fiftie men to be sent thither, under the charge of John White, whom hee appointed Governour, and also appointed unto him twelve Assistants, unto whom hee gave a Charter, and incorporated them by the name of Governour and Assistants of the Citie of Ralegh in Virginia.

April

Our Fleete being in number three saile, viz. the Admirall a shippe of one hundred and twentie Tunnes, a Flie-boate, and a Pinnesse, departed the sixe and twentieth of April from Portesmouth, and the same day came to an ancker at the Cowes in the Isle of Wight, where wee stayed eight dayes.

May

The fift of May, at nine of the clocke at night we came to Plimmouth, where we remained the space of two dayes.

The 8 we weyed anker at Plimmouth, and departed thence for Virginia.

The 16 Simon Ferdinando,[1] Master of our Admirall, lewdly

[1] Simon Ferdinando, so ill spoken of throughout this narrative, is lauded by Lane in one of his letters from America. *Archaeologia Americana,* IV. 11

forsooke our Fly-boate, leaving her distressed in the Bay of Portugal.

June

The 19 we fell with Dominica,[1] and the same evening we sayled betweene it, and Guadalupe: the 21 the Fly-boat also fell with Dominica.

The 22 we came to an anker at an Island called Santa Cruz,[2] where all the planters were set on land, staying there till the 25 of the same moneth. At our first landing on this Island, some of our women, and men, by eating a small fruit like greene Apples, were fearefully troubled with a sudden burning in their mouthes, and swelling of their tongues so bigge, that some of them could not speake. Also a child by sucking one of those womens breasts, had at that instant his mouth set on such a burning, that it was strange to see how the infant was tormented for the time: but after 24 houres it ware away of it selfe.

Also the first night of our being on this Island, we took five great Torteses, some of them of such bignes, that sixteene of our strongest men were tired with carying of one of them but from the sea side to our cabbins. In this Island we found no watring place, but a standing ponde, the water whereof was so evill, that many of our company fell sicke with drinking thereof: and as many as did but wash their faces with that water, in the morning before the Sunne had drawen away the corruption, their faces did so burne and swell, that their eyes were shut up, and could not see in five or sixe dayes, or longer.

The second day of our abode there, we sent forth some of our men to search the Island for fresh water, three one way, and two another way. The Governour also, with sixe others, went up to the top of an high hill, to viewe the Island, but could perceive no signe of any men, or beastes, nor any good-

---

[1] Twenty-nine miles south of Guadeloupe.
[2] St. Croix, a southerly island of the Virgin group.

nes, but Parots, and trees of Guiacum.[1] Returning backe to our cabbins another way, he found in the discent of a hill, certaine potsheards of savage making, made of the earth of that Island: whereupon it was judged, that this Island was inhabited with Savages, though Fernando had told us for certaine the contrary. The same day at night, the rest of our company very late returned to the Governour. The one company affirmed, that they had seene in a valley eleven Savages, and divers houses halfe a mile distant from the steepe, or toppe of the hill where they stayed. The other company had found running out of a high rocke a very fayre spring of water, whereof they brought three bottels to the company; for before that time, wee drank the stinking water of the pond.

The same second day at night Captaine Stafford, with the Pinnesse, departed from our fleete, riding at Santa Cruz, to an Island, called Beake,[2] lying neere S. John,[3] being so directed by Ferdinando, who assured him he should there find great plenty of sheepe. The next day at night, our planters left Santa Cruz, and came all aboord, and the next morning after, being the 25 of June we weyed anker, and departed from Santa Cruz.

The seven and twentieth we came to anker at Cottea,[4] where we found the Pinnesse riding at our comming.

The 28 we weyed anker at Cottea, and presently came to anker at S. Johns in Musketos Bay,[5] where we spent three dayes unprofitable in taking in fresh water, spending in the meane time more beere then the quantitie of the water came unto.

[1] Also Guaiacum, the heart-wood or the resin of the *Guaiacum officinale* or lignum-vitae.
[2] Vieques, a small island near Porto Rico, now belonging to the United States.
[3] *I.e.*, Porto Rico (San Juan de Porto Rico).
[4] In the narration of Sir Richard Grenville's voyage of 1585, Hakluyt, new edition, VIII. 311, we have this record under May 10, "Wee came to an anker at Cotesa, a little Iland situate neere to the Iland of St. John."
[5] A marginal note says, "Musketos Bay is a harbour upon the south side of S. Johns Island."

Julie

The first day we weyed anker at Musketoes Bay, where were left behind two Irish men of our company, Darbie Glaven, and Denice Carrell, bearing along the coast of S. Johns till evening, at which time wee fell with Rosse Bay.[1] At this place Ferdinando had promised wee should take in salte, and had caused us before, to make and provide as many sackes for that purpose, as we could. The Governour also, for that hee understood there was a Towne in the bottome of the Bay, not farre from the salt hils, appointed thirty shot, tenne pikes, and ten targets, to man the Pinnesse, and to goe aland for salt. Ferdinando perceiving them in a readines, sent to the Governour, using great perswasions with him, not to take in salt there, saying that hee knew not well whether the same were the place or not: also, that if the Pinnesse went into the Bay, she could not without great danger come backe, till the next day at night, and that if in the meane time any storme should rise, the Admirall were in danger to bee cast away. Whilest he was thus perswading, he caused the lead to be cast, and having craftily brought the shippe in three fadome and a halfe water, he suddenly began to sweare, and teare God in pieces, dissembling great danger, crying to him at the helme, beare up hard, beare up hard: so we went off, and were disappointed of our salt, by his meanes.

The next day sayling along the west end of S. John, the Governour determined to go aland in S. Germans[2] Bay, to gather yong plants of Orenges, Pines, Mameas, and Plantanos, to set at Virginia, which we knew might easily be had, for that they grow neere the shore, and the places where they grew, well knowen to the Governour, and some of the planters: but our Simon denied it, saying: he would come to an anker

[1] In the account of Sir Richard Grenville's voyage of 1585, Hakluyt, VIII. 312, this is given as Roxo Bay, and is located on the southwest side of Porto Rico.
[2] Probably the present port of Guayanilla, where the original town of St. Germans was built.

at Hispaniola, and there land the Governour, and some other of the Assistants, with the pinnesse, to see if he could speake with his friend Alanson, of whom he hoped to be furnished both of cattel, and all such things as we would have taken in at S. John: but he meant nothing lesse, as it plainely did appeare to us afterwards.

The next day after, being the third of July, we saw Hispaniola, and bare with the coast all that day, looking still when the pinnesse should be prepared to goe for the place where Ferdinando his friend Alanson was: but that day passed, and we saw no preparation for landing in Hispaniola.

The 4. of July, sayling along the coast of Hispaniola, untill the next day at noone, and no preparation yet seene for the staying there, we having knowledge that we were past the place where Alanson dwelt, and were come with Isabella:[1] hereupon Ferdinando was asked by the Governour, whether he meant to speake with Alanson, for the taking in of cattell, and other things, according to his promise, or not: but he answered that he was now past the place, and that Sir Walter Ralegh told him, the French Ambassador certified him, that the king of Spaine had sent for Alanson into Spaine: wherefore he thought him dead, and that it was to no purpose to touch there in any place, at this voyage.

The next day we left sight of Hispaniola, and haled off for Virginia, about foure of the clocke in the afternoone.

The sixt day of July we came to the Island Caycos,[2] wherein Ferdinando sayd were two salt pondes, assuring us if they were drie we might find salt to shift with, untill the next supply: but it prooved as true as finding of sheepe at Baque.[3] In this Island, whilest Ferdinando solaced himselfe ashore, with one of the company, in part of the Island, others spent the latter part of that day in other parts of the Iland, some to seeke the salt ponds, some fowling, some hunting Swans, whereof we caught many. The next day early in the morning

[1] On the north side of Hispaniola.   [2] One of the Turk's Island group.
[3] Beake above (Vieques).

we weyed anker, leaving Caycos, with good hope, that the first land that we saw next should be Virginia.

About the 16 of July we fel with the maine of Virginia, which Simon Ferdinando tooke to be the Island of Croatoan, where we came to anker, and rode there two or three dayes: but finding himselfe deceived, he weyed, and bare along the coast, where in the night, had not Captaine Stafford bene more carefull in looking out, then our Simon Ferdinando, we had bene all cast away upon the breach, called the Cape of Feare,[1] for we were come within two cables length upon it: such was the carelesnes, and ignorance of our Master.

The two and twentieth of July wee arrived safe at Hatorask, where our ship and pinnesse ankered: the Governour went aboord the pinnesse, accompanied with fortie of his best men, intending to passe up to Roanoak foorthwith, hoping there to finde those fifteene Englishmen, which Sir Richard Grinvile had left there the yeere before, with whom he meant to have conference, concerning the state of the Countrey, and Savages, meaning after he had so done, to returne againe to the fleete, and passe along the coast, to the Bay of Chesepiok where we intended to make our seate and forte, according to the charge given us among other directions in writing, under the hande of Sir Walter Ralegh: but assoone as we were put with our pinnesse from the ship, a Gentleman by the meanes of Ferdinando, who was appointed to returne for England, called to the sailers in the pinnesse, charging them not to bring any of the planters backe againe, but to leave them in the Island, except the Governour, and two or three such as he approved, saying that the Summer was farre spent, wherefore hee would land all the planters in no other place. Unto this were all the saylers, both in the pinnesse, and shippe, perswaded by the Master, wherefore it booted not the Governour to contend with them, but passed to Roanoak, and the same night at sunne-

---

[1] The name was probably given by Sir Richard Grenville, whose fleet narrowly escaped shipwreck there June 23, 1585. The record in the narrative of the voyage (Hakluyt, VIII. 315) says, "The 23, we were in great danger of wracke on a breach called the Cape of Feare."

set went aland on the Island, in the place where our fifteene men were left, but we found none of them, nor any signe that they had bene there, saving onely wee found the bones of one of those fifteene, which the Savages had slaine long before.

The three and twentieth of July the Governour with divers of his company, walked to the North ende of the Island, where Master Ralfe Lane had his forte, with sundry necessary and decent dwelling houses, made by his men about it the yeere before, where wee hoped to find some signes, or certaine knowledge of our fifteene men. When we came thither, we found the fort rased downe, but all the houses standing unhurt, saving that the neather roomes of them, and also of the forte, were overgrowen with Melons of divers sortes, and Deere within them, feeding on those Melons: so wee returned to our company, without hope of ever seeing any of the fifteene men living.[1]

The same day order was given, that every man should be employed for the repayring of those houses, which wee found standing, and also to make other new Cottages, for such as should neede.

The 25 our Flyboate and the rest of our planters arrived all safe at Hatoraske, to the great joy and comfort of the whole company: but the Master of our Admirall Ferdinando grieved greatly at their safe comming: for hee purposely left them in the Bay of Portugal, and stole away from them in the night, hoping that the Master thereof, whose name was Edward Spicer, for that he never had bene in Virginia, would hardly finde the place, or els being left in so dangerous a place as that was, by meanes of so many men of warre, as at that time were abroad, they should surely be taken, or slaine: but God disappointed his wicked pretenses.

The eight and twentieth, George Howe, one of our twelve Assistants was slaine by divers Savages, which were come over to Roanoak, either of purpose to espie our company, and what

[1] On the remains of early English colonization on Roanoke Island, see the paper of Dr. Talcott Williams in the *Annual Report of the American Historical Association*, for 1895, pp. 57–61.

we were, or else to hunt Deere, whereof were many in the Island. These Savages being secretly hidden among high reedes, where oftentimes they find the Deere asleep, and so kill them, espied our man wading in the water alone, almost naked, without any weapon, save only a smal forked sticke, catching Crabs therewithall, and also being strayed two miles from his company, and shot at him in the water, where they gave him sixteen wounds with their arrowes: and after they had slaine him with their woodden swords, they beat his head in pieces, and fled over the water to the maine.

On the thirtieth of July Master Stafford and twenty of our men passed by water to the Island of Croatoan, with Manteo, who had his mother, and many of his kindred dwelling in that Island, of whom wee hoped to understand some newes of our fifteene men, but especially to learne the disposition of the people of the countrey toward us, and to renew our old friendship with them. At our first landing they seemed as though they would fight with us: but perceiving us begin to march with our shot towardes them, they turned their backes, and fled. Then Manteo their countrey man called to them in their owne language, whom, assoone as they heard, they returned, and threwe away their bowes and arrowes, and some of them came unto us, embracing and entertaining us friendly, desiring us not to gather or spill any of their corne, for that they had but little. We answered them, that neither their corne, nor any other thing of theirs, should be diminished by any of us, and that our comming was onely to renew the old love, that was betweene us and them at the first, and to live with them as brethren and friends: which answer seemed to please them well, wherefore they requested us to walke up to their Towne, who there feasted us after their maner, and desired us earnestly, that there might bee some token or badge given them of us, whereby we might know them to be our friends, when we met them any where out of the Towne or Island. They told us further, that for want of some such badge, divers of them were hurt the yeere before, being found out of the Island by Master Lane his company, whereof they shewed us one, which

U

at that very instant lay lame, and had lien of that hurt ever since: but they sayd, they knew our men mistooke them, and hurt them instead of Winginos men, wherefore they held us excused.

August

The next day we had conference further with them, concerning the people of Secotan, Aquascogoc,[1] and Pomeiok, willing them of Croatoan to certifie the people of those townes, that if they would accept our friendship, we would willingly receive them againe, and that all unfriendly dealings past on both parts, should be utterly forgiven and forgotten. To this the chiefe men of Croatoan answered, that they would gladly doe the best they could, and within seven dayes, bring the Wiroances and chiefe Governours of those townes with them, to our Governour at Roanoak, or their answere. We also understood of the men of Croatoan, that our man Master Howe was slaine by the remnant of Winginos men dwelling then at Dasamonguepeuk, with whom Wanchese[2] kept companie: and also we understood by them of Croatoan, how that the 15 Englishmen left at Roanoak the yeere before, by Sir Richard Grinvile, were suddenly set upon, by 30 of the men of Secota, Aquascogoc, and Dasamonguepeuk in manner following. They conveyed themselves secretly behind the trees, neere the houses where our men carelesly lived: and having perceived that of those fifteene they could see but eleven onely, two of those Savages appeared to the 11 Englishmen calling to them by friendly signes, that but two of their chiefest men should come unarmed to speake with those two Savages, who seemed also to be unarmed. Wherefore two of the chiefest of our Englishmen went gladly to them: but whilest one of those Savages traiterously imbraced one of our men, the other with

---

[1] On White's charts this is set on the northeast side of the Pungo River, not far from the present site of Scranton, N.C.

[2] He was carried to England with Amadas and Barlowe, but had shown only bitter hostility to the English since his return.

his sworde of wood, which he had secretly hidden under his mantell, strooke him on the heade and slew him, and presently the other eight and twentie Savages shewed them selves: the other Englishman perceiving this, fled to his company, whom the Savages pursued with their bowes, and arrowes, so fast, that the Englishmen were forced to take the house, wherein all their victuall, and weapons were: but the Savages foorthwith set the same on fire: by meanes wherof our men were forced to take up such weapons as came first to hand, and without order to runne foorth among the Savages, with whom they skirmished above an howre. In this skirmish another of our men was shotte into the mouth with an arrow, where hee died: and also one of the Savages was shot into the side by one of our men, with a wild fire arrow, whereof he died presently. The place where they fought was of great advantage to the Savages, by meanes of the thicke trees, behinde which the Savages through their nimblenes, defended themselves, and so offended our men with their arrowes, that our men being some of them hurt, retyred fighting to the water side, where their boat lay, with which they fled towards Hatorask. By that time they had rowed but a quarter of a mile, they espied their foure fellowes coming from a creeke thereby, where they had bene to fetch Oysters: these foure they received into their boate, leaving Roanoak, and landed on a little Island on the right hand of our entrance into the harbour of Hatorask, where they remayned a while, but afterward departed, whither as yet we know not.

Having nowe sufficiently dispatched our businesse at Croatoan, the same day we departed friendly, taking our leave, and came aboord the fleete at Hatorask.

The eight of August, the Governour having long expected the comming of the Wiroanses of Pomeiok, Aquascogoc, Secota, and Dasamonguepeuk, seeing that the seven dayes were past, within which they promised to come in, or to send their answeres by the men of Croatoan, and no tidings of them heard, being certainly also informed by those men of Croatoan, that the remnant of Wingina his men, which were left alive, who dwelt at Dasamonquepeuk, were they which had slaine George Howe, and were also at the driving of our eleven Englishmen from Roanoak, hee thought to deferre the revenge thereof no longer. Wherefore the same night about midnight, he passed over the water, accompanied with Captaine Stafford, and 24 men, wherof Manteo was one, whom we tooke with us to be our guide to the place where those Savages dwelt, where he behaved himselfe toward us as a most faithfull Englishman.

The next day, being the 9 of August, in the morning so early that it was yet darke, we landed neere the dwelling place of our enemies, and very secretly conveyed our selves through the woods, to that side, where we had their houses betweene us and the water: and having espied their fire, and some sitting about it, we presently set on them: the miserable soules herewith amazed, fled into a place of thicke reedes, growing fast by, where our men perceiving them, shot one of them through the bodie with a bullet, and therewith we entred the reedes, among which we hoped to acquite their evill doing towards us, but we were deceived, for those Savages were our friends, and were come from Croatoan to gather the corne and fruit of that place, because they understood our enemies were fled immediatly after they had slaine George Howe, and for haste had left all their corne, Tobacco, and Pompions standing in such sort, that al had bene devoured of the birds, and Deere, if it had not bene gathered in time: but they had like to have payd deerely for it: for it was so darke, that they being naked, and their men and women apparelled all so like others, wee knew not but that they were al men: and if that one of them which was a Wiroances wife had not had a child at her backe, shee had bene slaine in stead of a man, and as hap was, another Savage knew master Stafford, and ran to him, calling him by his name, whereby hee was saved. Finding our selves thus disappointed of our purpose, we gathered al the corne, Pease, Pompions, and Tabacco that we found ripe, leaving the rest unspoyled, and tooke Menatoan his wife, with the yong child, and the other Savages with us over the water to Roanoak. Although the mistaking of these Savages somewhat grieved Manteo, yet he imputed their harme to their owne folly, saying to them, that if their Wiroances had kept their promise in comming to the Governour at the day appointed, they had not knowen that mischance.

The 13 of August our Savage Manteo, by the commandement of Sir Walter Ralegh, was christened in Roanoak, and called Lord thereof, and of Dasamonguepeuk, in reward of his faithfull services.

The 18 Elenor, daughter to the Governour, and wife to Ananias Dare one of the Assistants, was delivered of a daughter in Roanoak, and the same was christened there the Sonday following, and because this child was the first Christian borne in Virginia, shee was named Virginia.[1] By this time our ships had unladen the goods and victuals of the planters, and began to take in wood, and fresh water, and to new calke and trimme them for England: the planters also prepared their letters and tokens to send backe into England.

Our two ships, the Lion and the Flyboat almost ready to depart, the 21 of August, there arose such a tempest at Northeast, that our Admirall then riding out of the harbour, was forced to cut his cables, and put to sea, where he lay beating off and on sixe dayes before he could come to us againe, so that we feared he had bene cast away, and the rather for that at the time that the storme tooke them, the most and best of their sailers were left aland.

At this time some controversies arose betweene the Governour and Assistants, about choosing two out of the twelve Assistants, which should goe backe as factors for the company into England: for every one of them refused, save onely one, which all other thought not sufficient: but at length by much perswading of the Governour, Christopher Cooper only agreed to goe for England: but the next day, through the perswasion of divers of his familiar friends, hee changed his minde, so that now the matter stood as at the first.

[1] Her mother was a daughter of Governor John White. In the list of the colonists printed in Hakluyt the name of Ananias Dare is the second after that of John White.

The next day, the 22 of August, the whole company both of the Assistants and planters came to the Governour, and with one voice requested him to returne himselfe into England, for the better and sooner obtaining of supplies, and other necessaries for them: but he refused it, and alleaged many sufficient causes, why he would not: the one was, that he could not so suddenly returne backe againe without his great discredite, leaving the action, and so many whome hee partly had procured through his perswasions, to leave their native countrey, and undertake that voyage, and that some enemies to him and the action at his returne into England would not spare to slander falsly both him and the action, by saying, hee went to Virginia, but politikely, and to no other end but to leade so many into a countrey, in which hee never meant to stay himselfe, and there to leave them behind him. Also he alleaged, that seeing they intended to remove 50 miles further up into the maine presently, he being then absent, his stuffe and goods might be both spoiled, and most of them pilfered away in the cariage, so that at his returne he should be either forced to provide himselfe of all suche things againe, or else at his comming againe to Virginia find himselfe utterly unfurnished, whereof already he had found some proofe, being but once from them but three dayes. Wherefore he concluded that he would not goe himselfe.

The next day, not onely the Assistants but divers others, as well women as men, began to renew their requests to the Governour againe, to take upon him to returne into England for the supply, and dispatch of all such things as there were to be done, promising to make him their bond under all their handes and seales for the safe preserving of all his goods for him at his returne to Virginia, so that if any part thereof was spoyled or lost, they would see it restored to him, or his Assignes, whensoever the same should be missed and demanded: which bond, with a testimony under their hands and seales, they foorthwith made, and delivered into his hands. The copie of the testimony I thought good to set downe.

"May it please you, her Majesties subjects of England, we

your friends and countrey-men, the planters in Virginia, doe by these presents let you and every of you to understand, that for the present and speedy supply of certaine our knowen and apparent lackes and needes, most requisite and necessary for the good and happy planting of us, or any other in this land of Virginia, wee all of one minde and consent, have most earnestly intreated, and uncessantly requested John White, Governour of the planters in Virginia, to passe into England, for the better and more assured help, and setting forward of the foresayd supplies: and knowing assuredly that he both can best, and wil labour and take paines in that behalfe for us all, and he not once, but often refusing it, for our sakes, and for the honour and maintenance of the action, hath at last, though much against his will, through our importunacie, yeelded to leave his governement, and all his goods among us, and himselfe in all our behalfes to passe into England, of whose knowledge and fidelitie in handling this matter, as all others, we doe assure ourselves by these presents, and will you to give all credite thereunto, the 25 of August 1587."

The Governour being at the last through their extreame intreating constrayned to returne into England, having then but halfe a dayes respite to prepare himselfe for the same, departed from Roanoak the seven and twentieth of August in the morning and the same day about midnight, came aboord the Flieboat, who already had weyed anker, and rode without the barre, the Admirall riding by them, who but the same morning was newly come thither againe. The same day both the ships weyed anker, and set saile for England: at this weying their ankers, twelve of the men which were in the Flyboate were throwen from the Capstone, which by meanes of a barre [that] brake, came so fast about them, that the other two barres thereof strooke and hurt most of them so sore, that some of them never recovered it; neverthelesse they assayed presently againe to wey their anker, but being so weakened with the first fling, they were not able to weye it, but were throwen downe and hurt the second time. Wherefore having in all but fifteene men aboord, and most of them by this unfortunate beginning so bruised, and hurt, they were forced to cut their Cable, and leese their anker. Neverthelesse, they kept company with the Admirall, untill the seventeenth of September, at which time wee fell with Corvo, and sawe Flores.

September

The eighteenth, perceiving that of all our fifteene men in the Flyboat there remained but five, which by meanes of the former mischance, were able to stand to their labour: and that the Admirall meant not to make any haste for England but to linger about the Island of Tercera [1] for purchase: the Flyboate departed for England with letters, where we hoped by the helpe of God to arrive shortly: but by that time we had continued our course homeward about twentie dayes, having had sometimes scarse and variable windes, our fresh water also by leaking almost consumed, there arose a storme at Northeast, which for sixe dayes ceased not to blowe so exceeding, that we were driven further in those sixe then we could recover in thirteene daies: in which time others of our saylers began to fall very sicke and two of them dyed, the weather also continued so close, that our Master sometimes in foure dayes together could see neither sunne nor starre, and all the beverage we could make, with stinking water, dregs of beere, and lees of wine which remayned, was but three gallons, and therefore nowe we expected nothing but famine to perish at Sea.

October

The 16 of October we made land, but we knewe not what land it was, bearing in with the same land at that day: about sunne set we put into a harbour, where we found a Hulke of Dublin, and a pinnesse of Hampton riding, but we knew not as yet what place this was, neither had we any boate to goe

[1] Now Terceira, one of the Azores group.

ashore, untill the pinnesse sent off their boate to us with 6 or 8 men, of whom wee understood wee were in Smerwick in the West parts of Ireland: they also releeved us presently with fresh water, wine and other fresh meate.

The 18 the Governour and the Master ryd to Dingen a Cushe,[1] 5 miles distant, to take order for the new victualing of our Flieboat for England, and for reliefe of our sicke and hurt men, but within foure daies after the Boatswain, the Steward, and the Boatswains mate died aboord the Flieboat, and the 28 the Masters mate and two of our chiefe sailers were brought sicke to Dingen.

November

The first the Governour shipped himselfe in a ship called the Monkie, which at that time was ready to put to sea from Dingen for England, leaving the Flyboat and all his companie in Ireland. The same day we set sayle, and on the third day we fell with the North side of the lands end, and were shut up the Severne, but the next day we doubled the same for Mounts Bay.[2]

The 5 the Governour landed in England at Martasew,[3] neere Saint Michaels mount in Cornewall.

The 8 we arrived at Hampton,[4] where we understood that our consort the Admiral was come to Portsmouth, and had bene there three weekes before: and also that Ferdinando the Master with all his company were not onely come home without purchase, but also in such weaknesse by sicknesse, and death of their chiefest men, that they were scarse able to bring their ship into harbour, but were forced to let fall anker without, which they could not wey againe, but might all have perished there, if a small barke by a great hap had not come

---

[1] Now Dingle, County Kerry, on the southwestern coast of Ireland.

[2] The large bay between Land's End and the Lizard, on the southern coast of England.

[3] A hamlet on Mounts Bay.

[4] Southampton, still a principal port of departure for England's foreign trade.

to them to helpe them. The names of the chiefe men that died are these, Roger Large, John Mathew, Thomas Smith, and some other saylers, whose names I knew not at the writing hereof. An. Dom. 1587.

The names of all the men, women and children, which safely arrived in Virginia, and remained to inhabite there. 1587. Anno regni Reginæ Elizabethæ. 29

John White.
Ananias Dare.
Thomas Stevens.
Dyonis Harvie.
George How.
Nicholas Johnson.
Anthony Cage.
William Willes.
Cutbert White.
Clement Tayler.
John Cotsmur.
Thomas Colman.
Marke Bennet.
John Stilman.
John Tydway.
Edmond English.
Henry Berry.
John Spendlove.
Thomas Butler.
John Burden.
Thomas Ellis.
Michael Myllet.
Richard Kemme.
Richard Taverner.
Henry Johnson.
Richard Darige.
Arnold Archard.

Roger Baily.
Christopher Cooper.
John Sampson.
Roger Prat.
Simon Fernando.
Thomas Warner.
John Jones.
John Brooke.
John Bright.
William Sole.
Humfrey Newton.
Thomas Gramme.
John Gibbes.
Robert Wilkinson.
Ambrose Viccars.
Thomas Topan.
Richard Berry.
John Hemmington.
Edward Powell.
James Hynde.
William Browne.
Thomas Smith.
Thomas Harris.
John Earnest.
John Starte.
William Lucas.
John Wright.

William Dutton.
William Waters.
John Chapman.
Robert Little.
Richard Wildye.
Michael Bishop.
Henry Rufoote.
Henry Dorrell.
Henry Mylton.
Thomas Harris.
Thomas Phevens.
Thomas Scot.
John Wyles.
George Martyn.
Martin Sutton.
John Bridger.
Richard Shabedge.
John Cheven.
William Berde.

Mauris Allen.
Richard Arthur.
William Clement.
Hugh Taylor.
Lewes Wotton.
Henry Browne.
Richard Tomkins.
Charles Florrie.
Henry Paine.
William Nichols.
John Borden.
Peter Little.
Brian Wyles.
Hugh Pattenson.
John Farre.
Griffen Jones.
James Lasie.
Thomas Hewet.

Women

Elyoner Dare.
Agnes Wood.
Joyce Archard.
Elizabeth Glane.
Audry Tappan.
Emme Merrimoth.
Margaret Lawrence.
Jane Mannering.
Elizabeth Viccars.

Margery Harvie.
Wenefrid Powell.
Jane Jones.
Jane Pierce.
Alis Chapman.
Colman.
Joan Warren.
Rose Payne.

Boyes and children

John Sampson.
Ambrose Viccars.
Thomas Humfrey.
George How.
William Wythers.

Robert Ellis.
Thomas Archard.
Thomas Smart.
John Prat.

Children borne in Virginia

Virginia Dare.   Harvie.

Savages that were in England and returned home into Virginia with them

Manteo.   Towaye.

THE FIFTH VOYAGE OF M. JOHN WHITE
1590

INTRODUCTION

IN the spring of 1588 all England was busy with preparations for meeting the Spanish Armada. It was not a time for New World enterprises. So great, however, was Ralegh's interest in the colonists left by White at Roanoke Island, that he succeeded in getting ready a small relief fleet, which was placed under the charge of Sir Richard Grenville; but before the vessels were ready to sail they were impressed by the government. Strenuous effort on Ralegh's part, however, was successful in securing at length two small vessels, and these sailed from England April 22, under the command of Governor White; but in an encounter with Spanish ships not long after, they were so severely handled that they were obliged to return. In the following year, Ralegh made another attempt to send relief to the Roanoke Island colonists and failed. In 1590 three vessels of a London merchant, John Wattes, ready for a voyage to the West Indies, were held in port by an order prohibiting any vessel from leaving England. White, through Ralegh, obtained the release of the vessels, provided they would take him and some others, with supplies, to Virginia. When, however, the vessels sailed, the owners restricted passage to White; and before he could have his agreement with the owners enforced, the vessels put to sea, White being the only passenger for Virginia. The following narration records White's failure to find the colonists he left at Roanoke Island. All that he could learn concerning them was that the supply vessels failing to arrive, they at length removed to Croatoan. This was White's last voyage to the American coast. After his return to England, discouraged by the failure of the efforts already made, White seems to have abandoned hope. Ralegh, however, continued to send out vessels in search of the lost colonists. Nothing was learned concerning their fate, however, until after the settlement of the colony at Jamestown, when, according to Strachey, it was reported by the Indians that nearly all the Roanoke Island colonists were massacred by order of Powhatan only a little while before the Jamestown colonists arrived.

H. S. B.

THE FIFTH VOYAGE OF M. JOHN WHITE, 1590

To the Worshipful and my very friend Master Richard Hakluyt, much happinesse in the Lord.

SIR, as well for the satisfying of your earnest request, as the performance of my promise made unto you at my last being with you in England, I have sent you (although in a homely stile, especially for the contentation of a delicate eare) the true discourse of my last voyage into the West Indies, and partes of America called Virginia, taken in hand about the end of Februarie, in the yeare of our redemption 1590. And what events happened unto us in this our journey, you shall plainely perceive by the sequele of my discourse. There were at the time aforesaid three ships absolutely determined to goe for the West Indies, at the speciall charges of M. John Wattes of London Marchant. But when they were fully furnished, and in readinesse to make their departure, a generall stay was commanded of all ships thorowout England. Which so soone as I heard, I presently (as I thought it most requisite) acquainted Sir Walter Ralegh therewith, desiring him that as I had sundry times afore bene chargeable and troublesome unto him, for the supplies and reliefes of the planters in Virginia: so likewise, that by his endevour it would please him at that instant to procure license for those three ships to proceede on with their determined voyage, that thereby the people in Virginia (if it were Gods pleasure) might speedily be comforted and relieved without further charges unto him. Whereupon he by his good meanes obtained license of the Queenes Majestie, and order to be taken, that the owner of the 3 ships should be bound unto Sir Walter Ralegh or his assignes, in 3000 pounds, that those 3 ships in consideration of their releasement should take in, and transport a convenient number of passengers, with their furnitures and necessaries to be landed in Virginia. Neverthelesse that order was not observed, neither was the bond taken according to the intention aforesaid. But rather in contempt of the aforesaid order, I was by the owner and Commanders of the ships denied to have any passengers, or any thing els transported in any of the said ships, saving only my selfe and my chest; no not so much as a boy to attend upon me, although I made great sute, and earnest intreatie aswell to the chiefe Commanders, as to the owner of the said ships. Which crosse and unkind dealing, although it very much discontented me, notwithstanding the scarsity of time was such, that I could have no opportunity to go unto Sir Walter Ralegh with complaint: for the ships being then all in readinesse to goe to the Sea, would have bene departed before I could have made my returne. Thus both Governors, Masters, and sailers, regarding very smally the good of their countreymen in Virginia; determined nothing lesse then to touch at those places, but wholly disposed themselves to seeke after purchase and spoiles, spending so much time therein, that sommer was spent before we arrived at Virginia. And when we were come thither, the season was so unfit, and weather so foule, that we were constrained of force to forsake that coast, having not seene any of our planters, with losse of one of our ship-boates, and 7 of our chiefest men: and also with losse of 3 of our ankers and cables, and most of our caskes with fresh water left on shore, not possible to be had aboord. Which evils and unfortunate events (as wel to their owne losse as to the hinderance of the planters in Virginia) had not chanced, if the order set downe by Sir Walter Ralegh had bene observed, or if my dayly and continuall petitions for the performance of the same might have taken any place. Thus may you plainely perceive the successe of my fift and last voiage to Virginia, which was no lesse unfortunately ended then frowardly begun, and as lucklesse to many, as sinister to my selfe. But I would to God it had bene as prosperous to all, as noysome to the planters; and as joyfull to me, as discomfortable to them. Yet seeing it is not my first crossed voyage, I remaine contented. And wanting my wishes, I leave off from prosecuting that whereunto I would to God my wealth were answerable to my will. Thus committing the reliefe of my discomfortable company the planters in Virginia, to the merciful help of the Almighty, whom I most humbly beseech to helpe and comfort them, according to his most holy will and their good desire, I take my leave: from my house at Newtowne in Kylmore the 4 of February, 1593.

Your most welwishing friend,
JOHN WHITE.

The fift voyage of M. John White into the West Indies and parts of America called Virginia, in the yeere 1590.

The 20 of March the three shippes the Hopewell, the John Evangelist, and the little John, put to sea from Plymmouth with two small Shallops.

The 25 at midnight both our Shallops were sunke being towed at the ships stearnes by the Boatswaines negligence.

On the 30 we saw a head us that part of the coast of Barbary, lying East of Cape Cantyn, and the Bay of Asaphi.[1]

The next day we came to the Ile of Mogador,[2] where rode, at our passing by, a Pinnesse of London called the Mooneshine.

Aprill

On the first of Aprill we ankored in Santa Cruz rode;[3] where we found two great shippes of London lading in Sugar, of whom we had 2 shipboats to supply the losse of our Shallops.

On the 2 we set sayle from the rode of Santa Cruz, for the Canaries.

On Saturday the 4 we saw Alegranza, the East Ile of the Canaries.

[1] On the African coast, about latitude $32\frac{1}{2}°$.
[2] A short distance farther down the African coast.
[3] The most southerly seaport of Morocco, now Agadeer or Agadir.

On Sunday the 5 of Aprill we gave chase to a double flyboat, the which we also the same day fought with, and tooke her, with losse of three of their men slaine, and one hurt.

On Munday the 6 we saw Grand Canarie, and the next day we landed and tooke in fresh water on the Southside thereof.

On the 9 we departed from Grand Canary, and framed our course for Dominica.[1]

The last of Aprill we saw Dominica, and the same night we came to an anker on the Southside thereof.

May

The first of May in the morning many of the Salvages came aboord our ships in their Canowes, and did traffique with us; we also the same day landed and entered their Towne from whence we returned the same day aboord without any resistance of the Salvages; or any offence done to them.

The 2 of May our Admirall and our Pinnesse departed from Dominica leaving the John our Viceadmirall playing off and on about Dominica, hoping to take some Spaniard outwardes bound to the Indies; the same night we had sight of three smal Ilands called Los Santos,[2] leaving Guadalupe and them on our starboord.

The 3 we had sight of S. Christophers Iland, bearing Northeast and by East off us.

On the 4 we sayled by the Virgines, which are many broken Ilands, lying at the East ende of S. Johns Iland: and the same day towards evening we landed upon one of them called Blanca,[3] where we killed an incredible number of foules: here we stayed but three houres, and from thence stood into the shore Northwest, and having brought this Iland Southeast off us, we put towards night thorow an opening or swatch, called

---

[1] The course across the Atlantic was that of the voyage of 1587.
[2] Northwest of Guadeloupe.
[3] Probably Culebra, or Passage Island, one of the Virgin Islands off the east coast of Porto Rico.

FIFTH VOYAGE TO VIRGINIA

The passage,[1] lying betweene the Virgines, and the East end of S. John: here the Pinnesse left us, and sayled on the South side of S. John.

The 5 and 6 the Admirall sayled along the North side of S. John, so neere the shore that the Spaniards discerned us to be men of warre; and therefore made fires along the coast as we sailed by, for so their custome is, when they see any men of warre on their coasts.

The 7 we landed on the Northwest end of S. John, where we watered in a good river called Yaguana,[2] and the same night following we tooke a Frigate of tenne Tunne comming from Gwathanelo[3] laden with hides and ginger. In this place Pedro a Mollato, who knewe all our state, ranne from us to the Spaniards.

On the 9 we departed from Yaguana.

The 13 we landed on an Iland called Mona,[4] whereon were 10 or 12 houses inhabited of the Spaniards; these we burned and tooke from them a Pinnesse, which they had drawen a ground and sunke, and carried all her sayles, mastes, and rudders into the woods, because we should not take them away; we also chased the Spaniards over all the Iland; but they hid them in caves, hollow rockes, and bushes, so that we could not find them.

On the 14 we departed from Mona, and the next day after wee came to an Iland called Saona,[5] about 5 leagues distant from Mona, lying on the Southside of Hispaniola neere the East end: betweene these two Ilands we lay off and on 4 or 5 dayes, hoping to take some of the Domingo fleete doubling this Iland, as a neerer way to Spaine then by Cape Tyburon,[6] or by Cape S. Anthony.[7]

On Thursday being the 19 our Viceadmirall, from whom

[1] Passing through the Passage, the vessels proceeded along the northerly side of Porto Rico. The pinnace skirted the southern shores of the island.
[2] Probably the Yagüez.   [3] Guatemala.
[4] A small island in the Mona Passage.
[5] An island off the southeast end of Santo Domingo.
[6] Cape Tiburon, the western extremity of Hayti.
[7] Cape Antonio, the western extremity of Cuba.

we departed at Dominica, came to us at Saona, with whom we left a Spanish Frigate, and appointed him to lie off and on other five daies betweene Saona and Mona to the ende aforesaid; then we departed from them at Saona for Cape Tyburon. Here I was enformed that our men of the Viceadmirall, at their departure from Dominica brought away two young Salvages, which were the chiefe Casiques sonnes of that Countrey and part of Dominica, but they shortly after ran away from them at Santa Cruz Iland,[1] where the Viceadmirall landed to take in ballast.

On the 21 the Admirall came to the Cape Tyburon, where we found the John Evangelist our Pinnesse staying for us: here we tooke in two Spaniards almost starved on the shore, who made a fire to our ships as we passed by. Those places for an 100 miles in length are nothing els but a desolate and meere wildernesse, without any habitation of people, and full of wilde Bulles and Bores, and great Serpents.

The 22 our Pinnesse came also to an anker in Aligato Bay at cape Tyburon. Here we understood of M. Lane,[2] Captaine of the Pinnesse; how he was set upon with one of the kings Gallies belonging to Santo Domingo, which was manned with 400 men, who after he had fought with him 3 or 4 houres, gave over the fight and forsooke him, without any great hurt done on eyther part.

The 26 the John our Vizadmirall came to us to cape Tyburon and the Frigat which we left with him at Saona. This was the appointed place where we should attend for the meeting with the Santo Domingo Fleete.

On Whitsunday Even at Cape Tyburon, one of our boyes ranne away from us, and at tenne dayes end returned to our ships almost starved for want of food. In sundry places about this part of Cape Tyburon we found the bones and carkases of divers men, who had perished (as wee thought) by famine in those woods, being either stragled from their company, or landed there by some men of warre.

[1] The largest of the Virgin Islands.
[2] William Lane, not Ralph, according to an entry in the margin.

June

On the 14 of June we tooke a smal Spanish frigat which fell amongst us so suddenly, as he doubled the point at the Bay of Cape Tyburon, where we road, so that he could not escape us. This frigat came from Santo Domingo, and had but three men in her, the one was an expert Pilot, the other a Mountainer, and the thirde a Vintener, who escaped all out of prison at Santo Domingo, purposing to fly to Yaguana which is a towne in the West parts of Hispaniola where many fugitive Spaniards are gathered together.

The 17 being Wednesday Captaine Lane was sent to Yaguana with his Pinnesse and a Frigat to take a shippe, which was there taking in fraight, as we understood by the old Pylot, whom we had taken three dayes before.

The 24 the Frigat returned from Captaine Lane at Yaguana, and brought us word to cape Tyburon, that Captaine Lane had taken the shippe, with many passengers and Negroes in the same; which proved not so rich a prize as we hoped for, for that a Frenchman of warre had taken and spoyled her before we came. Neverthelesse her loading was thought worth 1000 or 1300 pounds, being hides, ginger, Cannafistula, Copperpannes, and Casavi.

July

The second of July Edward Spicer whom we left in England came to us at cape Tyburon, accompanied with a small Pinnesse, whereof one M. Harps was Captaine. And the same day we had sight of a fleete of 14 saile all of Santo Domingo, to whom we presently gave chase, but they upon the first sight of us fled, and separating themselves scattered here and there: Wherefore we were forced to divide our selves and so made after them untill 12 of the clocke at night. But then by reason of the darkenesse we lost sight of ech other, yet in the end the Admirall and the Moonelight happened to be together the same night at the fetching up of the Vizadmirall of the Spanish fleete, against whom the next morning we fought and tooke him,[1] with losse of one of our men and two hurt, and of theirs 4 slaine and 6 hurt. But what was become of our Viceadmirall, our Pinnesse, and Prize, and two Frigates, in all this time, we were ignorant.

The 3 of July we spent about rifling, romaging, and fitting the Prize to be sayled with us.

The 6 of July we saw Jamayca the which we left on our larboord, keeping Cuba in sight on our starboord.

Upon the 8 of July we saw the Iland of Pinos,[2] which lieth on the Southside of Cuba nigh unto the West end or Cape called Cape S. Anthony. And the same day we gave chase to a Frigat, but at night we lost sight of her, partly by the slow sayling of our Admirall, and lacke of the Moonelight our Pinnesse, whom Captaine Cooke had sent to the Cape the day before.

On the 11 we came to Cape S. Anthony, where we found our consort the Moonelight and her Pinnesse abiding for our comming, of whom we understood that the day before there passed by them 22 saile, some of them of the burden of 300 and some 400 tunnes loaden with the Kings treasure from the maine, bound for Havana: from this 11 of July untill 22 we were much becalmed: and the winde being very scarse, and the weather exceeding hoat, we were much pestered with the Spaniards we had taken: wherefore we were driven to land all the Spaniards saving three, but the place where we landed them was of their owne choise on the Southside of Cuba neere unto the Organes and Rio de Puercos.

The 23 we had sight of the Cape of Florida, and the broken Ilands thereof called the Martires.[3]

The 25 being S. James day in the morning, we fell in with the Matanças,[4] a head-land 8 leagues towards the East of Havana, where we purposed to take fresh water in, and make our abode two or three dayes.

[1] The fight, we are informed by the margin, took place in sight of Navassa, an island at the southwest entrance of the Windward Passage.
[2] Isle of Pines.   [3] The Florida Keys.   [4] Matanzas.

On Sunday the 26 of July plying too and fro betweene the Matanças and Havana, we were espied of three small Pinnasses of S. John de Ullua bound for Havana, which were exceedingly richly loaden. These 3 Pinnasses came very boldly up unto us, and so continued untill they came within musket shot of us. And we supposed them to be Captaine Harps Pinnesse, and two small Frigats taken by Captaine Harpe: wherefore we shewed our flag. But they presently upon the sight of it turned about and made all the saile they could from us toward the shore, and kept themselves in so shallow water, that we were not able to follow them, and therefore gave them over with expence of shot and pouder to no purpose. But if we had not so rashly set out our flagge, we might have taken them all three, for they would not have knowen us before they had beene in our hands. This chase brought us so far to leeward as Havana: wherfore not finding any of our consorts at the Matanças, we put over againe to the cape of Florida, and from thence thorow the chanel of Bahama.

On the 28 the Cape of Florida bare West of us.

The 30 we lost sight of the coast of Florida, and stood to Sea for to gaine the helpe of the current[1] which runneth much swifter a farre off then in sight of the coast. For from the Cape to Virginia all along the shore are none but eddie currents, setting to the South and Southwest.

The 31 our three ships were clearely disbocked,[2] the great prize, the Admirall, and the Mooneshine, but our prize being thus disbocked departed from us without taking leave of our Admirall or consort, and sayled directly for England.

August

On the first of August the winde scanted, and from thence forward we had very fowl weather with much raine, thundering, and great spouts, which fell round about us nigh unto our ships.

[1] The Gulf Stream.
[2] Meaning, apparently, "had got out into the open sea."

The 3 we stoode againe in for the shore, and at midday we tooke the height of the same. The height of that place we found to be 34 degrees of latitude. Towards night we were within three leagues of the Low sandie Ilands West of Wokokon. But the weather continued so exceeding foule, that we could not come to an anker nye the coast: wherefore we stood off againe to Sea untill Monday the 9 of August.

On munday the storme ceased, and we had very great likelihood of faire weather: therefore we stood in againe for the shore: and came to an anker at 11 fadome in 35 degrees of latitude, within a mile of the shore, where we went on land on the narrow sandy Island, being one of the Ilandes West of Wokokon: in this Iland we tooke in some fresh water and caught great store of fish in the shallow water. Betweene the maine (as we supposed) and that Iland it was but a mile over and three or foure foote deepe in most places.

On the 12 in the morning we departed from thence and toward night we came to an anker at the Northeast end of the Iland of Croatoan, by reason of a breach which we perceived to lie out two or three leagues into the Sea: here we road all that night.

The 13 in the morning before we wayed our ankers, our boates were sent to sound over this breach: our ships riding on the side thereof at 5 fadome; and a ships length from us we found but 4 and a quarter, and then deeping and shallowing for the space of two miles, so that sometimes we found 5 fadome, and by and by 7, and within two casts with the lead 9, and then 8, next cast 5, and then 6, and then 4, and then 9 againe, and deeper; but 3 fadome was the last, 2 leagues off from the shore. This breach is in 35. degr. and a halfe, and lyeth at the very Northeast point of Croatoan, whereas goeth a fret out of the maine Sea into the inner waters, which part the Ilandes and the maine land.

The 15 of August towards Evening we came to an anker at Hatorask, in 36 degr. and one third, in five fadom water, three leagues from the shore. At our first comming to anker on this shore we saw a great smoke rise in the Ile Roanoak neere the place where I left our Colony in the yeere 1587, which smoake put us in good hope that some of the Colony were there expecting my returne out of England.

The 16 and next morning our 2 boates went a shore, and Captaine Cooke, and Cap. Spicer, and their company with me, with intent to passe to the place at Roanoak where our countreymen were left. At our putting from the ship we commanded our Master gunner to make readie 2 Minions and a Falkon well loden, and to shoot them off with reasonable space betweene every shot, to the ende that their reportes might bee heard to the place where wee hoped to finde some of our people. This was accordingly performed, and our twoe boats put off unto the shore, in the Admirals boat we sounded all the way and found from our shippe untill we came within a mile of the shore nine, eight, and seven fadome: but before we were halfe way betweene our ships and the shore we saw another great smoke to the Southwest of Kindrikers mountes: we therefore thought good to goe to that second smoke first: but it was much further from the harbour where we landed, then we supposed it to be, so that we were very sore tired before wee came to the smoke. But that which grieved us more was that when we came to the smoke, we found no man nor signe that any had bene there lately, nor yet any fresh water in all this waye to drinke. Being thus wearied with this journey we returned to the harbour where we left our boates, who in our absence had brought their caske a shore for fresh water, so we deferred our going to Roanoak untill the next morning, and caused some of those saylers to digge in those sandie hills for fresh water whereof we found very sufficient. That night wee returned aboord with our boates and our whole company in safety.

The next morning being the 17 of August, our boates and company were prepared againe to goe up to Roanoak, but Captaine Spicer had then sent his boat ashore for fresh water, by meanes whereof it was ten of the clocke afternoone before we put from our ships which were then come to an anker within two miles of the shore. The Admirals boat was halfe way toward the shore, when Captaine Spicer put off from his ship. The Admirals boat first passed the breach, but not without some danger of sinking, for we had a sea brake into our boat which filled us halfe full of water, but by the will of God and carefull styrage of Captaine Cooke we came safe ashore, saving onely that our furniture, victuals, match and powder were much wet and spoyled. For at this time the winde blue at Northeast and direct into the harbour so great a gale, that the Sea brake extremely on the barre, and the tide went very forcibly at the entrance. By that time our Admirals boat was halled ashore, and most of our things taken out to dry, Captaine Spicer came to the entrance of the breach with his mast standing up, and was halfe passed over, but by the rash and undiscreet styrage of Ralph Skinner his Masters mate, a very dangerous Sea brake into their boate and overset them quite, the men kept the boat some in it, and some hanging on it, but the next sea set the boat on ground, where it beat so, that some of them were forced to let goe their hold, hoping to wade ashore: but the Sea still beat them downe, so that they could neither stand nor swimme, and the boat twise or thrise was turned the keele upward, whereon Captaine Spicer and Skinner hung untill they sunke, and were seene no more. But foure that could swimme a litle kept themselves in deeper water and were saved by Captaine Cookes meanes, who so soone as he saw their oversetting, stripped himselfe, and foure other that could swimme very well, and with all haste possible rowed unto them, and saved foure. There were 11 in all and 7 of the chiefest were drowned, whose names were Edward Spicer, Ralph Skinner, Edward Kelly, Thomas Bevis, Hance the Surgion, Edward Kelborne, Robert Coleman. This mischance did so much discomfort the saylers, that they were all of one mind not to goe any further to seeke the planters. But in the end by the commandement and perswasion of me and Captaine Cooke, they prepared the boates: and seeing the Captaine and me so resolute, they seemed much more willing. Our boates and all things fitted againe, we put off from Hatorask, being the number of 19 persons in both boates: but before we could get to the place where our planters were left, it was so exceeding darke, that we overshot the place a quarter of a mile: there we espied towards the North ende of the Island the light of a great fire thorow the woods, to which we presently rowed: when wee came right over against it, we let fall our Grapnel neere the shore and sounded with a trumpet a Call, and afterwardes many familiar English tunes of Songs, and called to them friendly; but we had no answere, we therefore landed at day-breake, and comming to the fire, we found the grasse and sundry rotten trees burning about the place. From hence we went thorow the woods to that part of the Iland directly over against Dasamongwepeuk, and from thence we returned by the water side, round about the North point of the Iland, untill we came to the place where I left our Colony in the yeere 1586. In all this way we saw in the sand the print of the Salvages feet of 2 or 3 sorts troaden the night, and as we entred up the sandy banke upon a tree, in the very browe thereof were curiously carved these faire Romane letters C R O: which letters presently we knew to signifie the place, where I should find the planters seated, according to a secret token agreed upon betweene them and me at my last departure from them, which was, that in any wayes they should not faile to write or carve on the trees or posts of the dores the name of the place where they should be seated; for at my comming away they were prepared to remove from Roanoak 50 miles into the maine. Therefore at my departure from them in An. 1587 I willed them, that if they should happen to be distressed in any of those places, that then they should carve over the letters or name, a Crosse ✠ in this forme, but we found no such signe of distresse. And having well considered of this, we passed toward the place where they were left in sundry houses, but we found the houses taken downe, and the place very strongly enclosed with a high palisado of great trees, with cortynes[1] and flankers very Fortlike, and one of the chiefe trees or postes at the right side of the entrance had the barke taken

---

[1] Curtains.

off, and 5 foote from the ground in fayre Capitall letters was graven CROATOAN without any crosse or signe of distresse; this done, we entred into the palisado, where we found many barres of iron, two pigges of Lead, foure yron fowlers, Iron sacker-shotte,[1] and such like heavie thinges, throwen here and there, almost overgrowen with grasse and weedes. From thence wee went along by the water side, towards the poynt of the Creeke to see if we could find any of their botes or Pinnisse, but we could perceive no signe of them, nor any of the last Falkons and small Ordinance which were left with them, at my departure from them. At our returne from the Creeke, some of our Saylers meeting us, told us that they had found where divers chests had bene hidden, and long sithence digged up againe and broken up, and much of the goods in them spoyled and scattered about, but nothing left, of such things as the Savages knew any use of, undefaced. Presently Captaine Cooke and I went to the place, which was in the ende of an olde trench, made two yeeres past by Captaine Amadas: wheere wee found five Chests, that had bene carefully hidden of the Planters, and of the same chests three were my owne, and about the place many of my things spoyled and broken, and my bookes torne from the covers, the frames of some of my pictures and Mappes rotten and spoyled with rayne, and my armour almost eaten through with rust; this could bee no other but the deede of the Savages our enemies at Dasamongwepeuk, who had watched the departure of our men to Croatoan; and assoone as they were departed digged up every place where they suspected any thing to be buried: but although it much grieved me to see such spoyle of my goods, yet on the other side I greatly joyed that I had safely found a certaine token of their safe being at Croatoan, which is the place where Manteo was borne, and the Savages of the Iland our friends.[2]

[1] Shot for sakers, or large cannon.
[2] On the theory, not generally held, that the colony was not wholly destroyed, and that descendants of some of its members are still to be found in North Carolina, see Weeks, "The Lost Colony of Roanoke: Its Fate and Survival," in *Papers of the American Historical Association*, V. 107.

When we had seene in this place so much as we could, we returned to our Boates, and departed from the shoare towards our shippes, with as much speede as we could: For the weather beganne to overcast, and very likely that a foule and stormie night would ensue. Therefore the same Evening with much danger and labour, we got our selves aboard, by which time the winde and seas were so greatly risen, that wee doubted our Cables and Anchors would scarcely holde untill Morning: wherefore the Captaine caused the Boate to be manned by five lusty men, who could swimme all well, and sent them to the little Iland on the right hand of the Harbour, to bring aboard sixe of our men, who had filled our caske with fresh water: the Boate the same night returned aboard with our men, but all our Caske ready filled they left behinde, unpossible to bee had aboard without danger of casting away both men and Boates: for this night prooved very stormie and foule.

The next Morning it was agreed by the Captaine and my selfe, with the Master and others, to wey anchor, and goe for the place at Croatoan, where our planters were: for that then the winde was good for that place, and also to leave that Caske with fresh water on shoare in the Iland untill our returne. So then they brought the cable to the Capston, but when the anchor was almost apecke, the Cable broke, by meanes whereof we lost another Anchor, wherewith we drove so fast into the shoare, that wee were forced to let fall a third Anchor: which came so fast home that the Shippe was almost aground by Kenricks mounts: so that we were forced to let slippe the Cable ende for ende. And if it had not chanced that wee had fallen into a chanell of deeper water, closer by the shoare then wee accompted of, wee could never have gone cleare of the poynt that lyeth to the Southwardes of Kenricks mounts. Being thus cleare of some dangers, and gotten into deeper waters, but not without some losse: for wee had but one Cable and Anchor left us of foure, and the weather grew to be fouler and fouler; our victuals scarse, and our caske and fresh water lost: it was therefore determined that we should goe for Saint John or some other Iland to the Southward for fresh water. And it was further purposed, that if wee could any wayes supply our wants of victuals and other necessaries, either at Hispaniola, Sant John, or Trynidad, that then we should continue in the Indies all the Winter following, with hope to make 2. rich voyages of one, and at our returne to visit our countreymen at Virginia. The captaine and the whole company in the Admirall (with my earnest petitions) thereunto agreed, so that it rested onely to knowe what the Master of the Moone-light our consort would doe herein. But when we demanded them if they would accompany us in that new determination, they alledged that their weake and leake Shippe was not able to continue it; wherefore the same night we parted, leaving the Moone-light to goe directly for England, and the Admirall set his course for Trynidad, which course we kept two dayes.

On the 28. the winde changed, and it was sette on foule weather every way: but this storme brought the winde West and Northwest, and blewe so forcibly, that wee were able to beare no sayle, but our fore-course halfe mast high, wherewith wee ranne upon the winde perforce, the due course for England, for that wee were driven to change our first determination for Trynidad, and stoode for the Ilands of Açores, where wee purposed to take in fresh water, and also there hoped to meete with some English men of warre about those Ilands, at whose hands wee might obtaine some supply of our wants. And thus continuing our course for the Açores, sometimes with calmes, and sometimes with very scarce windes, on the fifteenth of September the winde came South Southeast, and blew so exceedingly, that wee were forced to lye atry [1] all that day. At this time by account we judged our selves to be about twentie leagues to the West of Cuervo and Flores, but about night the storme ceased, and fayre weather ensued.

On Thursday the seventeenth wee saw Cuervo and Flores, but we could not come to anker that night, by reason the winde shifted. The next Morning being the eighteenth, stand-

[1] Heave to.

ing in againe with Cuervo, we escryed a sayle a head us, to whom we gave chase: but when wee came neere him, wee knew him to be a Spanyard, and hoped to make sure purchase of him: but we understood at our speaking with him, that he was a prize, and of the Domingo fleete already taken by the John our consort, in the Indies. We learned also of this prize, that our Viceadmirall and Pinnesse had fought with the rest of the Domingo fleete, and had forced them with their Admirall to flee unto Jamaica under the Fort for succour, and some of them ran themselves aground, whereof one of them they brought away, and tooke out of some others so much as the time would permit. And further wee understood of them, that in their returne from Jamaica about the Organes neere Cape Saint Anthony, our Viceadmirall mette with two Shippes of the mayne land, come from Mexico, bound for Havana, with whom he fought: in which fight our Viceadmirals Lieutenant was slaine, and the Captaines right arme strooken off, with foure other of his men slaine, and sixteene hurt. But in the ende he entred, and tooke one of the Spanish shippes, which was so sore shot by us under water, that before they could take out her treasure she sunke; so that we lost thirteene Pipes of silver which sunke with her, besides much other rich marchandize. And in the meane time the other Spanish shippe being pearced with nine shotte under water, got away; whom our Viceadmirall intended to pursue: but some of their men in the toppe made certaine rockes, which they saw above water neere the shoare, to be Gallies of Havana and Cartagena, comming from Havana to rescue the two Ships; Wherefore they gave over their chase, and went for England. After this intelligence was given us by this our prize, he departed from us, and went for England.

On Saturday the 19. of September we came to an Ancre neere a small village on the North side of Flores, where we found ryding 5. English men of warre, of whom we understood that our Viceadmirall and Prize were gone thence for England. One of these five was the Moonelight our consort, who upon the first sight of our comming into Flores, set sayle and went for England, not taking any leave of us.

On Sunday the 20. the Mary Rose, Admirall of the Queenes fleete, wherein was Generall Sir John Hawkins, stood in with Flores, and divers other of the Queenes ships, namely the Hope, the Nonpareilia, the Rainebow, the Swift-sure, the Foresight, with many other good merchants ships of warre, as the Edward Bonaventure, the Marchant Royal, the Amitie, the Eagle, the Dainty of sir John Hawkins, and many other good ships and pinnesses, all attending to meete with the king of Spaines fleete, comming from Terra firma of the West Indies.

The 22. of September we went aboard the Raynebow, and towards night we spake with the Swift-sure, and gave him 3. pieces. The captaines desired our company; wherefore we willingly attended on them: who at this time with 10. other ships stood for Faial. But the Generall with the rest of the Fleete were separated from us, making two fleetes, for the surer meeting with the Spanish fleete.

On Wednesday the 23. we saw Gratiosa,[1] where the Admiral and the rest of the Queenes fleete were come together. The Admirall put forth a flag of counsel, in which was determined that the whole fleete should go for the mayne, and spred themselves on the coasts of Spaine and Portugal, so farre as conveniently they might, for the surer meeting of the Spanish fleete in those parts.

The 26. we came to Faial, where the Admiral with some other of the fleete ankred, other some plyed up and downe betweene that and the Pico untill midnight, at which time the Anthony shot off a piece and weyed, shewing his light: after whom the whole fleete stood to the East, the winde at Northeast by East.

On Sunday the 27. towards Evening wee tooke our leave of the Admirall and the whole fleete, who stood to the East. But our shippe accompanied with a Flyboate stoode in again with

[1] Of the Azores group; so also are Fayal, Pico, São Jorge, and São Miguel, mentioned in the following paragraphs.

S. George, where we purposed to take in more fresh water, and some other fresh victuals.

On Wednesday the 30. of September, seeing the winde hang so Northerly, that wee could not atteine the Iland of S. George, we gave over our purpose to water there, and the next day framed our due course for England.

October

The 2. of October in the Morning we saw S. Michaels Iland on our Starre board quarter.

The 23. at 10. of the clocke afore noone, we saw Ushant in Britaigne.[1]

On Saturday the 24. we came in safetie, God be thanked, to an anker at Plymmouth.

[1] The most western of the islands of Brittany.

BRIEFE AND TRUE RELATION OF THE
DISCOVERIE OF THE NORTH PART OF
VIRGINIA, 1602, BY JOHN BRERETON

INTRODUCTION

ENGLISH voyagers to the American coast in the sixteenth century made their way thither by the island of Newfoundland, or the islands of the West Indies. Bartholomew Gosnold and Bartholomew Gilbert evidently aimed directly for the New England coast, avoiding the more northerly region visited by Cabot, and afterward by the French explorers, and the region visited by the expeditions sent out by Sir Walter Ralegh. They made at Cuttyhunk the first, though temporary, English settlement in New England. Brereton's *Relation*, which was printed in 1602, and is dedicated to Sir Walter Ralegh, states that the voyage was undertaken with Ralegh's permission. This is an error, although Ralegh allowed the statement to stand. The voyage was without Ralegh's knowledge. A fall in the price of sassafras, which had been held as high as twenty shillings a pound in the London market, occasioned an inquiry on Ralegh's part as to the cause of the lessening value of this New-World commodity. This inquiry led to the discovery of Gosnold's successful venture, and to a complaint on Ralegh's part that Gosnold and his associates had infringed on his rights as patentee. It was found, however, that persons of prominence had aided Gosnold and Gilbert in their enterprise; and as it was desirable that the matter should be set before the public in as favorable a light as possible, Ralegh consented to the statement that the expedition had his permission. Bartholomew Gilbert was a son of Sir Humphrey Gilbert. He at once made his peace with Ralegh, and the next year, in Ralegh's service, he came to Virginia, where he lost his life, some say in Chesapeake Bay, but more probably on the mainland. Gosnold, also, was again interested in New-World enterprises, and December 19, 1606, he sailed for Virginia with the Jamestown colonists. He was one of a large number of the colonists who died shortly after their arrival on the James. Brereton's *Relation* is the earliest English book relating to New England. Two editions of it were published in 1602, the one in twenty-four pages, the other in forty-eight, containing additional matter not deemed necessary to the present volume. The former issue, represented by a copy in the John Carter Brown Library at Providence, was reprinted in black-letter facsimile by Mr. L. S. Livingston in 1903, and is the one reprinted on the following pages. The other is reprinted in the third series of the *Collections of the Massachusetts Historical Society*, Vol. VIII., pp. 83–103, and in Winship's *Sailors' Narratives of New England Voyages*. There is also another "Relation" of this voyage, made by Gabriel Archer, who was "a gentleman in the said voyage." Purchas printed it in his fourth volume. A reprint of it will be found in the third Series of the *Collections of the Massachusetts Historical Society*, Vol. VIII., pp. 72–81.

BRIEFE AND TRUE RELATION OF THE DISCOVERIE OF THE NORTH PART OF VIRGINIA IN 1602

A Briefe and true Relation of the Discoverie of the North part of Virginia; being a most pleasant, fruitfull and commodious soile:
Made this present yeere 1602, by Captaine Bartholomew Gosnold, Captaine Bartholowmew Gilbert, and divers other gentlemen their associats, by the permission of the honourable knight, Sir Walter Ralegh, &c.
Written by M. John Brereton one of the voyage. . . .[1]

To the honourable, Sir Walter Ralegh, Knight, Captaine of her Majesties Guards, Lord Warden of the Stanneries, Lieutenant of Cornwall, and Governour of the Isle of Jersey.

Honourable sir, being earnestly requested by a deere friend, to put downe in writing, some true relation of our late performed voyage to the North parts of Virginia; at length I resolved to satisfie his request, who also imboldened me, to direct the same to your honourable consideration; to whom indeed of duetie it perteineth.

May it please your Lordship therefore to understand, that upon the sixe and twentieth of March 1602, being Friday, we went from Falmouth, being in all, two and thirtie persons,[2] in a small barke of Dartmouth, called *The Concord*, holding a course for the North part of Virginia: and although by chance the winde favoured us not at first as we wished, but inforced us so farre to the Southward, as we fell with S. Marie, one of

---

[1] These words in italics are taken from the title-page, which ends with the imprint: "Londini, Impensis Geor. Bishop, 1602."

[2] Archer says twelve were to return to England with the ship, and the rest were to remain "for population."

the islands of the Açores (which was not much out of our way) yet holding our course directly from thence, we made our journey shorter (than hitherto accustomed) by the better part of a thousand leagues, yet were wee longer in our passage than we expected; which happened, for that our barke being weake, we were loth to presse her with much saile; also, our sailers being few, and they none of the best, we bare (except in faire weather) but low saile; besides, our going upon an unknowen coast, made us not over-bolde to stand in with the shore, but in open weather; which caused us to be certeine daies in sounding, before we discovered the coast, the weather being by chance, somewhat foggie. But on Friday the fourteenth of May, early in the morning, we made the land,[1] being full of faire trees, the land somewhat low, certeine hummocks or hilles lying into the land, the shore ful of white sand, but very stony or rocky. And standing faire alongst by the shore, about twelve of the clocke the same day, we came to an anker, where sixe Indians, in a Baske-shallop[2] with mast and saile, an iron grapple, and a kettle of copper, came boldly aboord us, one of them apparelled with a waistcoat and breeches of blacke serdge, made after our sea-fashion, hose and shoes on his feet; all the rest (saving one that had a paire of breeches of blue cloth) were all naked. These people are of tall stature, broad and grim visage, of a blacke swart complexion, their eie-browes painted white; their weapons are bowes and arrowes: it seemed by some words and signes they made, that some Basks[3]

[1] Concerning Gosnold's landfall, Archer says, — "The fourteenth, about six in the morning, we descried Land that lay North, &c., the Northerly part we called the North Land, which to another Rocke upon the same lying twelve leagues West, that wee called Savage Rocke, (because the Savages first shewed themselves there)." It is admitted by all who have given any attention to this voyage that Gosnold made his approach to the land north of Massachusetts Bay. "North Land" is probably best identified as Cape Porpoise, and "Savage Rock," as Cape Neddock, — both on the southerly part of the Maine coast.

[2] This is evidence that Basque fishermen extended their voyages to the coast of Maine.

[3] They "could name Placentia of the New-found-land," says Archer. This is added evidence that French fishermen, visiting the Newfoundland fishing banks, came to the New England coast.

or of S. John de Luz, have fished or traded in this place, being in the latitude of 43 degrees. But riding heere, in no very good harbour, and withall, doubting the weather, about three of the clocke the same day in the afternoone we weighed, and standing Southerly off into sea the rest of that day and the night following, with a fresh gale of winde, in the morning we found our selves embayed with a mightie headland;[1] but comming to an anker about nine of the clocke the same day, within a league of the shore, we hoised out the one halfe of our shallop, and captaine Bartholmew Gosnold, my selfe, and three others, went ashore, being a white sandie and very bolde shore; and marching all that afternoon with our muskets on our necks, on the highest hilles which we saw (the weather very hot) at length we perceived this headland to be a parcell of the maine, and sundrie Islands lying almost round about it: so returning (towards evening) to our shallop (for by that time, the other part was brought ashore and set together) we espied an Indian, a young man, of proper stature, and of a pleasing countenance; and after some familiaritie with him, we left him at the sea side, and returned to our ship, where, in five or sixe hours absence, we had pestered our ship so with Cod fish, that we threw numbers of them over-boord againe: and surely, I am persuaded that in the moneths of March, April, and May, there is upon this coast, better fishing, and in as great plentie, as in Newfoundland: for the sculles of mackerell, herrings, Cod, and other fish,[2] that we dayly saw as we went and came from the shore, were woonderfull; and besides, the places where we tooke these Cods (and might in a few daies have laden our ship) were but in seven faddome water, and within lesse than a league of the shore; where, in New-found-land they fish in fortie or

---

[1] If Cape Ann was the starting-point, as some maintain, this "mightie headland," Cape Cod, would have been discovered much earlier by Gosnold in proceeding down the coast. Earlier voyagers, from the time of the Northmen, had descried this "mightie headland," "where wee tooke great store of Cod-fish," says Archer, "for which we altered the name, and called it Cape Cod."

[2] The abundance of fish on the New England coast is mentioned by all of the early explorers.

fiftie fadome water, and farre off. From this place, we sailed round about this headland, almost all the points of the compasse, the shore very bolde: but as no coast is free from dangers, so I am persuaded, this is as free as any; the land somwhat lowe, full of goodly woods, but in some places plaine: at length we were come amongst many faire Islands,[1] which we had partly discerned at our first landing; all lying within a league or two one of another, and the outermost not above sixe or seven leagues from the maine: but comming to an anker under one of the[m],[2] which was about three or foure leagues from the maine, captaine Gosnold, my selfe, and some others, went ashore, and going round about it, we found it to be foure English miles in compasse, without house or inhabitant, saving a little old house made of boughs, covered with barke, an olde piece of a weare of the Indians, to catch fish, and one or two places, where they had made fires. The chiefest trees of this Island, are Beeches and Cedars; the outward parts all overgrowen with lowe bushie trees, three or foure foot in height, which beare some kinde of fruits, as appeared by their blossomes; Strawberies, red and white, as sweet and much bigger than ours in England, Rasberies, Gooseberies, Hurtleberies, and such; an incredible store of Vines, aswell in the woodie part of the Island, where they run upon every tree, as on the outward parts, that we could not goe for treading upon them: also, many springs of excellent sweet water, and a great standing lake of fresh water, neere the sea side, an English mile in compasse, which is mainteined with the springs running exceeding pleasantly thorow the woodie grounds which are very rockie. Here are also in this Island, great store of Deere, which we saw, and other beasts, as appeared by their tracks, as also divers fowles, as Cranes, Hernshawes, Bitters, Geese; Mallards, Teales, and other fowles, in great plenty; also, great store of Pease, which grow in certeine plots all the Island over.

[1] Nantucket would be one of the first.
[2] A note in the margin of the original reads, "The first Island called Marthaes vineyard." The island was no doubt the present No Man's Land, near the larger island now called Martha's Vineyard.

On the North side of this Island we found many huge bones and ribbes of Whales. This Island, as also all the rest of these Islands, are full of all sorts of stones fit for building; the sea sides all covered with stones, many of them glistering and shining like minerall stones, and very rockie: also, the rest of these Islands are replenished with these commodities, and upon some of them, inhabitants; as upon an Island to the Northward, and within two leagues of this; yet wee found no townes, nor many of their houses, although we saw manie Indians, which are tall big boned men, all naked, saving they cover their privy parts with a blacke tewed skin, much like a Black-smithes apron, tied about their middle and betweene their legs behinde: they gave us of their fish readie boiled (which they carried in a basket made of twigges, not unlike our osier) whereof we did eat, and judged them to be fresh water fish: they gave us also of their Tabacco, which they drinke [1] greene, but dried into powder, very strong and pleasant, and much better than any I have tasted in England: the necks of their pipes are made of clay hard dried (whereof in that Island is great store both red and white) the other part, is a piece of hollow copper, very finely closed and semented together: we gave unto them certeine trifles, as knives, points, and such like, which they much esteemed. From thence we went to another Island,[2] to the Northwest of this, and within a league or two of the maine, which we found to be greater than before we imagined, being 16 English miles at the least in compasse; for it conteineth many pieces or necks of land, which differ nothing fro severall Islands, saving that certeine

[1] "We dranke of their excellent Tabacco," says Rosier, in his relation of Waymouth's voyage to the coast of Maine in 1605. "Drinking" tobacco was the term generally employed at that time, when the reference was to smoking it. Drake, *Book of the Indians*, p. 22, cites an entry in the Plymouth records in 1646 as follows, "Anthony Thatcher and George Pole were chosen a committee to draw up an order concerning disorderly drinking of tobacco."

[2] Cuttyhunk, one of the Elizabeth group of islands. A circumference of sixteen miles can be ascribed to it, however, only by combining with it the next island northward, now separated by a narrow strait. Archer says, "This Iland Captaine Gosnoll called Elizabeths Ile."

banks of small bredth do like bridges joyne them to this Island: on the outsides of this Island are many plaine places of grasse, abundance of Strawberies and other berries before mentioned: in mid May we did sowe in this Island (as for triall) in sundry places, Wheat, Barley, Oats, and Pease, which in foureteene daies were sprung up nine inches and more:[1] the soile is fat and lustie; the upper crust, of gray colour; but a foot or lesse in depth, of the colour of our hempe-lands in England; and being thus apt for these and the like graines; the sowing or setting (after the ground is cleansed) is no greater labour, than if you should set or sowe in one of our best prepared gardens in England. This Island is full of high timbered Oaks, their leaves thrise so broad as ours; Cedars, strait and tall; Beech, Elme, Hollie, Walnut trees in abundance, the fruit as bigge as ours, as appeared by those we found under the trees, which had lien all the yeere ungathered; Haslenut trees, Cherry trees, the leafe, barke and bignesse not differing from ours in England, but the stalke beareth the blossomes or fruit at the end thereof, like a cluster of Grapes, forty or fifty in a bunch; Sassafras trees [2] plentie all the Island over, a tree

[1] Other like statements concerning the remarkable fertility of the soil occur in the "Relations" of these early voyagers, and are indications of easy exaggeration. Shakespeare, in the *Tempest* (Act IV. Scene i.) makes Iris say to Ceres: —

"Ceres, most bounteous lady, thy rich leas
Of wheat, rye, barley, vetches, oats, and pease."

The *Tempest* was written, it is thought, in 1610–1611, and in this and other descriptions of the "uninhabited island," the scene of the play (which Shakespearian scholars have identified with Bermuda, Lampedusa, Pantalaria, and Corcyra), Edward Everett Hale finds intimations that Shakespeare was familiar with the story of Gosnold's Elizabeth Isle and used it in the play. In the *Tempest*, he says, "there is no allusion to an orange, a banana, a yam, or a potato, or a palm-tree, or a pineapple, or a monkey, or a parrot, or anything else which refers to the Gulf of Mexico or the tropics. Does not this seem as if he meant that the local color of the *Tempest* should be that which was suggested by the gentlemen adventurers and the seamen who were talking of Cuttyhunk, its climate and productions, as they told travellers' stories up and down London?" The Earl of Southampton, the patron and friend of Shakespeare, was the patron of Gosnold in this voyage.

[2] Sassafras was regarded as "a plant of Sovereigne vertue." Archer, in his "Relation," Purchas, IV. 1649 (*Mass. Hist. Soc. Coll.*, third series,

of high price and profit; also divers other fruit trees, some of them with strange barks, of an Orange colour, in feeling soft and smoothe like Velvet: in the thickest parts of the woods, you may see a furlong or more round about. On the Northwest side of this Island, neere to the sea side, is a standing Lake of fresh water, almost three English miles in compasse, in the middest whereof stands a plot of woodie ground, an acre in quantitie or not above: This Lake is full of small Tortoises, and exceedingly frequented with all sorts of fowles before rehearsed, which breed, some lowe on the banks, and others on lowe trees about this Lake in great abundance, whose young ones of all sorts we tooke and eat at our pleasure: but all these fowles are much bigger than ours in England. Also, in every Island, and almost in every part of every Island, are great store of Ground nuts, fortie together on a string, some of them as bigge as hennes egges; they grow not two inches under ground: the which nuts we found to be as good as Potatoes. Also, divers sorts of shell-fish, as Scallops, Muscles, Cockles, Lobsters, Crabs, Oisters, and Whilks, exceeding good and very great. But not to cloy you with particular rehearsall of such things as God and Nature hath bestowed on these places, in comparison wherof, the most fertil part of al England is (of it selfe) but barren; we went in our light-horsman fro this Island to the maine, right against this Island some two leagues off, where comming ashore, we stood a while like men ravished at the beautie and delicacie of this sweet soile; for besides divers cleere Lakes of fresh water (whereof we saw no end) Medowes very large and full of greene grasse; even the most woody places (I speake onely of such as I saw) doe grow so distinct and apart, one tree from another, upon greene grassie ground, somewhat higher than the Plaines, as if Nature would shew herselfe above her power, artificiall. Hard by, we espied seven Indians; and comming up to them, at first they expressed some feare; but being emboldned by our courteous

VIII. 77, 78), says, "The powder of Sassafrage in twelve houres cured one of our Company that had taken a great surfett by eating the bellies of Dogfish, a very delicious meate."

usage, and some trifles which we gave them, they followed us to a necke of land, which we imagined had beene severed from the maine; but finding it otherwise, we perceived a broad harbour or rivers mouth, which ranne up into the maine. but because the day was farre spent, we were forced to returne to the Island from whence we came, leaving the discoverie of this harbour, for a time of better leasure: of the goodnesse of which harbour, as also of many others thereabouts, there is small doubt, considering that all the Islands, as also the maine (where we were) is all rockie grounds and broken lands. Now the next day, we determined to fortifie our selves in the little plot of ground in the midst of the Lake above mentioned, where we built an house, and covered it with sedge, which grew about this lake in great abundance; in building whereof, we spent three weeks and more:[1] but the second day after our comming from the maine, we espied 9 canowes or boats, with fiftie Indians in them, comming towards us from this part of the maine, where we, two daies before, landed; and being loth they should discover our fortification, we went out on the sea side to meet them; and comming somewhat neere them, they all sat downe upon the stones, calling aloud to us (as we rightly ghessed) to doe the like, a little distance from them: having sat a while in this order, captaine Gosnold willed me to go unto them, to see what countenance they would make; but assoone as I came up unto them, one of them, to whom I had given a knife two daies before in the maine, knew me (whom I also very wel remembered) and smiling upon me, spake somewhat unto their lord or captaine, which sat in the midst of them, who presently rose up and tooke a large Beaver skin from one that stood about him, and gave it unto me, which I requited for that time the best I could: but I pointing towards captaine Gosnold, made signes unto him, that he was our captaine, and

[1] Noah Webster in 1797 (Belknap's *American Biography*, II. 114), Francis C. Gray in 1817 (*North American Review*, V. 313), and John Wingate Thornton in 1848 (*Cape Anne*, p. 21), maintained that they discovered on the islet plain outlines of Gosnold's fort and house; but the writer of this note, the general editor of the present series, found none in 1905. In 1902 a stone tower commemorative of Gosnold's sojourn was erected on the islet.

desirous to be his friend, and enter league with him, which (as
I perceived) he understood, and made signes of joy: whereupon captaine Gosnold with the rest of his companie, being
twentie in all, came up unto them; and after many signes of
gratulations (captaine Gosnold presenting their L.[1] with certeine trifles which they wondred at, and highly esteemed) we
became very great friends, and sent for meat aboord our shallop, and gave them such meats as we had then readie dressed,
whereof they misliked nothing but our mustard, whereat they
made many a sowre face. While we were thus merry, one of
them had conveied a target of ours into one of their canowes,
which we suffered, onely to trie whether they were in subjection to this L. to whom we made signes (by shewing him another
of the same likenesse, and pointing to the canowe) what one
of his companie had done: who suddenly expressed some feare,
and speaking angerly to one about him (as we perceived by
his countenance) caused it presently to be brought backe
againe. So the rest of the day we spent in trading with them
for Furres, which are Beavers, Luzernes, Marterns, Otters,
Wild-cat skinnes very large and deepe Furre, blacke Foxes,
Conie skinnes, of the colour of our Hares, but somewhat lesse,
Deere skinnes very large, Seale skinnes, and other beasts skinnes
to us unknowen. They have also great store of Copper, some
very redde, and some of a paler colour; none of them but have
chaines, earrings or collars of this mettall: they head some of
their arrows herewith, much like our broad arrow heads, very
workmanly made. Their chaines are many hollow pieces
semented together, ech piece of the bignesse of one of our
reeds, a finger in length, ten or twelve of them together on a
string, which they weare about their necks: their collars they
weare about their bodies like bandelieres a handfull broad,
all hollow pieces, like the other, but somewhat shorter, foure
hundred pieces in a collar, very fine and evenly set together.
Besides these, they have large drinking cups, made like sculles,
and other thinne plates of Copper, made much like our boare-

[1] Lord.

speare blades, all which they so little esteeme, as they offered their fairest collars or chaines, for a knife or such like trifle, but we seemed little to regard it; yet I was desirous to understand where they had such store of this mettall, and made signes to one of them (with whom I was verie familiar) who taking a piece of Copper in his hand, made a hole with his finger in the ground, and withall, pointed to the maine from whence they came. They strike fire in this maner; every one carrieth about him in a purse of tewed leather, a Minerall stone (which I take to be their Copper) and with a flat Emerie stone (wherewith Glasiers cut glasse, and Cutlers glase blades) tied fast to the end of a little sticke, gently he striketh upon the Minerall stone, and within a stroke or two, a sparke falleth upon a piece of Touchwood (much like our Spunge in England) and with the least sparke he maketh a fire presently. We had also of their Flaxe, wherewith they make many strings and cords, but it is not so bright of colour as ours in England: I am persuaded they have great store growing upon the maine, as also Mines and many other rich commodities, which we, wanting both time and meanes, could not possibly discover. Thus they continued with us three daies, every night retiring themselves to the furthermost part of our Island two or three miles from our fort: but the fourth day they returned to the maine, pointing five or six times to the Sun, and once to the maine, which we understood, that within five or six daies they would come from the maine to us againe: but being in their canowes a little from the shore, they made huge cries and shouts of joy unto us; and we with our trumpet and cornet, and casting up our cappes into the aire, made them the best farewell we could: yet sixe or seven of them remained with us behinde, bearing us company every day into the woods, and helpt us to cut and carie our Sassafras, and some of them lay aboord our ship. These people, as they are exceeding courteous, gentle of disposition, and well conditioned, excelling all others that we have seene; so for shape of bodie and lovely favour, I thinke they excell all the people of America; of stature much higher than we; of complexion or colour, much like a darke

Olive; their eie-browes and haire blacke, which they weare long, tied up behinde in knots, whereon they pricke feathers of fowles, in fashion of a crownet: some of them are blacke thin bearded; they make beards of the haire of beasts: and one of them offered a beard of their making to one of our sailers, for his that grew on his face, which because it was of a red colour, they judged to be none of his owne. They are quicke eied, and stedfast in their looks, fearlesse of others harmes, as intending none themselves; some of the meaner sort given to filching, which the very name of Salvages (not weighing their ignorance in good or evill) may easily excuse: their garments are of Deere skins, and some of them weare Furres round and close about their necks. They pronounce our language with great facilitie; for one of them one day sitting by me, upon occasion I spake smiling to him these words: How now (sirha) are you so saucie with my Tabacco? which words (without any further repetition) he suddenly spake so plaine and distinctly, as if he had beene a long scholar in the language. Many other such trials we had, which are here needlesse to repeat. Their women (such as we saw) which were but three in all, were but lowe of stature, their eie-browes, haire, apparell, and maner of wearing, like to the men, fat, and very well favoured, and much delighted in our compane; the men are very dutifull towards them. And truely, the holsomnesse and temperature of this Climat, doth not onely argue this people to be answerable to this description, but also of a perfect constitution of body, active, strong, healthfull, and very wittie, as the sundry toies of theirs cunningly wrought, may easily witnes. For the agreeing of this Climat with us (I speake of my selfe, and so I may justly do for the rest of our companie) that we found our health and strength all the while we remained there, so to renew and increase, as notwithstanding our diet and lodging was none of the best, yet not one of our company (God be thanked) felt the least grudging or inclination to any disease or sicknesse, but were much fatter and in better health than when we went out of England. But after our barke had taken in so much Sassafras, Cedar, Furres,

Skinnes, and other commodities, as were thought convenient; some of our company that had promised captaine Gosnold to stay,[1] having nothing but a saving voyage in their minds, made our company of inhabitants (which was small enough before) much smaller; so as captaine Gosnold seeing his whole strength to consist but of twelve men, and they but meanly provided, determined to returne for England, leaving this Island (which he called Elizabeths Island) with as many true sorrowfull eies, as were before desirous to see it. So the 18 of June, being Friday, we weighed, and with indifferent faire winde and weather came to anker the 23 of July, being also Friday (in all, bare five weeks) before Exmouth.[2]

Your Lordships to command,
JOHN BRERETON.

[1] Gosnold seems to have had in mind a permanent trading post. Archer says, "The eighth wee divided the victuals, *viz.*, the ships store for England, and that of the Planters, which by Captaine Gilberts allowance could be but sixe weekes for sixe moneths, whereby there fell out a controversie, the rather, for that some seemed secretly to understand of a purpose Captaine Gilbert had not to returne with supplie of the issue those goods should make by him to be carried home."

[2] A town in the county of Devon on the east side of the estuary of the Exe, and at present a celebrated watering-place.

A VOYAGE SET OUT FROM THE CITIE OF BRISTOLL, 1603, BY MARTIN PRING

INTRODUCTION

MARTIN PRING was only twenty-three years of age when, by "sundry of the chiefest merchants of Bristol," he was placed in command of an expedition to the American coast. In making this venture, these merchants evidently received encouragement from the reports brought back to England by Gosnold and his associates. Two vessels were employed in the expedition — one of about fifty tons, the *Speedwell*, commanded by Pring, with Edward Jones as mate; and another of twenty-six tons, the *Discoverer*, commanded by William Broune, with Samuel Kirkland as mate, Pring being "Master and Chief Commander." Robert Salterne, who was on the American coast with Gosnold the year before, was chief agent and supercargo; and another of Gosnold's best men, John Angell, accompanied Pring. The mistake of Gosnold and Gilbert the year before was not made by Pring's promoters, and permission for the undertaking was secured from Sir Walter Ralegh.

Pring made a voyage to the coast of Guiana in 1604. In 1606 he was again on the New England coast, and brought back with him such an encouraging report, with valuable information concerning the coast of Maine, that the Popham colony followed in 1607. It is supposed that Pring entered the East India service about that time, though no mention of him is found in that relation until 1614, when he was master of a large new ship. Purchas makes several extracts from manuscript journals of two voyages to the East Indies, made by him between 1614 and 1621. In the last of these voyages Pring commanded a squadron of five ships, one of which was of more than one thousand tons. In 1619, on the death of Dale,

Pring succeeded to the command of the whole English East India squadron. He returned to England in 1623. It is thought that he may have gone to Virginia two or three years later. If so, he died soon after his return to England, as his monument in St. Stephen's Church, Bristol, records his death in 1626.

The story of the voyage of 1603 was secured from Pring by Richard Hakluyt, but this of course was after the publication of Hakluyt's great work. Many of Hakluyt's papers, however, after his death, which occurred in 1616, passed into the hands of Samuel Purchas, and this narrative of Pring's voyage appeared in Purchas's *Pilgrimes*, fourth volume, published in 1625. The account of the voyage, though ascribed to Pring by Purchas, seems to have been written in part by other hands, as in the last paragraph, where mention of "our Captaine" is made. A careful reprint of the "Relation" appears in Winship's *Sailors' Narratives of New England Voyages*, pp. 53–63. A biographical account of Pring, by Professor Alfred L. P. Dennis, was printed by the Maine Historical Society in 1906, in its *Collections*, third series, II. 1–50.

H. S. B.

THE VOYAGE OF MARTIN PRING, 1603

A Voyage set out from the Citie of Bristoll at the charge of the chiefest Merchants and inhabitants of the said Citie with a small Ship and a Barke for the discoverie of the North part of Virginia.

WE set saile from Milford Haven [1] (where the winds had stayed us a fortnight, in which space we heard of Queen Elizabeths death) the tenth of April 1603. In our course we passed by the Iles of the Açores, had first sight of the Pike,[2] and afterward of the Iland of Cuervo [3] and Flores, and after we had runne some five hundred leagues, we fell with a multitude of small Ilands on the North Coast of Virginia, in the latitude of 43. degrees, the —— of June, which Ilands wee found very pleasant to behold, adorned with goodly grasse and sundry sorts of Trees, as Cedars, Spruce, Pine and Firre-trees. Heere wee found an excellent fishing for Cod, which are better then those of New-found-land, and withall we saw good and Rockie ground fit to drie them upon: also we see no reason to the contrary, but that Salt may bee made in these parts, a matter of no small importance. We sayled to the Southwest end of these Ilands, and there rode with our ships under one of the greatest. One of them we named Foxe Iland,[4] because we found those kind of beasts thereon. So passing through the rest with our Boates to the mayne Land, which lieth for a good space North-east and Southwest, we found very safe riding among them, in sixe, seven, eight, ten

[1] A harbor of Pembrokeshire, Wales. It was from this port that John Cabot, in 1497, made his voyage to America.
[2] The island called Pico, a high conical mountain.   [3] Or Corvo.
[4] An island on the coast of Maine, east of Penobscot Bay. The group still bears the name. The larger islands of the group are North Haven and Vinalhaven.

and twelve fathomes. At length comming to the Mayne in the latitude of 43. degrees and a halfe, we ranged the same to the South-west. In which course we found foure Inlets, the most Easterly whereof was barred at the mouth,[1] but having passed over the barre, wee ranne up into it five miles, and for a certaine space found very good depth, and comming out againe, as we sailed South-westward, we lighted upon two other Inlets, which upon our search we found to pierce not farre into the land, the fourth and most Westerly was the best, which we rowed up ten or twelve miles.

In all these places we found no people,[2] but signes of fires where they had beene. Howbeit we beheld very goodly Groves and Woods replenished with tall Okes, Beeches, Pine-trees, Firre-trees, Hasels, Wich-hasels and Maples. We saw here also sundry sorts of Beasts, as Stags, Deere, Beares, Wolves, Foxes, Lusernes, and Dogges with sharpe noses. But meeting with no Sassafras, we left these places with all the foresaid Ilands, shaping our course for Savage Rocke discovered the yeere before by Captaine Gosnold, where going upon the Mayne we found people, with whom we had no long conversation, because here also we could find no Sassafras. Departing hence [3] we bare into that great Gulfe which Captaine Gosnold over-shot the yeere before, coasting and finding people on the North side thereof. Not yet satisfied in our expectation, we left them and sailed over, and came to an Anchor on the South side in the latitude of 41. degrees and odde minute: where we went on Land in a certaine Bay, which we called Whitson Bay,[4] by the name of the Worshipfull Master John Whitson then Major of the Citie of Bristoll, and one of the

[1] It has been conjectured that this was the Saco River. The other inlets, then, would be the Kennebunk, York and Piscataqua rivers.

[2] Probably at that season of the year the Indians were fishing at the falls of the river.

[3] The language here does not necessarily locate Savage Rock at Cape Ann. The description evidently is generals not particular.

[4] Bancroft, following Belknap, identifies Whitson's Bay with the harbor of Edgartown, Martha's Vineyard, which is in the latitude of 41° 25'. The narrative implies that Pring passed from the north to the south side of the "greate Gulfe," and Dr. De Costa (*Magazine of American History*, VIII.

chiefe Adventurers, and finding a pleasant Hill thereunto adjoyning, we called it Mount Aldworth, for Master Robert Aldworths [1] sake a chiefe furtherer of the Voyage, as well with his Purse as with his travell.[2] Here we had sufficient quantitie of Sassafras.

At our going on shore, upon view of the people and sight of the place, wee thought it convenient to make a small baricado to keepe diligent watch and ward in, for the advertizement and succour of our men, while they should worke in the Woods. During our abode on shore, the people of the Countrey came to our men sometimes ten, twentie, fortie or threescore, and at one time one hundred and twentie at once. We used them kindly, and gave them divers sorts of our meanest Merchandize. They did eat Pease and Beanes with our men. Their owne victuals were most of fish.

We had a youth in our company that could play upon a Gitterne, in whose homely Music they tooke great delight, and would give him many things, as Tobacco, Tobacco-pipes, Snakes skinnes of sixe foot long, which they use for Girdles, Fawnes skinnes, and such like, and danced twentie in a Ring, and the Gitterne in the middest of them, using many Savage gestures, singing Io, Ia, Io, Ia, Ia, Io: him that first brake the ring, the rest would knocke and cry out upon. Some few of them had plates of Brasse a foot long, and halfe a foote broad before their breasts. Their Weapons are Bowes of five or six foot long of Wich-hasell, painted blacke and yellow, the strings of three twists of sinewes, bigger then our Bowstrings. Their Arrowes are of a yard and an handfull long not made of Reeds, but of a fine light wood very smooth and round with three long and deepe blacke feathers of some Eagle, Vulture, or Kite, as closely fastened with some bind-

807–819), more accurately, it would seem, identifies Whitson's Bay with Plymouth harbor.

[1] Robert Aldworth was a son of Thomas Aldworth, a prominent merchant of Bristol, and the patron of Hakluyt. He died in 1590. His son Robert inherited his father's interest in western discovery and colonization. With Giles Elbridge he obtained, in 1631, letters patent for a grant of land at Pemaquid. He died in 1634.   [2] *I.e.*, travail.

ing matter, as any Fletcher of ours can glue them on. Their Quivers are full a yard long, and made of long dried Rushes wrought about two handfuls broad above, and one handfull beneath with prettie workes and compartiments, Diamant wise of red and other colours.

We carried with us from Bristoll two excellent Mastives, of whom the Indians were more afraid, then of twentie of our men. One of these Mastives would carrie a halfe Pike in his mouth. And one Master Thomas Bridges a Gentleman of our company accompanied only with one of these Dogs, and passed sixe miles alone in the Countrey having lost his fellowes, and returned safely. And when we would be rid of the Savages company wee would let loose the Mastives, and suddenly with out-cryes they would flee away. These people in colour are inclined to a swart, tawnie, or Chestnut colour, not by nature but accidentally, and doe weare their haire brayded in foure parts, and trussed up about their heads with a small knot behind: in which haire of theirs they sticke many feathers and toyes for braverie and pleasure. They cover their privities only with a piece of leather drawne betwixt their twists and fastened to their Girdles behind and before: whereunto they hang their bags of Tobacco. They seeme to bee somewhat jealous of their women, for we saw not past two of them, who weare Aprons of Leather skins before them downe to the knees, and a Beares skinne like an Irish Mantle over one shoulder. The men are of stature somewhat taller then our ordinary people, strong, swift, well proportioned, and given to treacherie, as in the end we perceived.

Their Boats, whereof we brought one to Bristoll, were in proportion like a Wherrie of the River Thames, seventeene foot long and foure foot broad, and made of the Barke of a Birch-tree, farre exceeding in bignesse those of England: it was sowed together with strong and tough Oziers or twigs, and the seames covered over with Rozen or Turpentine little inferiour in sweetnesse to Frankincense, as we made triall by burning a little thereof on the coales at sundry times after our coming home: it was also open like a Wherrie, and sharpe at both ends, saving that the beake was a little bending roundly upward. And though it carried nine men standing upright, yet it weighed not at the most above sixtie pounds in weight, a thing almost incredible in regard of the largenesse and capacitie thereof. Their Oares were flat at the end like an Oven peele,[1] made of Ash or Maple very light and strong, about two yards long, wherewith they row very swiftly: Passing up a River we saw certaine Cottages together, abandoned by the Savages, and not farre off we beheld their Gardens and one among the rest of an Acre of ground, and in the same was sowne Tobacco, pompions, cowcumbers and such like; and some of the people had Maiz or Indian Wheate among them. In the fields we found wild Pease, Strawberries very faire and bigge, Gooseberries, Raspices, Hurts, and other wild fruits.

Having spent three Weeks upon the Coast before we came to this place where we meant to stay and take in our lading, according to our instructions given us in charge before our setting forth, we pared and digged up the Earth with shovels, and sowed Wheate, Barley, Oates, Pease, and sundry sorts of Garden Seeds, which for the time of our abode there, being about seven Weeks, although they were late sowne, came up very well, giving certaine testimonie of the goodnesse of the Climate and of the Soyle. And it seemeth that Oade, Hempe, Flaxe, Rape-seed and such like which require a rich and fat ground, would prosper excellently in these parts. For in divers places here we found grasse above knee deepe.

As for Trees the Country yeeldeth Sassafras a plant of sovereigne vertue for the French Poxe, and as some of late have learnedly written good against the Plague and many other Maladies; Vines, Cedars, Okes, Ashes, Beeches, Birch trees, Cherie trees bearing fruit whereof wee did eate, Hasels, Wichhasels, the best wood of all other to make Sope-ashes withall, Walnut-trees, Maples, holy to make Bird-lime with, and a kinde of tree bearing a fruit like a small red Peare-plum with a crowne or knop on the top (a plant whereof carefully wrapped

---

[1] A baker's wooden shovel.

up in earth, Master Robert Salterne brought to Bristoll.) We found also low trees bearing faire Cheries. There were likewise a white kind of Plums which were growne to their perfect ripenesse. With divers other sorts of trees to us unknowne.

The Beasts here are Stags, fallow Deere in abundance, Beares, Wolves, Foxes, Lusernes, and (some say) Tygres, Porcupines, and Dogges with sharpe and long noses, with many other sorts of wild beasts, whose Cases and Furres being hereafter purchased by exchange may yeeld no smal gaine to us. Since as we are certainly informed, the Frenchmen brought from Canada the value of thirtie thousand Crownes in the yeare 1604. Almost in Bevers and Otters skinnes only. The most usuall Fowles are Eagles, Vultures, Hawkes, Cranes, Herons, Crowes, Gulls, and great store of other River and Sea-fowles. And as the Land is full of Gods good blessings, so is the Sea replenished with great abundance of excellent fish, as Cods sufficient to lade many ships, which we found upon the Coast in the moneth of June, Seales to make Oile withall, Mullets, Turbuts, Mackerels, Herrings, Crabs, Lobsters, Creuises and Muscles with ragged Pearles in them.

By the end of July we had laded our small Barke called the *Discoverer*, with as much Sassafras[1] as we thought sufficient, and sent her home into England before, to give some speedie contentment to the Adventurers; who arrived safely in Kingrode[2] above a fortnight before us. After their departure we so bestirred our selves, that our shippe also had gotten in her lading, during which time there fell out this accident. On a day about noone tide while our men which used to cut down Sassafras in the Woods were asleepe, as they used to doe for two houres in the heat of the day, there came downe about seven score Savages armed with their Bowes and Arrowes, and environed our House or Barricado, wherein were foure of our men alone with their Muskets to keepe Centinell, whom they

[1] Evidently the voyage was not for discovery, but for this marketable commodity.
[2] A channel in the estuary of the Severn, near Bristol.

sought to have come downe unto them, which they utterly refused, and stood upon their guard. Our Master likewise being very carefull and circumspect having not past two with him in the shippe put the same in the best defence he could, lest they should have invaded the same, and caused a piece of great Ordnance to bee shot off, to give terrour to the Indians, and warning to our men which were fast asleepe in the Woods: at the noyse of which Peece they were a little awaked, and beganne a little to call for Foole and Gallant, their great and fearefull Mastives, and full quietly laid themselves downe againe, but beeing quickned up eftsoones againe with a second shot they rowsed up themselves, betooke them to their weapons and with their Mastives, great Foole with an halfe Pike in his mouth drew downe to their ship: whom when the Indians beheld afarre off, with the Mastive which they most feared, in dissembling manner they turned all to a jest and sport, and departed away in friendly manner: yet not long after, even the day before our departure, they set fire on the Woods where wee wrought, which wee did behold to burne for a mile space, and the very same day that wee weighed Anchor, they came downe to the shoare in greater number, to wit, very neere two hundred by our estimation, and some of them came in their Boates to our ship, and would have had us come in againe: but we sent them backe, and would none of their entertainment.

About the eighth or ninth of August, wee left this excellent Haven at the entrance whereof we found twentie fathomes water, and rode at our ease in seven fathomes being Landlocked, the Haven winding in compasse like the shell of a snaile, and it is in latitude of one and forty degrees and five and twentie minutes.

This by the way is not to be forgotten, that our Captaine fell so much to the Northward because he would find high grounds, where commonly the best Havens are: which also fell out to his expectation. We also observed that we could find no Sassafras but in sandie ground. In our returne we brought our selves into the latitude of eight and thirtie degrees about the Açores for certaine causes, and within five weekes space came from our Port of Virginia, into the Soundings of England, but there being long encountred with Easterly winds, we came at length into Kingrode, the second of October 1603. The *Discoverer* was out five moneths and an halfe. The *Speedwell*[1] was out sixe moneths upon the Voyage.

[1] A vessel bearing this name and with a like tonnage — also from the same part of England — was in Sir Francis Drake's fleet in 1587. In the fight with the Spanish Armada in 1588, also, Drake had a vessel of the same name and about the same tonnage — probably the one with Drake in the preceding year, and one of the many merchantmen engaged in that memorable contest. The *Speedwell* of Pring's voyage, therefore, may have been the vessel which was with Drake in 1587 and 1588.

A TRUE RELATION OF THE VOYAGE OF CAPTAINE GEORGE WAYMOUTH, 1605, BY JAMES ROSIER

INTRODUCTION

GEORGE WAYMOUTH was a native of Cockington, Devon. In the Introduction to "The Jewell of Artes," — a manuscript volume by Waymouth in the King's Library, British Museum, — Waymouth refers to the education he received on "four prentize shipps," and the volume shows in various ways that he was an accomplished draughtsman, mathematician, and engineer, and not merely a brave and resourceful sailor as was formerly supposed. In 1602, under the auspices of "the Worshipful Fellowship of the Merchants of London trading into the East Indies" (East India Company), Waymouth made a voyage in search of a northwest passage to India, but met with the usual insuperable difficulties. He reached Dartmouth Haven, on his return, August 5, 1602, a few days after Gosnold's arrival from his successful New England voyage. Waymouth's next venture was in this voyage of 1605, of which Henry Wriothesley, Earl of Southampton, and Thomas Arundell were the principal promoters. There must have been marked defects in Waymouth's character, for after his return from this successful voyage he failed to obtain the advancement he sought. A small government pension was at length awarded to him, but as no payment is recorded after 1612, it may be inferred that he died about that time. Concerning James Rosier, the author of the *Relation*, little is known except in connection with this voyage. A James Rosier was in Gosnold's expedition to the American coast in 1602 (Brown's *Genesis of the United States*, I. 26), and it is probable that he is to be identified with the author of the *Relation* of Waymouth's voyage. It is suggested by Baxter (*Sir Ferdinando Gorges*) that Rosier may have been a Catholic priest. The *Relation* was printed at London in 1605, and included by Purchas in his *Pilgrimes*, 1625. A reprint from a copy procured in England by Jared Sparks appeared in Volume VIII. of the third series of the *Collections of the Massachusetts Historical Society*, pp. 129-157, and this copy thus obtained was reprinted with notes, etc., at Bath, Maine, in 1860, by Captain George Prince. In 1887 the Gorges Society, of Portland, Maine, reprinted the *Relation* from an original printed copy of 1605, in the John Carter Brown Library, Providence, Rhode Island, the reprint being accompanied with introductions, notes, etc., by Henry S. Burrage, D.D. A careful reprint, also from the copy in the John Carter Brown Library, will be found in Winship's *Sailors' Narratives of New England Voyages*, 1906.

H. S. B.

TRUE RELATION OF WAYMOUTH'S VOYAGE, 1605

A True Relation of the most prosperous voyage made this present yeere 1605, by Captaine George Waymouth, in the Discovery of the Land of Virginia: Where he discovered 60 miles up a most excellent River; together with a most fertile land. Written by James Rosier, a Gentleman employed in the voyage. Londini, Impensis Geor. Bishop, 1605.[1]

TO THE READER

BEING employed in this Voyage by the right honourable Thomas Arundell [2] Baron of Warder, to take due notice, and make true report of the discovery therein performed: I became very diligent to observe (as much as I could) whatsoever was materiall or of consequence in the businesse which I collected into this briefe summe, intending upon our returne to publish the same. But he soone changed the course of his intendments; and long before our arrivall in England had so farre engaged himselfe with the Archduke,[3] that he was constrained to relinquish this action. But the commodities and profits of the countrey, together with the fitnesse of plantation, being by some honourable Gentlemen of good woorth and qualitie, and Merchants of good sufficiency and judgment duly considered, have at their owne charge (intending both

[1] This italic heading is copied from the title-page of the printed book.
[2] Thomas Arundell, first Lord Arundell of Wardour, was elevated to the peerage May 4, 1605.
[3] Meaning the Archduke Albert, who, jointly with his wife, the Infanta Isabella, sister of Philip III. of Spain, was regent of the Spanish Netherlands. In August, 1605, Arundell was appointed colonel of one of the Archduke's English regiments.

their private and the common benefit of their countrey)
undertaken the transporting of a Colony for the plantation
thereof;[1] being much encouraged thereunto by the gracious
favour of the KINGS MAJESTY himselfe, and divers Lords of his
Highnesse most Honourable Privie Councell. After these purposed designes were concluded, I was animated to publish this
briefe Relation, and not before; because some forrein Nation
(being fully assured of the fruitfulnesse of the countrie) have
hoped hereby to gaine some knowledge of the place, seeing
they could not allure our Captaine or any speciall man of our
Company to combine with them for their direction, nor obtaine their purpose, in conveying away our Salvages, which was
busily in practise. And this is the cause that I have neither
written of the latitude or variation most exactly observed by
our Captaine with sundrie instruments, which together with
his perfect Geographicall Map of the countrey, he entendeth
hereafter to set forth. I have likewise purposedly omitted
here to adde a collection of many words in their language
to the number of foure or five hundred, as also the names of
divers of their governours, as well their friends as their enemies:
being reserved to be made knowen for the benefit of those that
shal goe in the next Voyage. But our particular proceedings
in the whole Discoverie, the commodious situation of the
River, the fertilitie of the land, with the profits there to be
had, and here reported, I refer to be verified by the whole Company, as being eye-witnesses of my words, and most of them
neere inhabitants upon the Thames. So with my prayers to

[1] Prominent among them were Sir Ferdinando Gorges and Sir John
Popham, Lord Chief Justice of England. Sir Ferdinando, in August of the
following year, fitted out a vessel, under the command of Henry Challoung,
to renew the exploration. Before he had begun this, however, the vessel was
captured and confiscated by the Spaniards. Not long after Challoung's
departure, Sir John Popham sent out another vessel, of which Thomas
Hanham was commander and Martin Pring was master. They made "a
perfect discovery of all those rivers and harbors" to which their attention
had been directed by Gorges, and then returned to England. The report
brought back by them made such an impression on Sir John Popham,
Gorges, and their associates, that the Popham Colony was sent out in the
following year.

God for the conversion of so ingenious and well-disposed people, and for the prosperous successive events of the noble intenders the prosecution thereof, I rest

Your friend   J. R.

A TRUE RELATION

of Captaine George Waymouth his Voyage, made this present yeere 1605; in the Discoverie of the North part of Virginia.

Upon Tuesday the 5 day of March, about ten a clocke afore noone, we set saile from Ratcliffe,[1] and came to an anker that tide about two a clocke before Gravesend.[2]

From thence the 10 of March being Sunday at night we ankered in the Downes:[3] and there rode till the next day about three a clocke after noone, when with a scant winde we set saile; and by reason the winde continued Southwardly, we were beaten up and doune: but on Saturday the 16 day about foure a clocke after noon we put into Dartmouth Haven,[4] where the continuance of the winde at South and Southwest constrained us to ride till the last of this moneth. There we shipped some of our men and supplied necessaries for our Ship and Voyage.

Upon Easter day, being the last of March, the winde comming at North-North-East, about five a clocke after noone we wayed anker, and put to sea, In the name of God, being well victualled and furnished with munition and all necessaries: Our whole Company being but 29 persons; of whom I may boldly say, few voyages have beene manned forth with better Sea-men generally in respect of our small number.

Munday the next day, being the first of Aprill, by sixe a clocke in the morning we were sixe leagues South-South-East from the Lizarde.

[1] A hamlet on the Thames below London.
[2] Thirty miles below London on the Thames.
[3] North of Dover, between Goodwin Sands and the mainland.
[4] On the southern coast of England, two hundred and twenty-nine miles from London.

At two a clocke in the afternoone this day, the weather being very faire, our Captaine for his owne experience and others with him sounded, and had sixe and fiftie fathoms and a halfe. The sounding was some small blacke perrie sand,[1] some reddish sand, a match or two, with small shels called Saint James his Shels.[2]

The foureteenth of Aprill being Sunday, betweene nine and ten of the clocke in the morning our Captaine descried the Iland Cuervo:[3] which bare South-west and by West, about seven leagues from us: by eleven of the clocke we descried Flores to the Southward of Cuervo, as it lieth: by foure a clocke in the afternoone we brought Cuervo due South from us within two leagues of the shore, but we touched not, because the winde was faire, and we thought our selves sufficiently watered and wooded.

Heere our Captaine observed the Sunne, and found himselfe in the latitude of 40 degrees and 7 minutes: so he judged the North part of Cuervo to be in 40 degrees. After we had kept our course about a hundred leagues from the Ilands, by continuall Southerly windes we were forced and driven from the Southward, whither we first intended. And when our Captaine by long beating saw it was but in vaine to strive with windes, not knowing Gods purposes heerein to our further blessing, (which after by his especiall direction wee found) he thought best to stand as nigh as he could by the winde to recover what land we might first discover.

Munday, the 6 of May, being in the latitude of 39 and a halfe about ten a clocke afore noone, we came to a riplin,[4] which we discerned a head our ship, which is a breach of water caused either by a fall, or by some meeting of currents, which we judged this to be; for the weather being very faire, and a small gale of winde, we sounded and found no ground in a hundred fathoms.

[1] Sand mingled with grains of magnetic iron ore.
[2] The association of the name St. James with the scallop, here *Pecten opercularis*, owes its origin to a Spanish legend.   [3] Corvo.
[4] Well-marked tide-rips are observed off Nantucket during the flood and ebb tide, resembling breakers in shoal water.

Munday, the 13 of May, about eleven a clocke afore noone, our Captaine, judging we were not farre from land, sounded, and had a soft oaze in a hundred and sixty fathomes. At fowre a clocke after noone we sounded againe, and had the same oaze in a hundred fathoms.

From ten a clocke that night till three a clocke in the morning, our Captaine tooke in all sailes and lay at hull, being desirous to fall with the land in the day time, because it was an unknowen coast, which it pleased God in his mercy to grant us, otherwise we had run our ship upon the hidden rockes and perished all. For when we set saile we sounded in 100 fathoms: and by eight a clock, having not made above five or six leagues, our Captaine upon a sudden change of water (supposing verily he saw the sand) presently sounded, and had but five fathoms. Much marvelling because we saw no land, he sent one to the top, who thence descried a whitish sandy cliffe,[1] which bare West-North-West about six leagues off from us: but comming neerer within three or fowre leagues, we saw many breaches still neerer the land: at last we espied a great breach a head us al along the shore, into which before we should enter, our Captaine thought best to hoist out his ship boate and sound it. Which if he had not done, we had beene in great danger: for he bare up the ship, as neere as he durst after the boate: untill Thomas Cam, his mate, being in the boat, called to him to tacke about and stand off, for in this breach he had very showld water, two fathoms and lesse upon rockes, and sometime they supposed they saw the rocke within three or fowre foote, whereon the sea made a very strong breach: which we might discerne (from the top) to run along as we sailed by it 6 or 7 leagues to the Southward. This was in the latitude of 41 degrees, 20 minuts: wherefore we were constrained to put backe againe from the land: and sounding, (the weather being very faire and a small winde) we found our selves embaied with continuall showldes and rockes in a most

---

[1] Sankaty Head, the eastern extremity of Nantucket. Waymouth approached the Great Rip, and found himself on what is now known as Rose and Crown Shoal.

uncertaine ground, from five or sixe fathoms, at the next cast of the lead we should have 15 and 18 fathoms. Over many which we passed, and God so blessed us, that we had wind and weather as faire as poore men in this distresse could wish: whereby we both perfectly discerned every breach, and with the winde were able to turne, where we saw most hope of safest passage. Thus we parted from the land, which we had not so much before desired, and at the first sight rejoiced, as now we all joifully praised God, that it had pleased him to deliver us from so imminent danger.

Heere we found great store of excellent Cod fish, and saw many Whales, as we had done two or three daies before.

We stood off all that night, and the next day being Wednesday; but the wind still continuing between the points of South-South-West, and West-South-West: so as we could not make any way to the Southward, in regard of our great want of water and wood (which was now spent) we much desired land and therefore sought for it, where the wind would best suffer us to refresh our selves.

Thursday, the 16 of May, we stood in directly with the land, and much marvelled we descried it not, wherein we found our sea charts very false, putting land where none is.

Friday the 17 of May, about sixe a clocke at night we descried the land, which bare from us North-North-East; but because it blew a great gale of winde, the sea very high and neere night, not fit to come upon an unknowen coast, we stood off till two a clocke in the morning, being Saturday: then standing in with it againe, we descried it by eight a clocke in the morning, bearing North-East from us. It appeared a meane high land, as we after found it, being but an Iland[1] of some six miles in compasse, but I hope the most fortunate ever yet discovred. About twelve a clocke that day, we came to an anker on the North side of this Iland, about a league from the shore. About two a clocke our Captaine with twelve

[1] Monhegan, off the coast of Maine. It lies northeast and southwest, is a mile and a half long, high, with steep rocky or sloping shores. Close in with the western shore is an island called Manana, forming a small harbor.

men rowed in his ship boat to the shore, where we made no long stay, but laded our boat with dry wood of olde trees upon the shore side, and returned to our ship, where we rode that night.

This Iland is woody, grouen with Firre, Birch, Oke and Beech, as farre as we saw along the shore; and so likely to be within. On the verge grow Gooseberries, Strawberries, Wild pease, and Wild rose bushes. The water issued foorth downe the Rocky cliffes in many places: and much fowle of divers kinds breed upon the shore and rocks.

While we were at shore, our men aboord with a few hooks got above thirty great Cods and Hadocks, which gave us a taste of the great plenty of fish which we found afterward wheresoever we went upon the coast.

From hence [1] we might discerne the maine land from the West-South-West to the East-North-East, and a great way (as it then seemed, and as we after found it) up into the maine we might discerne very high mountaines,[2] though the maine seemed but low land; which gave us a hope it would please God to direct us to the discoverie of some good; although wee were driven by winds farre from that place, whither (both by our direction and desire) we ever intended to shape the course of our voyage.

The next day being Whit-Sunday; because we rode too much open to the sea and windes, we weyed anker about twelve a clocke, and came along to the other Ilands more adjoyning to the maine,[3] and in the rode directly with the mountaines, about three leagues from the first Iland where we had ankered.

[1] Possibly from Monhegan, but naturally from the deck of the *Archangel* at its anchorage north of the island. The name of Waymouth's vessel is not given by Rosier, but is mentioned in the account of the voyage found in *Purchas his Pilgrimes*.

[2] Union and Camden mountains. That they could not have been the White Mountains, as formerly maintained, see the edition of Rosier's *True Relation*, published by the Gorges Society, pp. 96–100.

[3] The St. George's Islands, sixteen in number, are in the direction indicated. Rosier's distance is an estimate, and, as usual with the estimates in the *Relation*, is in excess of actual measurements.

When we came neere unto them (sounding all along in a good depth) our Captaine manned his ship-boat and sent her before with Thomas Cam one of his Mates, whom he knew to be of good experience, to sound and search betweene the Ilands for a place safe for our shippe to ride in; in the meane while we kept aloofe at sea, having given them in the boat a token to weffe in the ship, if he found a convenient Harbour; which it pleased God to send us, farre beyond our expectation, in a most safe birth defended from all windes, in an excellent depth of water for ships of any burthen, in six, seven, eight, nine and ten fathoms upon a clay oaze very tough.

We all with great joy praised God for his unspeakable goodnesse, who had from so apparent danger delivered us, and directed us upon this day into so secure an Harbour: in remembrance whereof we named it Pentecost harbor,[1] we arriving there that day out of our last Harbour in England, from whence we set saile upon Easterday.

About foure a clocke, after we were ankered and well mored, our Captaine with halfe a dozen of our Company went on shore[2] to seeke fresh watering, and a convenient place to set together a pinnesse, which we brought in pieces out of England; both which we found very fitting.

Upon this Iland, as also upon the former, we found (at our first comming to shore) where fire had beene made: and about the place were very great egge shelles bigger than goose egges, fish bones, and as we judged, the bones of some beast.

Here we espied Cranes stalking on the shore of a little Iland adjoyning;[3] where we after saw they used to breed.

Whitsun-munday, the 20 day of May, very early in the morning, our Captaine caused the pieces of the pinnesse to be carried a shore, where while some were busied about her,

---

[1] St. George's Harbor, which fully answers the requirements of the *Relation*.   [2] Allen's Island.

[3] Benner's Island, which is separated from Allen's Island by a passage about two hundred yards wide.

others digged welles to receive the fresh water, which we found issuing downe out of the land in many places. Heere I cannot omit (for foolish feare of imputation of flattery) the painfull industry of our Captaine, who as at sea he is alwayes most carefull and vigilant, so at land he refuseth no paines; but his labour was ever as much or rather more than any mans: which not only encourageth others with better content, but also effecteth much with great expedition.

In digging we found excellent clay for bricke or tile.

The next day we finished a well of good and holesome cleere water in a great empty caske, which we left there. We cut yards, waste trees, and many necessaries for our ship, while our Carpenter and Cooper laboured to fit and furnish forth the shallop.

This day our boat went out about a mile from our ship, and in small time with two or three hooks was fished sufficiently for our whole Company three dayes, with great Cod, Haddocke, and Thornebacke.

And towards night we drew with a small net of twenty fathoms very nigh the shore: we got about thirty very good and great Lobsters, many Rockfish, some Plaise, and other small fishes, and fishes called Lumpes,[1] verie pleasant to the taste: and we generally observed, that all the fish, of what kinde soever we tooke, were well fed, fat, and sweet in taste.

Wednesday, the 22 of May, we felled and cut wood for our ships use, cleansed and scoured our wels, and digged a plot of ground, wherein, amongst some garden seeds, we sowed peaze and barley, which in sixteen dayes grew eight inches above ground; and so continued growing every day halfe an inch, although this was but the crust of the ground, and much inferior to the mould we after found in the maine.

Friday, the 24 of May, after we had made an end of cutting wood, and carying water aboord our shippe, with fourteene Shot and Pikes we marched about and thorow part of two of

[1] So called from the clumsiness of their form. They are still occasionally found in these waters.

the Ilands; the bigger of which we judged to be foure or five miles in compasse, and a mile broad.[1]

The profits and fruits which are naturally on these Ilands are these:

All along the shore and some space within, where the wood hindereth not, grow plentifully
{ Rasberries.
Gooseberries.
Strawberries.
Roses.
Currants.
Wild-Vines.
Angelica.[2]

Within the Ilands growe wood of sundry sorts, some very great, and all tall:
{ Birch.
Beech.
Ash.
Maple.
Spruce.
Cherry-tree.
Yew.
Oke very great and good.
Firre-tree, out of which

issueth Turpentine in so marvellous plenty, and so sweet, as our Chirurgeon and others affirmed they never saw so good in England. We pulled off much Gumme congealed on the outside of the barke, which smelled like Frankincense. This would be a great benefit for making Tarre and Pitch.

We stayed the longer in this place, not only because of our good Harbour, (which is an excellent comfort) but because every day we did more and more discover the pleasant fruitfulnesse; insomuch as many of our Companie wished themselves setled heere, not expecting any further hopes, or better discovery to be made.

Heere our men found abundance of great muscels among the

---

[1] Monhegan appeared to Rosier to be "some six miles in compasse." Allen's Island is longer than Monhegan, but not so wide.

[2] An umbelliferous plant, so called because of its supposed angelic virtues.

rocks; and in some of them many small Pearls: and in one muscell (which we drew up in our net) was found foureteene Pearles,[1] whereof one of prety bignesse and orient; in another above fiftie small Pearles; and if we had had a Drag, no doubt we had found some of great valew, seeing these did certainly shew, that heere they were bred: the shels all glistering with mother of Pearle.

Wednesday, the 29 day, our shallop being now finished, and our Captaine and men furnished to depart with hir from the ship: we set up a crosse[2] on the shore side upon the rockes.

Thursday, the 30 of May, about ten a clock afore noon, our Captaine with 13 men more, in the name of God, and with all our praiers for their prosperous discoverie, and safe returne, departed in the shallop; leaving the ship in a good harbour, which before I mentioned, well mored, and manned with 14 men.

This day, about five a clocke in the afternoone, we in the shippe espied three Canoas comming towards us, which went to the iland adjoining, where they went a shore, and very quickly had made a fire, about which they stood beholding our ships: to whom we made signes with our hands and hats, weffing unto them to come unto us, because we had not seene any of the people yet. They sent one Canoa with three men, one of which, when they came neere unto us, spake in his language very lowd and very boldly: seeming as though he would know why we were there, and by pointing with his oare towards the sea, we conjectured he ment we should be gone. But when

[1] When the Pilgrims anchored the *Mayflower* in Provincetown harbor, they found, according to Mourt's *Relation*, "great Mussles and very fat and full of Sea pearle."

[2] This is the only cross Rosier mentions as set up by Waymouth on any island, and Rosier says, farther on in the *Relation*, that no crosses were found that had been set up by others. The Popham colonists, coming to the coast, and anchoring in Pentecost harbor two years later, found a cross on one of the islands forming the harbor, "which we suppose," says the writer of the narrative of the voyage, "was Sett up by George Wayman." In commemoration of Waymouth's erection of a cross on one of the islands enclosing Pentecost harbor, a stone cross was erected on Allen's Island in the summer of 1905, the tercentenary of Waymouth's visit to the coast of Maine.

we shewed them knives and their use, by cutting of stickes and other trifles, as combs and glasses, they came close aboard our ship, as desirous to entertaine our friendship. To these we gave such things as we perceived they liked, when wee shewed them the use: bracelets, rings, peacocke feathers, which they stucke in their haire, and Tabacco pipes. After their departure to their company on the shore, presently came foure other in another Canoa: to whom we gave as to the former, using them with as much kindnes as we could.

The shape of their body is very proportionable, they are wel countenanced, not very tal nor big, but in stature like to us: they paint their bodies with blacke, their faces, some with red, some with blacke, and some with blew.

Their clothing is Beavers skins, or Deares skins, cast over them like a mantle, and hanging downe to their knees, made fast together upon the shoulder with leather; some of them had sleeves, most had none; some had buskins of such leather tewed: they have besides a peece of Beavers skin betweene their legs, made fast about their waste, to cover their privities

They suffer no haire to grow on their faces, but on their head very long and very blacke, which those that have wives, binde up behinde with a leather string, in a long round knot.

They seemed all very civill and merrie: shewing tokens of much thankefulnesse, for those things we gave them. We found them then (as after) a people of exceeding good invention, quicke understanding and readie capacitie.

Their Canoas are made without any iron, of the bark of a birch tree, strengthened within with ribs and hoops of wood, in so good fashion, with such excellent ingenious art, as they are able to beare seven or eight persons, far exceeding any in the Indies.

One of their Canoas came not to us, wherein we imagined their women were: of whom they are (as all Salvages) very jealous.

When I signed unto them they should goe sleepe, because it was night, they understood presently, and pointed that at the shore, right against our ship, they would stay all night: as they did.

The next morning very early, came one Canoa abord us againe with three Salvages, whom we easily then enticed into our ship, and under the decke: where we gave them porke, fish, bread and pease, all which they did eat; and this I noted, they would eat nothing raw, either fish or flesh. They marvelled much and much looked upon the making of our canne and kettle, so they did at a head-peece and at our guns, of which they are most fearefull, and would fall flat downe at the report of them. At their departure I signed unto them, that if they would bring me such skins as they ware I would give them knives, and such things as I saw they most liked, which the chiefe of them promised to do by that time the Sunne should be beyond the middest of the firmament; this I did to bring them to an understanding of exchange, and that they might conceive the intent of our comming to them to be for no other end.

About 10 a clocke this day we descried our Shallop returning toward us, which so soone as we espied, we certainly conjectured our Captaine had found some unexpected harbour, further up [1] towards the maine to bring the ship into, or some river; knowing his determination and resolution, not so suddenly else to make returne: which when they came neerer they expressed by shooting volleies of shot; and when they were come within Musket shot, they gave us a volley and haled us, then we in the shippe gave them a great peece and haled them.

Thus we welcomed them; who gladded us exceedingly with their joifull relation of their happie discoverie, which shall appeare in the sequele. And we likewise gave them cause of mutuall joy with us, in discoursing of the kinde civility we found in a people, where we little expected any sparke of humanity.

Our Captaine had in this small time discovered up a great

[1] A natural expression from the position of the *Archangel* in St. George's harbor.

river, trending alongst into the maine about forty miles.[1] The pleasantnesse whereof, with the safety of harbour for shipping, together with the fertility of ground and other fruits, which were generally by his whole company related, I omit, till I report of the whole discovery therein after performed. For by the breadth, depth and strong flood, imagining it to run far up into the land, he with speed returned, intending to flanke his light horsman [2] for arrowes, least it might happen that the further part of the river should be narrow, and by that meanes subject to the volley of Salvages on either side out of the woods.

Untill his returne, our Captaine left on shore where he landed in a path (which seemed to be frequented) a pipe, a brooch and a knife, thereby to know if the Salvages had recourse that way, because they could at that time see none of them, but they were taken away before our returne thither.

I returne now to our Salvages, who according to their appointment about one a clocke, came with 4 Canoas to the shoare of the iland right over against us, where they had lodged the last night, and sent one Canoa to us with two of those Salvages, who had beene a bord, and another, who then seemed to have command of them; for though we perceived their willingnesse, yet he would not permit them to come abord; but he having viewed us and our ship, signed that he would go to the rest of the company and returne againe. Presently after their departure it began to raine, and continued all that afternoone, so as they could not come to us with their skins and furs, nor we go to them. But after an houre or there about, the three which had beene with us before came againe, whom we had to our fire and covered them with our gownes.

[1] St. George's River. Some have conjectured that the river of Waymouth's discovery was the Kennebec, and some the Penobscot; but neither of these rivers meets the requirements of the narrative. Against the earlier views, Captain George Prince, in his reprint of Rosier's *Relation*, in 1860, was the first to call attention to the claims of the St. George's River. This river is indicated on the Simancas map of 1610 (Brown, *Genesis*, I. 445) under its Indian name, Tahanock. The length of the river, as given by Rosier, is only an estimate.

[2] *I.e.*, to raise its gunwale.

Our Captaine bestowed a shirt upon him, whom we thought to be their chiefe, who seemed never to have seene any before; we gave him a brooch to hang about his necke, a great knife, and lesser knives to the two other, and to every one of them a combe and glasse, the use whereof we shewed them: whereat they laughed and tooke gladly; we victualled them, and gave them aqua vitæ, which they tasted, but would by no meanes drinke; our beveridge they liked well, we gave them Sugar Candy, which after they had tasted they liked and desired more, and raisons which were given them; and some of every thing they would reserve to carry to their company. Wherefore we pittying their being in the raine, and therefore not able to get themselves victuall (as we thought) we gave them bread and fish.

Thus because we found the land a place answereable to the intent of our discovery, viz. fit for any nation to inhabit, we used the people with as great kindnes as we could devise, or found them capable of.

The next day, being Saturday and the first of June, I traded with the Salvages all the fore noone upon the shore, where were eight and twenty of them: and because our ship rode nigh, we were but five or sixe: where for knives, glasses, combes and other trifles to the valew of foure or five shillings, we had 40 good Beavers skins, Otters skins, Sables, and other small skins, which we knewe not how to call. Our trade being ended, many of them came abord us, and did eat by our fire, and would be verie merrie and bold, in regard of our kinde usage of them. Towards night our Captaine went on shore, to have a draught with the Sein or Net. And we carried two of them with us, who marvelled to see us catch fish with a net. Most of that we caught we gave them and their company. Then on the shore I learned the names of divers things of them: and when they perceived me to note them downe, they would of themselves, fetch fishes, and fruit bushes, and stand by me to see me write their names.

Our Captaine shewed them a strange thing which they woondred at. His sword and mine having beene touched with the Loadstone, tooke up a knife, and held it fast when they plucked it away, made the knife turne, being laid on a blocke, and touching it with his sword, made that take up a needle, whereat they much marvelled. This we did to cause them to imagine some great power in us: and for that to love and feare us.

When we went on shore to trade with them, in one of their Canoas I saw their bowes and arrowes, which I tooke up and drew an arrow in one of them, which I found to be of strength able to carry an arrow five or sixe score stronglie; and one of them tooke it and drew as we draw our bowes, not like the Indians.[1] Their bow is made of Wich Hazell, and some of Beech in fashion much like our bowes, but they want nocks, onely a string of leather put through a hole at one end, and made fast with a knot at the other. Their arrowes are made of the same wood, some of Ash, big and long, with three feathers tied on, and nocked very artificiallie: headed with the long shanke bone of a Deere, made very sharpe with two fangs in manner of a harping iron. They have likewise Darts, headed with like bone, one of which I darted among the rockes, and it brake not. These they use very cunningly, to kill fish, fowle and beasts.

Our Captaine had two of them at supper with us in his cabbin to see their demeanure, and had them in presence at service: who behaved themselves very civilly, neither laughing nor talking all the time, and at supper fed not like men of rude education, neither would they eat or drinke more than seemed to content nature; they desired pease to carry a shore to their women, which we gave them, with fish and bread, and lent them pewter dishes, which they carefully brought againe.

In the evening another boat came to them on the shore, and because they had some Tabacco, which they brought for their owne use, the other came for us, making signe what they

---

[1] Francis Parkman says, "The Indians in drawing the bow did not necessarily hold it perpendicularly, but often at a slant, and drew back the right hand, not to the level of the right ear, but to that of the shoulder, or sometimes below it."

had, and offered to carry some of us in their boat, but foure or five of us went with them in our owne boat: when we came on shore they gave us the best welcome they could, spreading fallow Deeres skins for us to sit on the ground by their fire, and gave us of their Tabacco in our pipes, which was excellent, and so generally commended of us all to be as good as any we ever tooke, being the simple leafe without any composition, strong, and of sweet taste; they gave us some to carry to our Captaine, whom they called our Bashabes;[1] neither did they require any thing for it, but we would not receive any thing from them without remuneration.

Heere we saw foure of their women, who stood behind them, as desirous to see us, but not willing to be seene; for before, whensoever we came on shore, they retired into the woods, whether it were in regard of their owne naturall modestie, being covered only as the men with the foresaid Beavers skins, or by the commanding jealousy of their husbands, which we rather suspected, because it is an inclination much noted to be in Salvages; wherefore we would by no meanes seeme to take any speciall notice of them. They were very well favoured in proportion of countenance, though coloured blacke, low of stature, and fat, bare headed as the men, wearing their haire long: they had two little male children of a yeere and half old, as we judged, very fat and of good countenances, which they love tenderly, all naked, except their legs, which were covered with thin leather buskins tewed, fastened with strops to a girdle about their waste, which they girde very streight, and is decked round about with little round peeces of red Copper; to these I gave chaines and bracelets, glasses, and other trifles, which the Salvages seemed to accept in great kindnesse.

At our comming away, we would have had those two that supped with us, to go abord and sleepe, as they had promised; but it appeared their company would not suffer them. Whereat we might easily perceive they were much greeved.

[1] A name, not a title (*Maine Hist. Soc. Coll.*, first series, VII. 96; Champlain's *Voyages*, Prince Society edition, II. 45; and *Relations des Jésuites*, I., ch. 3, 8). His seat was on the shores of the Penobscot.

but not long after our departure, they came with three more to our ship, signing to us, that if one of our company would go lie on shore with them, they would stay with us. Then Owen Griffin (one of the two we were to leave in the Country, if we had thought it needfull or convenient) went with them in their Canoa, and 3 of them staied aborde us, whom our whole company very kindly used. Our Captaine saw their lodging provided, and them lodged in an old saile upon the Orlop;[1] and because they much feared our dogs, they were tied up whensoever any of them came abord us.

Owen Griffin, which lay on the shore, reported unto me their maner, and (as I may terme them) the ceremonies of their idolatry; which they performe thus. One among them (the eldest of the Company, as he judged) riseth right up, the other sitting still, and looking about, suddenly cried with a loud voice, Baugh, Waugh:[2] then the women fall downe, and lie upon the ground, and the men all together answering the same, fall a stamping round about the fire with both feet, as hard as they can, making the ground shake, with sundry out-cries, and change of voice and sound. Many take the fire-sticks and thrust them into the earth, and then rest awhile: of a sudden beginning as before, they continue so stamping, till the yonger sort fetched from the shore many stones, of which every man tooke one, and first beat upon them with their fire sticks, then with the stones beat the earth with all their strength. And in this maner (as he reported) they continued above two houres.

After this ended, they which have wives take them apart, and withdraw themselves severally into the wood all night.

The next morning, assoone as they saw the Sunne rise, they pointed to him to come with them to our shippe: and having received their men from us, they came with five or six of their Canoas and Company hovering about

[1] The lowest deck in a vessel having three decks; or, sometimes, a temporary deck.
[2] Powwow, which came to be the name used to designate such ceremonies.

our ship; to whom (because it was the Sabbath day) I signed they should depart, and at the next Sun rising we would goe along with them to their houses; which they understood (as we thought) and departed, some of their Canoas coursing about the Iland, and the other directly towards the maine.

This day, about five a clocke after noone, came three other Canoas from the maine, of which some had beene with us before; and they came aboord us, and brought us Tabacco, which we tooke with them in their pipes, which were made of earth, very strong, blacke, and short, containing a great quantity: some Tabacco they gave unto our Captaine, and some to me, in very civill kind maner. We requited them with bread and peaze, which they caried to their Company on shore, seeming very thankefull. After supper they returned with their Canoa to fetch us a shore to take Tabacco with them there: with whom six or seven of us went, and caried some trifles, if peradventure they had any trucke, among which I caried some few biskets, to try if they would exchange for them, seeing they so well liked to eat them. When we came at shore, they most kindly entertained us, taking us by the hands, as they had observed we did to them aboord, in token of welcome, and brought us to sit doune by their fire, where sat together thirteene of them. They filled their Tabacco pipe, which was then the short claw of a Lobster, which will hold ten of our pipes full, and we dranke of their excellent Tabacco as much as we would with them; but we saw not any great quantity to trucke for; and it seemed they had not much left of old, for they spend a great quantity yeerely by their continuall drinking: and they would signe unto us that it was growen yet but a foot above ground, and would be above a yard high, with a leafe as broad as both their hands. They often would (by pointing to one part of the maine Eastward) signe unto us, that their Bashabes (that is, their King) had great plenty of Furres, and much Tabacco. When we had sufficiently taken Tabacco with them, I shewed some of our trifles for trade; but they made signe that they had there nothing to exchange; for (as I after conceived) they had beene fishing and fowling, and so came thither to lodge that night by us: for when we were ready to come away, they shewed us great cups made very wittily of barke, in forme almost square, full of a red berry[1] about the bignesse of a bullis,[2] which they did eat, and gave us by handfuls; of which (though I liked not the taste) yet I kept some, because I would by no meanes but accept their kindnesse. They shewed me likewise a great piece of fish, whereof I tasted, and it was fat like Porpoise; and another kinde of great scaly fish, broiled on the coales, much like white Salmon, which the French-men call Aloza,[3] for these they would have had bread; which I refused, because in maner of exchange, I would always make the greatest esteeme I could of our commodities whatsoever; although they saw aboord our Captaine was liberall to give them, to the end we might allure them still to frequent us. Then they shewed me foure yoong Goslings, for which they required foure biskets, but I offered them two; which they tooke and were well content.

At our departure they made signe, that if any of us would stay there on shore, some of them would go lie aboord us: at which motion two of our Company stayed with them, and three of the Salvages lodged with us in maner as the night before.

Early the next morning, being Munday the third of June, when they had brought our men aboord, they came about our ship, earnestly by signes desiring that we would go with them along to the maine, for that there they had Furres and Tabacco to traffique with us. Wherefore our Captaine manned the light-horseman with as many men as he could well, which were about fifteene with rowers and all; and we went along with them. Two of their Canoas they sent away before, and they which lay aboord us all night, kept company with us to direct us.

This we noted as we went along, they in their Canoa with three oares, would at their will go ahead of us and about us,

[1] Not the checkerberry, which is pleasant to the taste. Probably the partridge-berry. [2] The wild plum. [3] The American shad.

when we rowed with eight oares strong; such was their swiftnesse, by reason of the lightnesse and artificiall composition of their Canoa and oares.

When we came neere the point [1] where we saw their fires, where they intended to land, and where they imagined some few of us would come on shore with our merchandize, as we had accustomed before; when they had often numbered our men very diligently, they scoured away to their Company, not doubting we would have followed them. But when we perceived this, and knew not either their intents, or number of Salvages on the shore, our Captaine, after consultation, stood off, and wefted them to us, determining that I should go on shore first to take a view of them and what they had to traffique: if he, whom at our first sight of them seemed to be of most respect among them, and being then in the Canoa, would stay as a pawne for me. When they came to us (notwithstanding all our former courtesies) he utterly refused; but would leave a yoong Salvage: and for him our Captaine sent Griffin in their Canoa, while we lay hulling a little off. Griffin at his returne reported, thay had there assembled together, as he numbered them, two hundred eighty three Salvages, every one his bowe and arrowes, with their dogges, and wolves which they keepe tame at command, and not anything to exchange at all; but would have drawne us further up into a little narrow nooke [2] of a river, for their Furres, as they pretended.

These things considered, we began to joyne them in the ranke of other Salvages, who have beene by travellers in most discoveries found very trecherous; never attempting mischiefe, untill by some remisnesse, fit opportunity affoordeth them certaine ability to execute the same. Wherefore after good advice taken, we determined so soone as we could to take some of them, least (being suspitious we had discovered their plots) they should absent themselves from us.

Tuesday, the fourth of June, our men tooke Cod and Had-

---

[1] Probably the entrance to New Harbor, on the eastern side of the Pemaquid peninsula. [2] The creek at New Harbor.

ocke with hooks by our ship side, and Lobsters very great; which before we had not tried.

About eight a clocke this day we went on shore with our boats, to fetch aboord water and wood, our Captaine leaving word with the Gunner in the shippe, by discharging a musket, to give notice if they espied any Canoa comming; which they did about ten a clocke. He therefore being carefull they should be kindly entreated, requested me to go aboord, intending with dispatch to make what haste after he possibly could. When I came to the ship, there were two Canoas, and in either of them three Salvages; of whom two were below at the fire, the other staied in their Canoas about the ship; and because we could not entice them abord, we gave them a Canne of pease and bread, which they carried to the shore to eat. But one of them brought backe our Canne presently and staid abord with the other two; for he being yoong, of a ready capacity, and one we most desired to bring with us into England, had received exceeding kinde usage at our hands, and was therefore much delighted in our company. When our Captaine was come, we consulted how to catch the other three at shore which we performed thus.

We manned the light horseman with 7 or 8 men, one standing before carried our box of Marchandise, as we were woont when I went to traffique with them, and a platter of pease, which meat they loved: but before we were landed, one of them (being too suspitiously feareful of his owne good) withdrew himselfe into the wood. The other two met us on the shore side, to receive the pease, with whom we went up the Cliffe to their fire and sate downe with them, and whiles we were discussing how to catch the third man who was gone, I opened the box, and shewed them trifles to exchange, thinking thereby to have banisht feare from the other, and drawen him to returne: but when we could not, we used little delay, but suddenly laid hands upon them. And it was as much as five or sixe of us could doe to get them into the light horseman. For they were strong and so naked as our best hold was by their long haire on their heads; and we would have beene very loath to have done them any hurt, which of necessity we had beene constrained to have done if we had attempted them in a multitude, which we must and would, rather than have wanted them, being a matter of great importance for the full accomplement of our voyage.

Thus we shipped five Salvages, two Canoas, with all their bowes and arrowes.

The next day we made an end of getting our wood aboord, and filled our empty caske with water.

Thursday, the 6 of June, we spent in bestowing the Canoas upon the orlop safe from hurt, because they were subject to breaking, which our Captaine was carefull to prevent.

Saturday the eight of June (our Captaine being desirous to finish all businesse about this harbour) very early in the morning, with the light horseman, coasted five or sixe leagues about the Ilands adjoining, and sounded all along wheresoever we went. He likewise diligently searched the mouth of the Harbour, and about the rocks [1] which shew themselves at all times, and are an excellent breach of the water, so as no Sea can come in to offend the Harbour. This he did to instruct himselfe, and thereby able to direct others that shall happen to come to this place. For every where both neere the rocks, and in all soundings about the Ilands, we never found lesse water than foure and five fathoms, which was seldome; but seven, eight, nine and ten fathoms is the continuall sounding by the shore. In some places much deeper upon clay oaze or soft sand: so that if any bound for this place, should be either driven or scanted with winds, he shall be able (with his directions) to recover safely his harbour most securely in water enough by foure [2] severall passages, more than which I thinke no man of judgement will desire as necessarie.

[1] The Dry Ledges between Allen's Island and Burnt Island. The depth of water, as recorded on the Coast Survey chart, corresponds with the figures given by Rosier.
[2] St. George's Harbor has four entrances: (1) that between Allen's and Burnt Islands; (2) that between Allen's and Benner's Islands; (3) that between Benner's and Davis's Islands; and (4) the wide passage between Davis's and Burnt Islands. In all four there is water enough to enter safely.

Upon one of the Ilands (because it had a pleasant sandy Cove for small barks to ride in) we landed, and found hard by the shore a pond [1] of fresh water, which flowed over the banks, somewhat over growen with little shrub trees, and searching up in the Iland, we saw it fed with a strong run, which with small labour, and little time, might be made to drive a mill. In this Iland, as in the other, were spruce trees of excellent timber and height, able to mast ships of great burthen.

While we thus sounded from one place to another in so good deepes, our Captaine to make some triall of the fishing himselfe, caused a hooke or two to be cast out at the mouth of the harbour, not above halfe a league from our ship, where in small time only, with the baits which they cut from the fish and three hooks, we got fish enough for our whole Company (though now augmented) for three daies. Which I omit not to report, because it sheweth how great a profit the fishing would be, they being so plentifull, so great and so good, with such convenient drying as can be wished, neere at hand upon the Rocks.

This day, about one a clocke after noone, came from the Eastward,[2] two Canoas abord us, wherein was he that refused to stay with us for a pawne, and with him six other Salvages which we had not seene before, who had beautified themselves after their manner very gallantly, though their clothing was not differing from the former, yet they had newly painted their faces very deep, some all blacke, some red, with stripes of excellent blew over their upper lips, nose and chin. One of them ware a kinde of Coronet about his head, made very cunningly, of a substance like stiffe haire coloured red, broad, and more than a handfull in depth, which we imagined to be some ensigne of superioritie; for he so much esteemed it as he would not for anything exchange the same. Other ware the white feathered skins of some fowle, round about their head, jewels in their

---

[1] There is a pond on Allen's Island fed in this way.
[2] It is stated farther on that the Indians came from "the Bashabes." As his abode was on the Penobscot, they would naturally come from the eastward.

ears, and bracelets of little white round bone, fastened together upon a leather string. These made not any shew that they had notice of the other before taken, but we understood them by their speech and signes, that they came sent from the Bashabes, and that his desire was that we would bring up our ship (which they call as their owne boats, a Quiden [1]) to his house, being, as they pointed, upon the main towards the East, from whence they came, and that he would exchange with us for Furres and Tabacco. But because our Company was but small, and now our desire was with speed to discover up the river, we let them understand, that if their Bashabes would come to us, he should be welcome, but we would not remove to him. Which when they understood (receiving of us bread and fish, and every of them a knife) they departed; for we had then no will to stay them long abord, least they should discover the other Salvages which we had stowed below.

Tuesday, the 11 of June, we passed up [2] into the river with our ship, about six and twenty miles. Of which I had rather not write, then by my relation to detract from the worthinesse thereof. For the River, besides that it is subject by shipping to bring in all traffiques of Marchandise, a benefit alwaies accounted the richest treasury to any land: for which cause our Thames hath that due denomination, and France by her navigable Rivers receiveth hir greatest wealth; yet this place of itselfe from God and nature affoordeth as much diversitie of good commodities, as any reasonable man can wish, for present habitation and planting.

The first and chiefest thing required, is a bold coast and faire land to fall with; the next, a safe harbour for ships to ride in.

The first is a speciall attribute to this shore, being most free from sands or dangerous rocks in a continuall good depth, with a most excellent land-fall, which is the first Iland we fell

---

[1] *Aquiden* is the Abnaki word for canoe. Rosier inferred that "a" was the indefinite article.

[2] An accurate statement of the course of a vessel passing from St. George's Harbor into the St. George's River.

with, named by us, Saint Georges Iland.[1] For the second, by judgement of our Captaine, who knoweth most of the coast of England, and most of other Countries, (having beene experienced by imployments in discoveries and travels from his childhood) and by opinion of others of good judgement in our shippe, heere are more good harbours for ships of all burthens, than England can affoord, and far more secure from all winds and weathers than any in England, Scotland, France or Spaine. For besides without the River in the channell, and sounds about the ilands adjoining to the mouth thereof, no better riding can be desired for an infinite number of ships. The River it selfe as it runneth up into the main very nigh forty miles toward the great mountaines, beareth in bredth a mile, sometime three quarters, and halfe a mile is the narrowest, where you shall never have under 4 and 5 fathoms water hard by the shore, but 6, 7, 8, 9, and 10 fathoms[2] all along, and on both sides every halfe mile very gallant Coves, some able to conteine almost a hundred saile, where the ground is excellent soft oaze with a tough clay under for anker hold, and where ships may ly without either Cable or Anker, only mored to the shore with a Hauser.

It floweth by their judgement eighteen or twenty foot at high water.[3]

Heere are made by nature most excellent places, as Docks to grave or Carine ships of all burthens; secured from all windes, which is such a necessary incomparable benefit, that

---

[1] The first island Waymouth "fell with" was Monhegan, to which he gave the name St. George. There is no evidence that Waymouth set up a cross at Monhegan; nor does the narrative of the Popham colony make any mention of an anchorage at Monhegan. The narrative shows that there was a definitely appointed rendezvous in case of separation, namely, Pentecost harbor, to which both of Popham's ships came. The island on which the Popham colonists found Waymouth's cross, therefore, was not Monhegan, but one of the St. George's Islands.

[2] These statements with reference to the breadth and depth of the river, also concerning the character of its bottom and the boldness of its shores, are true of the St. George's River.

[3] An erroneous estimate. The mean rise and fall of the tide in the St. George's River is nine and four-tenths feet.

in few places in England, or in any parts of Christendome, art, with great charges, can make the like.

Besides, the bordering land is a most rich neighbour trending all along on both sides, in an equall plaine, neither mountainous nor rocky, but verged with a greene bordure of grasse, doth make tender unto the beholder of hir pleasant fertility, if by clensing away the woods she were converted into meddow.

The wood she beareth is not shrubbish fit only for fewell, but goodly tall Firre, Spruce, Birch, Beech, Oke, which in many places is not so thicke, but may with small labour be made feeding ground, being plentifull like the outward Ilands with fresh water, which streameth doune in many places.

As we passed with a gentle winde up with our ship in this River, any man may conceive with what admiration we all consented in joy. Many of our Company who had beene travellers in sundry countries, and in the most famous Rivers, yet affirmed them not comparable to this they now beheld. Some that were with Sir Walter Ralegh [1] in his voyage to Guiana, in the discovery of the River Orenoque, which echoed fame to the worlds eares, gave reasons why it was not to be compared with this, which wanteth the dangers of many Shoules, and broken ground, wherewith that was incombred. Others before that notable River in the West Indies called Rio Grande; some before the River of Loyer,[2] the River Seine, and of Burdeaux in France, which, although they be great and goodly Rivers, yet it is no detraction from them to be accounted inferiour to this, which not only yeeldeth all the foresaid pleasant profits, but also appeared infallibly to us free from all inconveniences.

I will not prefer it before our river of Thames, because it is Englands richest treasure; but we all did wish those excellent Harbours, good deeps in a continuall convenient breadth and small tide-gates, to be as well therein for our countries good, as we found them here (beyond our hopes) in certaine, for those to whom it shall please God to grant this land for

[1] In 1595.   [2] Loire.

habitation; which if it had, with the other inseparable adherent commodities here to be found; then I would boldly affirme it to be the most rich, beautifull, large and secure harbouring river that the world affoordeth.[1]

Wednesday, the twelfth of June, our Captaine manned his light-horseman with 17 men, and ranne up from the ship riding [2] in the river up to the codde thereof, where we landed, leaving six to keepe the light-horseman till our returne. Ten of us with our shot, and some armed, with a boy to carry powder and match, marched up into the countrey towards the mountaines, which we descried at our first falling with the land.[3] Unto some of them the river brought us so neere, as we judged our selves when we landed to have beene within a league of them; but we marched up about foure miles in the maine, and passed over three hilles: and because the weather was parching hot, and our men in their armour not able to travel farre and returne that night to our ship, we resolved not to passe any further, being all very weary of so tedious and laboursom a travell.

In this march we passed over very good ground, pleasant and fertile, fit for pasture, for the space of some three miles, having but little wood, and that Oke like stands left in our pastures in England, good and great, fit timber for any use. Some small Birch, Hazle and Brake, which might in small time with few men be cleansed and made good arable land: but as it now is will feed cattell of all kindes with fodder enough for Summer and Winter. The soile is blacke, bearing sundry hearbs, grasse, and strawberries bigger than ours in England.

---

[1] This is evidently the language of contagious enthusiasm; yet one sailing up the St. George's River on a beautiful day in May or June, at full tide, or nearly full tide, would find himself in entire sympathy with Rosier in this description.

[2] Waymouth anchored his vessel near the present ruins of Fort St. George. "The codde" is said to mean a bay in the river. Such a "codde" there is at Thomaston. But Winship, *Sailors' Narratives of New England Voyages*, gives as the meaning "a bend or narrow portion."

[3] Such mountains are the Union and Camden mountains. The White Mountains are not visible at any point on the St. George's River, nor are they visible from the deck of a vessel ascending the Kennebec.

In many places are lowe Thicks like our Copisses of small yoong wood. And surely it did all resemble a stately Parke, wherein appeare some old trees with high withered tops, and other flourishing with living greene boughs. Upon the hilles grow notable high timber trees, masts for ships of 400 tun: and at the bottome of every hill, a little run of fresh water; but the furthest and last we passed, ranne with a great streame able to drive a mill.

We might see in some places where fallow Deere and Hares had beene, and by the rooting of ground we supposed wilde Hogs had ranged there, but we could descrie no beast, because our noise still chased them from us.

We were no sooner come aboord our light-horseman, returning towards our ship, but we espied a Canoa comming from the further part of the Cod of the river Eastward, which hasted to us: wherein, with two others, was he who refused to stay for a pawne: and his comming was very earnestly importing to have one of our men to go lie on shore with their Bashabes (who was there on shore, as they signed) and then the next morning he would come to our ship with many Furres and Tabacco. This we perceived to be only a meere device to get possession of any of our men, to ransome all those which we had taken, which their naturall policy could not so shadow, but we did easily discover and prevent. These meanes were by this Salvage practised, because we had one of his kinsemen prisoner, as we judged by his most kinde usage of him being aboord us together.

Thursday, the 13 of June, by two a clocke in the morning (because our Captaine would take the helpe and advantage of the tide) in the light-horseman with our Company well provided and furnished with armour and shot both to defend and offend; we went from our ship up to that part of the river which trended westward into the maine,[1] to search that: and

[1] The St. George's River makes such a trend westward at Thomaston. In recognition of the tercentenary of Waymouth's voyage, a memorial tablet on a large boulder was unveiled at Thomaston, July 6, 1905, at a celebration under the auspices of the citizens of Thomaston and the Maine Historical Society.

2 c

we carried with us a Crosse, to erect at that point, which (because it was not daylight) we left on the shore untill our returne backe; when we set it up in maner as the former.[1] For this (by the way) we diligently observed, that in no place, either about the Ilands, or up in the maine, or alongst the river, we could discerne any token or signe, that ever any Christian had beene before; of which either by cutting wood, digging for water, or setting up Crosses (a thing never omitted by any Christian travellers) we should have perceived some mention left.

But to returne to our river, further up into which we then rowed by estimation twenty miles, the beauty and goodnesse whereof I can not by relation sufficiently demonstrate. That which I can say in generall is this: What profit or pleasure soever is described and truly verified in the former part of the river, is wholly doubled in this; for the bredth and depth is such, that any ship drawing 17 or 18 foot water, might have passed as farre as we went with our light-horsman, and by all our mens judgement much further, because we left it in so good depth and bredth; which is so much the more to be esteemed of greater woorth, by how much it trendeth further up into the maine: for from the place of our ships riding in the Harbour at the entrance into the Sound, to the furthest part we were in this river, by our estimation was not much lesse than threescore miles.

From ech banke of this river are divers branching streames into the maine, whereby is affoorded an unspeakable profit by the conveniency of transportation from place to place, which in some countries is both chargeable; and not so fit, by cariages on waine, or horse backe.

Heere we saw great store of fish, some great, leaping above water, which we judged to be Salmons. All along is an excellent mould of ground. The wood in most places, especially on the East side, very thinne, chiefly oke and some small

[1] On the Simancas map of 1610 there is at this point the mark of a cross. What was it intended to represent if not the cross which Waymouth erected, and which he doubtless marked on his "perfect geographicall map"?

young birch, bordering low upon the river; all fit for medow and pasture ground: and in that space we went, we had on both sides the river many plaine plots of medow, some of three or foure acres, some of eight or nine: so as we judged in the whole to be betweene thirty and forty acres of good grasse, and where the armes run out into the Maine, there likewise went a space on both sides of cleere grasse, how far we know not, in many places we might see paths made to come downe to the watering.

The excellencie of this part of the River, for his good breadth, depth, and fertile bordering ground, did so ravish us all with variety of pleasantnesse, as we could not tell what to commend, but only admired; some compared it to the River Severne, (but in a higher degree) and we all concluded (as I verily thinke we might rightly) that we should never see the like River in every degree equall, untill it pleased God we beheld the same againe. For the farther we went, the more pleasing it was to every man, alluring us still with expectation of better, so as our men, although they had with great labour rowed long and eat nothing (for we carried with us no victuall, but a little cheese and bread) yet they were so refreshed with the pleasant beholding thereof, and so loath to forsake it, as some of them affirmed, they would have continued willingly with that onely fare and labour 2 daies; but the tide not suffering us to make any longer stay (because we were to come backe with the tide) and our Captaine better knowing what was fit then we, and better what they in labour were able to endure, being verie loath to make any desperate hazard, where so little necessitie required, thought it best to make returne, because whither we had discovered was sufficient to conceive that the River ran very far into the land. For we passed six or seven miles, altogether fresh water (whereof we all dranke) forced up by the flowing of the Salt: which after a great while eb, where we left it, by breadth of channell and depth of water was likely to run by estimation of our whole company an unknowen way farther: the search whereof our Captaine hath left till his returne, if it shall so please God to dispose of him and us.

For we having now by the direction of the omnipotent disposer of all good intents (far beyond the period of our hopes) fallen with so bold a coast, found so excellent and secure harbour, for as many ships as any nation professing Christ is able to set forth to Sea, discovered a River, which the All-creating God, with his most liberall hand, hath made above report notable with his foresaid blessings, bordered with a land, whose pleasant fertility bewraieth it selfe to be the garden of nature, wherein she only intended to delight hir selfe, having hitherto obscured it to any, except to a purblind generation, whose understanding it hath pleased God so to darken, as they can neither discerne, use, or rightly esteeme the unvaluable riches in middest whereof they live sensually content with the barke and outward rinds, as neither knowing the sweetnes of the inward marrow, nor acknowledging the Deity of the Almighty giver: having I say thus far proceeded, and having some of the inhabitant nation (of best understanding we saw among them) who (learning our language) may be able to give us further instruction, concerning all the premised particulars, as also of their governours, and government, situation of townes, and what else shall be convenient, which by no meanes otherwise we could by any observation of our selves learne in a long time: our Captaine now wholy intended his provision for speedy returne. For although the time of yeere and our victuall were not so spent, but we could have made a longer voyage, in searching farther and trading for very good commodities, yet as they might have beene much profitable, so (our company being small) much more prejudiciall to the whole state of our voyage, which we were most regardfull now not to hazard. For we supposing not a little present private profit, but a publique good, and true zeale of promulgating Gods holy Church, by planting Christianity, to be the sole intent of the Honourable setters foorth of this discovery;[1] thought it generally most expedient, by our speedy returne, to give the longer space of time to make provision for so weighty an enterprise.

[1] A like purpose was expressed by the Pilgrims in the compact signed in the cabin of the *Mayflower* in the harbor of Provincetown.

Friday, the 14 day of June, early by foure a clocke in the morning, with the tide, our two boats, and a little helpe of the winde, we rowed downe to the rivers mouth and there came to an anker about eleven a clocke. Afterward our Captaine in the light horseman searched the sounding all about the mouth and comming to the River, for his certaine instruction of a perfect description.

The next day, being Saturday, we wayed anker, and with a briese from the land, we sailed up to our watering place, and there stopped, went on shore and filled all our empty caske with fresh water.

Our Captaine upon the Rocke[1] in the middest of the harbour observed the height, latitude, and variation exactly upon his instruments.

1 Astrolabe.
2 Semisphere.
3 Ringe instrument.
4 Crosse Staffe.
5 And an excellent compasse made for the variation.

The certainty whereof, together with the particularities of every depth and sounding, as well at our falling with the land, as in the discovery, and at our departure from the coast; I refer to his owne relation in the Map[2] of his Geographicall description, which for the benefit of others he intendeth most exactly to publish.

The temperature of the Climate (albeit a very important matter) I had almost passed without mentioning, because it affoorded to us no great alteration from our disposition in England; somewhat hotter up into the Maine, because it lieth open to the South; the aire so wholesome, as I suppose not any of us found our selves at any time more healthfull, more able to labour, nor with better stomacks to such good fare, as we partly brought, and partly found.

Sunday, the 16 of June, the winde being faire, and because we had set out of England upon a Sunday, made the Ilands

[1] Such a rock is Carey's Rock in St. George's Harbor.
[2] This map has disappeared, but evidently the Simancas map of 1610 has preserved its main features.

upon a Sunday, and as we doubt not (by Gods appointment) happily fell into our harbour upon a Sunday; so now (beseeching him still with like prosperity to blesse our returne into England our country, and from thence with his good will and pleasure to hasten our next arrivall there) we waied Anker and quit the Land upon a Sunday.

Tuesday, the 18 day, being not run above 30 leagues from land, and our Captaine for his certaine knowledge how to fall with the coast, having sounded every watch, and from 40 fathoms had come into good deeping, to 70, and so to an hundred: this day the weather being faire, after the foure a clocke watch, when we supposed not to have found ground so farre from land, and before sounded in about 100 fathoms, we had ground in 24 fathomes. Wherefore our sailes being downe, Thomas King boatswaine, presently cast out a hooke, and before he judged it at ground, was fished and haled up an exceeding great and well fed Cod: then there were cast out 3 or 4 more, and the fish was so plentifull and so great, as when our Captaine would have set saile, we all desired him to suffer them to take fish a while, because we were so delighted to see them catch so great fish, so fast as the hooke came down: some with playing with the hooke they tooke by the backe, and one of the Mates with two hookes at a lead at five draughts together haled up tenne fishes; all were generally very great, some they measured to be five foot long, and three foot about.

This caused our Captaine not to marvell at the shoulding for he perceived it was a fish banke, which (for our farewell from the land) it pleased God in continuance of his blessings to give us knowledge of: the abundant profit whereof should be alone sufficient cause to draw men againe, if there were no other good both in present certaine, and in hope probable to be discovered. To amplifie this with words, were to adde light to the Sunne: for every one in the shippe could easily account this present commodity; much more those of judgement, which knew what belonged to fishing, would warrant (by the helpe of God) in a short voyage with few good fishers to make a more profitable returne from hence than from Newfoundland: the fish being so much greater, better fed, and abundant with traine;[1] of which some they desired, and did bring into England to bestow among their friends, and to testifie the true report.

After, we kept our course directly for England and with ordinary winds, and sometime calmes, upon Sunday the 14 of July about sixe a clocke at night, we were come into sounding in our channell, but with darke weather and contrary winds, we were constrained to beat up and downe till Tuesday the 16 of July, when by five a clocke in the morning we made Sylly;[2] from whence, hindered with calmes and small winds, upon Thursday the 18 of July about foure a clocke after noone, we came into Dartmouth: which Haven happily (with Gods gracious assistance) we made our last and first harbour in England.

Further, I have thought fit here to adde some things worthy to be regarded, which we have observed from the Salvages since we tooke them.

First, although at the time when we surprised them, they made their best resistance, not knowing our purpose, nor what we were, nor how we meant to use them; yet after perceiving by their kinde usage we intended them no harme, they have never since seemed discontented with us, but very tractable, loving, and willing by their best meanes to satisfie us in any thing we demand of them, by words or signes for their understanding: neither have they at any time beene at the least discord among themselves; insomuch as we have not seene them angry but merry; and so kinde, as if you give any thing to one of them, he will distribute part to every one of the rest.

We have brought them to understand some English, and we understand much of their language; so as we are able to aske them many things. And this we have observed, that if we shew them anything, and aske them if they have it in their

---

[1] Oil made from the livers of cod.   [2] The Scilly Islands.

countrey, they will tell you if they have it, and the use of it, the difference from ours in bignesse, colour, or forme; but if they have it not, be it a thing never so precious, they wil denie the knowledge of it.

They have names for many starres, which they will shew in the firmament.

They shew great reverence to their King, and are in great subjection to their Governours: and they will shew a great respect to any we tell them are our Commanders.

They shew the maner how they make bread of their Indian wheat, and how they make butter and cheese of the milke they have of the Rain-Deere and Fallo-Deere, which they have tame as we have Cowes.

They have excellent colours. And having seene our Indico, they make shew of it, or of some other like thing which maketh as good a blew.

One especiall thing is their maner of killing the Whale, which they call Powdawe;[1] and will describe his forme; how he bloweth up the water; and that he is 12 fathoms long; and that they go in company of their King with a multitude of their boats, and strike him with a bone made in fashion of a harping iron fastened to a rope, which they make great and strong of the barke of trees, which they veare out after him; then all their boats come about him, and as he riseth above water, with their arrowes they shoot him to death; when they have killed him and dragged him to shore, they call all their chiefe lords together, and sing a song of joy: and those chiefe lords, whom they call Sagamos, divide the spoile, and give to every man a share, which pieces so distributed they hang up about their houses for provision: and when they boile them, they blow off the fat, and put to their peaze, maiz, and other pulse, which they eat.

[1] Abnaki for "he blows."

A Briefe Note of what Profits we saw the Country yeeld in the small time of our stay there.

Trees

Oke of an exellent graine, strait, and great timber.
Elme.
Beech.
Birch, very tall and great; of whose barke they make their Canoas.
Wich-Hazell.
Hazell
Alder.
Cherry-tree.
Ash.
Maple.
Yew.
Spruce.
Aspe.
Firre.
Many fruit trees, which we knew not.

Fowles

Eagles.
Hernshawes.
Cranes.
Ducks great.
Geese.
Swannes.
Penguins.
Crowes.
Sharks.
Ravens.
Mewes.
Turtle-doves.
Many birds of sundrie colours.
Many other fowls in flocks, unknown.

Beasts

Reine-Deere.
Stagges.
Fallow-Deere.
Beares.
Wolves.
Beaver.
Otter.
Hare.
Cony.
Hedge-Hoggs.
Polcats.
Wilde great Cats.
Dogges; some like Wolves, some like Spaniels.

Fishes

Whales
Seales.
Cod very great.
Haddocke great.
Herring great.
Plaise.
Thornebacke.
Rockefish.
Lobstar great.
Crabs.

Muscles great, with pearles in them.
Cockles.
Wilks.
Cunner-fish.
Lumps.
Whiting.
Soales.
Tortoises.
Oisters.

Fruits, Plants and Herbs

Tobacco, excellent sweet and strong.
Wild-Vines.

Strawberries ⎫
Raspberries ⎪
Gooseberries ⎬ abundance.
Hurtleberries⎪
Currant trees⎭

Rose-bushes.
Peaze.
Ground-nuts.
Angelica, a most soveraigne herbe.
An hearbe that spreadeth the ground and smelleth like Sweet Marjoram, great plenty.
Very good Dies, which appeare by their painting; which they carrie with them in bladders.

The names of the five Salvages which we brought home into England, which are all yet alive, are these.

1. Tahanedo, a Sagamo or Commander.
2. Amoret   ⎫
3. Skicowaros ⎬ Gentlemen.
4. Maneddo   ⎭
5. Saffacomoit, a servant.[1]

---

[1] Three of these Indians were given to Gorges when Waymouth reached England. In his *Briefe Narration* their names are Manida, Skettwarroes, and Tasquantum. The first two are found in Rosier's list. Tasquantam is the name of an Indian captured by Thomas Hunt, master of a vessel with Captain John Smith, in 1614, and it is erroneously introduced here by Gorges writing many years afterward. Tahanedo, whom Gorges calls Dehamda, returned with Pring in 1606, and Skicowaros accompanied the Popham colonists. Sir John Popham received two of Waymouth's Indians. Probably they were with Challoung in 1606, when he set out for the Maine coast, and were captured by the Spaniards with Challoung and his vessel. Saffacomoit, one of the two, was recovered, and possibly the other.

A RELATION OF A VOYAGE TO SAGADA-
HOC 1607–1608

INTRODUCTION

ON April 10, 1606, James I. affixed his signature to a charter for two colonies in America. The promoters of the northern colony — "knights, gentlemen and merchants" in the west of England, prominent among whom were Sir Ferdinando Gorges and Sir John Popham, Chief Justice of England — sent out two vessels for exploration in the summer following the issuance of the charter. One of these vessels, commanded by Captain Henry Challoung, and in which Sir Ferdinando Gorges was especially interested, was captured by a Spanish fleet. The other, of which Thomas Hanham was the nominal commander, with Captain Martin Pring as navigator (Gorges, in his account of the voyage, makes no mention of Hanham), reached the coast of Maine, and was so successful in his exploration of it — his report bringing to Gorges and others full and satisfactory information — that it was decided to establish the northern colony there; and in May, 1607, two vessels, the *Gift of God* and the *Mary and John*, were despatched to the coast of Maine with colonists. Prominent in the expedition were George Popham, a nephew of Sir John Popham, and Raleigh Gilbert, a son of Sir Humphrey Gilbert. The manuscript of the following *Relation of a Voyage to Sagadahoc* was discovered in 1875 in the library of Lambeth Palace, London, by the late Rev. B. F. De Costa, D.D., and was first printed in 1880 by John Wilson and Son, University Press, Cambridge, Massachusetts, being reprinted in advance from the *Proceedings of the Massachusetts Historical Society*, Vol. XVIII. (1880–1881). In 1892, under title *The Sagadahoc Colony*, and with introductions, notes, and appendices, by Rev. Henry O. Thayer, A.M., it was reprinted by the Gorges Society of Portland, Maine, from an exact transcription of the Lambeth Palace manuscript. The manuscript does not give its author's name. It contains statements, however, that afford strong support to the conjecture that it was written by James Davies, probably the navigator of Gilbert's vessel, the *Mary and John* (Thayer's *Sagadahoc Colony*, pp. 17-20).

The manuscript ends abruptly at the foot of a page, leaving the narrative unfinished. But it happens that William Strachey, when writing his *Historie of Travaile into Virginia Britannia*, used this narrative before it was mutilated; and as he followed it closely in the parts of it which have been preserved, we may assume that he did the same in the parts now lost. Therefore in this present volume, after the reprint of the *Relation* (from the Gorges Society's text), Strachey's version of the rest of the story is added, being reprinted from the volume of the Hakluyt Society in which it was first printed, in 1849.

H. S. B.

RELATION OF A VOYAGE TO SAGADAHOC
1607–1608

In the nam of God, Amen.
The Relation of a Voyage, unto New England. Began from the Lizard, the first of June 1607, By Captn. Popham in the ship the Gift, and Captn. Gilbert in the Mary and John:
Written by............and found amongst the Papers of the truly Wor^{nfull}:[1] *S^r. Ferdinando Gorges, K^{nt}. by me William Griffith.*[2]

DEPARTED from the Lyzard the firste daye of June Ano Domi[3] 1607,[4] beinge Mundaye about 6 of the Cloke in the afternoon and ytt bore of [5] me then Northeste and by North eyght Leags of.

from thence Directed our Course for the Illands of flowers and Corve[6] in the wch we wear 24 dayes attainynge of ytt. All wch time we still kept the Sea and never Saw but on Saill beinge a ship of Salcom[7] bound for the New Foundland whearin was on[8] tosser of Dartmoth M^r.[9] in her.

The 25th daye of June we fell wth the Illand of Gersea [10] on of The Illands of the Assores and ytt bore of us then South and by est ten Leags of, our M^r. and his matts makinge ytt to be flowers but my Selffe wth stood them and reprooved them

---

[1] Worshipful.
[2] Gorges died in 1647, and the manuscript of the *Relation* did not come into Mr. Griffith's hand until after that date — possibly not until many years after.
[3] Anno Domini.
[4] According to Gorges the vessels left the harbor of Plymouth the day before. [5] Off.
[6] Flores and Corvo, islands of the Azores group.
[7] Salcombe, a village on the Devon coast.
[8] One.   [9] Master.   [10] Terceira, or Graciosa?

in thear errour as afterward ytt appeared manyfestly and then stood Roome[1] for flowers.

The 26th of June we had Seight of flowers and Corvo and the 27th in the mornynge early we wear hard abord flowers and stod in for to fynd a good rod for to anker Whearby to take in wood and watter. the 28th we Descryed to Sailles, standinge in for flowers Whearby we presently Wayed Anker and stood towards the rod of Sainta Cruse[2] beinge near three Leags from the place. Whear we wattered. thear Capt popham ankered to take in wood and watt^r but ytt was So calme that we Could nott recover or gett unto hem beffor the daye cam on.

The 29th of June beinge Mundaye early in the morning those to Sailles we had seen the nyght beffore Wear neare unto us and beinge Calme they Sent thear bots beinge full of men towards us. And after the orders of the Sea they hailled us demandynge us of whense we wear the wch we told them: and found them to be flemens[3] and the stats shipes.[4] on of our Company named John Goyett of plymoth knew the Capt. of on of the shipes for that he had ben att Sea wth hem. havinge aquainted Capt. Gilbert of this and beinge all frinds he desyered the Capt. of the Dutch to com near and take a can of bear the wch hee thankfully excepted we still keepinge our Selves in a redynesse both of our small shott and greatt; the Dutch Capt. beinge Com to our ships syde Capt. Gilbert desyered hem to com abord hem and entertand hem in the beste Sort he Could. this don they to requytt his kind entertainment desyered hem that he wold go abord wth them. And uppon thear earnest intreaty he went wth them takinge three or 4 gentell wth hem, but when they had hem abord of them they thear kept hem per Forse charginge him that he was a pyratt and still threatnynge hemselffe and his gentellmen wth hem to throw them all overbord and to take our ship from us. in this Sort they kept them from ten of the Clok mornynge untill eyght of the Clok

---

[1] An old nautical term, meaning to come about before the wind.
[2] A town on Flores.   [3] People of Flanders.
[4] Ships of the States, *i.e.*, of the United Provinces of the Netherlands.

nyght ussinge Som of his gent in most wild maner as Settinge Som of them in the bibowes [1] and buffettinge of others and other most wyld and shamffull abusses but in the end havinge Seene our Comission the wch was proffered unto them att the firste but they reffused to See yt and the greatest Cause doutinge of the Inglyshe men beinge of thear owne Company who had promist Capt. Gilbert that yf they proffered to perfform that wch they still threatned hem that then they all woold Rysse wth hem and either end thear Lyves in his deffence or Suppresse the shipe, the wch the Dutch perseavinge presently Sett them att Lyberty and Sent them abord unto us aggain to our no small Joye.   Capt. popham all this tyme beinge in the Wind of us never woold Com roome unto us not withstandinge we makinge all the Seignes that possybell we myght by strykinge on topsaill and hoissinge ytt aggain three tymes and makinge towards hem all that ever we possybell could.   so hear we lost Company of hem beinge the 29th daye of June about 8 of the Clok att nyght beinge 6 Leags from flowers West norwest wee standinge our Course for Vyrgenia the 30th wee laye in Seight of the Illand.

The firste Daye of Jully beinge Wesdaye wee depted [2] from the Illand of flowers beinge ten Leags South weste from ytt.

From hence we allwayes kept our Course to the Westward as much as wind and weather woold permytt untill the 27th daye of Jully duringe wch time wee often times Sounded but could never fynd grounde.   this 27th early in the mornynge we Sounded and had ground [3] but 18 fetham beinge then in the Lattitud of 43 degrees and $\frac{2}{3}$ hear w . . . fysht three howers and tooke near to hundred of Cods very great and large fyshe bigger and larger fyshe then that wch coms from the bancke of the New Found Land. hear wee myght have lodden our shipe in Lesse time then a moneth.

From hence the Wynd beinge att South west wee sett our Saills and stood by the wind west nor west towards the Land

[1] Bilboes or stocks.   [2] Departed.
[3] Sable Island Bank, about twenty miles southwest of Sable Island.

allwayes Soundinge for our better knowledg as we ran towarde the main Land from this bancke.

From this bancke we kept our Course west nor west 36 Leags wch ys from the 27th of July untill the 30th of July in wch tyme we ran 36 L as ys beffore sayed and then we Saw the Land [1] about 10 of the Clok in the mornynge bearinge norweste from us About 10 Leags and then we Sounded and had a hundred fethams blacke oze. hear as we Cam in towards the Land from this bancke we still found deepe watt^r. the deepest within the bancke ys 160 fethams and in 100 fetham you shall See the Land yf ytt be Clear weather after you passe the bancke the ground ys still black oze untill yo Com near the shore. this daye wee stood in for the Land but Could nott recover ytt beffor the night tooke us so we stood a Lyttell from ytt and thear strok a hull [2] untill the next daye beinge the Laste of July. hear Lyeinge at hull we tooke great stor of cod fyshes the bigeste and largest that I ever Saw or any man in our ship. this daye beinge the Last of July about 3 of the Clok in the after noon we recovered the shor and cam to an anker under an Illand [3] for all this Cost ys full of Illands and broken Land but very Sound and good for shipinge to go by them the watt^r deepe. 18 and 20 fetham hard abord them.

This Illand standeth in the lattitud of 44 d and ½ and hear we had nott ben att an anker past to howers beffore we espyed a bisken [4] shallop Cominge towards us havinge in her eyght Sallvages and a Lyttell salvage boye they cam near unto us and spoke unto us in thear Language. and we makinge Seignes to them that they should com abord of us showinge unto them knyves glasses beads and throwinge into thear bott Som bisket

---

[1] Aspotogeon, a conspicuous mountain, or the steep cliffs of Cape La Hève.
[2] Struck a hull, *i.e.*, lay to with all sails furled.
[3] Thayer (*The Sagadahoc Colony*, p. 42, note) says that while Macnab Island, at the entrance of Halifax harbor, Tancook and Green Islands, guarding Mahone Bay, and Cross Island, at Lunenburg Bay, clearly meet the requirements of latitude, he thinks Ironbound Island, from its proximity to the harbor of La Hève, has the preference.   [4] Biscayan.

but for all this they wold nott com abord of us but makinge show to go from us, we suffered them. So when they wear a Lyttell from us and Seeinge we proffered them no wronge of thear owne accord retorned and cam abord of us and three of them stayed all that nyght wth us the rest depted in the shallope to the shore makinge Seignes unto us that they wold retorn unto us aggain the next daye.

The next daye the Sam Salvages wth three Salvage wemen beinge the fryst daye of Auguste retorned unto us bringinge wth them Som feow skines of bever in an other bisken shallop and propheringe thear skines to trook wth us but they demanded over muche for them and we Seemed to make Lyght of them So then the other three wch had stayed wth us all ngyht went into the shallop and So they depted. ytt Seemth that the french hath trad wth them for they use many french words. the Cheeff Comander of these p^{ts} ys called Messamott and the ryver or harbor ys called emannett.[1] we take these peopell to be the tarentyns[2] and these peopell as we have Learned sence do make wars wth Sasanoa[3] the Cheeffe Comander to the westward whea . . . we have planted and this Somer they kild his Sonne. So the Salvages depted from us and cam no mor unto us. After they wear depted from us we hoyssed out our bot whearin my Selffe was wth 12 others and rowed to the shore and landed on this Illand that we rod under the wch we found to be a gallant Illand full of heigh and myghty trees of Sundry Sorts. hear we allso found aboundance of gusberyes, strawberyes, rasberyes and whorts. So we retorned and Cam abord.

Sondaye beinge the second of Auguste after dyner our bott went to the shore again to fille freshe watt^r whear after they had filled thear watt^r thear cam fower Salvages unto them havinge thear bowes and arowes in thear hands makinge show unto them to have them Com to the shore but our

---

[1] Afterward called Cape La Hève, from a bluff in Normandy which bears that name.
[2] An Indian tribe occupying the country east of the Penobscot.
[3] A Kennebec sachem.

Saillers havinge filled thear watt' wold nott go to the shore unto them but retorned and cam abord beinge about 5 of the Clock in the afternoon. So the bott went presently from the ship unto a point of an Illand and thear att Lo watt' in on hower kild near .50. great Lopsters. you shall See them Whear they Ly in shold[1] Watt' nott past a yeard deep and wth a great hooke mad faste to a staffe you shall hitch them up. thear ar great store of them you may near Lad a Ship wth them, and they are of greatt bignesse. I have nott Seen the Lyke in Ingland. So the bott retorned a bord and wee toke our bott in and about myd nyght the wynd cam faier att northest we Sett Saill and depted from thence keepinge our Course South west for So the Cost Lyeth.

Mundaye being the third of Auguste in the morninge we wear faier by the shore and So Sailled alongste the Coste. we Saw many Illands all alonge the Cost and great Sounds, goinge betwyxt them. but We could make prooffe of non for want of a penyshe.[2] hear we found fyshe still all alonge the Cost as we Sailled.

Tusdaye being the 4th of Auguste in the morninge 5 of the Clok we wear theawart of a Cape or head Land[3] Lyeing in the Latitud of 43 degrees and cam very near unto ytt. ytt ys very Low Land showinge Whytt Lyke sand but ytt ys Whytt Rocks and very stronge tides goeth hear from the place we stopt att beinge in 44 de and ½. untill this Cape or head land ytt ys all broken Land and full of Illands and Large Sounds betwixt them and hear we found fyshe aboundance so large and great as I never Saw the Lyke Cods beffor nether any man in our shipe.

After we paste this Cape or head Land the Land falleth awaye and Lyeth in norwest and by north into a greatt deep baye.[4] We kept our course from this head Land West and Weste and by South 7 Leags and cam to thre Illands[5] whear cominge near unto them we found on the Southest Syd of

[1] Shoal.   [2] A pinnace.   [3] Cape Sable.   [4] Bay of Fundy.
[5] Seal Island and Mud Islands, five in all, but appearing, from the position of the observer, as one.

them a great Leadge of Rocks Lyeinge near a Leage into the Sea the wch we perseavinge tackt our ship and the wynde being Large att northest Cleared our Selves of them kepinge still our course to the westward west and by South and west Southwest untill mydnyght. then after we hald in more northerly.

Wensdaye being the 5th of Auguste from after mydnyght we hald in West norwest untill 3 of the Clok afternoon of the Sam and then we Saw the Land aggain bearinge from us north weste and by north and ytt Risseth in this forme hear under.[1] ten or 12 Leags from yo they ar three heigh mountains [2] that Lye in upon the main Land near unto the ryver of penobskot in wch ryver the bashabe makes his abod the cheeffe Comander of those pts and streatcheth unto the ryver of Sagadehock [3] under his Comand. yo shall see theise heigh mountains when yo shall not perseave the main Land under ytt they ar of shutch an exceedinge heygts: And note, that from the Cape or head Land beffor spoken of untill these heigh mountains we never Saw any Land except those three Illands also beffor mensyoned. We stood in Right wth these mountains untill the next daye.

Thursdaye beinge the 6th of Auguste we stood in wth this heigh Land untill 12 of the Cloke noon and then I found the shipe to be in 43 d and ½ by my observatio[4] from thence we Sett our Course and stood awaye dew weste and Saw three other Illands [5] Lyenge together beinge Lo and flatt by the watt^r showinge whytt as yff ytt wear Sand but ytt ys whytt Rocks makinge show a far of allmoste Lyke unto Dover Cleeves [6] and these three Illands Lye dew est and west on of the other. so we Cam faier by them and as we Cam to the Westward the heygh Land beffor spoken of shewed ytt selffe in this form as followith.[7]

[1] The reference is to sketches in the manuscript.
[2] The Camden Hills.   [3] Kennebec.
[4] An indication of the official position of the writer of the *Relation*. He was the pilot of the vessel.
[5] Ragged, Wooden Ball and Seal Islands of the Matinicus group. Matinicus itself was hidden from view by the islands mentioned.
[6] Cliffs.   [7] Sketches in the manuscript.

From hence we kept still our Course West and Weste by North towards three other Illands[1] that we Sawe Lyenge from these Illands beffor spoken of 8 Leags and about ten of the Clok att nyght we recovered them and havinge Sent in our bott beffor nyght to vew ytt for that ytt was Calme a[nd] to Sound ytt and See whatt good ankoringe was under ytt we bor in wth on of them the wch as we cam in by we still sounded and founde very deep watt^r 40 fetham hard abord of yt. So we stood in into a Cove In ytt and had 12 fetham watt^r and thear we ankored untill the mornynge. And when the daye appeared We Saw we weare environed Round about with Illands. yo myght have told neare thirty Illands round about us from abord our shipe. this Illand we Call S^t. Georges Illand for that we hear found a Crosse Sett up the wch we Suposse was Sett up by George Wayman.[2]

Frydaye beinge the 7th of Auguste we wayed our Ankor whereby to bringe our shipe in mor bett^r Safty how Soever the wynd should happen to blow and about ten of the Cloke in the mornynge as we weare standinge of a Lyttell from the Illand we descried a saill standinge in towards this Illand and we presently mad towards her and found ytt to be the *gyfte* our Consort So beinge all Joye full of our happy meetinge we both stood in again for the Illand we ryd under beffor and theare anckored both together.[3]

This night followinge about myd nyght Capt. Gilbert caussed his ships bott to be maned and took to hemselffe 13 other my Selffe beinge on, beinge 14 persons in all, and tooke the Indyan skidwarres wth us[4] the weather beinge faier and

---

[1] Of the St. George's group.

[2] Probably Allen's Island. Waymouth, when on the coast in 1605, gave the name St. George to Monhegan. Finding here, on one of the islands forming Pentecost Harbor, Waymouth's cross, the Popham colonists transferred to the island on which the cross was erected the name St. George, and so we find in the *Relation* the words, "We Call St. Georges Illand."

[3] Evidently here was the rendezvous that had been agreed upon before leaving England. The *Mary and John* preceded the *Gift* only about twelve hours.

[4] Skicowaros (so Rosier wrote the name), one of the Indians captured by Waymouth.

the wynd Calme we rowed to the Weste in amongst many gallant Illands and found the ryver of pemaquyd to be but 4 Leags weste from the Illand we Call S^t. Georges whear our ships remained still att anckor. hear we Landed in a Lyttell Cove [1] by skyd warres Direction and marched over a necke of the Land near three mills. So the Indyan skidwarres brought us to the Salvages housses whear they did inhabitt although much against his will for that he told us that they wear all removed and gon from the place they wear wont to inhabitt, but we answered hem again that we wold nott retorn backe untill shutch time as we had spoken with Som of them. At Length he brought us whear they did inhabytt whear we found near a hundreth of them men wemen and Children. And the Cheeffe Comander of them ys Nahanada.[2] att our fryste Seight of them uppon a howlinge or Cry that they mad they all presently Isued forth towards us wth thear bowes and arrows and we presently mad a stand and Suffered them to Com near unto us. then our Indyan skidwarres spoke unto them in thear language showinge them what we wear wch when nahanada thear Comander perseaved what we wear he Caussed them all to laye assyd thear bowes and arrowes and cam unto us and imbrassed us and we did the lyke to them aggain. So we remained wth them near to howers and wear in thear housses. Then we tooke our Leave of them and retorned wth our Indyan skidwarres wth us towards our ships the 8th Daye of August being Satterdaye in the after noon.

Sondaye being the 9th of Auguste in the morninge the most p^t of our holl company of both our shipes Landed on this Illand the wch we call S^t. Georges Illand whear the Crosse standeth and thear we heard a Sermon delyvred unto us by our preacher [3] gyvinge god thanks for our happy metinge and Saffe aryvall into the Contry and So retorned abord aggain.

[1] The landing was probably at New Harbor.
[2] Another of the Indians captured by Waymouth. He returned the previous year with Pring. Rosier says, "Tahanedo, a Sagamo or Commander."
[3] Rev. Richard Seymour. Bishop Burgess identifies him as a great-grandson of the Protector Somerset.

Mundaye beinge the Xth of Auguste early in the morninge Capt. popham in his shallope wth thirty others and Capt. Gilbert in his ships bott wth twenty others Acompanede Depted from thear shipes and sailled towards the ryver of pemaquyd[1] and Caryed wth us the Indyan skidwarres and Cam to the ryver ryght beffore thear housses whear they no Sooner espyed us but presently Nahanada wth all his Indians wth thear bowes and arrows in thear hands Cam forth upon the Sands. So we Caussed skidwarres to speak unto hem and we our Selves spok unto hem in Inglyshe givinge hem to understand our Cominge tended to no yvell towards hem Selffe nor any of his peopell. he told us again he wold nott thatt all our peopell should Land. So beccause we woold in no sort offend them, hearuppon Som ten or twelffe of the Cheeff gent Landed and had Some parle together and then afterward they wear well contented that all should Land. So all landed we ussinge them with all the kindnesse that possibell we Could. neverthelesse after an hower or to they all Soddainly withdrew them Selves from us into the woods and Lefte us. we perseavinge this presently imbarked our Selves all except skidwarres who was nott Desyerous to retorn with us. We Seeinge this woold in no Sort proffer any Violence unto hem by drawing hem perfforce Suffered hem to remain, and staye behinde us, he promyssinge to retorn unto us the next Daye followinge but he heald not his promysse. So we imbarked our Selves and went unto the other Syd of the ryver and thear remained uppon the shore the nyght followinge.

Tuesdaye beinge the xith of Auguste we retorned and cam to our ships whear they still remained att ankor under the Illand we call S^t. Georges.

Wensdaye being the xiith of Auguste we wayed our anckors and Sett our saills to go for the ryver of Sagadehock. we kept our Course from thence dew Weste until 12 of the Clok mydnyght of the Sam. then we stroke our Saills and layed a hull untill the mornynge Doutinge for to over shoot ytt.

[1] The boats passed around Pemaquid Point.

Thursdaye in the mornynge breacke of the daye beinge the xiii[th] of Auguste the Illand of Sutquin [1] bore north of us nott past halff a leage from us and ytt rysseth in this form hear under followinge [2] the w[ch] Illand Lyeth ryght beffore the mouth of the ryver of Sagadehocke South from ytt near 2 Leags but we did not make ytt to be Sutquin so we Sett our saills and stood to the westward for to Seeke ytt 2 Leags farther and nott fyndinge the ryver of Sagadehocke we knew that we had overshott the place. then we wold have retorned but Could nott and the nyght in hand the *gifte* Sent in her shallop and mad ytt and went into the ryver this nyght but we wear constrained to remain att Sea all this nyght and about mydnight thear arosse a great storme and tempest uppon us the w[ch] putt us in great daunger and hassard of castinge awaye of our ship and our Lyves by reason we wear so near the shore. the wynd blew very hard att South right in uppon the shore so that by no means we could nott gett of. hear we sought all means and did what possybell was to be don for that our Lyves depended on ytt. hear we plyed ytt wth our ship of and on all the nyght often times espyeinge many soonken rocks and breatches hard by us enforsynge us to put our ship about and stand from them bearinge saill when ytt was mor fytter to have taken ytt in but that ytt stood uppon our Lyves to do ytt and our bott Soonk att our stern yet woold we nott cut her from us in hope of the appearinge of the daye. thus we Contynued untill the daye cam. then we perseaved our Selves to be hard abord the Lee shore and no waye to escape ytt but by Seekinge the Shore. then we espyed 2 Lyttell Illands [3] Lyeinge under our lee. So we bore up the healme and steerd in our shipe in betwyxt them whear the Lord be praised for ytt we found good and sauffe ankkoringe and thear anckored the storme still contynuinge untill the next daye followynge.

[1] Seguin. It was known on the *Mary and John* that Seguin was opposite the entrance to the river. But as the Kennebec is not discernible from the ocean, the officers of the *Gift*, who evidently had not been on the coast before, sought the entrance to the river farther to the westward.

[2] Sketches in the manuscript.

[3] Cape Small Point (which from the vessel seemed to be an island) and Seal Island.

Frydaye beinge the xiiii[th] of August that we anckored under these Illands thear we repaired our bott being very muche torren and spoilled. then after we Landed on this Illand and found 4 salvages and an old woman. this Illand ys full of pyne trees and ocke and abundance of whorts of fower Sorts of them.

Satterdaye beinge the 15th of Auguste the storme ended and the wind Cam faier for us to go for Sagadehock. so we wayed our anckors and Sett Saill and stood to the estward and cam to the Illand of Sutquin w[ch] was 2 Leags from those Illands we rod att anker beffor, and hear we anckored under the Illand of Sutqin in the estersyd of ytt for that the wynd was of the shore that wee could no gett into the ryver of Sagadehock and hear Cap[t]. pophams ships bott cam abord of us and gave us xx freshe Cods that they had taken beinge Sent out a fyshinge.

Sondaye beinge the 16th of Auguste Cap[t]. popham Sent his Shallop unto us for to healp us in. So we wayed our anckors and beinge Calme we towed in our ship and Cam into the Ryver of Sagadehocke and anckored by the *gyfts* Syd about xi of the Cloke the Same daye.

Mundaye beinge the 17th Auguste Cap[t]. popham in his shallop wth 30 others and Cap[t]. Gilbert in his shipes bott accompaned wth 18 other persons depted early in the morninge from thear ships and sailled up the Ryver of Sagadehock for to vew the Ryver and allso to See whear they myght fynd the most Convenyent place for thear plantation my Selffe beinge wth Cap[t]. Gilbert. So we Sailled up into this ryver near 14 Leags and found ytt to be a most gallant ryver very brod and of a good depth. we never had Lesse Watt[r] then 3 fetham when we had Least and abundance of greatt fyshe [1] in ytt Leaping above the Watt[r] on eatch Syd of us as we Sailled. So the nyght aprochinge after a whill we had refreshed our Selves uppon the shore about 9 of the Cloke we sett backward to retorn and Cam abourd our shipes the next day following about 2 of the Clok in the afternoon. We fynd this ryver to be very

[1] Sturgeon.

pleasant wth many goodly Illands in ytt and to be both Large and deepe Watt^r havinge many branches in ytt. that wch we tooke bendeth ytt Selffe towards the northest.

Tuesdaye beinge the 18th after our retorn we all went to the shore and thear mad Choies of a place for our plantation[1] wh^ch ys at the very mouth or entry of the Ryver of Sagadehocke on the West Syd of the Ryver beinge almoste an Illand of a good bygness. whylst we wear uppon the shore thear Cam in three Cannoos by us but they wold not Com near us but rowed up the Ryver and so past away.

Wensday beinge the 19th Auguste we all went to the shore whear we mad Choise for our plantation and thear we had a Sermon delyvred unto us by our precher and after the Sermon our pattent was red wth the orders and Lawes thearin prescrybed and then we retorned abord our ships again.

Thursdaye beinge the 20th of Auguste all our Companyes Landed and thear began to fortefye. our presedent Capt. popham Sett the fryst spytt of ground unto ytt and after hem all the rest followed and Labored hard in the trenches about ytt.

Frydaye the 21th of Auguste all hands Labored hard about the fort Som in the trentch Som for fagetts and our ship Carpenters about the buildinge of a small penis [2] or shallop.

Satterdaye the 22th Auguste Capt. popham early in the morninge depted in his shallop to go for the ryver of paship-skoke.[3] thear they had parle wth the Salvages again who delyvred unto them that they had ben att wars wth Sasanoa and had slain his Soone in fyght. skidwares and Dehanada wear in this fyght.

Sondaye the 23th our presedent Capt. popham retorned unto us from the ryver of pashipscoke.

The 24th all Labored about the fort.

---

[1] Strachey gives the Indian name of the place as Sabino. A plan of the fort erected by the Popham colonists (discovered in the royal archives of Spain at Simancas, by the Hon. J. L. M. Curry, United States Minister to Spain, and reproduced in Brown's *Genesis of the United States*, I. 190) makes the location of the fort certain. A better copy of the plan will be found in Thayer's *Sagadahoc Colony*, p. 186. It is reproduced in the present volume.
[2] Pinnace.   [3] The Pejepscot or Androscoggin.

Tuesdaye the 25th Capt. Gilbert imbarked hem Selffe wth 15 other wth hem to go to the Westward uppon Som Discovery but the Wynd was contrary and forsed hem backe again the Sam daye.

The 26th and 27th all Labored hard about the fort.

Frydaye the 28th Capt. Gilbert wth 14 others my Selffe beinge on Imbarked hem to go to the westward again. So the wynd Servinge we Sailled by many gallant Illands [1] and towards nyght the winde Cam Contrary against us So that we wear Constrained to remain that nyght under the head Land called Semeamis [2] whear we found the Land to be most fertill. the trees growinge thear doth exceed for goodnesse and Length being the most p^t of them ocke and wallnutt growinge a greatt space assoonder on from the other as our parks in Ingland and no thickett growinge under them. hear wee also found a gallant place to fortefye whom Nattuer ytt Selffe hath already framed wth out the hand of man wth a runynge stream of watt^r hard adjoyninge under the foott of ytt.

Satterdaye the 29th Auguste early in the mornynge we depted from thence and rowed to the westward for that the wind was againste us. but the wynd blew so hard that forsed us to remain under an Illand [3] 2 Leags from the place we remayned the night beffore. whilst we remayned under this Illand thear passed to Cannoos by us but they wold nott Com neare us. after mydnyght we put from this Illand in hope to have gotten the place we dessyered but the wind arose and blew so hard at Southwest Contrary for us that forsed us to retorn.

Sondaye beinge the 30th Auguste retornynge beffore the wynd we sailled by many goo[d]ly Illands for betwixt this head Land called Semeamis and the ryver of Sagadehock ys a great baye in the wch Lyeth So many Illands and so thicke and neare together that yo Cannott well desern to Nomber them. yet may yo go in betwixt them in a good ship for yo shall have never Lesse Watt^r the[n] 8 fethams. these Illands ar all over

---

[1] Islands of Casco Bay. [3] Richmond's Island.
[2] Evidently some headland on Cape Elizabeth.

growen wth woods very thicke as ocks wallnut pyne trees and many other things growinge as Sarsaperilla hassell nuts and whorts in aboundance. So this day we retorned to our fort att Sagadehock.

Munday being the Last of Auguste nothinge hapened but all Labored for the buildinge of the fort and for the storhouse to reseave our vyttuall.

Tuesday the first of September thear Cam a Canooa unto us in the wch was 2 greatt kettells of brasse. Som of our Company did parle wth them but they did rest very doutfull of us and wold nott Suffer mor then on att a tyme to Com near unto them. So he depted. The Second daye third and 4th nothinge hapened worth the wryttinge but that eatch man did his beste endevour for the buildinge of the fort.

Satterdaye beinge the 5th of Septemb^r thear Cam into the entraunce of the ryver of Sagadehocke nine Canoos in the wch was Dehanada and skidwarres wth many others in the wholl near fortye persons men women and Children. they Cam and parled wth us and we aggain ussed them in all frindly maner We Could and gave them vyttaills for to eatt. So skidwarres and on more of them stayed wth us untill nyght the rest of them withdrew them in thear Canooas to the farther Syd of the ryver. but when nyght Cam for that skidwares woold needs go to the rest of his Company Capt. Gilbert acompaned wth James Davis and Capt. ellis best took them into our bott and Caryed them to thear Company on the farther syd the ryver and thear remained amongst them all the nyght and early in the mornynge the Sallvages depted in thear Canooas for the ryver of pemaquid promyssinge Capt. Gilbert to accompany hem in thear Canooas to the ryver of penobskott whear the bashabe remayneth.

The 6th nothinge happened. the 7th our ship the *Mary and John* began to discharge her vyttualls.

Tuesday beinge the 8th Septemb^r Capt. Gilbert acompaned wth xxii others my Selffe beinge on of them depted from the fort to go for the ryver of penobskott takinge wth hem divers Sorts of M^{r}chandise for to trad wth the Bashabe who ys the

Cheeffe Comander of those p^{ts} but the wind was Contrary againste hem so that he could nott Com to dehanada and skidwares at the time apointed for ytt was the xith daye beffor he Could gett to the ryver of pemaquid Whear they do make thear abbod.

Frydaye beinge the xith in the mornynge early we Cam into the ryver of pemaquyd thear to Call nahanada and skidwares as we had promyste them. but beinge thear aryved we found no Lyvinge Creatuer. they all wear gon from thence. the wch we perseavinge presently depted towards the ryver of penobskott Saillinge all this daye and the xiith and xiiith the Lyke yett by no means Could we fynd ytt. So our vitall beinge spent we hasted to retorn. So the wynd Cam faier for us and we Sailled all the 14th and 15th dayes in retornynge the Wind blowinge very hard att north and this mornynge the 15th daye we pseaved [1] a blassing star in the northest of us.

The 16th 17th 18th 19th 20th 21th 22th nothinge hapened but all Labored hard about the fort and the store house for to Land our wyttaills.

The 23th beinge Wensdaye Capt. Gilbert acompaned wth 19 others my Selffe on of them depted from the fort to go for the head of the ryver of Sagadehock. we Sailled all this daye. So did we the Lyke the 24th untill the evenynge. then we Landed thear to remain that Nyght. hear we found a gallant Champion Land and exceeddinge fertill. So hear we remayned all nyght.

The 25th beinge frydaye early in the mornynge we depted from hence and sailled up the ryver about eyght Leags farther untill we Cam unto an Illand [2] beinge Lo Land and flatt. att this Illand ys a great down Fall of watt^r the wch runeth by both Sydes of this Illand very swyfte and shallow. in this Illand we found greatt store of grapes exceedinge good and sweett of to Sorts both red butt the on of them ys a mervellous deepe red.

[1] Perceived.
[2] At Augusta. There was formerly an island, near the eastern bank of the river just below the falls, known as Cushnoc Island. This island is so marked on the 1750 survey of the Plymouth Company. It was just below the present dam.

by both the syds of this ryver the grapes grow in aboundance and allso very good Hoppes and also Chebolls [1] and garleck. and for the goodnesse of the Land ytt doth so far abound that I Cannott allmost expresse the Sam. hear we all went ashore and wth a stronge Rope made fast to our bott and on man in her to gyde her aggainst the Swyfte stream we pluckt her up throwe ytt pforce.[2] after we had past this down-Fall we all went into our bott again and rowed near a Leage farther up into the ryver and nyght beinge att hand we hear stayed all nyght, and in the fryst of the night about ten of the Cloke thear Cam on the farther syd of the ryver sartain Salvages Callinge unto us in broken inglyshe. we answered them aggain. So for this time they depted.

The 26th beinge Satterdaye thear Cam a Canooa unto us and in hear fower salvages those that had spoken unto us in the nyght beffore. his name that Came unto us ys Sabenoa. he macks hemselffe unto us to be Lord of the ryver of Sagadehock.

End: The relation of Whole Voyage to Virginia,
New England,
1607.[3]

[*The remainder of the narration is taken from Chapter X. of the "Historie of Travaile into Virginia," by William Strachey.*]

They entertayned him friendly, and tooke him into their boat and presented him with some triffling things, which he accepted; howbeyt, he desired some one of our men to be put into his canoa as a pawne of his safety, whereupon Captain Gilbert sent in a man of his, when presently the canoa rowed away from them with all the speed they could make up the

[1] Onions.   [2] Perforce.
[3] This subscription must have been added at the end of the manuscript by a later hand, perhaps by Griffith, who wrote the title.

river. They followed with the shallop, having great care that the Sagamo should not leape overbourd. The canoa quickly rowed from them and landed, and the men made to their howses, being neere a league on the land from the river's side, and carried our man with them. The shallop making good waye, at length came to another downefall,[1] which was so shallowe and soe swift, that by noe meanes they could passe any further, for which, Captain Gilbert, with nine others, landed and tooke their fare, the salvadge Sagamo, with them, and went in search after those other salvages, whose howses, the Sagamo told Captain Gilbert, were not farr off; and after a good tedious march, they came indeed at length unto those salvages' howses wheere found neere fifty able men very strong and tall, such as their like before they had not seene; all newly painted and armed with their bowes and arrowes. Howbeyt, after that the Sagamo had talked with them, they delivered back again the man, and used all the rest very friendly, as did ours the like by them, who shewed them their comodities of beads, knives, and some copper, of which they seemed very fond; and by waye of trade, made shew that they would come downe to the boat and there bring such things as they had to exchange them for ours. Soe Captain Gilbert departed from them, and within half an howre after he had gotten to his boat, there came three canoas down unto them, and in them some sixteen salvages, and brought with them some tobacco and certayne small skynes, which where of no value; which Captain Gilbert perceaving, and that they had nothing ells wherewith to trade, he caused all his men to come abourd, and as he would have putt from the shore; the salvadges perceiving so much, subtilely devised how they might put out the fier in the shallop, by which meanes they sawe they should be free from the danger of our men's picces, and to performe the same, one of the salvadges came into the shallop and taking the fier brand which one of our company held in his hand thereby to light the matches, as if he would

---

[1] Bacon's Rips, five miles above Cushnoc.

light a pipe of tobacco, as sone as he had gotten yt into his hand he presently threw it into the water and leapt out of the shallop. Captain Gilbert seeing that, suddenly commanded his men to betake them to their musketts and the targettiers too, from the head of the boat, and bad one of the men before, with his targett on his arme, to stepp on the shore for more fier; the salvages resisted him and would not suffer him to take any, and some others holding fast the boat roap that the shallop could not pott off. Captain Gilbert caused the musquettiers to present their peeces, the which, the salvages seeing, presently let go the boatroap and betooke them to their bowes and arrowes, and ran into the bushes, nocking their arrowes,[1] but did not shoot, neither did ours at them. So the shallop departed from them to the further side of the river, where one of the canoas came unto them, and would have excused the fault of the others. Captain Gilbert made shew as if he were still friends, and entertayned them kindlye and soe left them, returning to the place where he had lodged the night before, and there came to an anchor for that night. The head of the river standeth in 45 degrees and odd mynutts. Upon the continent they found aboundance of spruse trees such as are able to maast the greatest ship his majestie hath, and many other trees, oake, walnutt, pineaple;[2] fish, aboundance; great store of grapes, hopps, chiballs, also they found certaine codds[3] in which they supposed the cotton wooll to grow, and also upon the bancks many shells of pearle.

27. Here they sett up a crosse and then returned homeward, in the way seeking the by river of some note called Sasanoa.[4] This daye and the next they sought yt, when the weather turned fowle and full of fog and raine, they made all hast to the fort before which, the 29th, they arrived.

30. and 1 and 2 of October, all busye about the fort.

[1] *I.e.*, laying the arrow to the bowstring.
[2] A variety of pine with cones.   [3] Pods.
[4] The tidal river opening from the Kennebec opposite Bath, and connecting the waters of the Kennebec with those of Sheepscot Bay.

3. There came a canoa unto some of the people of the fort as they were fishing on the sand, in which was Skidwares, who badd them tell their president that Nahanada, with the Bashabaes brother, and others, were on the further side of the river, and the next daie would come and visitt him.

4. There came two canoas to the fort, in which were Nahanada and his wife, and Skidwares, and the Basshabaes brother, and one other called Amenquin, a Sagamo; all whome the president feasted and entertayned with all kindnes, both that day and the next, which being Sondaye, the president carried them with him to the place of publike prayers, which they were at both morning and evening, attending yt with great reverence and silence.

6. The salvadges departed all except Amenquin the Sagamo, who would needes staye amongst our people a longer tyme. Upon the departure of the others, the president gave unto every one of them copper beades, or knives, which contented them not a little, as also delivered a present unto the Basshabae's brother, and another for his wife, giving him to understand that he would come unto his court in the river of Penobscot, and see him very shortly, bringing many such like of his country commodityes with him.

You maie please to understand how, whilst this busines was thus followed here, soone after their first arrivall, that had dispatch't away Capt. Robert Davies, in the *Mary and John*,[1] to advertise of their safe arrival and forwardness of their plantacion within this river of Sachadehoc, with letters to the Lord Chief Justice, ymportuninge a supply for the most necessary wants to the subsisting of a colony, to be sent unto them betymes the next yeare.

After Capt. Davies' departure they fully finished the fort, trencht and fortefied yt with twelve pieces of ordinaunce, and built fifty howses,[2] therein, besides a church and a storehowse; and the carpenters framed a pretty Pynnace of about some

---

[1] A letter written by Sir Ferdinando Gorges records the sailing of one of the vessels in October. This would indicate that the first vessel to return was the *Mary and John*.   [2] Evidently an error.

thirty tonne, which they called the *Virginia;* the chief ship wright beinge one Digby of London.

Many discoveries likewise had been made both to the mayne and unto the neghbour rivers, and the frontier nations fully discovered by the diligence of Capt. Gilbert, had not the wynter proved soe extreame unseasonable and frosty; for yt being in the yeare 1607, when the extraordinary frost was felt in most parts of Europe, yt was here likewise as vehement, by which noe boat could stir upon any busines. Howbeyt, as tyme and occasyon gave leave, there was nothing omitted which could add unto the benefitt or knowledg of the planters, for which when Capt. Davies arrived there in the yeare following (sett out from Topsam, the port towne of Exciter,[1] with a shipp laden full of vitualls, armes, instruments and tooles, etc.,) albeyt he found Mr. George Popham, the president, and some other dead, yet he found all things in good forwardness, and many kinds of furrs obteyned from the Indians by way of trade; good store of sarsaparilla gathered,[2] and the new pynnace all finished. But by reason that Capt. Gilbert received letters that his brother was newly dead,[3] and a faire portion of land fallen unto his share, which required his repaier home, and noe mynes discovered, nor hope thereof, being the mayne intended benefit expected to uphold the charge of this plantacion, and the feare that all other wynters would prove like the first, the company by no means would stay any longer in the country, especyally Capt. Gilbert being to leave them, and Mr. Popham, as aforesaid, dead; wherefore they all [4] ymbarqued in this new arrived shipp, and in the new pynnace, the *Virginia*, and sett saile for England.[5] And this was the end of that northerne colony uppon the river Sachadehoc.

[1] Exeter.   [2] For medicinal uses.
[3] Sir John Gilbert, who died July 8, 1608.
[4] None of the colonists were left behind. It has erroneously been claimed that some of them remained on the coast.
[5] The *Virginia* was built by the colonists. In the following year this vessel was in the fleet that sailed from England for Virginia. A letter from Jamestown, Virginia, written August 31, 1609, says, "In the boat of Sir George Somers, called the *Virginia*, which was built in the North Colony, went one Captain Davies and one Master Davies."

INDEX

INDEX

Acorns, used by French in Florida for food, 123.
Adhothuis, 71.
Africa, William Hawkins brings slaves from, 113; John Hawkins obtains slaves from, 135.
Agona, ruler of Canada, visits Cartier, 95–96; inquires about Donnacona, 96; makes presents to Cartier, 96; dissimulation, 96; ruler of Hochelay seeks conference with, 102.
Agouhanna, name applied to Donnacona, 46; meaning, 61.
Agouhanna, of Hochelaga, appearance, 61; greets Cartier, 62.
Aguatulco, see Guatulco.
Alanson, Ferdinando promises he will try to obtain cattle from, 286; reported to have been called to Spain by the king, 286.
Albemarle Sound, and name Occam, 237 n.; Lane passes through, 248 n.; same as the broad Sound of Weapomeiok, 251 n.
Albert, Archduke, Thomas Arundell's connection with, 357.
Albion, name given by Drake to California, 171.
Aldworth, Robert, 347; obtained, with Giles Elbridge, letters patent for a grant of land at Pemaquid, 347 n.
Aldworth, Thomas, 347 n.
Alegranza, one of the Canaries, 307.
Alezai, named by Cartier, 15.
Aligato Bay, 310.
Allen's Island, 364 n.; size, 366 n.; stone cross in commemoration of Waymouth's visit erected on, 367 n.; mentioned, 379 n.; has pond like that seen on island by Rosier, 380 n.; Waymouth's cross probably found on, 406 n.

Alligator River, 237 n.
Amadas, sent out by Ralegh, 227, 240; goes ashore on island, 230; in Grenville's voyage of 1585, 245; mentioned, 262 n., 277 n.; White finds trench made by, 318.
Amenquin, Indian ruler, visits fort of Popham colonists, 418.
Amitie, arrives at Flores, 322.
Amoret, Indian, brought to England by Waymouth, 394.
Andacon, appointed to kill Lane, 263.
Andrewes, William, in command of the *Squirrel*, 192; return to England, 192 n., 207.
Androscoggin River, 411 n.
Angell, John, in Pring's expedition, 343.
Anghiera, Pietro Martire d', 119 n., 182 n.
Angolesme, lake of, 55 n., 72 n.
Anticosti, 26 n., 27 n., 28 n., 40 n.; named the island of the Assumption, 41.
Aporath, name given by Cartier to bird seen at Isle of Birds, 5.
Apponatz, 13.
Aquascogoc, Indian town, visited by Grenville, 247 n.; White sends offer of friendship to natives of, 290; men left by Grenville reported to have been attacked by natives of, 290; no reply received by White from natives of, 291.
Aquiden, 381 n.
Archangel, name of Waymouth's vessel, 363 n.; in St. George's Harbor, 369 n.
Archer, Gabriel, account of voyage of Gosnold and Gilbert, 328; quoted, 329 n., 330 n., 331 n., 333 n., 334 n.–335 n., 340 n.
Arundell, Thomas, a promoter of

423

Waymouth's voyage, 355, 357; and the Archduke Albert, 357; first Lord Arundell of Wardour, 357 n.
Asia, New France supposed to be part of, 91.
Aspotogeon, mountain, 402 n.
Assumption, island of the, named, 41; mentioned, 43, 69.
Atinas, Martin, Hawkins's pilot, 120 n.
Augusta, Me., 414 n.
Auk, possible identity with Cartier's "Aporath," 5 n.
Avezac, M. d', edited *Brief Récit*, 35.
Ayraste, Indian town, 70.
Azores, 218; Sir Richard Grenville's encounter with Spanish fleet off, 245; Grenville's depredations at, 278; White near, 320; English ships at, 321–322; Gosnold and Gilbert near, 330; passed by Pring, 345; Popham colonists at, 399–401.

Baccalaos, Roberval viceroy of, 91; name applied to what is now Baccalieu Island, 195; application of term, 200.
Baccalieu Island, origin of name, 195 n.
Bacchus Island, described, 48.
Bacon's Rips, 416 n.
Bahama, channel of, Hawkins passes through, 147; White passes through, 213.
Baie Royal, 7 n.
Baltimore, in Ireland, 191.
Bancroft, George, 346 n.
Baque Island, *see* Vieques.
Barbary coast, sighted by White, 307.
Barlowe, Captain Arthur, narrative of voyage, 225, 227–241; departure from England, 227; at Canaries, 227; at West Indies, 227–228; along coast of North Carolina, 228; with Amadas, takes possession of land, 228; rows ashore to see Indian, 230; evidence that narrative was written by, 230 n.; trade with Indians, 232; visits Indian village at Roanoke Island, 235–236; return to England, 240; his companions, 241; Ralegh encouraged by report of, 245; Grenville aided in sending out Amadas and, 245, 277 n.; mentioned, 262 n.

Bashabes, Indian king, 373 n.; reported to have quantity of furs and tobacco, 375; Indians sent to visit Waymouth by, 380 n., 381; abode on Penobscot, 380 n., 405; offers to exchange furs and tobacco with Waymouth and his men, 381, 385; Waymouth and his men refuse to go to see, 381; Captain Gilbert brings merchandise to trade with, 413; brother of, comes to fort of Popham colonists, 418.
Basque fishermen, along Maine coast, 330 n.
Bath, Earl of, some survivors of Hore's expedition visit, 110.
Bath, Me., 417 n.
Baxter, James P., 3, 35, 40 n., 66 n., 95 n., 355.
Bay of Asaphi, 307.
Bay of Castles, *see* Chateau Bay.
Bay of Chaleur, 18 n.; Cartier at, 20–22; described, 21; natives, 21; named, 22; mentioned, 85.
Bay of Fundy, 404 n.
Bay of Heat, *see* Bay of Chaleur.
Bay of Islands, 11 n.
Bay of Placentia, 208, 330 n.
Bay of Portugal, Fernando deserted fly-boat in, 283, 288.
Bay of St. Julian, 11.
Beake, *see* Vieques.
Bear Haven, in Ireland, 191.
Bears, at Island of Birds, 6; on Brion's Island, 14; killed by Indians, 69; on Penguin Island, 107.
Beaupré, Viscount of, on Cartier's third voyage, 95, 99.
Belknap, Jeremy, 346 n.
Belle Isle, 7 n., 91.
Belle Isle, Strait of, 6 n.
Benner's Island, 364 n., 379 n.
Best, Captain Ellis, accompanies Gilbert in visit to Indians, 413.
Bevis, Thomas, drowned, 316.
Bibliothèque Nationale, manuscript relation of Cartier's first voyage discovered in, 3.
Bic Islands, 43 n.
Bird Rocks, 13 n.
Biron, Mr., accompanies Hore, 106.
Blackland Point, 17 n.
Blanc Sablon, *see* White Sands.

INDEX

Blanca, island, 308; probable identity of, 308 n.
Blount Bay, 237 n.
Bluff Head, 11 n.
Bohier, Bishop, of St. Malo, blesses Cartier and his men, 37 n.
Bolivar, state of, 139 n.
Bonavista Bay, Cartier at, 4 n.
Bonne Bay, 11 n.
Bonner, bark, offered to Lane by Drake, 269–270.
Bradore Bay, 8 n.
Brazil, William Hawkins sells slaves in, 113.
Bread, made of corn by Indians, 57, 59; method used by Indians in making, 59–60; called Carraconny, 59.
Brereton, John, 325; goes ashore on "a white sandie and very bolde shore," 331; goes ashore on an island, 332; communicates with Indians, 336–337; found climate healthful, 339.
Brereton, John, *Briefe and true relation of the discoverie of the North Part of Virginia in 1602*, 325–340; states that voyage was undertaken with Ralegh's permission, 327; the earliest English book relating to New England, 328; editions, 178, 328.
Bridges, Thomas, on Pring's voyage, 348.
Brion, Sieur de, *see* Chabot, Philippe de.
Brion's Island, Cartier at, 13–14; named, 14; described, 14; products, 14; mentioned, 15; Cartier visits on second voyage, 85.
Bristol, Cabot and merchants of, 180 n.; mentioned, 192, 344, 346, 348, 350; Pring and merchants of, 343, 345.
Briton, William, on Cartier's second voyage, 57.
Brittany, Cartier returns to, 30; ships of, at St. Pierre, 86 n.; Donnacona in, 93; mentioned, 95, 99, 323 n.
Broune, William, in Pring's expedition, 343.
Browewich, James, in expedition of Amadas and Barlowe, 241.
Brown, Alexander, 355, 370 n., 411 n.

Brown, Richard, in Hawkins's voyage of 1568, 146 n.
Browne, Maurice, in command of the *Swallow*, 192; of honest and religious character, 195, 212; permitted crew to board fishing vessel, 196; appointed captain of the *Delight*, 207; fate, 192 n., 212.
Burnt Island, 379 n.
Burrage, Henry S., 356.
Butler, Captain, of bark *Raleigh*, in Gilbert's second expedition, 192; fell sick, 193.
Buts, Thomas, accompanies Hore, 106; entertained by Sir Thomas Luttrell, 110; changed by voyage, 110.
Buts, Sir William, 106, 110.
Byron Island, 14 n.

Cabo de la Vela, 139.
Cabot, John, landfall, 4 n.; discoveries, 180, 182, 327; set sail from Milford Haven in 1497, 345 n.
Cabot, Sebastian, sailed down coast of America, 131 n.; accompanied father in voyage of 1498, 180 n.; in service of Spain, 180 n.; return to England, 180 n.; extent of discoveries in America, 182 n.
Cade, master of the *Squirrel*, 192.
California, Drake on coast of, 153, 173; climate, 156–158; natives, 159–173; named Albion by Drake, 171; Drake sets up monument in, 171; foundation of English claim to sovereignty of, 171 n.
Cam, Thomas, 361; sent in boat to sound among islands, 364.
Camden Hills, 363 n., 384 n., 405 n.
Canada, voyage of Cartier to, 37; Indians tell Cartier way to reach, 41; Cartier seeks, 44; beginning of land of, 45; Donnacona, lord of, 46, 93; Cartier twenty-five leagues from, 54. Indian lord came to visit Cartier in, 55; natives of, travel out of their country, 60; Cartier sails towards, 64; Cartier invited by Donnacona to see, 65; natives of, 65–69, 81–83, 95–96; animals of, 69, 71; described, 70; language of natives, 86–88; natives of, report land where cinnamon grows, 88; Roberval

INDEX

viceroy of, 91; reports of Cartier about, 93; Roberval "Lieutenant and Governor" of, 93; Cartier delayed in reaching, 95; Cartier's arrival, 95; Cartier greeted by natives of, 95–96; mentioned, 99, 185, 201; journey of ruler of Hochelay to, 102.
Canaries, Hawkins at, 137; Amadas and Barlowe at, 227; White at, 307–308.
Cannibalism, reported among Hore's men, 108–109.
Cannon, Indians frightened by, 51.
Cap d'Esperance, 18.
Cape Anguille, 13 n.
Cape Ann, 331 n., 346 n.
Cape Breton Island, Cartier's conjecture of passage between Newfoundland and, 14 n.; mentioned, 85 n., 187, 188, 191; Hore near, 107; origin of name, 107 n.; Gilbert seeks, 208; reckonings of course of *Hind* from Cape Race to, 209; *Delight* wrecked near, 211 n.
Cape Cantyn, 307.
Cape Cod, discovered by Gosnold and Gilbert, 331 n.
Cape Degrad, 6, 7; identified with northern extremity of Quirpon, 6 n.
Cape des Monts, 41 n.
Cape Dolphin, 13; named, 14; identified with North Point, 14 n.
Cape Elizabeth, in Maine, 412 n.
Cape Fear, White and his company in danger off, 287; origin of name, 287 n.
Cape Finisterre, 137.
Cape Hatteras, 182 n.
Cape Kildare, 16 n.
Cape La Hève, 402 n., 403 n.
Cape Loreine, same as Cape St. Lawrence, 85.
Cape Memorancie, 27; identified with Table Head, 27 n.
Cape Neddock, 330 n.
Cape of Bonavista, 4, 5.
Cape of Good Hope, 105; Drake returns by way of, 151.
Cape of Hope, named, 18.
Cape of Milk, 10; named, 12; same as Cape St. George, 12 n.
Cape of Prato, 22; same as White Head. 22 n.; mentioned, 85.

Cape Orleans, 15, 16; identified with Cape Kildare, 16 n.
Cape Porpoise, 330 n.
Cape Prat, *see* Cape of Prato.
Cape Rabast, Cartier approaches, 40; identified with Cow Point, 40 n.
Cape Race, Cartier at, 86; mentioned, 188, 201, 216; appointed as meeting-place for Gilbert's ships, 190, 191; climate, 202; Gilbert at, 207; distance to Cape Breton, 208; reckonings of course of *Golden Hind* to Cape Breton from, 209; Gilbert's ships pass, 215.
Cape Razo, 6; same as Cape Rouge, 6 n.
Cape Rouge, 6 n.
Cape Rouge River, Cartier in, 96 n.; described, 97–98.
Cape Royal, 10; named by Cartier, 11; Cartier leaves, 12; mentioned, 13.
Cape Sable, 404 n.
Cape St. Alvise, named, 26; identification of, 26 n.; mentioned, 27.
Cape St. Anthony, *see* Cape San Antonio.
Cape St. Francis, 195, 196.
Cape St. George, 12 n.
Cape St. John, named, 13; same as Cape Anguille, 13 n.
Cape St. Lawrence, 85 n.
Cape St. Loys, 26 n.
Cape San Antonio, mentioned, 114 n., 309 n.; *Moonlight* and her pinnaces found waiting at, 312; the *John* met ships from Mexico near, 321.
Cape San Francisco, Drake at, 151.
Cape Small Point, 409 n.
Cape Thiennot, *see* Cape Tiennot.
Cape Tiburon, 309; English ships meet at, 310; human bones found at, 310; White at, 310–311; Spanish frigate captured at, 311; Edward Spicer arrives at, 311.
Cape Tiennot, 28; natives, 29; named by Cartier, 29; identity of, 29 n., 39 n.; Cartier sights, on second voyage, 39; mentioned, 40.
Cape Tyburon, *see* Cape Tiburon.
Cape Verde, Hawkins at, 137.
Cape Verde Islands, Ralegh has fight off, 225.

INDEX   427

Cape Whittle Islands, 39 n.
Capo de la Vela, *see* Cabo de la Vela.
Carey's Rock, in St. George's Harbor, 389 n.
Caribbean Sea, Hawkins in, 139 n.
Carpunt, 5; Cartier at, 6; mentioned, 7; Roberval viceroy of, 91; Cartier's ships meet at, 95.
Carrell, Denice, left at Musketos Bay, 285.
Cartagena, 139; Hawkins forbidden to sell slaves at, 140; Drake returns from, 249 n., 276; mentioned, 321.
Carter, Mr., accompanies Hore, 106.
Cartier, Jacques, early years, 3; letter to Philippe de Chabot, 3; sails from St. Malo, 3, 4; accounts of first voyage, 3; *The First Relation of*, 4–31; reaches Newfoundland, 4; at Bonavista, 4; enters St. Katherine's Haven, 4; at Island of Birds, 5–6; at Carpunt, 6; names St. Katherine's Island, 7; enters Port of Brest, 8; names St. Antony's Port, 9; sets up cross at St. Servans, 9; meets French ship in St. James River, 9; leaves Brest, 10; near Bay of Islands, 11; goes towards Cape Royal, 12; strikes out into the sea, 12; sees Cape St. John, 13; at Islands of Margaulx, 13; at Brion's Island, 14; at Alezai, 15; at St. Peter's Cape, 15; sees Cape Orleans, 16; enters River of Boats, 16; sees savage at Wild Men's Cape, 16; names S. Lunarios Bay, 17; at Cape of Hope and St. Martin's Creek, 18–19; encounter with natives, 19; in Bay of Chaleur, 20–22; trades with natives, 21; near Cape of Prato, 22; gives presents to natives, 23, 24; sets up cross, 24; nears island of Anticosti, 26; names Cape S. Alvise, 26; along coast of Anticosti, 26–27; decides to return home, 28; names Cape Tiennot, 29; approaches Newfoundland, 29; leaves Newfoundland, 30; arrival at St. Malo, 30, 35; report to king, 35; receives new commission, 35; accounts of second voyage, 35–36; narrative of second voyage, 37–88; receives sacrament, 37; sails from St. Malo, 37; encounters storms, 38; his ships are separated, 38; arrival in Newfoundland, 38; at Island of Birds, 38; meets other ships in Bay of Castles, 38; names St. Martha's Islands, 39; passes St. German's Islands, 39; passes Cape Tiennot, 39; sets up cross at St. Nicolas Haven, 40; names Bay of St. Lawrence, 40; approaches Anticosti, 40; near Anticosti, 41; search of northwest passage, 42; reaches Round Islands, 42; at St. John's Islets, 43; seeks Canada, 44; at Island of Filberts, 45; anchors near Isle of Orleans, 46 n.; visited by natives of Isle of Orleans, 46–47; visited by natives of Stadacona, 46–49; names Bacchus Island, 48; arrives at place of the Holy Cross, 48; brings ships to river of the Holy Cross, 48–49; desires to reach Hochelaga, 49, 50; talks with Donnacona, 49; urges Taignoagny to go to Hochelaga, 50; receives present of Indian children, 51; makes present to Donnacona, 51; orders cannon fired, 51; trick of Indians to hinder, from going to Hochelaga, 52–53; at Hochelay, 54–55; Indian lord gives child to, 55; anchors at lake, 55; prepares to go to Hochelaga, 56–58; welcomed by Indians of Hochelaga, 58–59; meets a lord of Hochelaga, 58–59; reads service to Indians, 62; gives presents to Indians, 62; goes back to boat, 62; on top of Mont Royal, 63; leaves Hochelaga, 64; reaches port of the Holy Cross, 65; visited by Indians of Stadacona, 65; visits Stadacona, 65; intercourse with Indians, 71; his men catch disease from Indians, 73; orders service of prayer, 73; makes promise of pilgrimage, 73; effort to prevent Indians from learning weakness of his men, 74; sees natives coming from Stadacona, 75; learns from Domagaia cure for pestilence, 76; suspects Donnacona of treachery, 77, 78; sends men to investigate, 78; hears of assembling of Indians

428   INDEX

at Stadacona, 79; plans to capture Indians, 79; asks Taignoagny to visit him, 79; refuses Taignoagny's request that he capture an Indian, 80; desires visit from Donnacona, 80; capture of Donnacona and other Indians, 80–81; promises safe return to Donnacona, 82, 83; gives present to Donnacona, 82; leaves port of St. Croix, 84; exchanges gifts with Donnacona's subjects, 84; comes to Island of Filberts, 84; sails to Honguedo, 84; at Brion's Island, 85; at Cape Loreine, 85; along Cape Breton Island, 85 n.; meets French ships at St. Peter's Islands, 86; at Cape Race, 86; arrival in St. Malo, 86; third voyage, 91–102; account of third voyage, 92; discovery of St. Lawrence, 91; sufferings at St. Croix, 91; desire to take possession of land discovered, 91; sails from St. Malo, 91; winters at Charlesbourg Royal, 92; decides to return, 92; finds Indians unfriendly, 92; meets Roberval in harbor of St. John's, 92; supposed by some to have led expedition to relief of Roberval, 92; death, 92; reports to king, 93; authorized by Roberval to sail in advance of him, 94; date of departure, 95 n.; his ships are separated, 95; meets his other ships at Carpunt, 95; in Newfoundland, 95; arrives at St. Croix, 95; Indians visit, 95–96; in Cape Rouge River, 96 n., 98 n.; sends back letters to king, 97, 99; builds fort, 98, 99; leaves Charlesbourg Royal for exploring trip, 99–102; visits ruler of Hochelay, 99–100; arrives at Lachine Rapids, 100 n.; reaches Courant de Ste. Marie, 100 n.; leaves boats, 100; reaches Indian villages, 100; guided by Indians, 100; learns that river is not navigable to Saguenay, 101; returns to boats, 101; welcomed by Indians, 101; gives presents, 101; hears of departure of lord of Hochelay, 101–102; returns to fort, 102; finds Indians unfriendly, 102; prepares for defence, 102; discoveries of reported in England, 105.

Cartier, Jacques, *Brief Récit et Succincte Narration*, 35.

Casco Bay, 412 n.

Castles, The, strait, 18.

Catalina, 4 n.

Causand, Gilbert's ships at, 186; Gilbert's departure from, 191, 192.

Caycos, White and his company at, 286–287.

Chabot, Philippe de, Sieur de Brion, Cartier's letter to, 3; island named for, 14 n.

Challoung, Henry, in command of vessels sent out by Sir Ferdinando Gorges, 358 n.; captured by Spaniards, 394 n., 397.

Chanoists, *see* Chaonists.

Chanter, John R., *Sketches of the Literary History of Barnstaple*, 277 n.

Chaonists, warned against Lane by Pemisapan, 252; part of Lane's company reported to have been killed by, 260; feared by other Indians, 260; Lane proposes to rely on, 264.

Charles I., of Spain, 91.

Charlesbourg Royal, Cartier spends winter at, 92; Roberval locates colony at, 92; Cartier leaves, for exploring trip, 99.

Chateau Bay, 7 n., 38.

Chatham, England, Hawkins founded hospital at, 136.

Chaunis Temoatan, Indian reports of, 254–255; Lane prevented from searching for mine of, 257; method proposed for reaching, 258.

Chawanoac, Indian town, 237 n.; English colonists visit, 248; mentioned, 249; king of, promises to give guides to Lane, 250; assembly of Weroances at, 252; country of Chaunis Temoatan known to natives of, 254; distance to country of Mangoaks from, 255, 258.

Chawanook, *see* Chawanoac.

Chawanook, river of, mentioned, 248, 249, 250, 258; same as Chowan River, 248 n.; shows no current, 251.

Chepanoc, *see* **Chepanum.**

INDEX

Chepanum, Indian town, 248 n.; Lane hopes to obtain food at, 253; Lane arrives at, 257.
Chesapeake Bay, Roanoke colonists to go to, 230 n.; mentioned, 247 n., 249 n.; White to find location for colony on, 281, 287; Bartholomew Gilbert thought by some to have lost his life in, 327.
Chesepians, 247, 263, 266.
Chesepiook, *see* Chesapeake Bay.
Chester, John, in voyage of John Hawkins in 1565, 132.
Cheticamp, 85 n.
Chipanum, *see* Chepanum.
Chypanum, *see* Chepanum.
Choanists, *see* Chaonists.
Chowan River, 248 n.
Christianity, need of its introduction into New World, 181; Waymouth s purpose to establish, in America, 388.
Cipo River, 237.
Clarke, Richard, 192; in wreck of *Delight*, 213.
Cockington, Devon, Waymouth a native of, 355.
Codde, meaning, 384 n.
Coleman, Robert, drowned, 316.
Colombia, 139 n.
Columbus, Christopher, discovery of West Indies, 182.
Conception Bay, Gilbert's ships at, 195.
Concord, The, in expedition of Gosnold and Gilbert, 329.
Consolacion del Norte, 116 n.
Cooke, Captain, joins White in search for Roanoke colonists, 315–318.
Cooper, Christopher, agrees to go to England as factor, 293; changes his mind, 293; in list of colonists who accompanied John White, 298.
Copper, 72, 263, 264; mines reported to be in Florida, 127; Indians wore, 232, 337–338.
Corbett, Julian S., *Drake and the Tudor Navy*, cited, 135, 152, 155 n.
Cornibotz, river, wampum found in, 60.
Cornwall, arrival of Hore's expedition in, 110; Hawkins's arrival in, 131; Hawkins at, 147; White lands in, 297; Ralegh lieutenant of, 329.

Cortereal, Gaspar, landfall, 4 n.
Corvo, White at, 296, 320, 321; sighted by Pring, 345; Waymouth near, 360; Popham colonists direct course for, 399, 400.
Cossine, accompanies Lane on exploring expedition, 260.
Cotesa, Sir Richard Grenville at, 284 n.
Courant de Ste. Marie, Cartier reaches, 100 n.
Cow Head, 11 n.
Cow Point, 40 n.
Cowes, White anchors at, 282.
Cox, William, master of *Golden Hind*, 192; reckonings of course from Cape Race to Cape Breton kept by, 209; objects to keeping course near land, 210; unwilling to return to England, 214; assigned by Gilbert to south discovery, 217; urges Gilbert not to return to frigate, 218.
Craney Island, 249 n.
Croatoan, Manteo a native of, 241 n.; Captain Stafford sent to, 264; Lane announces intention of going to, 266; mainland of Virginia mistaken for, 287; Captain Stafford goes to, 289; natives of, 289–292; destruction of men left by Grenville reported by natives of, 290–291; White hears that Roanoke colonists removed to, 303; White at anchor off, 314; White believes colonists to be at, 318; White plans to go to, 319.
Cross Island, 402 n.
Cuba, Hawkins reaches, 114; Hawkins sails towards, 115; Hawkins passes by, 140; mentioned, 309 n.; captured Spaniards landed on, 312.
Cudruaigny, Indian god, 52, 53, 66, 67.
Cuervo, *see* Corvo.
Culebra, 308 n.
Cumberland Bay, 9 n.
Currituck Sound, 235 n.
Curry, J. L. M., discovered, in archives at Simancas, plan of fort erected by the Popham colonists, 411 n.
Cushnoc Island, 414 n., 416 n.
Cuttyhunk, first English settlement in New England at, 327; Gosnold and Gilbert at, 333; called by Gos-

nold Elizabeth's Island, 333 n., 340; described, 334–335; Indians come to, 336–339; stone tower erected at, 336 n.; climate, 339.

Daniel, of Buda, claims to have found silver, 205; death, 212; mentioned, 216.
Dare, Ananias, 293, 298.
Dare, Elenor, daughter of Governor John White, 293, 299.
Dare, Virginia, born at Roanoke, 293, 300.
Dartmouth, Edward Hayes lands at, 219; mentioned, 329, 399; Waymouth at, 359; Waymouth's return to, 355, 391.
Dasamonguepeuk, Manteo made lord of, 241 n., 293; plan to gather Indians at, 263; Pemisapan caused Indians to sow ground in, 262; Pemisapan goes to, 264, 265; Lane orders his men to capture canoes going to, 266; Lane goes to, 267; men left in 1586 by Grenville reported to have been attacked by natives of, 290–291, 292; White receives no reply to message sent to natives of, 291; natives of, suspected of despoiling property of Roanoke colonists, 318.
Davidson, George, quoted, 155 n.
Davies, James, probable author of *Relation of a Voyage to Sagadahoc*, 398.
Davies, Captain Robert, returns to England from river of Sagadahoc, 418; returns to fort, 419; brings back ship laden with supplies, 419.
Davis, James, accompanies Gilbert in visit to Indians, 413.
Davis, Robert, in Gilbert's voyage of 1583, 192.
Davis's Island, mentioned, 379 n.
Dawbeney, Oliver, accompanies Hore, 107; gives information concerning Hore's voyage, 107–108; reported that men killed companions for food, 108.
Deadman s Island, 15 n.
Deane, Charles, editor Hakluyt's *Discourse*, 226.
De Costa, B. F., 346 n., 397.

Dehamda, *see* Tahanedo.
Dehanada, *see* Tahanedo.
Degrad, harbor, 6.
Delight, ship of Sir Humphrey Gilbert, 192; loss of, 205 n., 208, 210–213; return of captain of, to England, 207; Maurice Browne made captain of, 207; music aboard, 210; wrecked, 211; fate of survivors of, 213; grief of Gilbert for loss of, 216.
Dennis, Alfred, biographical account of Pring, cited, 344.
Diamonds, Cartier thinks he has found, 98, 99.
Digby, shipwright, and building of pinnace *Virginia*, 419.
Dingen a Cushe, 297.
Dingle, Governor White at, 297 n.
Discoverer, in Pring's expedition, 343; loaded with sassafras, 350; sent ahead to England, 350; duration of voyage, 352.
Domagaia, 26 n.; greeted by natives of Isle of Orleans, 46; talks with Donnacona, 46; refuses to come to Cartier's ship, 48–49; comes aboard ship, 50; agrees to go to Hochelaga, 51; quarrel with Taignoagny, 51; in ruse to hinder Cartier's journey to Hochelaga, 53; visits Cartier, 65; desires baptism, 67; illness of, 75; remedy used by, 76; announces approach of Donnacona, 78; Cartier's plan to recapture, 79; speaks with Cartier, 80; reports unfriendliness of Taignoagny, 81; taken prisoner, 81; reports capture of Donnacona to his subjects, 84; mentioned, 100.
Dominica, Hawkins near, 139; White reaches, 283; Englishmen trade with natives of, 308; men on the *John* capture two natives of, 310.
Donnacona, visits Cartier, 46; village of, 47, 70; welcomes Cartier, 48; objects to Cartier's carrying weapons, 49; visit to Cartier, 50; presents Indian children to Cartier, 50–51; device to prevent Cartier's journey to Hochelaga, 52–54; desires Cartier to leave hostage, 54; visits Cartier, 65; house of, 65–66; desires baptism, 67; account of Saguenay

INDEX

River, 71; suspected of treachery, 77; assembles many Indians at Stadacona, 78; feigns illness, 78; Cartier's plan to capture, 79; said he had travelled, 79; refuses to visit Cartier, 80; visits Cartier, 81; taken prisoner, 81; talks with his people, 82; promised safe return, 82; orders people to bring him food, 83; receives present from Cartier, 83; promises to return, 84; in France, 93; king appointed by, 95; death of, reported to Indians by Cartier, 96.
Double Cape, Cartier near, 10, 11, 29.
Dove Houses, islands, 10; named, 11; same as Bay of Islands, 11 n.
Drake, Francis, afterwards Sir Francis, in Hawkins's third voyage, 135, 151; expedition against Spanish settlements in West Indies, 136, 152, 249 n.; bitterness against Spaniards, 151; crossed Isthmus of Panama, 151; voyage around world, 151–152; sources of information about voyage of circumnavigation, 151–152; knighted by Elizabeth, 152; in harbor of Cadiz, 152; present at destruction of Armada. 152; death, 152; account of last voyage of, 152; on coast of California, 153–173; leaves Guatulco, 153; encounters extreme cold, 153–154, 155, 156; anchors in a bay, 154; goes southward, 155; anchors in a "convenient and fit harborough," 155, 158; probable identity of anchorage of, 155 n.; visited by natives, 159, 162–163; building of fort of, 160, 162; relations with Indians, 160, 161–162, 168; Indians appear to worship, 163, 169; prays for Indians, 163; visited by Indian king, 164–168; gives food to Indians, 170; explores inland, 170–171; names country Albion, 171; sets up monument, 171; Indians say farewell to, 173; and the Virginia colonists, 246, 249, 257, 259, 268, 271, 276–277; mentioned, 352 n.
Drake, Samuel, *The Book of the Indians*, cited, 333 n.

Drake's Bay, attempt to identify Drake's "convenient and fit harborough" with, 155 n.
Dry Ledges, 379 n.
Du Petit Val, Raphael, *Discours du Voyage fait par le Capitaine Jaques Cartier*, 3.
East Cape, 26 n.
East India Company, Waymouth's search for a northwest passage under auspices of, 355.
East India service, Pring in, 343.
East Indies, search for northwest passage to, 105.
Eden, Richard, translation of Peter Martyr's *De Rebus Oceanicis*, 119 n.
Edenton, 248 n.
Edgartown, Martha's Vineyard, 346 n.
Edward Bonaventure, arrives at Flores, 322.
Elbridge, Giles, obtained, with Robert Aldworth, letters patent for a grant of land at Pemaquid, 347 n.
Elizabeth, queen of England, knights Drake, 152; patent to Sir Humphrey Gilbert, 177, 185, 185 n.; Gilbert takes possession of harbor and surrounding country in name of, 199; Amadas and Barlowe take possession of land in name of, 228; names Virginia, 230 n.; knighted Ralegh, 231 n.; Indian king Okisko announces intention of doing homage to, 261; granted license to ships of John Wattes to depart for West Indies, 305.
Elizabeth Islands, 333 n.
Elizabeth Isle, Cuttyhunk named, by Gosnold, 333 n., 340; and Shakespeare's *Tempest*, 334 n.
El Mina, Hawkins considers going to, 138 n.
Emannett, 403.
Engelhard, N.C., 237 n.
England, Cartier's discoveries reported in, 105; fishing interests in Newfoundland, 109 n.; and colonization in America, 179, 182–183; and discoveries of Cabots, 180, 183; support of Netherlands in conflict with Spain, 270, 275; Grenville wishes to secure claim of, to Virginia, 275,

278; preparations to meet Armada, 305.
English voyagers to the American coast, in the sixteenth century, routes of, 327.
Enríquez, Don Martín, viceroy of Nueva España, 142; replies to Hawkins's message, 143; gives assurance of protection, 144; attack on Hawkins, 144.
Ensenore, friendliness to English, 259, 260-261; death of, 259, 262; persuades Pemisapan to have ground sown to provide English with food, 262; mentioned, 263.
Eracano, accompanied Lane on exploring expedition, 260.
Estero Limantour, 155 n.
Exeter, England, 419.
Exmouth, Gosnold and Gilbert near, 340.

Falcon, Ralegh in command of, 225.
Falmouth, Golden Hind arrives at, 219; Gosnold's expedition leaves, 329.
Fayal, part of English fleet anchor at, 322.
Ferdinando, Simon, in expedition of Amadas and Barlowe, 230, 241; and Roanoke colonists, 230 n.; forsook fly-boat, 282-283; reported that St. Croix was not inhabited by savages, 284; said there were many sheep on Vieques, 284; prevented White from stopping for salt, 285; did not wish White to land at St. Germans, 285; promised to land on Hispaniola, 286; said he would try to obtain cattle from friend Alanson, 286; claimed that he heard Alanson had left, 286; reported that there were saltponds on Caycos, 286; mistook location of Croatoan, 287; to return to England, 287; displeased at reappearance of fly-boat, 288; return voyage, 297; mentioned, 298.
Fermeuse, 190 n.
Fire, Indian method of obtaining, 120, 338.
Fishing vessels off Newfoundland, 109 n., 187, 194.

Fitzwilliam, Mr., in voyage of John Hawkins in 1565, 132.
Flamingo, Hawkins describes, 129-130.
Flanders, war in, 270, 275.
Flax, use by Indians, 338.
Flores, seen by White, 296; sighted, 320; White at, 321-322; English men-of-war at, 321-322; Pring passes, 345; Waymouth near, 360; Popham colonists direct course towards, 399; Captain Popham anchors at, 400; Captain Gilbert leaves, 401.
Florida, 72; information derived from Hawkins's voyage about, 113; Hawkins near, 114; dangers of coast, 116; Hawkins at islands near, 117, 119; French settlement in, 118, 119, 120, 122-125, 126, 127, 128, 131; cruelty of natives of, 119; Hawkins along coast of, 119-120; regarded by Hawkins as an island, 120; products of, 120, 125-130; Indians of, 120-121, 125-127; French deserters from fort returned to, 123; Hawkins seeks coast of, 140; mentioned, 147, 179, 180, 182, 227; ill success of Spanish attempts in, 182; currents off coast of, 187, 188; Drake passes coast of, 276; White near, 312-313.
Floridians, cruelty of, 119; houses of, 120; clothing, 120-121; weapons, 121; French obliged to aid a king of the, 122-123; wars with French colony, 124; food, 125; use of tobacco, 125-126; paint their bodies, 126; ornaments, 127.
Florio, Jean, 3.
Flying fish, 129.
Foresight, arrives at Flores, 322.
Fort St. George, 384 n.
Fouetz, river of, 64; same as the St. Maurice, 64 n.
Fox Island, named, 345.
France, Taignoagny and Domagaia tell what they saw in, 46; Cartier sets upon fort the arms of, 81; Donnacona in, 93, 96; activity in America, 179; alleged encroachment on English rights in America, 182; ill success of early attempts at

INDEX

settlement in America, 182; Ralegh fights with Huguenots in, 225; value of her navigable rivers to, 381.
Francis I., king of France, interest in Cartier's enterprise, 3; Cartier's men sworn to service of, 4; hears Cartier's report, 35; gives Cartier new commission, 35; mentioned, 37, 50, 79, 80; name inscribed on Cartier's fort, 81; Donnacona to relate travels to, 82; hesitated to encourage Cartier to return, 91; attention of, occupied by Spanish invasion, 91; letters patent to Roberval, 91; considered New France to be part of Asia, 91; heard reports of Cartier's voyages, 93; decides to send expedition under Roberval, 93; provided money for fitting out ships, 94; desired early departure of Cartier, 94.
Francis, bark, provisioned for Lane by Drake, 269; loss of, 269.
French fishing vessels, off Newfoundland, 109, 194, 330 n.; on New England coast, 330 n.
French settlement in Florida, 118, 119, 120, 122–125, 126, 127, 128, 131; relieved by Hawkins, 124.
French ship met by Hore, 109–110; receives redress from king of England, 110.
Frobisher, Martin, Hawkins joined, in voyage for purpose of harassing Spanish commerce, 136.
Frosmont, Thomas, master of the great *Hermina*, 37.
Funk Island, 5 n.
Furs, obtained in trade from Indians, 337; worn by Indians, 339; Gosnold's bark carries, 339; value of French trade in, 350; Waymouth's men obtained, from Indians in trade, 371; Bashabes reported to have quantity of, 375; Indians report that on the mainland they have, 376, 377; Bashabes offers to exchange, 381, 385.

Galicia, Hawkins approaches, 147.
Gannets, identity of Margaulx with, 6 n.

Gaspé Bay, Cartier puts into, 22; natives of, 22–24, 25; Cartier sets up cross at, 24–25; Cartier leaves, 26; mentioned, 41 n.
George, The, another name for Gilbert's ship *Delight*, 192.
Gift of God, despatched to coast of Maine with colonists, 397; George Popham captain of, 399; arrived in Pentecost Harbor, 406 n.; went into river of Sagadahoc, 409; officers of, not familiar with coast, 409 n.
Gilbert, Bartholomew, route of, 327; persons of prominence aided voyage of, 327; makes peace with Ralegh, 327; accompanied Ralegh to Virginia, 327; fate, 327; and division of food, 340 n.; mentioned, 343.
Gilbert, Sir Humphrey, quoted, 109; wrote *A Discourse of Discovery for a new Passage to Cataia*, 177; early life, 177; service in Ireland, 177; in Parliament, 177; in Netherlands, 177; received royal patent, 177, 185; unsuccessful attempt at voyage of discovery, 177, 185, 225; last voyage, 177–178; account of last voyage, 178–222; purpose to colonize northern part of America, 179, 197; first Englishman to "carry people to erect an habitation and government in those Northerly countreys of America," 178, 183; grants assignments out of his commission, 185, 186; preparations for second voyage, 186; orders agreed upon by captains and masters of fleet of, 189–191; proposed route, 190; sets sail, 192; ships of, 192; abandoned by the *Raleigh*, 193; meets unfavorable winds, 193; separated from two of his ships, 193; at Grand Banks, 194; near Penguin Island, 195; joined by *Swallow*, 195; reaches harbor of St. John's, 196; meets *Squirrel*, 196; sends boat into harbor, 197; shows commission to masters and owners of English fishing vessels, 197; on land, 198; takes formal possession, 199; erects arms of England, 199; makes grants of land, 200; assigns tasks to men, 200; hears report of silver, 205–206;

decides to go in *Squirrel*, 207; leaves harbor of St. John's, 207; at Cape Race, 207; orders sounding to be made, 210; confers with captain and master of *Golden Hind*, 214; besought by men to return, 214; resolves to return to England, 214; promises to return to America in spring, 214; sees strange fish, 215; starts on return voyage, 215; comes aboard *Golden Hind*, 215; return to frigate *Squirrel*, 216; spends day aboard *Golden Hind*, 216; laments loss of *Delight*, 216; rage at boy for forgetting something he was ordered to bring from the *Delight*, 216; believed to have had hopes of finding silver mine in Newfoundland, 216–217; plans for another voyage, 217; warned not to return to frigate, 217; insists on continuing in frigate, 218; courage, 219; fate, 219; character, 221–222; firmness of purpose, 221–222; mentioned, 327, 397.

Gilbert, Sir John, brother of Sir Humphrey, 205; hears of Sir Humphrey Gilbert's fate, 219; mentioned, 220.

Gilbert, Sir John, son of Sir Humphrey, Captain Gilbert hears of death of, 419 n.

Gilbert, Sir Otho, 177.

Gilbert, Raleigh, in expedition to Maine coast, 397, 398; captain of the *Mary and John*, 399; held as pirate by Flemish captain, 400–401; released, 401; goes on shore to see Indians, 406–407; sails towards river of Pemaquid, 408; sails up river of Sagadahoc, 410; embarks to go to westward upon some discovery, 412–413; spends night with Skidwarres and other Indians, 413; Indians promise to accompany, to river of Penobscot, 413; leaves fort to go to trade with Bashabes, 413; delayed in reaching river of Pemaquid, 414; fails to find Skidwarres, 414; leaves fort to go for head of river of Sagadahoc, 414; sends man to Indian canoe as hostage for Sabenoa, 415; goes to see Indian houses, 416; refuses to trade with Indians, 416; orders men to present muskets at Indians, 417; resumes friendly attitude towards Indians, 417; sets up cross near head of river, 417; hears news of brother's death, 419; obliged to return to England, 419.

Glaven, Darbie, left at Musketos Bay, 285.

Godetz, 5; named by Cartier, 6; at Island of Birds, 8; at Islands of Margaulx, 13.

Gold, reported to be in Saguenay, 72; of Florida Indians, 126, 127.

Gold coast, 138 n.

Golden Hind, one of Gilbert's ships, 192; becomes vice-admiral, 193; reckonings of course from Cape Race to Cape Breton, 209; porpoise caught by men in, 210; escapes from shoals, 211; crew of, desire to return to England, 214; strange fish approaches, 215; Gilbert aboard, 216–217; provisions furnished to frigate from, 218; arrival in Falmouth, 219; goes to Dartmouth, 219; crew of, impatient to depart, 220; arrives at Weymouth, 220.

Goldsmid, Edmund, 226.

Gomera, Hawkins at, 137.

Gorges, Sir Ferdinando, fitted out vessel, 358 n.; Indians given to, 394 n.; especially interested in vessel commanded by Challoung, 397; makes no mention of Hanham in his account of voyage of 1606, 397; manuscript of *Relation of a Voyage to Sagadahoc*, found among papers of, 399; mentioned, 418 n.

Gorges Society, 356, 398.

Gosnold, Bartholomew, voyage to New England coast, 327–340; route, 327; Ralegh hears of voyage of, 327; Ralegh complains of, 327; persons of prominence aided, 327; sailed for Virginia with Jamestown colonists, 328; fate, 328; landfall, 330 n.; goes ashore on a "white sandie and very bolde shore," 331; goes ashore on island, 332; calls Cuttyhunk Elizabeth's Island, 333 n., 340; Earl of Southampton patron of, 334 n.; directs Brereton to go to

INDEX 435

Indians, 336; fort, 336 n.; his sojourn on Cuttyhunk commemorated by erection of tower, 336 n.; makes presents to Indians, 337; return to England, 340; probably desired to establish a permanent trading post, 340 n.; mentioned, 343, 346, 355.
Gouion, John, accompanies Cartier to Hochelaga, 57.
"Governour and Assistants of the Citie of Ralegh in Virginia," 282.
Goyett, John, knew captain of one of the Flemish ships met by Captain Gilbert, 400.
Graciosa, 322, 399 n.
Gran Canaria, 308.
Grand Bay, 194, 201.
Granganimeo, greets Amadas and Barlowe, 230; receives presents, 231; comes aboard ships, 232; apparel of, 232; wife of, 232, 233, 235-236; offers pearl in exchange for armor, 234; sends food, 234; Barlowe and his companions entertained by wife of, 235-236; Barlowe's suspicion of Indians grieves wife of, 236; death of, 252, 259.
Granges, hills, 11, 29.
Gratiosa, see Graciosa.
Gravesend, Hore embarks at, 107; Waymouth's expedition at, 359.
Gray, Francis C., 336 n.
Great Meccatina, 38 n.
Green Island, 402 n.
Greene, Henry, in expedition of Amadas and Barlowe, 241.
Greenevile, William, in expedition of Amadas and Barlowe, 241.
Greenish harbor, 7 n.
Grenville, Sir Richard, 230 n.; Manteo returned with, 241 n.; early life, 245; aided in sending Amadas and Barlowe to America, 245, 277 n.; in command of expedition of colonists to America, 245; death, 245; relation of his voyage of 1585, 245; anchors at Wocokon, 246 n.; lands colonists, 247 n.; return, 247 n.; Lane fails to receive supplies from, 270; disappointed at not finding Roanoke colonists, 275; institutes measures for maintaining England's claim to

Virginia, 275, 278; return to England, 275; arrival in Virginia, 277; hunts for colonists and relief ship, 277; lands fifteen men on Roanoke Island, 278, 281, 290; departs for England, 278; captures Spaniards off Azores, 278; return, 278; placed in charge of relief fleet Ralegh prepared to send to Virginia, 303.
Griffin, Owen, spends night ashore with Indians, 374; gives account of powwow ceremonies, 374; sent ashore to meet Indians, 377; reports seeing large number of armed Indians, 377.
Griffith, William, 399.
Guadeloupe, 283, 308.
Guatemala, 153 n., 309 n.
Guatulco, Drake at, 151, 153.
Guayanilla, in Porto Rico, 285 n.
Guiana, voyage of Pring to, 343; Ralegh's voyage to, 383.
Guinea, Hawkins procures slaves at, 113; mentioned, 114; Hawkins sails to, 137; Hawkins along coast of, 138-139.
Gulf Stream, 117 n., 313 n.
Gwathanelo, see Guatemala.

Hakluyt, Richard, *Principal Navigations*, 3, 36, 72 n., 92, 95 n., 105, 146 n., 185 n., 186 n., 192 n., 196 n., 212 n., 225, 226, 229 n., 241 n., 245, 246 n., 247 n., 258 n., 275, 281, 284 n., 285 n., 287 n., 293 n.; and Pretty's narrative, 152; mentioned, 212 n., 305, 347 n.
Hakluyt, Richard, of the Middle Temple, 105, 107, 110.
Hakluyt Society, 113, 135, 146 n., 152, 186 n., 212 n., 229 n., 241 n., 398.
Hale, Edward Everett, opinion of identity of "convenient and fit harborough" where Drake anchored, 155 n.
Halifax Harbor, 402 n.
Hance, Mr., surgeon, drowned, 316.
Hanham, Thomas, in command of vessel sent out by Sir John Popham, 358 n., 397.
Hardie, Mr., accompanied Hore, 106.
Hare Island, 44 n., 84.
Hariot, Thomas, see Harriot, Thomas

2F

436 INDEX

Harps, Mr., captain of pinnace brought by Edward Spicer, 311, 313.

Harriot, Thomas, among Roanoke colonists, 258; *A briefe and true report of the new found land of Virginia*, 258 n.; Indians plan to kill, 263.

Hatorask, Pridiox sent to, 264; probable location, 264 n.; relief expedition of 1586 arrives at, 277; White comes to, 287; fly-boat arrives at, 288; Englishmen left in 1586 fled to, 291; White near, 314; White sets out from, 316.

Havana, Hawkins seeks, 115; Hawkins passes, 116; mentioned, 227, 312, 321; White near, 313.

Hawkins, John, early life, 113; invention, 113; voyage to Guinea, 113; brought slaves to West Indies, 113; despatched ships to Spain, 113; account of voyage of 1565, 113-132; sails from Plymouth, 114; reaches Cuba, 114; sails towards Florida, 114; at Tortugas, 115; sails towards Cuba, 115; searches for Mesa de Mariel, 115-116; decides to go to Rio de Puercos, 116; overshoots Havana, 116; reaches islands near Florida, 117; rejoices at recovery of boats, 119; sails along shore of Florida in a pinnace, 119; speaks with natives, 119; seeks French settlement, 119-120; finds French, 120, 122; entertained at French fort, 122; relieves Frenchmen, 124; leaves Florida, 131; buys fish from French ships at Newfoundland, 131; arrival in Cornwall, 131; return to England, 135; his account of third voyage, 135-148; member of Parliament, 135; made a grandee of Spain, 135; equipped vessels for operations against Spain, 135; made treasurer of navy, 135; prepared royal fleet to meet Armada, 135; knighted, 136; voyage of 1590, 136; founded hospital, 136; in expedition against Spanish settlements in West Indies, 136; death, 136; sets sail from Plymouth, 137; at Canaries, 137; reaches Cape Verde, 137; captures negroes, 137; shot by poisoned arrow, 138; along coast of Guinea, 138; helps negro king to capture enemy's town, 138; captures many prisoners, 138; deceived by negro, 138; leaves Guinea, 139; sights Dominica, 139; difficulty in trading with Spaniards, 139; goes from Margarita Island to Cartagena, 139; at Cabo de la Vela, 139; enters Rio de la Hacha by force, 139; not allowed to trade at Cartagena, 140; passes Cuba, 140; encounters storms, 140; seeks coast of Florida, 140; captures ships, 140; enters port of San Juan de Ulua, 140; visited by Spanish officials, 140; finds ships laden with gold and silver, 141; sends messenger to Mexico, 141; sees Spanish fleets approaching, 141; in perplexity, 142; receives reply of viceroy, 142; proposes conditions to viceroy, 142; suspects Spanish treachery, 143; attacked by viceroy and other Spaniards, 144-145; boards *Minion*, 145; abandons *Jesus of Lubec*, 145; escape from Spaniards, 145; lands half of his men on shore of Gulf of Mexico, 146; in storm, 147; passes through channel of Bahama, 147; loses men by famine, 147; arrival in Galicia, 147; helped by English ships at Vigo, 147; arrival in Cornwall, 147; sufferings on voyage of, 147-148; at Azores awaiting arrival of Spanish fleet, 322.

Hawkins, William, voyages to Africa for slaves, 113.

Hayes, Edward, narrative of voyage of Sir Humphrey Gilbert, 178-222; *A Treatise . . . conteining important inducements for the planting of these parts and finding a passage that way to the South sea and China*, 178; admonition to would-be colonizers of America, 181; in command of *Golden Hind*, 192; unwillingness to return to England, 214; opinion that Gilbert had hopes of finding mine in Newfoundland, 216-217; assigned to south discovery, 217; urges Gilbert not to continue in

INDEX

frigate, 218; lands at Dartmouth, 219; informs Gilbert's brother of his fate, 219; urged by men to leave Dartmouth, 220; sails to Weymouth, 220.
Hayti, 309 n.
Headly, Edward, survives wreck of *Delight*, 213; death, 213.
Henry VII., patent to Cabots, 180 n.; aid to Cabot, 183.
Henry VIII., favors voyage of Hore, 106; gave recompense to French ship despoiled by Hore, 110.
Henry, William Wirt, quoted, 233 n.
Hermerillon, in Cartier's second voyage, 37.
Hermina, the *Great*, ship, in Cartier's second voyage, 37.
Hermina, the *Little*, ship, in Cartier's second voyage, 37.
Herne, Griffith, 269.
Hewes, John, in expedition of Amadas and Barlowe, 241.
Hispaniola, slaves sold by Hawkins at, 113; French from Florida fort went to, 123; Ferdinando promises to land at, 286; White passes, 286; mentioned, 309, 311, 320.
Hochelaga, 37; Indians captured by Cartier tell of river of, 41; Indians promise to go to, 49; Cartier's wish to reach, 49; Donnacona wishes Cartier not to go to, 50; Donnacona's ruse to prevent Cartier from going to, 52–54; Indians direct Cartier to, 56; Cartier reaches, 57; natives of, 57, 60; site of town of, 58 n.; town of, described, 59; Cartier in town of, 61–63; mentioned, 69, 72, 75; language of natives of, 86–88; Roberval lieutenant-governor of, 91, 93; Cartier decides to go to, 99.
Hochelaga, river of, same as St. Lawrence River, 41.
Hochelay, Cartier at, 54; little girl given to Cartier by ruler of, 55; mentioned, 70; Cartier visits ruler of, 99–100; Cartier fails to find ruler of, 101.
Hognedo, *see* Honguedo.
Holy Cross, port of, *see* St. Croix.
Honfleur, Roberval goes to, 94.

Honguedo, 41; same as Gaspé, 41 n.; mentioned, 66; Cartier sails to, 84.
Honguedo, mountains of, 69.
Hope, comes to Flores to await Spanish fleet, 322.
Hopewell, ship, 307.
Hore, Robert, probable interest in search for a northwest passage to the East Indies, 105; study of "cosmographie," 105, 106; sufferings of expedition of, 105; Hakluyt's narrative of voyage of, 106–110; companions of, 106; embarks, 107; near Cape Breton, 107; at Penguin Island, 107; in Newfoundland, 107–110; hears reports of cannibalism among his men, 109; makes speech exhorting men to repentance, 109; meets with French ship, 110; return, 110.
Hortop, Job, in Hawkins's voyage of 1568, 146 n.
Howe, George, killed by Indians, 288–289; reported to have been slain by Wingina's men, 290, 292; in list of colonists who came with John White, 298.
Hudson River, 72 n.
Hunt, Thomas, captured Tasquantam, 394 n.

Icebergs, seen by Hore's men, 110
Indians, of White Sands, 10; appearance of, 10; dress of, 10; paint themselves, 10; catch seals, 10; of Wild Men's Cape, 16; come in boats to St. Martin's creek, 19, 20; afraid of Cartier's guns, 19; trade with Cartier, 20; of Bay of Chaleur, 21; trade with Cartier, 21; of Gaspé Bay, 23–25; appearance of, 23; food of, 23, 24; captured by Cartier, 25; of Cape Tiennot, 29; tell Cartier of river of Hochelaga, 41; of Isle of Orleans, 46; of Stadacona, 46–54, 65–72, 75–83, 95–97; frightened by cannon, 51; of Hochelay, 54–55, 99–100; of Hochelaga, 57–64; bring food to Cartier, 57; village of, 59; manner of making bread, 59–60; apparel, 60; use of wampum, 60; occupations of, 60; bring sick to Cartier to be healed,

INDEX

62; hear service read, 62; food of, 62; houses of those of Stadacona, 66; have scalps of enemies, 66; manners and customs of, 66–69; beliefs of, 66–67; apparel of, 67; have two or three wives, 67; food of, 68; use tobacco, 68; clothing of, 71; reports of a country to the southwest, 72; captured, 81; use of wampum, 82, 83, 84, 96; of river of Saguenay, 84; language of, 86–88; bring food to Cartier, 101; unfriendly, 102; in boat near Newfoundland, 108; of Florida, 119–127; of California, 158–173; regard Drake and his men as gods, 159–163, 169, 172; houses of, 161, 171; appearance, 161; hear singing of psalms, 163; apparel, 164–165; a king of, 165–167; paint their faces, 165; baskets of, 166; weapons of, 170; show grief at Drake's departure, 172–173; of the country near Roanoke, 230–239, 241, 247–267, 277, 288, 293, 318; rulers reverenced by, 231; trade with Amadas and Barlowe, 232; have ornaments of copper, 232, 233; appearance of, 232; signal-fires, 233; boats of, 233–234; food of, 235–236; fear of guns, 238; weapons, 238; civil dissensions, 238, 239; visit English, 247–248; towns of, 248; of Chawanoac, 248–252, 254, 255, 261; prepare to attack Roanoke, 252; give accounts of mine of Chaunis Temoatan, 254–255; make attack on Lane, 255; Lane's colonists dependent on, for food, 259; belief that white men after death would injure them, 261; of Weapemeoc, 261, 263, 265; conspire against Lane, 262–266; treatment of, by Lane's colony, 277, 277 n.; killed men left by Grenville, 288, 290–291; kill George Howe, 288–289, 292; of Croatoan, 289–292; greet White and his men, 289; of Dominica, 308, 310; of New England, 330–331, 333, 336–339, 347–351, 367–381, 385, 391, 392, 405, 407, 408, 411–418; come aboard boats of Gosnold and Gilbert, 330; appearance, 330; weapons, 330; report having seen Basque fishermen, 330–331; of islands near Cape Cod, 333; appearance, 333; give fish and tobacco to English, 333; pipes of, 333; of Cape Cod, 336–339; visit Englishmen at Cuttyhunk, 336–338; dislike of mustard, 337; trade furs with English at Cuttyhunk, 337; have ornaments of copper, 337–338; manner of striking fire, 338; return to mainland, 338; help English cut and carry sassafras, 338; disposition and appearance of, 338–339; aptitude at learning English, 339; treatment of women, 339; come to see Englishmen with Pring, 347; food of, 347; delight in music, 347; weapons of, 347–348; afraid of mastiffs, 348, 351; appearance, 348; boats of, 348–349; surround Pring's fort, 350–351; dissemble friendly manner, 351; mentioned, 358; visit Waymouth's ship, 367–368; appearance of, 368; paint their bodies and faces, 368; clothing, 368; found to be of quick understanding, 368; boats of, 368; believed to be jealous of their women, 368, 373; would eat nothing raw, 369; Rosier offers to trade with, 369; afraid of guns, 369; kindly disposition shown by, 369; come to visit Englishmen, 370; treated with kindness by English, 371; trade with Rosier, 371; marvel to see English catch fish by net, 371; wonder at use of loadstone, 371–372; at supper and at service with Waymouth, 372; offer tobacco to English, 373; call Waymouth "Bashabes," 373; children of, 373; fear dogs, 374; powwow ceremonies of, 374; bring tobacco to English, 375; use great quantity of tobacco, 375; have cups of bark, 376; trade food with English, 376; desire English to accompany them to mainland, 376; swiftness of boats of, 376–377; suspected of treachery, 377; captured by Waymouth, 378–379, 391; sent from Bashabes, 380–381; wore white-feathered skins, 380; device for ransoming men cap-

INDEX

tured by Waymouth, 385; respect for rulers, 392; manner of killing whale, 392; seen in shallop by Raleigh Gilbert and his men, 402; come aboard Gilbert's ship, 403; try to trade beaver skins, 403; use French words, 403; promise to accompany Gilbert to Penobscot, 413; try to escape with Englishman given as hostage, 415–416; offer to trade with Gilbert, 416; try to put out fire in shallop, 416–417; betake themselves to bows and arrows, 417; entertained kindly by Gilbert, 418; attend prayers, 418.

Ingram, David, landed on shore of Gulf of Mexico, 146 n.; narrative, 146 n.

Ireland, services of Sir Humphrey Gilbert in, 177; Ralegh's services in, 225; White in, 297.

Ironbound Island, 402 n.

Iron mine, found near Cartier's fort, 98.

Iroquois Indians, 66 n.

Iroquois, river of, 72 n.

Isabella, in Hispaniola, 286.

Isabella, Infanta, sister of Philip III., of Spain, 357 n.

Island of Birds, Cartier at, 5; identified with Funk Island, 5 n.; mentioned, 8; Cartier visits, ons econd voyage, 38.

Island of Filberts, 45, 84.

Island of Brest, 8; now called Old Fort, 8 n.

Islands of Margaulx, 13; now Bird Rocks, 13 n.

Isle of Orleans, Cartier lands on, 46 n.; natives of, 46; Cartier's idea of size of, 46 n., 48 n.; named Bacchus Island, 48; Cartier approaches, 84.

Isle of Pines, 312.

Isle of Wight, White at, 282.

Jalobert, Marc, a captain on Cartier's second voyage, 37; accompanies Cartier to Hochelaga, 57; sent back to France, 97.

Jamaica, French deserters from Florida fort plunder at, 123; passed by White, 312; Spanish fleet from Santo Domingo forced to flee to, 321.

James I., of England, charter for two colonies in America, 397.

James Carthiers Sound, named, 9; same as Cumberland Bay, 9 n.

Jamestown, in Virginia, 281; colony at, 304; pinnace *Virginia* at, 419 n.

Jersey, Ralegh governor of, 329.

Jesus of Lubec, in Hawkins's voyage of 1565, 114; pinnace of, sent ashore after water, 117; carried ahead by current, 118; joined by other boats, 119; on third voyage, 137; injured by storm, 137; disabled by storm, 140; in fight with Spaniards at San Juan de Ulua, 144–145; abandoned, 145.

John, ship, 307; off Dominica, 308; joins other ships at Saona, 310; ordered to remain five days between Saona and Mona, 310; reported capture of two Indians at Dominica, 310; arrives at Cape Tiburon, 310; fight with Santo Domingo fleet, 321; encounter with ships from Mexico, 321; return to England, 321.

John the Evangelist, 307; along southern shore of Porto Rico, 309; awaiting other ships at Cape Tiburon, 310;

John Carter Brown Library, 328.

Jolloberte, Mace, see Jalobert, Marc.

Jones, Edward, in Pring's expedition, 343.

Joy, Mr., accompanies Hore, 107.

Judith, bark of Hawkins, escapes from Spaniards, 145; commanded by Drake, 151.

Kelborne, Edward, drowned, 316.

Kelly, Edward, drowned, 316.

Kendall, Abraham, 269.

Kenrick's Mount, 315, 319.

Kennebec, attempt to identify great river discovered by Waymouth with, 370 n.; mentioned, 384 n., 403 n., 405 n., 409 n., 417 n. *See also* Sagadahoc, river of.

Kennebunk River, 346 n.

King, Thomas, Waymouth's boatswain, 390.

Kingrode, arrival of *Discoverer* in, 350; *Speedwell* reaches, 352.

Kingsley, Charles, use of material furnished by relations of Hawkins's voyage in *Westward Ho*, 146 n.

INDEX

Kirkland, Samuel, in Pring's expedition, 343.
Labrador, coast sighted by Cartier, 27 n.; mentioned, 28 n.; Roberval viceroy of, 91; Cabot's discovery of, 180 n.
Lachine Rapids, Cartier sees, on second voyage, 63 n.; Cartier arrives at, on third voyage, 100 n.
Lacie, Edward, in Hawkins's voyage of 1565, 132.
La Hève, harbor, 402 n.
Lake Champlain, 72 n.
Lake Ontario, 72 n.
Lambeth Palace Library, manuscript of *Relation of a Voyage to Sagadahoc* found in, 397–398.
Lane, Ralph, tobacco introduced into England by, 125 n., 159 n.; account of the Englishmen left in Virginia, 1585–1586, 243–271; in charge of colonists sent to America, 245; knighted, 245; gets information from King Menatonon, 249–250; proposed trip to country of pearls described by Menatonon, 250–251; has Menatonon's son a prisoner, 250, 261, 265; dismisses Menatonon for a ransom, 252; resolves to go to river of Moratoc, 252; finds assembly of Indians at Chawanoac, 252; fails to find Moratocs and Mangoaks, 253; suspects Indians, 253; in need of food, 253, 257, 260, 262, 264; reasons for wishing to see Mangoaks, 254, 255; hears reports of a country which abounds in a strange mineral, 254; attacked by Indians, 256; return to mouth of river, 256; at Chepanum, 257; arrival at Roanoke, 257; desire to find mine, 257; commends soil and climate, 257; prevented from searching for better harbor, 257; proposes mode of extending discoveries, 258; dependence on Indians for food, 259; Pemisapan surprised by return of, 260; Menatonon sends pearl to, 261; Okisko sends messenger to, 261; fear of starving, 262; Indians plan to kill, 263; sends men to various places to get food, 264; sends messenger to Pemisapan, 265–266; prepares to meet attack of Indians, 266; encounter with Indians at Dasamonguepeuk, 267; hears news of Drake's fleet, 268; asks Drake for supplies, 268; loses ships and provisions in storm, 269; reasons for return, 270; requests passage with Drake, 270; returns to England, 271, 275; mentioned, 278, 288, 289.
Lane, William, Captain, attacked by Spanish galley, 310; captures ship at Yaguana, 311.
Large, Roger, death, 298.
Laudonnière, René de, colony of, on St. John River, 122; receives Hawkins, 122; superseded by Ribault, 122 n.; escape from Spaniards, 122 n.
Le Poil Bay, 86 n.
Lescarbot, Marc, edition of Cartier's first voyage, 3.
Limehouse, 192, 209.
Limoïlou, mentioned, 92.
Lion, in Governor John White's expedition, prepares for departure from Roanoke, 293.
Little Meccatina, 39 n.
Livingston, L. S., 328.
Lizard, The, 297 n., 359, 399.
Loire River, 383.
Louis IX., king of France, Cartier names cape for, 26 n.
Lucayos, 147.
Lunenburg Bay, 402 n.
Luttrell, Sir John, entertains some of the survivors of Hore's voyage, 110.

Macnab Island, 402 n.
Magdalena, Hawkins along coast of, 139 n.
Mahone Bay, 402 n.
Maine, Gosnold on coast of, 330 n.; Basque fishermen along coast of, 330 n.; mentioned, 333 n.; Pring brings information concerning, 343; Pring near coast of, 345 n.; Waymouth near coast of, 362 n.; tercentenary of Waymouth's visit to, 367 n.; Rosier notes products of 393–394; Hanham explored coast of,

INDEX

397; colonists sent to, 397; Popham colonists approach, 405.
Maine Historical Society, *Documentary Series*, 226; and tercentenary of Waymouth's voyage, 385 n.
Maisouna, 102.
Manana, island, 362 n.
Mandoages, visit English colonists, 248; Pemisapan's plan to enlist, in conspiracy against Lane, 263; join Pemisapan's conspiracy, 265, 266.
Maneddo, brought to England by Waymouth, 394; given to Gorges, 394 n.
Mangoaks, warned against Lane by Pemisapan, 252, 253; reported to have entered into confederacy against English, 252; retire from towns, 253; reported to have traffic with natives of Chaunis Temoatan, 254; said to have much copper, 255; Skiko a prisoner among, 255; Lane's desire to find, 254, 255; mentioned, 258; Indians report part of Lane's company killed by, 260; feared by other Indians, 260, 261.
Manida, *see* Maneddo.
Manteo, brought to England, 241; return, 241 n.; made lord of Roanoke and Dasamonguepeuk, 241 n., 293; warns Lane of Indian attack, 256; on exploring expedition, 260; mentioned, 267, 300, 318; goes to Croatoan, 289; calls to countrymen, 289; accompanies White as guide in expedition against Wingina's men, 292.
Marchant Royal, at Flores, 322.
Margarita, Hawkins at, 139.
Margaulx, 5; Cartier's name for birds seen at Island of Birds, 6.
Marie, William, 37.
Martasew, Governor John White lands at, 297.
Martha's Vineyard, 332 n., 346 n.
Martires, 312; same as the Florida Keys, 312 n.
Martyr, Peter, *see* Anghiera, Pietro Martire d'.
Mary and John, despatched to Maine coast with colonists, 397;

James Davies probably the navigator of, 398; Raleigh Gilbert captain of, 399; arrived in Pentecost harbor only about twelve hours before the *Gift*, 406 n.; in great danger from storm, 409; finds anchorage between two islands, 409; anchored near Seguin Island, 410; towed into river of Sagadahoc, 410; unloads provisions, 413; despatched to England, 418.
Mary Rose, comes to Flores to await Spanish fleet, 322; anchors at Fayal, 322.
Mary Stuart, queen of the Scots, deceived by Hawkins, 135.
Mascomenge, Indian town, 248, 248 n.
Massachusetts Bay, 330 n.
Massachusetts Historical Society, Proceedings of, 398.
Matanzas, White at, 312, 313.
Mathew, John, death, 298.
Matinicus Island, 405 n.
Mayflower, in Provincetown Harbor, 367 n., 388 n.
Maynarde, Thomas, manuscript account of Drake's last voyage, 152.
Meilleraye, Sir Charles de Mouy, Sieur de, 4.
Menatoan, wife of, brought to Roanoke, 292.
Menatonon, Indian king, 237; taken prisoner by Lane, 248, 260; well informed, 248; gives account of neighboring country where pearls abound, 249–250; gives pearls to Lane, 249; promises to provide guides to country of pearls, 250; report of river of Moratoc, 251; released by Lane, 252; reported to be holding assembly of Weroances, 252; promises to provide guides to conduct Lane to Chaunis Temoatan, 255; sends pearl to Lane, 261; Lane puts trust in, 264–265.
Menendez, Don Pedro, captured French fort in Florida, 122 n.
Mesa de Mariel, Hawkins seeks, 115–116; Hawkins reaches, 116.
Messamott, Indian ruler, 403.
Metackwem, Indian town, 248.

INDEX

Mexico, arrival of viceroy of, 142. See also Enríquez, Don Martín.
Mexico, city of, 140; Hawkins sends messenger to, 141.
Mexico, Gulf of, Hawkins lands part of his men on shore of, 146; Amadas and Barlowe fear currents of, 227; head of river of Moratoc thought to be near, 258.
Meylleraye, Lord of, see Meilleraye, Sir Charles de Mouy, Sieur de.
Milford Haven, Pring sails from, 345.
Minion, ship in voyage of Hore, 106, 107.
Minion, ship of Hawkins on third voyage, 137; in fight with Spaniards at San Juan de Ulua, 144–145.
Miramichi, 17 n.
Mogador, island, 307.
Moisie River, 69 n.
Mona, Englishmen burn Spanish house on, 309.
Monhegan, Waymouth near, 362 n.; described, 363; Rosier's estimate of size of, 362, 366 n.; called by Waymouth "St. George," 382 n., 406 n.; no evidence that Waymouth set up cross on, 382 n.
Monkey, ship, 297.
Mont Joli, 39 n.
Mont Royal, 58 n.; named by Cartier, 59, 63; view from top of, 63.
Montreal, origin of name of, 58 n.
Moonlight, at Cape Tiburon, 311; reports seeing Spanish ships laden with treasure bound for Havana, 312; to return directly to England, 320; leaves Flores upon arrival of the admiral, 321–322. See also *Moonshine*.
Moonshine, English pinnace off Morocco, 307; in the open sea, 313. See also *Moonlight*.
Moratico, river, see Moratoc, river.
Moratoc, Indian town, 251.
Moratoc Indians, retire from towns, 253.
Moratoc, river, violence of current, 251; same as Roanoke River, 251 n.; Lane goes up, 253–257; Lane desires the exploration of, 258.
Morgan, Miles, fate, 185.
Mount Aldworth, 347.

Mount St. Genevieve, 40 n.
Mount's Bay, Hawkins arrives at, 147; White lands in, 297.
Mouy, Sir Charles de, see Meilleraye, Sir Charles de Mouy, Sieur de.
Mud Islands, 404 n.
Munster, Sir Humphrey Gilbert governor of, 177.
Murres, identity with Cartier's "Godetz," 6 n.
Muscamunge, see Mascomenge.
Mushkoniatawee Bay, 40 n.
Musketos Bay, White and his colonists stop at, 284–285.

Nahanada, see Tahanedo.
Nantucket, 332 n.; tide-rips off, 360 n.; Waymouth near, 361 n.
Narwhal, 45 n.
Natashquan Point, 29 n., 39 n.
Navassa, island, 312 n.
Negroes, of West Africa, captured by Hawkins, 137–139; used poisoned arrows, 138 n.; captured from Spanish ships by Captain William Lane, 311.
Neuse River, 239.
Newasiwac, situation of, 239 n.
New England, first English settlement in, 327; Gosnold aimed directly for coast of, 327; earliest English book relating to, 328; French fishing vessels came to coast of, 330 n.; abundance of fish on coast of, 331 n.; Pring's second voyage to, 343; Gosnold's return from, 355.
New France, Cartier's first relation of, 4–31; language of natives, 30–31, 86–88; Cartier's second voyage to, 37–88; name given by Cartier, 88; application of name, 91; supposed by Francis I. to be part of Asia, 91; Cartier's third voyage to, 93–102.
New Harbor, 377 n., 407 n.
Newfoundland, Cartier reaches, 4; description of, 6–7; Cartier along northwestern shore, 11 n.; Cartier's conjecture of passage between Cape Breton Island and, 14 n.; mentioned, 28; Cartier approaches, 29; Cartier leaves, 30; Cartier arrives at, on second voyage, 38; men-

INDEX

tioned, 80, 327, 399; Cartier touches at, 86 n.; Roberval viceroy of, 91; Cartier meets Roberval, at, 92; Cartier at, on third voyage, 95; Hore in, 107–110; fishing vessels at, 109 n., 131, 187 n., 194, 195 n., 196–198, 330 n.; icebergs near, 110 n.; Hawkins fishes off, 131; French ships at, 131; and the Cabots, 180; Gilbert decides to head for, 188, 190; Gilbert's ships meet at, 193, 195, 196; Basque fishermen at, 195 n.; Gilbert at, 195–207; Gilbert's men made maps of, 200; described, 200–206; climate, 201–202; products, 203–206; supposed existence of silver in, 205, 216, 217; survivors of wreck of *Delight* reach, 213; fishing off New England coast compared with that of, 331, 345, 391, 401.
Newsiok, *see* Newasiwac.
No Man's Land, island, 332 n.
Nomopana, river, 237; same as the Chowan, 237 n.
Nonpareilia, comes to Flores to await Spanish fleet, 322.
Normandy, some of Roberval's supplies to be procured in, 94.
North Cape, 40 n.
North Carolina, Amadas and Barlowe along coast of, 228; changes in coast of, 228 n.; mentioned, 318 n.
North Haven, 345 n.
"North Land," probable identity of, 330 n.
North Point, 14 n., 16 n., 27 n.
Northwest passage to East Indies, and the Cabots, 105; Sir Humphrey Gilbert desires permission to search for, 177.
Norumbega, Roberval called lord of, 91.
Nova Hispania, *see* Mexico.
Nova Scotia, 107 n.
Nueva España, *see* Mexico.
Nugent, Irishman with Lane, kills Pemisapan, 267.

Occam, 235, 237; probable application of name, 235 n., 237 n.
Ocracoke Inlet, 247 n.
Ohanoak, Indian town, 248.

Ohaunoock, 248 n.
Okisko, Indian king, 248; announces intention of doing homage to queen of England, 261; Indians plan to enlist, against English, 263; refuses to join conspiracy, 265.
Old Fort, 8 n.
Opossians, visit English colonists, 248.
Orenoque, *see* Orinoco.
Organes, 312, 321.
Orinoco River, discovery of, 383.
Osacan, unfriendliness to English, 262; mentioned, 267.
Ottawa, river, 63 n.

Pacific Ocean, Drake views, 151; crossed by Drake, 151.
Padstow Bay, Hawkins arrives at, 131.
Painpont, Martin de, accompanies Cartier on voyage of exploration, 99.
Pamlico River, 237 n.
Pamlico Sound, 229 n., 235 n.; Sir Richard Grenville crossed, 247 n.
Panama, Isthmus of, Drake crosses, 151.
Pananuaioc, *see* Pomooik.
Parkhurst, Anthony, in voyage of John Hawkins, 1565, 132.
Parkman, Francis, quoted, 372 n.
Parmenius, Stephen, fate, 212.
Pashipskoke, *see* Pejepscot.
Pasquenoke, Indian town, 248.
Passage Island, 308 n.
Passaquenoke, *see* Pasquenoke.
Paul, John, mate of *Golden Hind*, 192 n.; reckonings of course from Cape Race to Cape Breton, 209.
Pearl-fishing, by Spaniards, 127.
Pearls, found in mussels, 367.
Peckham, Sir George, furnished aid to Gilbert's expedition, 186.
Pedro, deserts to Spaniards at Porto Rico, 309.
Pejepscot, river, Captain Popham goes to, 411.
Pemaquid, 347 n., 377 n.; Captain Gilbert lands at, 407; Popham colonists at, 408; Indians of, 408, 413; Captain Gilbert finds Indians gone from, 414.
Pemisapan, *see* Wingina.
Penguin Island, Hore at, 107; abun-

444   INDEX

dance of birds on, 107, 195; sighted by Gilbert's expedition, 195.
Penobscot Bay, 345 n.
Penobscot River, attempt to identify great river discovered by Waymouth with, 370 n.; Bashabes' abode on, 373 n., 380 n., 405, 418; mentioned, 403 n.; Skidwarres and other Indians promise to accompany Gilbert to, 413; Captain Gilbert starts for, 413; Gilbert fails to find, 414; Popham promises to go to, 418.
Pentecost Harbor, 364; identified with St. George's Harbor, 364 n.; Waymouth anchored in, 364, 366; Popham colonists in, 367 n., 406 n.; appointed as rendezvous for Popham's ships, 382 n.
Pestilence among Cartier's men, 73–76; Cartier finds cure for, 76–77.
Petit Val, Raphael du, see Du Petit Val, Raphael.
Petman, Nicholas, in expedition of Amadas and Barlowe, 241.
Philip II., sends Pedro Menendez to destroy French colonists in Florida, 122 n.; deceived by Hawkins, 135; mentioned, 139, 141, 286.
Philippines, Drake goes to, 151.
Phillips, Miles, in Hawkins's voyage of 1568, 146 n.; narrative of, 146 n.
Piamacum, Indian king, 238; at war with Wingina, 239; hated by inhabitants of Secotan, 239; inhabitants of Secotan wish Englishmen to attack, 239.
Pico, island of Azores group, 322, 345 n.
Picquemians, reports of, 79.
Pilgrims, in Provincetown Harbor, 367 n., 388 n.
Pillage Bay, 40 n.
Pinar del Rio, 116 n.
Pipes of Indians, described, 333, 375.
Piscataqua River, 346 n.
Plymouth, England, Hawkins a native of, 113; Hawkins sails from, in 1564, 114; Hawkins leaves, on third voyage, 137; Drake sails from, 151; Drake returns to, 151; White at, 282; mentioned, 307, 323; Popham colonists sail from, 399 n.

Plymouth Company, survey, 414 n.
Plymouth Harbor, Whitson's Bay identified with, 347 n.
Point Miscou, 18 n.
Point Reyes, 155 n.
Point Rich, 11 n.
Pointed Cape, 10; named, 11; same as Cow Head, 11 n.
Pomeiock, see Pomeiok.
Pomeiok, Indian village, 237; visited by Grenville, 247 n.; White sends offer of friendship to, 290; no reply received from message to natives of, 291.
Pomeyooc, see Pomeiok.
Pommeraye, Charles de, 37, 57.
Pomooik, 238.
Ponce de Leon, Juan, experience with currents off Florida, 118 n.
Pont Briand, Claudius de, 37; accompanies Cartier to Hochelaga, 57.
Pooneno, Indian ruler, 237.
Popham, George, in expedition to Maine coast, 397; in the ship *Gift of God*, 399; anchors at Flores, 400; leaves Gilbert's ship, 401; sailed towards river of Pemaquid, 408; sends shallop to help other boat into river of Sagadahoc, 410; sails up the river, 410; starts work on fortification, 411; goes in shallop to river of Pejepscot, 411; entertained Bashabes' brother and other Indians, 418; takes Indians to prayers, 418; died, in New England, 419.
Popham, Sir John, sent out vessel in command of Hanham, 358 n., 397; received two of Waymouth's Indians, 394 n.; joined Gorges in sending out colonists, 358 n., 397; letters sent from Popham colony to, 418.
Popham colonists, sent out, 343; anchored in Pentecost Harbor, 367 n., 382 n., 406; find cross which they suppose was set up by Waymouth, 367 n., 382 n., 406; no mention of anchorage at Monhegan in account of, 382 n.; rendezvous at Pentecost Harbor appointed for, 382 n.; Skicowaros accompanied, 394 n.; leave the Lizard, 399; date of departure, 399 n.; at the Azores, 399–401;

INDEX

meet Flemish ships, 400–401; ships of, are separated, 401; voyage of those in Gilbert's ship, 402–406; ships of, meet, 406; hold service on St. George's Island, 407; sail towards river of Pemaquid, 408; deserted by Skicowaros, 408; return to ships near St. George's Island, 408; set sail to go to river of Sagadahoc, 408; overshoot the place, 409; arrive in river of Sagadahoc, 410; make choice of place for settlement, 411; holds services and read patent, 411; work upon fortification, 411, 413, 414; plan of fort of, found in archives at Simancas, 411 n.; visited by Indians, 413; expedition to head of river, 414–417; visited by Bashabes' brother, 418; send back news of safe arrival, 418; pass winter of extreme cold, 419; build pinnace *Virginia*, 419; obtained fur from Indians, 419; gathered sarsaparilla : 419 ; reasons for return of, 419; departure, 419.

Port Mariel, 115 n.
Port of Balances, 7; same as Baie Royal, 7 n.
Port of Brest, Cartier enters, 8; a ship passes, 9; Cartier leaves, 10; mentioned, 11, 38.
Port of Gutte, 7; now Greenish Harbor, 7 n.
Port of Islettes, 8 ; same as Bradore Bay, 8 n.; Cartier at, 9.
Port Rognoso, Cartier leaves boat, at 86.
Port St. Julian, Drake at, 151.
Porto Rico, see San Juan de Puerto Rico.
Portsmouth, England, Lane arrives in, 271; White sails from, 282; mentioned, 297.
Portsmouth, Virginia, 235 n.
Portuguese fishing vessels off Newfoundland, 194.
Portus Novae Albionis, 155 n.
Poulet, John, with Cartier on second voyage, 37; accompanies Cartier to Hochelaga, 57; goes to visit Donnacona, 78; reports to Cartier results of embassy, 79.
Powdawe, 392.

Powhatan, and Roanoke colonists, 230 n., 304.
Powlet, John, see Poulet, John.
Powwow ceremonies, 374.
Pretty, Francis, narrative of Drake's voyage of circumnavigation, 151.
Pridiox, Mr., sent to Hatorask, 264.
Prince, George, 356, 370 n.
Pring, Martin, voyage, 341–352; placed in command of expedition to American coast, 343; accompanied by two of Gosnold's men, 343; voyage to Guiana, 343; later voyage to New England coast, 343, 358 n., 397; in East India service, 343–344; in command of whole English East India squadron, 344; return to England, 344; death, 344; a biographical account of, mentioned, 344; sets out from Milford Haven, 345; outward voyage, 345; arrives on coast, 345; goes up river, 346; finds no people, 346; at Whitson's Bay, 346–351; reason for northerly course, 351; arrival at Kingrode, 352; mentioned, 394 n., 407 n.
Pring, Martin, narrative of voyage of 1603, editions of, 344.
Provincetown Harbor, the Pilgrims in, 367 n., 388 n.
Pungo River, 290 n.

Quebec, 47 n., 54 n.
Quiden, see Aquiden.
Quirpon, 6 n.

Ragged Island, 405 n.
Rainbow, 322; at the Azores, 322.
Ralegh, Sir Walter, in first expedition of Sir Humphrey Gilbert, 177, 225; and Gilbert's second expedition, 192, 193, 225; military services, 225; fits out expedition, 225; and Hakluyt's "discourse," 226; mentioned, 227, 286; sends out ships with colonists, 230 n.; Manteo rewarded by order of, 241 n., 293; preparations for sending Lane and his companions, 245; supplies failed to arrive from, 257, 258; Indian king proposes to do homage to, 261; sends supplies to Roanoke in 1586, 275–277; grants privileges to John White and others

INDEX

for planting colony in Virginia, 281, 282; directed that White's settlement be made at Chesapeake Bay, 281, 287; attempts to send relief to Roanoke Island colonists who went in White's expedition, 303–305; and voyage of Gosnold and Gilbert, 327; Brereton's Relation addressed to, 329; permission for Pring's voyage obtained from, 343; voyage to Guiana, 383.

Raleigh, one of Sir Humphrey Gilbert's ships, 192; abandons expedition, 193; arrival at Plymouth, 193.

Ramusio, *Navigationi*, 3, 35, 36.

Raonoak, *see* Roanoke.

Rastall, Mr., accompanies Hore, 106; entertained by Sir Thomas Luttrell, 110.

Ratcliffe, Waymouth's expedition sails from, 359.

Redclyffe, Cartier's fort near, 98 n.

Relation of a Voyage to Sagadahoc, 395–415; discovery of manuscript, 397; editions, 397–398; possible authorship of, 398, 405 n.; manuscript used by Strachey before it was mutilated, 398; manuscript came into hands of William Griffith, 399, 399 n.

Renapoaks, Indians report part of Lane's company killed by, 260.

Renewse, 190 n.

Revenge, Sir Richard Grenville in the, 245.

Ribault, Jean, on coast of South Carolina, 122 n.; in Florida, 122 n.

Richelieu River, 72 n.

Richmond Bay, 16 n.

Richmond's Island, 412 n.

Ridley, Mr., accompanies Hore, 106.

Rio de la Hacha, resistance of treasurer of, to Hawkins, 139; inhabitants of, trade secretly, 140.

Rio de Puercos, 116, 312.

Rio Grande, in Africa, Hawkins at, 138.

River of Boats, 15; Cartier enters, 16; identified with the Narrows in Richmond Bay, 16 n.

River of May, French colony in, 120; same as St. John River, 120 n.;

French ship seen by Hawkins in, 122.

Roanoke Island, 159 n., 230 n., 239; Barlowe visits Indian village on, 235–236; praised, 240; Manteo made lord of, 241, 293; colonists at, 247 n.; mentioned, 248, 262 n., visited by Drake, 249 n., 268–271, 276–277; Indians reported to be preparing to attack, 252, 265; Lane and his party return to, 257; Okisko sends men to, 261; plan of Indians to attack, 263; Indians assemble at, 266; Grenville lands men on, 278; White to relieve men left in 1586 at, 281; White arrives at, 287; remains of early English colonization on, 288 n.; natives of Croatoan promise to bring other Indian rulers to, 290; Englishmen left in 1586 forced to leave, 291, 292; White's departure from, 295; Ralegh's attempts to send relief to, 303–305; colonists believed to have gone to Croatoan from, 303, 318; smoke seen at, 314–315; White finds remains of settlement at, 317–318.

Roanoke River, 251 n.

Roberval, Jean François de la Rocque de, letters patent, 91; to establish colony in New France, 91; located colony at Charlesbourg Royal, 92; sent to France for supplies, 92; explored Saguenay, 92; return to France, 92; appointed "Lieutenant and Governour of Canada and Hochelaga," 93; preparations for expedition, 94; sent Cartier ahead, 94; Cartier waited for, 95; date of Cartier's meeting with, 95 n.; mentioned, 97.

Rochelle, 9.

Rocky Bay, 9 n.

Rocquemado, 73.

Rogneux, *see* Renewse.

Rognoso, *see* Port Rognoso.

Rose and Crown Shoal, 361 n.

Rosier, James, 355; reasons for publishing narrative of Waymouth's voyage, 357–358; reasons for omitting details about latitude and language of natives, 358; departure, 359; near Azores, 360; among

INDEX

shoals, 360-361 at anchor off Monhegan, 362; at islands near mainland, 363; estimates of distance, 363 n.; comes to good harbor, 364; communicates with Indians, 368; offers to trade with Indians, 369; trades with Indians for skins, 371; writes down Indian names for things, 371; tries Indian bow and arrow, 372; gives presents to Indian children, 373; signs to Indians to leave vicinity of ship, 375; Indians give tobacco to, 375; trades with Indians, 376; Waymouth plans to send ashore, 377; helps capture Indians, 378-379; praises river found by Waymouth, 381-384, 386-387; sums up what has been accomplished on voyage, 388; found climate healthful, 389; return voyage, 390-391; observations made of Indians, 391-392; quoted, 407 n.
Rosier, James, *True Relation of Waymouth's Voyage*, 1605, editions, 356.
Rosse Bay, *see* Roxo Bay.
Rouen, Roberval decides to go to, 94.
Rougemont, Philip, 73; death, 74.
Round Islands, the, Cartier approaches, 42.
Roxo Bay, 285 n.

Sabenoa, calls himself lord of the river of Sagadahoc, 415; taken into Captain Gilbert's boat, 415; accompanies Gilbert to houses of Indians, 416.
Sable Island, 208 n., 401 n.
Sable Island Bank, 401 n.
Sablon, island of, *see* Sable Island.
Sachadehoc, *see* Sagadahoc.
Saco River, 346 n.
Saffacomoit, brought to England by Waymouth, 394; recovered from Spaniards, 394 n.
Sagadahoc, river of, 405; same as Kennebec, 405 n.; Popham colonists seek, 408, 409; the *Gift* comes into, 409; the *Mary and John* towed into, 410; Popham and Gilbert sail up, 410; found to be broad and deep, 410, 411; place for settlement selected near mouth of, 411; mentioned, 412; canoes come to entrance of, 413; Captain Gilbert leaves fort to go for head of, 414; Sabenoa calls himself lord of, 415; cross set up near head of, 417; news sent to England from, 418; colonists leave, 419.
Saguenay, beginning of the way to, 41, 71-72; mentioned, 63, 66, 69, 99; copper of, 41, 64, 72, 79; Indians of, 60, 72; described by Donnacona, 72, 79; reported wealth of, 79, 93; Donnacona to describe, in France, 82; Roberval viceroy of, 91; Roberval and Cartier to explore, 93; Cartier seeks, 100-101.
Saguenay River, Cartier in, 44; reports of, 71; mentioned, 84.
St. Antony's Port, named, 9; same as Rocky Bay, 9 n.
St. Augustine, 249 n., 276.
St. Charles River, 47 n.
St. Christopher's, 308.
St. Croix, harbor of, Cartier in, on second voyage 47, 48; Cartier returns to, 64, 65; mentioned, 70, 92; Cartier's sufferings in, 75, 91; Cartier leaves, 84; Cartier arrives at, on third voyage, 95; Cartier greeted by natives at, 95-96.
St. Croix, one of Virgin Islands, 283, 284, 310.
St. George's Harbor, 364 n., 379 n., 381 n., 389 n. *See also* Pentecost Harbor.
St. George's Island, name given by Waymouth to Monhegan, 382 n., 406 n.; name given by Popham colonists to island where they found Waymouth's cross, 406, 406 n.; ships anchored at, 407, 408; services held by colonists on, 407.
St. George's Islands, 363 n., 382 n., 406 n.; products, 366.
St. George's River, " great river," discovered by Waymouth identified with, 370 n., mentioned, 381 n., 384 n., 385 n.
St. Germans, in Porto Rico, White wishes to stop at, 285.
St. German's Islands, 39; same as Cape Whittle Islands, 39 n.
St. Ives, arrival of Hore's expedition at, 110.

St. James River, Cartier in, 9.
St. John, cape of, 27.
St. John de Luz, 331.
St. John River, French settlement on, 120, 122–128, 131; Hawkins in, 122–131.
St. John's, Newfoundland, 95 n.; Gilbert's expedition reaches, 196; fishing vessels in, 197–198; Gilbert takes possession of, 199; Gilbert makes grants of land on, 200; Gilbert departs from, 207; mentioned, 208, 217.
St. John's Islets, 43; same as Bic Islands, 43 n.
St. Katherine's Haven, 4.
St. Katherine's Island, named, 7.
St. Lawrence's Bay, named, 40; same as Pillage Bay, 40 n.; mentioned, 42.
St. Lawrence, Gulf of, 5 n., 30 n., 201, 214.
St. Lawrence River, 26 n., 27 n.; same as river of Hochelaga, 41 n.; mentioned, 185 n., 201.
St. Lunario's Bay, named, 17.
St.-Malo, Cartier sails from, 3, 4; Cartier returns to, 30; Cartier and his men receive sacrament at, 37; mentioned, 80 n., 92; return of Cartier to, 86; Cartier's departure from, on third voyage, 91, 94; ships sent back to, 97.
St. Margaret River, 69 n.
St. Marie, one of the Azores, Gosnold and Gilbert near, 329.
St. Martha's Islands, 39.
St. Martin's Creek, 18; named, 19; Cartier's ships at anchor in, 20; Cartier leaves, 22.
St. Maurice River, 64 n.
St. Michael's Mount, 297.
St. Nicholas Haven, named, 40; same as Mushkoniatawee Bay, 40 n.
St. Paul's Cape, named, 85; same as Cheticamp, 85 n.
St. Pierre, 86 n.
St. Peter's Cape, named, 15; same as Deadman's Island, 15 n.
St. Peter's Islands, Cartier at, 86; same as St. Pierre, 86 n.
St. Peter's Lake, 55 n.
St. Peter's Strait, Cartier in, 28.
St. Servans, port, 9.

St. Spiritus Port, 86; same as Le Poil Bay, 86 n.
St. Williams Islands, 38.
Salcombe, 399 n.
Salobert, Mace, see Jalobert, Marc.
Salomon, ship of Hawkins, 114; mentioned, 117; near shore of Florida. 118; joins the *Jesus of Lubec*, 119.
Salterne, Robert, in Pring's expedition, 343, 350.
San Francisco, 155 n.
San Francisco Bay, attempt to identify Drake's "convenient and fit harborough" with, 155 n.
San Juan de Puerto Rico, 136; White lands at, 284; White along coast of, 285; mentioned, 286, 308, 309, 319, 320.
San Juan de Ulua, Hawkins enters port of, 140; thirteen ships enter, 141; described, 141–142; Hawkins obtains promise of possession of, during his stay, 143; ordnance of, directed against Hawkins, 144; Drake at, 151; mentioned, 313.
Sankaty Head, 361 n.
Santa Cruz, town on Flores, Captain Popham anchored at, 400.
Santa Cruz, see St. Croix.
Santa Cruz, in Morocco, 307.
Santo Domingo, city, ship from, seizes some of French from Florida, 123; Drake at, 249 n., 276; mentioned, 309, 310, 311, 321.
Santos, Los, 308.
São Jorge, island of Azores group, 322 n., 323.
São Miguel, island of Azores group, 322 n., 323.
Saona, 309; ship *John* ordered to remain near, 310.
Sasanoa, Indian sachem, 403, 411.
Sasanoa River, Gilbert seeks, 417.
Sassafras, 76, 257, 351; fall in price of, in London market, 327; abundant in Cuttyhunk, 334–335; Indians help English cut and carry, 338; not found near Whitson's Bay, 346, 347; the *Discoverer* loaded with, 350.
Sault de St. Louis, Cartier seeks, 100 n.
"Savage Rock," probable identity of, 330 n.; Pring goes to, 346.

INDEX

Schooner Island, 7 n.
Scilly Islands, 190, 391.
Scitadin, Indian village, 70, 80.
Scranton, N.C., 290 n.
Seal Island, 404 n., 405 n., 409 n.
Secotan, Indian village, wreck of white people near, 237–238; inhabitants of, 238, 239, 290, 291; mentioned, 247; visited by Grenville, 247 n.
Seguin Island, 409, 410.
Semeamis, a headland, described, 412.
Sequotan, see Secotan.
Seven Islands, the, 42 n.
Severn River, John White in the, 297; mentioned, 387.
Seymour, Rev. Richard, 407 n.
Shakespeare, William, probable use of story of Gosnold's Elizabeth Isle in *Tempest*, 334 n.
Shecatica Bay, 9 n.
Sheepscot Bay, 417 n.
Sidatin, see Scitadin.
Sidney, Sir Henry, 177.
Sierra Leone, 138.
Silver, of Florida Indians, 126, 127; believed by Gilbert to exist in Newfoundland, 205–206, 216–217.
Skettwarroes, see Skicowaros.
Skicoak, Indian village, 235; location of, 235 n.; Barlowe hears report of, 237.
Skicowaros, brought to England by Waymouth, 394; accompanied Popham colonists, 394 n., 406, 406 n.; leads Captain Gilbert to where Indians are, 407; accompanies Captains Popham and Gilbert ashore, 408; assures Indians that colonists do not mean to hurt them, 408; deserts colonists, 408; in fight with Sasanoa, 411; comes to see Popham colonists, 413; Captain Gilbert accompanies, to his companions, 413; Gilbert delayed in going to see, 414; accompanies Bashabes' brother to fort, 418.
Skidwarres, see Skicowaros.
Skiko, son of Indian king, Menatonon, held captive by Lane, 250; tells of mineral country, 255; Menatonon sends messenger to visit, 261; reports conspiracy of Pemisapan, 265.

Skinner, Ralph, poor steering, 316; drowned, 316.
Skyco, see Skiko.
Slafter, Carlos, memoir of Sir Humphrey Gilbert, 178.
Slave-trade, John Hawkins engaged in, 113, 135, 137–140; no intimation by Hawkins of disgrace attached to, 135; forbidden by Spanish king, 139; forbidden by governor of Cartagena, 140.
Smerwick, 297.
Smith, Thomas, in Governor White's colony, 298.
Somers, Sir George, 419 n.
South Carolina, Jean Ribault on coast of, 122 n.
Southampton, England, 297 n.
Southampton, Earl of, patron of Gosnold in voyage to New England, 334 n.; and Waymouth's voyage, 355.
Southwest Cape, 15 n.
Spain, and vessels sent by Hawkins, 113; unsuccessful attempts in Florida, 119, 182; war in the Netherlands, 177, 275; the Armada of, 152, 303, 352 n.
Sparke, John, wrote account of 1565 voyage of John Hawkins, 113, 132; mentioned, 135.
Sparks, Jared, 356.
Speedwell, in Pring's expedition, 343; duration of voyage, 352; may have been vessel which was with Drake in 1587 and 1588, 352 n
Spicer, Edward, in White's expedition to Virginia, 288; arrives at Cape Tiburon, 311; joins White in search for Roanoke colonists, 315; drowned, 316.
Squirrel, in Gilbert's voyage of 1583, 192; separated from Gilbert's ship, 193; at St. John's, 196; Gilbert decides to go in, 207; reports of strange voices heard by men of, 210; escapes from shoals, 211; crew of, desires to return home, 214; endangered by rough sea, 215; overweighted, 217; Gilbert insists on continuing in, 218 ; wreck of, 219.
Stadacona, described, 47; natives of, 46–54, 65–72, 75–83, 95–97; Car-

INDEX

tier visits, 65–66; location, 70; gathering of Indians at, 102.
Stafford, Captain, sent to Croatoan, 264; reports arrival of fleet, 267; praised, 267; brings letter from Sir Francis Drake, 268; goes to Vieques, 284; mentioned, 287; goes to Croatoan, 289; accompanies White to Dasamonguepeuk to take vengeance on Indians, 292.
Starnatan, Indian town, 70.
Stevens, Henry, 258 n., 281.
Strachey, William, 304; used manuscript of *Relation of a Voyage to Sagadahoc* before it was mutilated, 398; *Historie of Travaile into Virginia Britannia*, 398; quoted, 411 n., 415–419.
Strait of Canso, 107 n.
Strait of Northumberland, supposed by Cartier to be a bay, 17 n.
Straits of Magellan, Drake at, 151, 229 n.; mentioned, 229.
Sutquin, *see* Seguin.
Swallow, ship of Hawkins, 114.
Swallow, in Gilbert's voyage of 1583, 192; separated from Gilbert's ship, 193; at Newfoundland, 195; originally captured from pirates, 195; character of crew, 195, 196, 207; despoiled fishing vessel, 196; Gilbert decides to leave, 206.
Swift-sure, arrives at Flores, 322.

Tahanedo, Indian sagamore, brought to England by Waymouth, 394; returned with Pring in 1606, 394 n., 407 n.; called by Gorges Dehamda, 394 n.; same as Nahanada, 407 n.; caused Indians to lay aside bows and arrows, 407; comes forth to see colonists, 408; in fight with Sasanoa, 411; visits Popham colonists, 413; Gilbert delayed in coming to, 414; accompanies Bashabes' brother to fort, 418.
Tahanock, Indian name for St. George's River, 370 n.
Taignoagny, captured by Cartier, 25, 26 n., 40, 41; greeted by natives of Isle of Orleans, 46; talks with Donnacona, 46; refuses to return to Cartier's ship, 48–49; acts as interpreter, 49, 50; refuses to go to Hochelaga, 50; quarrels with Domagaia, 51; suspected of treachery, 51; in device to prevent Cartier from going to Hochelaga, 52–54; exchanges visits with Cartier, 65; desires baptism, 67; pretends to go hunting, 77; Poulet visits, 78; refuses Cartier's men entrance to his house, 79; wishes Cartier to capture Agonna, 79, 80; Cartier's plan to recapture, 79; promises to bring Donnacona to visit Cartier, 79, 80; visits Cartier, 81; reported unfriendliness of, 81, 100; seized by Cartier, 81.
Tailla, Indian town, 70.
Tanaquiny, unfriendly to English, 262.
Tancook Island, 402 n.
Tarentyn Indians, 403.
Tarraquine, appointed to kill Lane, 263.
Tasquantam, captured by Thomas Hunt, 394 n.
Tavistock, England, 151.
Teguenondahi Indians, 70.
Terceira, 296 n., 399 n.
Tetepano, accompanies Lane on exploring expedition, 260.
Thames River, value to England, 381, 383.
Thayer, Henry O., edited *The Sagadahoc Colony*, 398; quoted, 402 n.
Thomaston, Me., 384 n.; westward trend of St. George's River at, 385 n.; memorial tablet in recognition of tercentenary of Waymouth's voyage unveiled at, 385 n.
Thornton, John Wingate, 336 n.
Tiennot, 29.
Tiger, ship of Hawkins, 114.
Tobacco, use by Indians of Stadacona, 68; use by Florida Indians, 125–126; introduction into England, 125 n., 159 n.; probably unknown to Drake when in California, 159 n.; mentioned, 292, 347, 348, 349, 372, 394; given to Gosnold and Gilbert by Indians, 333; term "drinking" in connection with, 333 n.; brought by Indians to Waymouth, 373, 375; Bashabes reported to have much, 375; Indians say that on the mainland they have, 376; Bashabes offers to exchange, 381, 385.

INDEX

Topsham, England, Captain Davies sails from, 419.
Tortoises, at Island of Filberts, 45; at the Tortugas, 115; at St. Croix, 283; on Cuttyhunk, 335.
Tortugas, Hawkins at, 115.
Toudamani Indians, 65.
Treble Hill, 38 n.
Trepassa, bay, 208.
Trinidad, 320.
Trinitie, ship of Hore, 106, 107.
Trinity Bay, 4 n.
Tripanicks, visit English colonists, 248.
Trout River, Cartier enters, 42 n.
Tucke, Mr., accompanies Hore, 106.
Tuckfield, Mr., accompanies Hore, 106.
Turk's Island, 286 n.
Tutonaguy, Indian town, 100.
Twide, Richard, in Hawkins's expedition of 1568, 146 n.

Union Mountains, 363 n., 384 n.
Ushant, 323.

Vardöhuus, 158 n.
Vaux, W. S. W., editor *The World Encompassed by Sir Francis Drake*, 152.
Venezuela, 139 n.
Verrazano, Giovanni de, voyage, 3.
Vieques, 284 n., 286 n.
Vigo, Hawkins at, 147.
Vimeux, 91.
Vinalhaven, 345 n.
Virgin Islands, 283 n., 308, 309, 310 n.
Virginia, discovery of a part of, by Amadas and Barlowe, 227-241; named, 230, 230 n.-231 n.; Lane's colonists in, 242-271; described by Lane, 246-259; the third voyage to, 276-278; voyage of White and his company to, 281-300; first Christian born in, 293; White's last voyage to, 305-323; voyage of Gosnold and Gilbert to north part of, 325-340; voyage of Pring to the north part of, 345-352; Waymouth's voyage to the north part of, 357-394; voyage of Popham colonists to north part of, 399-419.
Virginia, pinnace built by Popham colonists, 411, 419; sets sail for England, 419; in fleet that sailed for Virginia, 419 n.
Virginia Company, 281.

Wade, Armigil, accompanies Hore, 106.
Wade, William, 107.
Wampum, manner of obtaining, 60; presented to Cartier, 82, 83, 84, 96.
Wanchese, brought to England by Amadas and Barlowe, 241; unfriendly to English, 262, 290 n.; kept company with remnants of Wingina's men, 290.
Wattes, John, vessels of, bound for West Indies, 303, 305.
Wayman, George, *see* Waymouth, George.
Waymouth, George, early life, 355; "The Jewell of Artes," 355; voyage in search of a northwest passage to India, 355; voyage of 1605, 355, 357-394; failed to obtain advancement, 355; sights Azores, 360; observes latitude, 360; takes sounding, 361; desire to come upon the land in the daytime, 361; sends boat ahead, 361; near Monhegan, 362 n.; name of vessel of, 363 n.; sends boat to sound among islands, 364; goes ashore on Allen's Island, 364 n.; industry of, 365; cross set up by, 367; departs in shallop, 367; return to ship, 369; discovery of a "great river," 370, 388; goes ashore to have draught with seine, 371; shows loadstone to Indians, 371-372; entertains Indians at supper, 372; called by Indians "Bashabes," 373; has Indians spend night aboard ship, 374; Indians give tobacco to, 375; liberal to Indians, 376; goes in boat to mainland with Indians, 376; sends Owen Griffin ashore to see what Indians have to trade, 377; takes Indians captive, 378-379; coasts about adjoining islands, 379; makes trial of the fishing, 380; passes up the river, 381, 383, 385; named his landfall St. George, 382, 382 n.; knowledge derived from early travels, 382; praises harbors along coast, 382; not known to have set up a cross on Monhegan, 382 n;

2 G

Popham colonists found cross set up by, 382 n., 406; explores on land. 384–385; set up cross on shore of river, 386; decides to return, 387, 388; purpose of voyage, 388; takes soundings at mouth and approach to river, 389; intended to publish map, 389; departure, 389–390; comes on a fish bank, 390; mentioned, 394 n., 407 n.
Weapemeoc, Indian town, 248; Pemisapan sends messengers to, 265; some of the natives of, join comspiracy, 265, 266.
Weapemeoc, king of, see Okisko.
Weapomeiok, see Weapemeoc.
Weapomeiok Sound, 251, 253; same as Albemarle Sound, 251 n.
Webster, Noah, 336 n.
Weopomiok, king of, see Okisko.
West Indies, slaves brought by Hawkins to, 113; mentioned, 114, 303, 305, 327; expedition of Drake against, 136; and third voyage of Hawkins, 137, 138, 139; discovery, 182; Amadas and Barlowe at, 227–228.
White, John, and cartography of Ralegh voyages, 229, 235 n., 237 n., 239 n., 246 n., 247 n., 248 n.
White, Governor John, voyage to Virginia, 279–300; granted privileges for planting a colony in Virginia, 281, 282; to bring relief to men left by Grenville, 281; to seek new location for colony on shores of Chesapeake Bay, 281, 287; journal of voyage of 1587, 279–300; departure, 282; near Dominica, 283; at St. Croix, 283–284; at anchor at Cottea, 284; at San Juan, 284–285; hindered from landing on Hispaniola, 286; at Caycos, 286–287; approaches Virginia, 287; in danger off Cape Fear, 287; arrival at Hatorask, 287; hindered from going to Chesapeake Bay, 287; goes to Roanoke, 287; searches for men left by Grenville, 288; orders men to prepare houses, 288; entertained by natives of Croatoan, 289; hears account of Indian attack on men left by Grenville, 290–291; proposes to avenge attack, 292; controversy with his company, 293; urged to go to England for supplies, 294–295; sets sail for England, 295; near Azores, 296; encounters storm, 296; return to England, 297; mentioned, 298; unsuccessful attempt in 1588, 303; last voyage to American coast, 303–323; takes passage in vessels bound for West Indies, 303, 305; misfortunes of voyage, 306; sets sail, 307; along African coast, 307; at Canaries, 308; at Dominica, 308; at Blanca, 308; at San Juan, 309; on Mona, 309; at Saona, 309; at Cape Tiburon, 310–311; near Cuba, 312; along coast of Florida, 313; on island west of Wocokon, 314; at anchor at northeast end of Croatoan, 314; at Hatorask, 314; encouraged by seeing smoke at Roanoke, 314–315; search for colonists, 315–319; believes colonists to have gone to Croatoan, 317–319; plans to go to Croatoan, 319; obtains promise that he will be brought back to Virginia, 320; departure, 320; at Flores, 321–322; arrival, 323.
White Head, 22 n.
White Mountains, 363 n., 384 n.
White Sands, 7; described, 8, 10; inhabitants of, 10; Cartier returns to, 29–30; Cartier comes to, on second voyage, 38.
Whitson, John, bay named for, 346.
Whitson's Bay, 346; probable identity, 346 n.–347 n.; Pring leaves, 351.
Wild Men's Cape, 15; named, 16; same as North Point, 16 n.; native seen at, 16.
Williams, Talcott, 235 n., 288 n.
Windward Passage, 312 n.
Wingandacoa, mistaken for name of country of Wingina, 230, 237, 277 n.
Wingina, Indian king, comes to see Amadas and Barlowe, 230–231; Pooneno not subject to, 237; conspiracy of, 246, 259–267; changed name to Pemisapan, 252; treachery

INDEX

of, 252; desire to starve English, 259; hears report that Lane has suffered at hands of Chaonists and Mangoaks, 260; contemptuous demeanor towards English, 260; effect of Lane's return on, 260–261; says pearl sent by Menatonon is for ransom of son, 261; persuaded by Ensenore to order ground sown, 262; to kill Lane, 263; reasons for going to Dasamonguepeuk, 264–265; sends messengers to Weopomeiok and to the Mandoages, 265; receives Skiko, 265; promises to go over to Roanoke, 266; killed, 267; Englishmen reported to have been killed by followers of, 290–291, 292.

Winship, George Parker, *Sailors' Narratives of New England Voyages*, 328, 356, 384 n.

Winter, John, on Drake's voyage around the world, 229.

Winter, William, in expedition of Sir Humphrey Gilbert, 192; return to England, 192 n., 207.

Wocokon, island, described, 228–229; mentioned, 237, 238, 314.

Wood, Benjamin, in expedition of Amadas and Barlowe, 241.

Wood, John, in expedition of Amadas and Barlowe, 241.

Wooden Ball Island, 405 n.

Woods, Leonard, found manuscript copy of Hakluyt's "discourse," 226.

Woorley, Thomas, in voyage of John Hawkins, 1565, 132.

Wright, Mr., accompanies Hore, 106.

Wriothesley, Henry, *see* Southampton, Earl of.

Wyngandecora, *see* Wingandacoa.

Yaguana, river, 309; probable identity of, 309 n.

Yaguana, town in Hispaniola, 311; Captain William Lane captures Spanish ship at, 311.

Yagüez River, 309 n.

York River, 346 n.

Youghan, Mr., among colonists with Lane, 258.